GRAND HOTEL ABYSS

Grand Hotel Abyss

The Lives of the Frankfurt School

Stuart Jeffries

VERSO

London • New York

First published by Verso 2016
© Stuart Jeffries 2016

1 3 5 7 9 10 8 6 4 2

Verso
UK: 6 Meard Street, London W1F 0EG
US: 20 Jay Street, Suite 1010, Brooklyn, NY 11201
versobooks.com

Verso is the imprint of New Left Books

ISBN-13: 9-781-78478-568-0
ISBN-13: 9-781-78478-571-0 (US EBK)
ISBN-13: 9-781-78478-570-3 (UK EBK)

British Library Cataloguing in Publication Data
A catalogue record for this book is available from the British Library

Library of Congress Cataloging-in-Publication Data

Names: Jeffries, Stuart, 1964–
Title: Grand Hotel Abyss : the lives of the Frankfurt School / Stuart
Jeffries.
Description: London ; Brooklyn, NY : Verso, 2016. | Includes bibliographical
references and index.
Identifiers: LCCN 2016015391| ISBN 9781784785680 (hardcover : alkaline paper)
| ISBN 9781784785703 (ebook)
Subjects: LCSH: Frankfurt school of sociology – History. | Critical
theory – History – 20th century. | Frankfurt school of sociology – Biography.
| Sociologists – Germany – Biography. | Philosophers – Germany – Biography. |
Sociology – Germany – History – 20th century. | Germany – Intellectual
life – 20th century.
Classification: LCC HM467 .J44 2016 | DDC 301.01 – dc23
LC record available at https://lccn.loc.gov/2016015391

Typeset in Minion by Hewer Text UK Ltd, Edinburgh, Scotland
Printed and bound by CPI Group (UK) Ltd, Croydon, CR0 4YY

For Juliet and Kay

Contents

Introduction: Against the Current

Not long before he died in 1969, Theodor Adorno told an interviewer: 'I established a theoretical model of thought. How could I have suspected that people would want to implement it with Molotov cocktails?'[1] That, for many, was the problem with the Frankfurt School: it never stooped to revolution. 'The philosophers have only interpreted the world in various ways; the point is to change it', wrote Karl Marx.[2] But the intellectuals of the Frankfurt School turned Marx's eleventh thesis on Feuerbach upside down.

From its inception in 1923, the Marxist research institute that became known as the Frankfurt School was aloof from party politics and sceptical about political struggle. Its leading members – Theodor Adorno, Max Horkheimer, Herbert Marcuse, Erich Fromm, Friedrich Pollock, Franz Neumann and Jürgen Habermas – were virtuosic at critiquing the viciousness of fascism and capitalism's socially eviscerating, spiritually crushing impact on western societies, but not so good at changing what they critiqued.

The Frankfurt School's apparent inversion of Marx exasperated other Marxists. The philosopher György Lukács once charged that Adorno and other members of the Frankfurt School had taken up residence in what he called the Grand Hotel Abyss. This beautiful hotel was, he wrote, 'equipped with every comfort, on the edge of an abyss, of nothingness, of absurdity'. Previous residents included that earlier, pessimistic, Frankfurt philosopher Arthur Schopenhauer, whose work, Lukács suggested, involved musing on the suffering of the world from a safe distance. 'The daily contemplation of the abyss between excellent meals or artistic entertainments', Lukács wrote sarcastically, 'can only heighten the enjoyment of the subtle comforts offered.'[3]

The thinkers of the Frankfurt School were no different, Lukács argued. Like Schopenhauer, the latest guests of the Hotel Grand Abyss took perverse pleasure in suffering – in their case, though, in the spectacle of monopoly capitalism that was destroying the human spirit below as they reclined on the terrace. For Lukács, the Frankfurt School had abandoned the necessary connection between theory and praxis, where the latter means the realisation in action of the former. If either was to be justifiable, they had to be united – the one reinforcing the other in dialectical relationship. Otherwise, he argued, theory became merely an elitist exercise in interpretation – like all philosophy before Marx.

When Adorno made his remark about Molotov cocktails, he was accounting for the Frankfurt School's retreat into theory at a time when many around him and his colleagues were calling for action. The student movement and the New Left were at their height and many were convinced, wrongly as it turned out, that radical political change was imminent thanks to just such praxis. It was certainly a period of intense political turbulence. Students were revolting from Berkeley to Berlin, protests against the American war in Vietnam at the Democratic Party convention in Chicago had been attacked by the police, and Soviet tanks had recently rolled into Prague to put down the Czechoslovak experiment in 'socialism with a human face'.

At the University of Frankfurt, Adorno himself, this self-admittedly paunchy, sixty-five-year-old professor and the most prominent figure of the Frankfurt School in Germany, was targeted by leaders of the Sozialistischer Deutscher Studentenbund for being insufficiently radical. His lectures were disrupted by protestors, one of whom wrote on the blackboard: 'If Adorno is left in peace, capitalism will never cease.'[4]

Emblematically, the university's Sociology Department was briefly taken over by protesters and renamed the Spartacus Department, after the movement led by Rosa Luxemburg and Karl Liebknecht, the German revolutionaries murdered fifty years earlier. The name change served as rebuke and reminder: rebuke since the Spartacists of 1919 had done what the Frankfurt School of 1969, apparently, did not dare to do; reminder, since the Frankfurt School had come into being in part because of Marxist theorists' attempts to understand the Spartacists' failure to emulate in Germany what the Bolsheviks had acheived in Russia two years earlier.

In 1969, student leaders such as Rudi Dutschke and Daniel Cohn-Bendit believed it was time to unite theory and practice, revolutionise universities and destroy capitalism. It was precisely not time for the German intelligentsia to fail, once more, at its moment of reckoning. Adorno demurred. His compunctions explain a great deal about what the Frankfurt School was and is like and why it was and still some-times is viewed so sceptically by many on the left. In his 1969 paper 'Marginalia to Theory and Praxis', Adorno noted that a student had had his room destroyed because he preferred to work rather than take part in student protests. Someone had even scrawled on his wall: 'Whoever occupies himself with theory without acting practically is a traitor to socialism.'

To Adorno, that student was clearly a kindred spirit – critical theo-rist rather than street-fighting man – and he sought to defend him. He did so by pitting theory against the kind of praxis that he discerned in the student movement and the New Left. 'It is not only against him [the student who had his room trashed] that praxis serves as an ideo-logical pretext for exercising moral constraint', Adorno wrote.[5] That paradox, the oppressive call for liberating action, made Adorno and many other thinkers of the Frankfurt School queasy. Jürgen Habermas called it 'left fascism', and Adorno, his former teacher, saw in it the rise of a grisly new mutation of the authoritarian personality that had thrived in Nazi Germany and Stalinist Russia.

Adorno and the rest of the Frankfurt School knew something about authoritarian personalities. If you were a Jewish Marxist intel-lectual forced to flee into exile in order to avoid being murdered by Nazis, and most of the Frankfurt School were, it was pretty much your specialist subject. All the Frankfurt School's leading lights spent a great deal of time theorising Nazism and trying to account for how the German people in particular had come to desire their own domination rather than rising up in socialist revolution against their capitalist oppressors.

What is striking about Adorno's critical thinking in 1969 is that he took the authoritarian personality type that thrived under Hitler and its attendant spirit of conformism to be alive and well in the New Left and the student movement. Both postured as anti-authoritarian but replicated the repressive structures they ostensibly sought to overthrow. 'Those who protest most vehemently', wrote Adorno, 'are similar to authoritarian personalities in their aversion to introspection.'[6]

Only one member of the Frankfurt School did not pour cold water on the ambitions of late 1960s radicals. Herbert Marcuse, then working at the University of California, San Diego, dabbled in political militancy even as his Frankfurt School colleagues mocked it. Though he disdained the honorific Father of the New Left, Marcuse was for a while caught up in the movement's enthusiasms, daring to imagine that a non-repressive utopia was near at hand. For that he was venerated by students, but also forced to go into hiding after experiencing death threats. In Paris, student protesters held up a banner emblazoned with the words 'Marx, Mao, Marcuse' hailing a new revolutionary trinity.

In terms of the Frankfurt School, though, Marcuse was exceptional. Adorno was more characteristic in arguing, sometimes in topical essays, sometimes in angry correspondence with Marcuse, that now was not the time for the easy posturing of action, but for the hard work of thinking. 'The thinking denigrated by actionists apparently demands too much undue effort: it requires too much work, is too practical', he wrote.[7] Against such misplaced praxis, theory was not reactionary retreat into a Grand Hotel Abyss, but principled withdrawal into a fortress of thought, a citadel from which, periodically, radical jeremiads were issued. For Adorno, thinking rather than sit-ins and barricades was the true radical act. 'Whoever thinks, offers resistance; it is more comfortable to swim with the current, even when one declares oneself to be against the current.'[8]

Even more significantly, Adorno detected in the student movement the very thing the Frankfurt School was charged with – impotence. 'Barricades', he argued, 'are ridiculous against those who administer the bomb.'[9] It's an eviscerating remark, suggesting that the New Left and the student revolutionaries had ineptly borrowed the revolutionary tactics that worked in 1789, 1830 and 1845, but which in 1969 could only be irrelevant to any effective struggle to destroy advanced western capitalism. Or, as Marx put it in another context, history was repeating itself as farce. Perhaps if the New Left had tooled itself up with nuclear weapons, Adorno's analysis might have been different.

But, just possibly, there was method in what Adorno took to be the students' ridiculousness. Certainly, for anyone interested in the Frankfurt School's brand of critical theory, there is more to be said about radical students' appropriation of the revolutionary heritage of the barricades in the late 1960s. That great influence on the Frankfurt School, the philosopher and critic Walter Benjamin, noted in his late essay 'Theses on the Philosophy of History', how revolutionaries self-consciously borrow from past heroes. To do so is to reach back in time to express solidarity with previous role models, to honour their struggles by co-opting their iconography into new revolutionary service.

For instance, the French Revolution of 1789 appropriated the fashions and institutions of ancient Rome. Benjamin called this 'a tiger's leap into the past'. That leap was across time to a historical moment that now resonated with topicality. 'Thus, to Robespierre ancient Rome was a past charged with the time of the now which he blasted out of the continuum of history.'[10] That continuum, or what Benjamin described as 'homogeneous, empty time', was the temporal order of the ruling classes, and it was negated by such time-travelling leaps of radical solidarity.

Similarly, perhaps, the *enragés* who took to the streets and built barricades in late 1960s Paris expressed thereby their solidarity with the revolutionaries of nearly two centuries earlier. But the tiger's leap was a perilous one, likely to end in failure. Benjamin explained: 'This jump, however, takes place in an arena where the ruling class gives the commands.' And yet that leap, he added, was how Marx understood revolution. The leap was dialectical, since by means of it the past was redeemed by the present action and the present by its association with its counterpart in the past.

This suggests that, had he not died in 1940 but survived to witness the student rebellions of the late 1960s, Walter Benjamin might well have championed those who took to the barricades, in all their supposed ridiculousness. Perhaps he would have been more amenable to implementing theory with bombs than his friend Theodor Adorno. It is probably an oversimplification to argue that Benjamin romanticised praxis while Adorno romanticised theory, but there is something in it. Certainly, the Frankfurt School over which Adorno prevailed as the leading intellectual force venerated theory as offering the only space in which the prevailing order could be indicted, if not overthrown. Theory retained – unlike everything tainted by exposure to the real, fallen world – its lustre and its untameable spirit. 'Theory speaks for what is not narrow minded', Adorno wrote. 'Despite all of its unfreedom, theory is the guarantor of freedom in the midst of unfreedom.'[11]

This was where the Frankfurt School felt most comfortable – instead of getting caught up in delusive revolutionary euphoria, they preferred to retreat into a non-repressive intellectual space where they could think freely. That kind of freedom is, to be sure, a melancholy one since it is borne of a loss of hope in real change. But to explore the history of the Frankfurt School and critical theory is to discover how increasingly impotent these thinkers, Marcuse notwithstanding, thought themselves to be against forces they detested but felt powerless to change.

There is, though, a rival history of the Frankfurt School, a counterpart to this narrative of programmatic impotence. It's a conspiracy theory that alleges that a small group of German Marxist philosophers called the Frankfurt School developed something called Cultural Marxism that overturned traditional values by encouraging multiculturalism, political correctness, homosexuality and collectivist economic ideas.[12] The leading thinkers of the Institute for Social Research would have been surprised to learn that they had plotted the downfall of western civilisation, and even more so to learn how successful they had been at it. But then they were mostly

Holocaust survivors, and as such they knew a little about how conspiracy theories that serve psychic needs have disastrous real-world consequences.

One of those who accepted that conspiracy was the right-wing terrorist Anders Breivik. When he set out on a murderous rampage that resulted in the deaths of seventy-seven Norwegians in July 2011, he left behind a 1,513-page manifesto entitled '2083: A European Declaration of Independence'. In it, he blamed supposed European Islamisation on Cultural Marxism. Breivik's ideas, if that's not too strong a word, drew on a conspiracy theory that had its origins in an essay called 'The Frankfurt School and Political Correctness', written by Michael Minnicino in *Fidelio*, a journal of the Schiller Institute.[13] But Minnicino missed a trick in his account of how the Frankfurt School destroyed the West. Given that some of the Frankfurt School worked in the secret services during the Second World War, perhaps those men learned there to become virtuosos, not just at critical theory, but at hiding their diabolical intentions. That, too, seems unlikely.

The truth about the Frankfurt School is less gaudy than the one conspiracy theorists tout. The School came into being in part to try to understand failure, in particular the failure of the German Revolution in 1919. As it evolved during the 1930s, it married neo-Marxist social analysis to Freudian psychoanalytical theories to try to understand why German workers, instead of freeing themselves from capitalism by means of socialist revolution, were seduced by modern consumer capitalist society and, fatefully, Nazism.

While in Los Angeles exile in the 1940s, Adorno helped develop the California F-scale, a personality test designed to discover those likely to fall prey to fascist or authoritarian delusions. Breivik would have been the perfect example of the authoritarian personality Adorno wrote about, one who was 'obsessed with the apparent decline of traditional standards, unable to cope with change, trapped in a hatred of all those not deemed part of the in-group and prepared to take action to "defend" tradition against degeneracy'.[14] In his introduction to *The Authoritarian Personality*, Adorno sounded a warning note:

[P]ersonality patterns that have been dismissed as 'pathological' because they were not in keeping with the most common manifest trends or the most dominant ideals within a society, have, on closer investigation, turned out to be but exaggerations of what was almost universal below the surface in that society. What is 'pathological' today may, with changing social conditions, become the dominant trend of tomorrow.[15]

His experience of Nazism made him especially attuned to such tragic trends.

You don't need to be Anders Breivik to misunderstand the Frankfurt School. 'Cultural Marxism does tremendous damage because, while fantastic at analysis, it is weak on human nature and so fails to antici-pate consequences (when institutions, whether country, church, families or law, fall to pieces, it is the weakest who usually suffer).'[16] So wrote Ed West in the right-wing British newspaper the *Daily Telegraph*. In fact, nearly all the institutions West charged Cultural Marxism with undermining, the Frankfurt School sought to defend. Adorno and Horkheimer defended the institution of the family as a zone of resist-ance against totalitarian forces; Habermas sought out the Catholic Church as an ally for his project of making modern multicultural soci-eties work; Axel Honneth, the Frankfurt School's current director, stresses equality before the law as a precondition of human flourishing and individual autonomy. Yes, Habermas does hope for the dissolution of the German state in favour of a European-wide polity, but chiefly because this former Hitler Youth fears a return of the kind of evil nationalism that thrived in his homeland between 1933 and 1945.

The Frankfurt School, in short, deserves to be freed from its detrac-tors, from those who have wittingly or otherwise misconstrued its works for their own ends. It also deserves to be liberated from the idea that it has nothing to say to us in the new millennium.

These are some of the things I try to do in this book. Although there are many excellent histories of the Frankfurt School and critical theory, and many fine biographies of its leading thinkers, I hope this book offers a different and fruitful approach, a new and, just maybe, compelling way into their distinctive perspective on the world.

Grand Hotel Abyss is in part a group biography, one that tries to describe how the leading figures of the school influenced and intellectually sparred with each other and how their similar experiences of being raised by mostly wealthy Jewish businessmen contributed to their rejection of Mammon and embrace of Marxism. But I also hope the book recounts a narrative that stretches from 1900 to now, from the era of horse-drawn transport to the age of war by unmanned drone. It travels through the cosseted German childhoods of these thinkers as they were raised by and rebelled against their fathers, their experiences of the First World War, their exposure to Marxism in the failed German Revolution and in the neo-Marxist theory they developed to account for that failure, the intensification of mass industrial production and mass-produced culture during the 1920s, the rise of Hitler, their resultant exile to an America which nauseated and seduced them, their bitter returns to a post-Second World War Europe eternally scarred by the Holocaust, their queasy confrontation in the 1960s with youthful revolutionary euphoria, and the Frankfurt School's struggle in the new millennium to comprehend what might stop the multicultural societies of the west from collapsing.

It's a story that offers some unlikely contrasts and paradoxes, embracing as it does a young Herbert Marcuse in Berlin in 1919 as a member of a communist defence force shooting at right-wing snipers; Jürgen Habermas finding a spiritual ally in fellow ex-Hitler Youth member Joseph Ratzinger, better known as Pope Benedict XVI, in the early years of the new millennium; Marxist thinkers working for the forerunner of the CIA during the Second World War; Adorno playing piano for Charlie Chaplin at Hollywood parties while eviscerating the comedian's work in his books; the Frankfurt School erasing the M word from its research papers so as not to affront its American hosts and potential sponsors.

What attracted me to the Frankfurt School in the first place was how its thinkers developed a compelling critical apparatus to understand the times they lived through. They re-conceptualised Marxism by bringing in ideas from Freudian psychoanalysis the better to comprehend how the dialectical movement of history towards a socialist utopia seemed to have stalled. They engaged with the rise of

what they called the culture industry and thereby explored a new relationship between culture and politics, where the former served as a
lackey of capitalism and yet had the potential, mostly unrealised, to be
its gravedigger. In particular, they reflected on how everyday life could
become the theatre of revolution and yet in fact was mostly the opposite, involving a conformism that thwarted any desire to overcome an
oppressive system.

Arguably, we still live in a world like the one the Frankfurt School
excoriated – if one in which we have more freedom to choose than
ever before. Adorno and Horkheimer thought that the freedom to
choose that was the great boast of the advanced capitalist societies in
the west was chimerical. We had 'the freedom to choose what was
always the same', they argued in *Dialectic of Enlightenment*.[17] There,
too, they argued that human personality had been so corrupted by
false consciousness that there was scarcely anything worth the name
any more: 'personality', they wrote, 'scarcely signifies anything more
than shining white teeth and freedom from body odour and emotions'.
Humans had been transformed into desirable, readily exchangeable,
commodities, and all that was left to choose was the option of knowing that one was being manipulated. 'The triumph of advertising in
the culture industry is that consumers feel compelled to buy and use
its products even though they see through them.'[18] The Frankfurt
School is relevant to us now because such critiques of society are even
more possible today than when those words were written.

Why? Arguably because human domination by the culture industry and consumerism is more intense today than ever. Worse, what
was once a system of domination of European and North American
societies has expanded its remit. We no longer live in a world where
nations and nationalism are of key significance, but in a globalised
market where we are, ostensibly, free to choose – but, if the Frankfurt
School's diagnosis is right, free only to choose what is always the same,
free only to choose what spiritually diminishes us, keeps us obligingly
submissive to an oppressive system.

In 1940, Max Horkheimer wrote to a friend: 'In view of what is
now threatening to engulf Europe and perhaps the world, our work is
essentially designed to pass things down through the night that is

approaching: a kind of message in a bottle.'[19] The night he meant was, of course, the Second World War and the Holocaust.

But the writings of the Frankfurt School are useful to us now as we live in a different kind of darkness. We don't live in a hell that the Frankfurt School created, but in one they can help us understand. It is a good time to open their message in a bottle.

PART I:

1900–1920

1

Condition: Critical

Outside, it is a wintry morning in Berlin in 1900. Inside, the maid has put an apple to bake in the little oven at eight-year-old Walter Benjamin's bedside. Perhaps you can imagine the fragrance, but even if you can, you won't be able savour it with the manifold associations that Benjamin experienced when he memorialised the scene thirty-two years later. That baking apple, Benjamin wrote in his memoir *Berlin Childhood Around 1900*, extracted from the oven's heat

> the aromas of all the things the day had in store for me. So it was not surprising that, whenever I warmed my hands on its shining cheeks, I would always hesitate to bite in. I sensed that the fugitive knowledge conveyed by its smell could all too easily escape me on the way to my tongue. That knowledge which sometimes was so heartening that it stayed to comfort me on my trek to school.[1]

But comfort was quickly displaced: at school he was overtaken by 'a desire to sleep my fill . . . I must have made that wish a thousand times, and later it actually came true. But it was a long time before I recognised its fulfilment in the fact that all my cherished hopes for a position and proper livelihood had been in vain'.[2]

So much of Walter Benjamin is in this vignette, starting with the cursed Adamantine apple, whose aromas prefigure his expulsion from childhood Eden, which in turn prefigures his adult exile from Germany into picaresque vagabondage and tragic death on the run from the Nazis aged forty-eight in 1940. There is the vulnerable figure who struggles to impose himself on the difficult world beyond his charmed, fragrant bedroom. There is the melancholic who gets what he wants (sleep) only when it is irredeemably associated with the frustration of other wishes. There is the jump-cut (from bed to school to disenchanted adulthood) echoing the modernist writing techniques he brought to his 1928 book *One-Way Street* and prefiguring his championing, in his 1936 essay 'The Work of Art in the Age of Mechanical Reproduction', of cinematic montage and its revolutionary potential. In particular, there is in Benjamin's remembrance of his childhood at the beginning of the twentieth century the very strange, counterintuitive critical move that he makes again and again in his writings – namely to tear events out of what he called the continuum of history, to look back and mercilessly expose the delusions that sustained earlier eras, to retrospectively detonate what, at the time, looked natural, unproblematic, sane. He may have looked as though he was nostalgically basking in an idyllic childhood made possible by daddy's money and the work of hired help, but really he was figuratively putting sticks of dynamite into its foundations and, indeed, the Berlin of his early years. There is also in this memoir of a lost childhood much of what made this great critic and philosopher so impressive and influential to the mostly younger, fellow German Jewish intellectuals who worked for the Institute for Social Research – or what has become known as the Frankfurt School. Although Benjamin was never on the School's staff, he was its most profound intellectual catalyst.

Like many of the childhood homes of the leading members of the Frankfurt School, the comfortable, bourgeois apartments and villas in the west of Berlin that Emil, a successful art dealer and antiquarian, and Pauline Benjamin lived in were the fruits of business success. Like the Horkheimers, the Marcuses, the Pollocks, the Wiesengrund-Adornos and other families of assimilated Jews from which the thinkers of the Frankfurt School came, the Benjamins lived in unprecedented luxury amid the Wilhelmine pomp and pretension of the rapidly industrialising early twentieth-century German state.

That was one reason Benjamin's writings resonated so profoundly for many of the leading members of the Frankfurt School: they shared his privileged, secular Jewish background in the new Germany and, like him, rebelled against the commercial spirit of their fathers. Max Horkheimer (1895–1973), the philosopher, critic and, for more than thirty years, director of the Institute for Social Research, was the son of a textile factory owner in Stuttgart. Herbert Marcuse (1898–1979), the political philosopher and darling of the 1960s student radicals, was the son of a well-off Berlin businessman and was raised as an upper-middle-class youth in a Jewish family integrated into German society. The father of the social scientist and philosopher Friedrich Pollock (1894–1970) turned away from Judaism and became a successful businessman as the owner of a leather factory in Freiburg im Breisgau. As a boy, the philosopher, composer, music theorist and sociologist, Theodor Wiesengrund Adorno (1903–1969), lived in an ease comparable to that of the young Walter Benjamin. His mother, Maria Calvelli-Adorno, had sung opera and his father, Oscar Wiesengrund, was a successful assimilated Jewish wine merchant in Frankfurt, from whom, as the historian of the Frankfurt School Martin Jay puts it, '[Theodor] inherited a taste for the finer things in life, but little interest in commerce'[3] – a remark that applies to several members of the Frankfurt School who were dependent on their fathers' commerce but queasy about becoming contaminated by its spirit.

The Frankfurt School's leading psychoanalytical thinker, Erich Fromm (1900–1980), was slightly different from his colleagues, not because his father was only a moderately successful travelling fruit-wine salesman based in Frankfurt, but because he was an Orthodox Jew who served as cantor in the local synagogue and carefully observed all the Jewish holidays and customs. But Fromm certainly shared with his colleagues a temperamental distaste for Mammon and a rejection of the world of business.

Henryk Grossman (1881–1950), at one point the Frankfurt School's leading economist, had his childhood home in Krakow, in what was then a Galicia colonised by the Austrian Habsburg Empire. It was materially lavish thanks to the work of his father, a bar owner who had become a successful small industrialist and mine owner. Henryk's biographer, Rick Kuhn, writes that: 'The prosperity of the Grossman family buffered it from the consequences of social prejudices, political currents and laws that discriminated against Jews.'[4] Many of the Frankfurt School's leading thinkers shared that buffering in their childhood, though none of course were spared discrimination entirely, especially when the Nazis came to power. That said, Grossman's parents, though assimilated into Krakow society, ensured that their sons were circumcised and registered as members of the Jewish community: there were limits to assimilation.

All were intelligent men, alive to the irony of their historical situation, namely that it was thanks to the business acumen of their fathers that they were able to choose the life of critical writing and reflection, even if those writings and reflections were Oedipally fixated on bringing down the political system that had made their lives possible. The comfortable worlds in which these men had been born and raised may well have seemed to childish eyes eternal and secure. But while Benjamin's memoir was an elegy to one of those worlds – the materially sumptuous world of his childhood – it also revealed the unbearable truth that it was neither eternal nor secure, but rather had existed only briefly and was doomed to disappear. The Berlin of Benjamin's childhood was a recent phenomenon. The city that had been a relatively provincial Prussian backwater only half a century earlier had by 1900 arguably supplanted Paris as mainland Europe's most modern city. Its rage for reinventing itself and erecting very nearly bombastic architecture (the Reichstag building, for instance, opened in 1894) stemmed from the swaggering self-confidence that came from the city becoming capital of the newly unified Germany in 1871. Between then and the turn of the century Berlin's population rose from 800,000 to two million. As it grew, the new capital was modelled on the city it sought to supplant in grandiosity. The Kaiser-Galerie that connected Friedrichstrasse and Behrenstrasse was an arcade modelled on those of Paris. Berlin's Paris-style grand boulevard, the Kufürstendamm, was newly developed when Benjamin was a boy; the city's first department store at Leipziger Platz opened in 1896, apparently modelled on Au Bon Marché and La Samaritaine, the grand temples to shopping that had opened in Paris more than half a century earlier.

In writing his childhood memoir, Benjamin was attempting something that might on the face of it seem merely a nostalgic escape from a difficult adulthood, but on closer inspection appears as a revolutionary act of writing. For Benjamin, history was not, in Alan Bennett's words, one fucking thing after another, just a sequence of events without sense. Rather, narrative sense had been imposed on those events – that was what made them history. But imposing meaning was hardly an innocent act. History was written by the victors and its triumphalist narrative had no place for losers. To tear events out of that history as Benjamin did and set them in other temporal contexts – or what he would call constellations – was both a revolutionary Marxist act and also a Jewish one: the former because it sought to expose the hidden delusions and exploitative nature of capitalism; the latter because it was inflected with Judaic rituals of mourning and redemption.

Crucially, then, what Benjamin was doing involved a new conception of history, one that would break with the belief in the kind of progress that capitalism took to be an article of faith. In this, he was following Nietzsche's critique of historicism, that soothing, triumphalist, positivistic sense that the past could be scientifically apprehended as it was. In German idealist philosophy, that belief in progress was underpinned by the dialectical, historical unfolding of the Spirit. But that historicist fantasy erased elements of the past that didn't fit the narrative. Benjamin's task was therefore to retrieve what had been consigned to oblivion by the victors. The subversive Benjamin, then, aimed at breaking through this widespread amnesia, shattering this delusive notion of historical time, and awakening those who lived under capitalism from their illusions. Such a breakthrough was, he hoped, what would result from what he called 'a new, dialectical method of history'.[5] For this method, the present is haunted by the ruins of the past, by the very detritus capitalism had sought to airbrush from its history. Benjamin scarcely wrote in Freudian terms of the return of the repressed, but that is what his project sets in motion. That's why, for example, in *Berlin Childhood* he recalled as a little boy visiting something called the Kaiserpanorama in a Berlin arcade. The panorama was a dome-like apparatus that presented stereoscopic images of historical events, military victories, fjords, cityscapes, all painted on a circular wall that trundled slowly around the seated audience. Modern critics have drawn a parallel between such panoramas and today's multiplex cinematic experience, and Benjamin would doubtless have appreciated the comparison: the way in which examining an obsolete technology-driven form of entertainment that was once the last word can make us reflect on a later technology with similar pretensions.

The Kaiserpanorama had been built between 1869 and 1873 and now was consigned to obsolescence. But not before its final audiences, mainly children, had appreciated it, especially when it was raining outside. 'One of the great attractions of the travel scenes found in the Kaiserpanorama', Benjamin wrote, 'was that it did not matter where you began the cycle. Because the viewing screen, with places to sit before it, was circular, each picture would pass through all the stations . . . [E]specially towards the end of my childhood, when fashion was already turning its back on the Kaiserpanorama, one got used to taking the tour in a half empty room.'[6] For Benjamin, it was such out-of-date things, as well as the aborted attempts and abject failures that had been erased from the narratives of progress, that drew his critical attention. His was a history of the losers, not just of defeated humans, but of expendable things that, back in the day, had been the last word. So when he recalled the Kaiserpanorama he wasn't merely indulging in bittersweet reminiscence of what he did one rainy afternoon in his childhood, but doing what he often did in his writings – studying the overlooked, the worthless, the trashy, the very things that didn't make sense within the official version of history but which, he maintained, encoded the dream wishes of the collective consciousness. By way of recovering the abject and obsolete from historical oblivion, Benjamin sought to awaken us from the collective dream by means of which capitalism had subdued humanity.

The Kaiserpanorama had once been the newest thing on the scene, a projection of utopian fantasies as well as a projector of them too. By the time little Walter visited the panorama, it was heading for the scrap heap of history. It was, as the grown-up Benjamin realised while writing his reminiscences, an allegory of the delusions of progressive history: the panorama revolves endlessly, its history being repetition, precluding real change. Like the notion of progressive history itself, the panorama was a phantasmagoric tool to keep its spectators subdued, passive and fatuously dreaming, longing (as did Walter when he visited) for new experiences, distant worlds and diverting journeys; for lives of endless distraction rather than confrontation with the realities of social inequality and exploitation under capitalism. Yes, the Kaiserpanorama would be replaced by newer, better technologies, but that was what always happened under capitalism: we were always confronting the new, never turning our gaze to contemplate the fallen, the obsolete, the rejected. It was as if we were the torture victim in *A Clockwork Orange* or Dantesque denizens in some ring of hell, doomed to keep consuming the newest commodities for eternity.

Writing his childhood memoirs, then, was for him part of a more general literary project that was also a political act. A political act that was the basis for the Marxist-inflected, multidisciplinary work called critical theory that Benjamin's fellow German Jewish intellectuals would undertake during the twentieth century in the face of the three great (as they saw it) benighted triumphalist narratives of history delivered by the faithful proselytisers for capitalism, Stalinist communism and National Socialism.

IF CRITICAL THEORY means anything, it means the kind of radical re-thinking that challenges what it considers to be the official versions of history and intellectual endeavour. Benjamin initiated it, perhaps, but it was Max Horkheimer who gave it a name when he became the director of the Frankfurt School in 1930: critical theory stood in opposition to all those ostensibly craven intellectual tendencies that thrived in the twentieth century and served as tools to keep an irksome social order in place – logical positivism, value-free science, positivist sociology, among others. Critical theory stood in opposition, too, to what capitalism in particular does to those it exploits – buying us off cheaply with consumer goods, making us forget that other ways of life are possible, enabling us to ignore the truth that we are ensnared in the system by our fetishistic attention and growing addiction to the purportedly must-have new consumer good.

When Benjamin recalled a childhood winter's morning in 1900, then, he may initially have seemed to be lost in reverie over his privileged childhood, but in reality he was writing like a Marxist, albeit a very oddball one. The new morning and the new century into which little Walter was lured into consciousness by the sweet aromas made possible by a woman's work in 1900 seemed to promise lovely possibilities and material security, but they were exposed by Benjamin as illusions. 'Capitalism', he once wrote, 'was a natural phenomenon with which a new dream-filled sleep came over Europe, and, through it, a reactivation of mythic forces.'[7] The aim of his writing aim was to shake us from those dogmatic slumbers. The world his parents had established in their villa in West Berlin needed to be exposed: it was a life that seemed secure, permanent and natural, but which in fact was based on complacency combined with a ruthless exclusion of those who didn't fit the triumphalist narrative, notably the poor.

He described, for instance, his birthplace in a large apartment in a then elegant district south of Berlin's Tiergarten, choosing to write in the third person, perhaps as a distancing technique to suggest the communist writer's alienation from his earlier self: 'the class that had pronounced him one of its number resided in a posture compounded of self-satisfaction and resentment that turned it into something of a ghetto held on lease. In any case, he was confined to this affluent quarter without knowing of any other. The poor? For the rich children of his generation, they lived in the back of beyond.'[8]

In a section of a *Berlin Childhood* called 'Beggars and Whores', he described encountering a poor man. Until that moment for little Walter, the poor had existed only as beggars. But then, as if to prove the point that only by writing could he truly experience something, he recalled doing a little piece of writing, 'perhaps the first I composed entirely for myself', about a man who distributes leaflets and 'the humiliations he suffers in encountering a public that has no interest in his literature':

So the poor man (this is how I ended it) secretly jettisons the whole pack of leaflets. Certainly the least promising solution to the problem. But at the same time I could imagine no other form of revolt than

sabotage – something rooted, naturally, in my own personal experience, and to which I had recourse whenever I sought escape from my
mother.[9]

Projecting on to a struggling worker the modes of protest he had
deployed against an overbearing mother may hardly count as the most
sophisticated form of revolt for someone who would become a self-
styled communist, but Benjamin's youthful if limited empathy was at
least a start. He was repeatedly drawn into reflections on how his privileged childhood was premised on a ruthless airbrushing of the
unpalatable and the unfortunate, and how its bourgeois security
involved a monstrous, more or less intentional, act of forgetting of
what lay beyond the lowered blinds of the family's apartments. In *A
Berlin Chronicle*, for instance, a series of newspaper articles from the
1920s that predate the writing of *Berlin Childhood*, Benjamin remembered the sense of bourgeois security that suffused his family's
apartment:

> Here reigned a species of things that was, no matter how compliantly it
> bowed to the minor whims of fashion, in the main so wholly convinced
> of itself and its permanence that it took no account of wear, inheritance,
> or moves, remaining forever equally near to and far from its ending,
> which seemed the ending of all things. Poverty could have no place in
> these rooms where even death had none.[10]

In his last essay, Benjamin wrote: 'There is no document of civilisation
that is not at the same time a document of barbarism.'[11] That sense of
the repression of the unacceptable, the embarrassing, the awkward, of
the ideological disappearing of that which doesn't fit the master narrative, had come early to him and remained with him lifelong: barbarism
for, Walter Benjamin, began at home. And the Frankfurt School, too,
was committed to uncovering the barbarism that they thought underpinned capitalism's putative civilisation, even if they didn't excavate it
quite so assiduously in their own families as did Benjamin.

Certainly, his childhood sounds as though it teemed with consumer
durables, as though his parents were unwitting victims of what Marx

called the fetishism of commodities, expressing their faith in the profane religion of capitalism through protracted bouts of shopping, accumulating the articles that their son would imaginatively repurpose both as a child and as a Marxist adult. 'Around him', write his biographers, 'was a multifarious *Dingwelt*, a world of things appealing to his well nurtured imagination and omnivorous imitative abilities: delicate china, crystal, and cutlery that emerged on festive days, while antique furniture – large, ornate armoires and dining tables with carved legs – readily served in games of masquerade.'[12] At thirty-two years' remove, Benjamin wrote of how little Walter pierced this sumptuous surface, describing for example a table laid out for a lavish dinner: 'As I gazed at the long, long rows of coffee spoons and knife rests, fruit knives and oyster forks, my pleasure in this abundance was tinged with anxiety, lest the guests we had invited would turn out to be identical to one another, like our cutlery.'[13] An insightful thought: when the Frankfurt School thinkers and other leading Marxists such as György Lukács considered the nature of reification under capitalism, they would worry that persons as much as cutlery became commodities, compelled to bow before the all-consuming principle of exchange, dehumanised and endlessly substitutable for articles of equivalent value.

But what particular need prompted Walter Benjamin in 1932 to write about his childhood in Berlin at the turn of the century? To be sure, he returned again and again in his writings during the 1920s and 1930s to those childhood scenes that fired his imagination. But, in the summer of 1932 in particular, he memorialised his childhood in the first draft of what became *Berlin Childhood Around 1900*, in order to satisfy a very specific psychic need and, moreover, to satisfy it in a particularly strange way. That summer he was wandering around Europe, keeping away from Berlin, finally pitching up in the Tuscan seaside resort of Poveromo.[14] The Berlin of his childhood was poised to disappear, the Jews and communists of the city murdered or forced into exile by the Nazis. Benjamin had the misfortune to be both a Jew and a communist. *Berlin Childhood* was written, then, as Benjamin suggested in its introduction, as 'it became clear to me that I would have to bid a long, perhaps lasting farewell to the city of my birth.'[15]

Nostalgia is typically decadent, delusive and conservative, particularly when it involves an adult looking back on childhood. But Benjamin's nostalgia for his Berlin childhood at the turn of the century was that of a revolutionary Marxist and, even more importantly, that of a Jew seeking to give the traditional Judaic rituals of mourning and remembrance a new twist. The Marxist critic and Benjamin scholar Terry Eagleton recognised as much when he wrote that:

> Today, nostalgia is almost as unacceptable as racism. Our politicians speak of drawing a line under the past and turning our back on ancient quarrels. In this way, we can leap forward into a scrubbed, blank, amnesiac future. If Benjamin rejected this kind of philistinism, it was because he was aware that the past holds vital resources for the renewal of the present. Those who wipe out the past are in danger of abolishing the future as well. Nobody was more intent on eradicating the past than the Nazis, who would, like the Stalinists, simply scrub from historical record whatever they found inconvenient.[16]

There was work to be done on the past: for the Nazis it involved scrubbing and airbrushing; for Benjamin it was the delicate spadework of the archaeologist. 'Memory is not an instrument for surveying the past but its theatre', he wrote in *Berlin Childhood*. 'It is the medium of past experience, just as the earth is the medium in which dead cities lie buried. He who seeks to approach his own buried past must conduct himself like a man digging. Above all, he must not be afraid to return again and again to the same matter; to scatter it as one scatters earth, to turn it over as one turns over soil.'[17] This is what Benjamin did: he returned again and again to the same scene, digging through layers of repression until he got to the treasure.

'Remembering was not merely an inventorying of the past', writes his biographer Esther Leslie. 'Memory's significance depended on the strata that smothered it, right up to the present, the moment of and place of their rediscovery. Memory actualises the present.'[18] There was, in other words, what Benjamin was to call in *The Arcades Project*, a 'now of recognisability'[19] – as if the significance of things long buried could only be recognised much later. We look to the past, in part, to understand the now. For instance, as Benjamin reminisced about his boyhood in the 1920s and 1930s, he returned again and again to one particular childhood scene in which his father Emil came into five-year-old Walter's bedroom:

> He had come to say goodnight to me. It was perhaps half against his will that he gave me the news of a cousin's death. The cousin had been an older man who did not mean a great deal to me. My father filled out the account with details. I did not take in everything that he said. But I did take special note, that evening, of my room, as though I were aware that one day I would again be faced with trouble there. I was well into adult-hood when I learned that the cause of the cousin's death had been syphilis. My father had come by in order not to be alone. He had sought out my room, however, and not me. The two of them could have wanted no confidant.[20]

Benjamin excavated and re-excavated this scene: in different drafts for *Berlin Childhood Around 1900* and its precursor, *Berlin Chronicle*, he wrote about it four times, each time focusing on different aspects. Here and elsewhere the premonitions of the child and the knowledge of the grown man remembering his past in writing bring past and future together in a dialectical relationship. Only as he wrote his remi-niscences could he understand the full significance of why his father had visited him in his bedroom; only as an adult did the event have a now of recognisability.

This obsessive remembrance of childhood makes one think of one of Benjamin's favourite writers, Marcel Proust, and in particular another bedroom scene at the start of *À la recherche du temps perdu* in which another privileged little boy – neurotic, Jewish, Victorian, obsessive Marcel – sits awaiting his beloved mother's goodnight kiss. 'We know that in his work Proust did not describe life as it actually was', wrote Benjamin in his essay 'The Image of Proust', 'but a life as it was remembered by the one who had actually lived it. And yet even this statement is imprecise and far too crude. For the important thing for the remembering author is not what he experienced, but the weaving of his memory, the Penelope work of recollection.'[21] Benjamin thus seized on Proust's notion of *mémoire involontaire*, the work of spontaneous recollection contrasting with the purposive recollection of *mémoire volontaire*. Benjamin took dreams to be key in such remembrance. 'When we awake each morning we hold in our hands, usually weakly and loosely, but a few fringes of the tapestry of lived life, as loomed for us by forgetting', he wrote in the same essay. 'However, with our purposeful activity and, even more, our purposive remembering each day unravels the web and the ornaments of forgetting. This is why Proust finally turned his days into nights, devoting all his hours to undisturbed work in his darkened room with artificial illumination, so that none of those intricate arabesques might escape him.'[22]

It was when Proust tasted a Madeleine dipped in a tisane that his childhood was opened up in hitherto unyielding detail. It was through such moments that what Benjamin called 'Proust's blind, senseless, frenzied quest for happiness'[23] could be realised. Benjamin, as he recalled the aroma of baked apple, may seem at first reading to be engaged in a similar quest to save his childhood from the ravages of time, but in truth he was engaged upon something stranger. Proust's search for 'lost time' was undertaken to escape from time altogether; Benjamin's project was aimed at putting his childhood in a new temporal relationship with the past. As the literary scholar Peter Szondi puts it, Proust's 'real goal is escape from the future, filled with dangers and threats, of which the ultimate one is death'. Benjamin's project is different and, to my mind, less delusive: there can be no inoculation nor escape, ultimately, from death. 'In contrast, the future is precisely what Benjamin seeks in the past. Almost every place that his memory wishes to rediscover bears "traces of what was to come" as he puts it . . . Unlike Proust, Benjamin does not want to free himself from temporality; he does not wish to to see things in their ahistorical essence.'[24] Rather, in looking into the past, and finding there the forgotten, the obsolete, the allegedly irrelevant, Benjamin sought not just to redeem the past by means of the kind of revolutionary work of nostalgia Terry Eagleton liked, but to redeem the future. 'The past', Benjamin wrote in 'Theses on the Philosophy of History', 'carries with it a secret index by which it is referred to redemption.'[25] Benjamin's task, as critical archaeologist, was to recover and decipher that index.

In this, what he was doing was very Jewish. Proust, himself a great Jewish writer, had sought to redeem his childhood from the ravages of time by taking it, through the novel's imaginative work, out of the continuum of history. Benjamin found inspiration in that project, but his memoir had a different purpose. He was seeking to understand himself and his historical condition as a function of capitalism's class system through meditating on his privileged childhood. For Proust, memory was a means of recreating bliss, of stopping time's arrow; for Benjamin, the act of remembrance through writing had a palimpsest, dialectical character that raced backwards and forwards in time, weaving temporally disparate events together in what he called the Penelope work of memory.

But *Berlin Childhood* was supposed to do something more in Benjamin's estimation – to be a kind of spiritual prophylactic against what was to come, the Nazi takeover of his homeland and the exile that would most likely entail. 'Several times in my inner life', he wrote in the book's introduction,

> I had already experienced the process of inoculation as something salutary. In this situation, too, I resolved to follow suit, and I deliberately called to mind those images which, in exile, are most apt to waken homesickness: images of childhood. My assumption was that the feeling of longing would no more gain mastery over my spirit than a vaccine does over a healthy body. I sought to limit its effect through insight into the irretrievability – not the contingent autobiographical but the necessary social irretrievability – of the past.[26]

When one first reads this, it's hard not to think that the project seems hopeless, more likely to infect and enfeeble a troubled exile than steel him against the rigours to come; or at least to resemble more putting one's finger into a wound and stirring it rather than helping the process of healing. True, philosophers in adversity sometimes strive to gain solace by contemplating happier times – consider the philosopher Epicurus, who wrote to a friend saying that on this, the last day of his life, he was in excruciating pain from kidney stones and unable to urinate, but was nonetheless cheerful because 'the recollection of all my philosophical contemplation, counterbalances all these afflictions'.[27] Philosophical detachment had, or so Epicurus claimed, overcome the pain caused by kidney stones.

But Benjamin's project of self-inoculation against suffering is weirder than Epicurus'. For a start, he is aware that recalling the past is apt to encourage a longing for that happier time, a longing that cannot be realised. Epicurus overcomes the effects of physical pain through philosophical detachment; Benjamin seems bent on overcoming the psychic pain of loss and homesickness through a different crypto-Marxist kind of detachment. Not for Walter Benjamin the Proustian project of satisfying longing by taking childhood out of time through writing and thereby making it imperishable. Rather, for him the images of homesickness he evokes in his memoir are meant to make him realise that what is lost is lost, and that meditating on the irretrievability of his childhood will – somehow – soothe him and inoculate him against suffering.

But there is an important twist: Benjamin was writing, as he noted, not about the contingent, autobiographical nature of loss – a loss, after all, that each one of us experiences as we grow up and look back, perhaps fondly, to the childhoods that we will never again live through, except by means of the relatively pallid movement of imaginative recreation. Rather, he is writing about the necessary social irretrievability of the past, by which he means to reflect, as a Marxist historical materialist, on the loss, not just of his, Walter Benjamin's, privileged childhood, but on the loss of the world that sustained it. This was what made Benjamin's lovely memoir so exquisitely suggestive to the leading lights of the Frankfurt School, since it evoked a lost world of material comfort for secular Jews in that new-born German Empire of the last years of the nineteenth century and the early years of the twentieth, a world that had seemed permanent and stable to childish eyes but which Benjamin revealed as having, a little like summer's lease in Shakespeare's sonnet, all too short a date.

There was, then, no Proustian escape from lost time for Benjamin, merely the consolation – if that's the right word – of meditating on the necessity of loss. Theodor Adorno, Benjamin's friend and arguably the Frankfurt School's greatest thinker, wrote the most insightful words about Benjamin's memoir, suggesting that it 'laments the irretrievabil- ity of what, once lost, congeals into an allegory of its own demise'.[28] Fine, but how is one supposed to find solace or inoculation from such a lament? How to inoculate oneself from past and future woes by recalling a more materially secure past forever obliterated? The project seems esoteric, counter-productive and yet, at the same time, compel- lingly subversive and political. Benjamin sought succour from the remembrance but also discovered its opposite – that his childhood was precarious, a little world that tottered even as it seemed secure, before it collapsed entirely.

What's also odd about Benjamin's memoirs of childhood as he remembered and re-remembered it in his writings is that he increas- ingly purges them of people. In *A Berlin Chronicle* of 1924 he revisited family and schoolfriends from a quarter of a century earlier. But with *Berlin Childhood Around 1900*, written in 1932, his remembrances become like the literary equivalent of a neutron bomb – purging people, and filling their places with things. It was a baked apple, the loggias of his grandmother's apartment block, the Victory column in Berlin's Tiergarten that triggered his associations, that opened up his past, that served his needs in Poveromo. In his essay on Proust he wrote that *À la Recherche* 'has at its centre a loneliness which pulls the world down into its vortex with the force of a maelstrom'. As Eiland and Jennings put it, Proust's novel involves for Benjamin the 'transfor- mation of existence into a preserve of memory centred in the vortex of solitude'.[29] Benjamin's memoirs have a similar tenor. You could read these remembrances believing he was what he was not, an only child. His parents are mute presences (apart from the image of his father uttering threats and curses into the telephone when the complaints department was on the line). And the portrait of his childhood is one in which the sitter scarcely appears, his presence taken by objects.

'Everything in the courtyard became a sign or hint to me', Benjamin wrote in a section of *Berlin Childhood* entitled 'Loggias'. 'Many were the messages embedded in the skirmishing of the green roller blinds drawn up high, and many the ominous dispatches that I prudently left unopened in the rattling of the roll-up shutters that came thundering down at dusk.'[30] But this depopulated memoir, which could be read as an elegy to the fetishised commodities of his parental home, is more apparent than real. Each object contains the ghost of human presence, a history, the heat of attachment.

Frankfurt School thinkers were serially impressed by the way things carry the heat of our attachment to persons. Adorno, years later, was to write of the potency of objects, of how the libidinal cathexis of one's attachment to a beloved person can be replicated in our attachment to non-human objects. 'The more second person attitudes a subject can attach to this same object in the course of its libidinal cathexis', wrote the current director of the Frankfurt School, Axel Honneth, of Adorno's account in his essay *Reification*, 'the more rich in aspects the object will ultimately appear in its objective reality.'[31] Adorno was convinced it was possible to speak of recognition with non-human objects, a conviction that Benjamin surely shared. But in this memoir, Benjamin wasn't merely drawing up an inventory of the treasure trove of the past:

> the man who merely makes an inventory of his findings, while failing to establish the exact location of where in today's ground the ancient treasures have been stored up, cheats himself of his richest prize. In this sense, for authentic memories, it is far less important that the investigator report on them than that he mark, quite precisely, the site where he gained possession of them. Epic and rhapsodic in the strictest sense, genuine memory must therefore yield an image of the person who remembers, in the same way a good archaeological report not only informs us about the strata from which its findings originate, but also gives an account of the strata which first had to be broken through.[32]

As Benjamin dug into his past, he was revealing himself to himself: he wasn't just recording the past, but actualising the present. That said, it is important to recognise that he was recording the past, in particular a past in which privileged boys were born and raised in families of materially successful, mostly secularised, Jewish businessmen in the years leading up to the First World War. From that privileged position, then, Walter Benjamin and the Frankfurt School sought to indict what had made that privileged position possible. In developing the multidisciplinary intellectual movement called critical theory, they indicted, too, the values for which their fathers' stood.

When the critic T. J. Clark reviewed Benjamin's posthumously published, uncompleted *The Arcades Project* – a great wreck of a book teeming with data about the phantasmagoric nature of consumer capitalism in Paris in the nineteenth century that Benjamin had laboriously written onto cards in the French capital's Bibliothèque Nationale – he noted that 'there was from the beginning a shadow spreading across the notecards, of a larger, more wonderful study in which all the great dreams of his father's generation, and his father's father's, would be related and denounced'.[33] That book never got written by Benjamin, but the impulse to write it remained. 'We have to wake up from the existence of our parents', he wrote in *The Arcades Project*.[34] But why? Arguably because some of the most ardent of capitalism's faithful were the fathers of the Frankfurt School's leading thinkers. As a result, the troubles Benjamin and many of the Frankfurt School scholars had with their fathers during their childhoods and adolescence, which we will turn to in the next chapter, were crucially important to the way in which critical theory developed during the twentieth century.

2

Fathers and Sons, and Other Conflicts

I|f Freud had lived and carried on his inquiries in a country and
language other than the German-Jewish milieu which supplied his
patients', wrote the philosopher Hannah Arendt, 'we might never have
heard of an Oedipus complex.'[1] What she meant is that thanks to the
father–son tensions unleashed by the very specific conditions that
prevailed among the families of some of the most materially successful Jews in Wilhelmine Germany and the Habsburg Empire in the last
years of the nineteenth century and the first years of the twentieth,
Freud developed a notion of patriarchal society and Oedipal struggle
as natural facts about humankind. Nearly all the leading lights of the
Frankfurt School – Benjamin, Adorno, Horkheimer, Löwenthal,
Pollock, Fromm, Neumann – were resistant to the *Weltanschauung*
transmitted by paternal authority, and many rebelled in various ways
against their fathers who had become very materially successful.

Without such Oedipal struggles, critical theory would not have
developed in quite the way it did. Thomas Mann's schema of German
bourgeois familial development in *Buddenbrooks* – the first generation makes the money, the second cements the family's social position,
and the third withdraws into something like aesthetic malaise[2] – was
unwittingly subverted by these Frankfurt scholars. Sceptics about the
merits of the Frankfurt School and critical theory might suggest that
the Benjamin, Adorno and Horkheimer families skipped a generation – going straight from money to aesthetic malaise, but that would
arguably be unfair. Rather, if Frankfurt scholars skipped a generation,
it was to turn immediately against the previous generation who had

made the money and, as a result, made their for the most part privileged sons comfortable. In so doing they were enacting not Thomas Mann, but Franz Kafka. As Peter Demetz notes in his introduction to a collection of Benjamin's essays called *Reflections*:

> In many Jewish families of late nineteenth-century Europe, gifted sons turned against the commercial interests of their fathers who were largely assimilated (after moving from the provinces to the more liberal cities) to bourgeois success and, in building their counterworlds in spiritual protest, they incisively shaped the future of science, philosophy and literature.[3]

Even if Freud is right and every son wants to symbolically castrate his father – and must do so for the sake of his mental health and adult flourishing – the Oedipal struggles of the precocious, cultured German-speaking Jews of late nineteenth-century and early twentieth-century Europe took a very particular turn, involving them rejecting the materialistic values their businessman fathers ostensibly espoused, values which those fathers had often adopted in their own struggles with their fathers.

One of the founders of the Institute for Social Research, the sociologist of literature Leo Löwenthal (1900–1993), recalled how this dynastic struggle and counterstruggle played out in his own life in *An Unmastered Past: The Autobiographical Reflections of Leo Löwenthal*, and in particular in a section of the book entitled 'I Never Wanted to Play Along' (which surely could have been a motto for the Frankfurt School). Leo's own father Victor wanted to be a lawyer, but his father (Leo's paternal grandfather), a strict orthodox Jew who taught at a Jewish school in Frankfurt, refused to grant his permission because he thought that might mean Victor working and writing on the Sabbath. Instead he insisted that Victor study medicine, which he obligingly did though his heart was not in it. 'But then', recalled Löwenthal, 'he took his revenge – either consciously or unconsciously – when he later became totally "free": not just irreligious, but decidedly antireligious.'

For Leo Löwenthal, his father typified the nineteenth-century mindset against which he and his colleagues in the Frankfurt School rebelled, what he called the 'mechanistic-materialistic, positivist way of thinking'. He recalled that the atmosphere at home was secular. 'I hardly knew anything about Judaism . . . I still remember when they divided us up for religious instruction in sixth grade. When the teacher told the Protestants to gather in one part of the classroom, the Catholics in another, and the Jews in a third, I remained seated – I really didn't know what religion I belonged to!'[4]

Later in his youth, Löwenthal learned about and appropriated his Jewish heritage, much to the disgust of his father. As a student at Marburg, he was taught by Hermann Cohen, a liberal Jew steeped in Judaism and in Jewish religious philosophy. For the intellectual German Jew of that time, there was no shortage of surrogate fathers who could give precocious sons the sustenance they could not get at home. At Heidelberg, Leo fell in with a group of left-wing Zionist students who bitterly opposed another Jewish group at the university, the Syndicate of Organisations of German Students of the Jewish Faith, an assimilationist student organisation. Löwenthal loathed the latter group because they believed in total integration into the German nation. 'Only now do I realise what I hated about that assimilationist group', Löwenthal recalled. 'Not that they as Jews wanted to be human beings like everyone else, but that their convictions were essentially capitalist.'[5]

Again and again, with members of the Frankfurt School, we see this rejection of assimilation thus conceived, a rejection of an ideology that had enabled their own fathers to do well in German society and that was contrary to their own nascent socialism. These intellectual sons revolted against the Enlightenment heritage to which their secular fathers were drawn precisely because it provided the intellectual gloss to their material success.

In 1923, Löwenthal married Golda Ginsburg, a woman from Königsberg who came from a relatively orthodox Jewish family. The couple decided to keep a kosher household, to go to synagogue, and to observe Jewish holidays. 'Of course, this had a catastrophic effect on my father, who took an immediate dislike to my wife.' Löwenthal's father disdained any Jews who lived east of the Elbe, calling them *Ostjuden* (a snobbery the established, materially successful Jews of

German cities such as Frankfurt felt towards the immigrant Jews from eastern Europe). Near the end of his own life, Löwenthal recalled his father's upset at the fact that his son chose to keep a kosher house. 'I still remember it very well – he broke out in tears of anger. It was a terrible disappointment for him that his son, whom he, the father, the true scion of the enlightenment, had raised so "progressively", was now being pulled into the "nonsensical", "obscure", and "deceitful" clutches of a positive religion.'[6]

This refusal to do what was expected, to be obedient and to earn one's father's love, was characteristic of many of the Jewish intellectuals who were members of the Frankfurt School as well as of their friends and peers. If the father was a practising Jew, the son might rebel by expressing atheism; if the father was a secular Jew steeped in German nationalism, the son might rebel by reclaiming his Jewish religious heritage or embracing the gathering movement of political Zionism.

Ernst Bloch (1885–1977), the German Jewish writer whose esoteric utopian Marxist philosophy profoundly influenced the Frankfurt School and with whom Walter Benjamin smoked hashish in the 1920s, made his first clumsy act of rebellion against his father's religion at his bar mitzvah by declaring himself an atheist.[7] Benjamin's close friend, the German-born, Israeli philosopher and historian Gershom Scholem (1897–1982), was one of three sons who rebelled against their father Arthur, an assimilated Berlin Jew and German nationalist who ran a successful printing business. Werner Scholem became a communist, Reinhold became a member of the nationalist Deutsche Volkspartei, while Gershom rejected his father's politics and became a Zionist, learning Hebrew, studying the Talmud and any Kabbalistic writings he could find. There is even a story that a portrait of the founder of modern political Zionism, Theodor Herzl, which Gershom's mother had bought him, was hung in the same room as the Scholems' Christmas tree – a symbolic rebuke, it would seem, from a Zionist son to his assimilationist father.[8]

Max Horkheimer, who, on becoming director of the Institute for Social Research in 1930, transformed it from an orthodox Marxist institution into a multidisciplinary, psychoanalytically inclined and revisionist Marxist one, is the prototypical example of a German Jewish intellectual of this era who disappointed his father's wishes. A successful and respected businessman who owned several textile factories in Stuttgart's Zuffenhausen district, Moritz Horkheimer expected his son to follow in his footsteps. 'I was intended from the very first year of my life to be my father's successor as director of an industrial company', Max would write later.[9] He attended, not an intellectually inclined Gymnasium, but a Realgymnasium, whose function was to prepare students for practical careers. As a result of this paternal wish, Max was taken out of school aged fifteen in 1910 to work in the family business, and later became a junior manager. His father arranged for him to work as an unpaid intern in Brussels and Manchester, in order that the young Max could learn the business as well as French and English. But these foreign trips liberated Horkheimer: freed from parental shackles and the stifling bourgeois atmosphere of Stuttgart, he wrote to a friend: 'We have escaped from the world in which you suffer and our memory of it is a constant joy at being rid of it.'[10]

In Brussels, he was joined by Friedrich Pollock (1894–1970). Like Max, Freidrich was the son of a rich industrialist father, and was also gaining business experience at another factory in the Belgian capital. 'Fritz', who became an economist and social scientist and was Horkheimer's predecessor as director of the Institute of Social Research in the late 1920s, was to become a lifelong friend, even a soulmate. 'I had an ideal of having a friend with whom I could share everything that was important to me', he recalled in later life.[11] There was a third member of this party in what Horkheimer described as an *isle heureuse* – an intellectually, emotionally and erotically charged zone beyond the constraints of bourgeois norms – namely, Horkheimer's cousin Suze Neumeier. Max knew Suze from the annual visits her family made to Stuttgart from their home in Paris. But their relationship took a different turn as she became part of the coterie. Horkheimer visited her in Paris and she followed him to Calais. His father's plan was that, after Brussels, his son would go to Manchester to familiarise himself with the latest production techniques. Instead, Horkheimer and Pollock rented a flat in London and Suze soon joined them there. By this stage, Max had fallen in love with his cousin and she with him: 'Je suis à vous', she wrote to Horkheimer in her blood, 'corps et âme'. The Neuemeier and Horkheimer families were scandalised and notified the British police. Suze's father packed a pistol and headed across the Channel. In London, the parents found that Pollock was already in police custody. The families broke up what Jon Abromeit calls the trio's *bateau ivre*, returning Max and Fritz to Stuttgart and Suze to Paris.[12]

Back in Stuttgart, though, Horkheimer continued to rebel against his father's authority. He started working for the family firm, but soon began another erotic relationship, this time with his father's private secretary. As far as his parents were concerned, Rose Riekher was not a suitable woman for the Horkheimers' only son: she was eight years Max's senior, economically lower class and a gentile. She had come to the Horkheimer firm only because her own businessman father had gone bankrupt, necessitating that she take a secretarial post after graduating from trade school. But when the affair came to Max's parents' attention, she was dismissed.

From the first, Horkheimer's romantic liaison was wedded to his burgeoning social criticism – something that found expression in the novellas he wrote during the First World War. In one, entitled *Spring*, a young student leaves his wealthy parents for a woman from a nearby village with whom he has fallen in love. They walk to a hilltop chapel, past a vagrant whom the woman knows and fears. Inside the chapel, they try to keep thoughts about the impoverished man from ruining their romantic bliss. But he appears in the pulpit and delivers a sermon about injustice, which upsets the couple. He then approaches them and says: 'I feel sorry for you, you now know the truth . . . But it is not enough to take off the rose-tinted glasses and then to stand there confused and helpless. You have to use your eyes and learn to walk in the colder world. Intoxicate yourselves and praise every minute that you spend without being conscious, for consciousness is terrible; only Gods can possess it clear and undistorted and still smile.'[13] The religion of love, then, that the young student took as replacement for the religion of his parents in which he could no longer believe, is itself insufficient in a world that is unjust.

In another novella from this time, *Leonhard Steirer*, Horkheimer imagined a rebellion against such injustice. In it, the eponymous labourer finds his girlfriend Johanna Estland in the arms of the industrialist boss's son and kills him. He steals the son's money and then goes on the run with Johanna. 'If people like him can be "good",' Leonhard explains to Johanna bitterly,

> people whose pleasures, whose education, the very days of whose life are purchased at the cost of so much unhappiness to others, then what I did can't be evil. The difference between him and me is that I had to act and had courage and strength, while he was able to sit in comfort and enjoy himself and never discover what his pleasure was costing and that it was tainted with blood . . . Johanna, if you are not inhuman and cruel you must belong to me, just as you belonged to him! [14]

They spend a doomed, blissful day together, spending the murdered son's money in boutiques and restaurants before the police arrive and arrest Leonhard, who is later condemned to death.

Leonhard isn't so much a character as a type not uncommon in European fiction in the first decades of the twentieth century: an intellectually, economically and sexually frustrated worker in an intensely socially stratified capitalist system that crushes his hopes and dreams. Leonhard is a soulmate to the impoverished insurance clerk, Leonard Bast in E. M. Forster's 1910 novel *Howards End*. But, while Bast is wreathed in immobilising sadness and *ressentiment* ('I don't want your patronage. I don't want your tea. I was perfectly happy', he tells the unwittingly patronising Schlegel sisters who've invited him to their home to 'help him'[15]), Steirer takes action. For Leonhard at least then, the barbarity of civilisation personified by his effete rival is plain, but it is a barbarity that could be answered with courage and strength – in this case murder.

And Johanna? She reflects on the 'vague, mysterious sense of guilt' her dead lover had had and which 'she had never understood and thought was just a symptom of his illness'. She considers that Leonard deserved her love no more and no less than the son of the industrialist, 'and the thought made her shudder. For a moment she saw into the heart of the world – with wide, horrified eyes – she saw the insatiable, cruel greed of everything that lives, the hard inescapable fate of every creature, the obsession with desire, which burns and tortures forever, which is the source of all evils and will never be put out.'[16] A chastening passage that reads as though it were borrowed from Schopenhauer, whose philosophy captivated many German artists and intellectuals before Horkheimer.

It is as though behind the courageous struggle against an inhumane social order that Horkheimer is imagining here there lies a hideous spectre: the indestructible, insatiable will that governs all creatures and which necessarily expresses itself through greed and cruelty. It is that will to which we are all, Marxists or otherwise, in thrall: we are bound, thought Schopenhauer, on the wheel of Ixion, enduring the penal servitude of willing – from which we can escape only by artistic appreciation or through the Buddhist project of renouncing the will. But then Schopenhauer was a political reactionary, a German idealist philosopher who didn't share his contemporary Marx's belief that the purpose of philosophy was not to interpret the world but to change it, to eliminate the injustice and inequality upon which capitalism is founded.

This novella, which was only published along with others from the time in a volume called *Aus der Pubertät* (From Puberty) a year after Horkheimer's death in 1973, is intriguing since it involves the shotgun marriage of a temperamentally unsuited couple – proto-Marxist social critique and Schopenhauerian despair. Leonhard represents a critique of the capitalist values of an industrialist father and his privileged, complicit son (whose real-world analogues are Moritz and Max Horkheimer). Joanna stands for a pessimistic sense that the struggle against injustice is undone by the irredeemableness of evil and the inescapable human fate of being both possessed and demeaned by desire. It's not, you'd think, a marriage that's going to last.

But does Schopenhauerian pessimism undermine the raison d'être of Marxist struggle? Writing of these early novellas, Alfred Schmidt in *Max Horkheimer's Intellectual Physiognomy* argues that:

The ensnarement of humanity in eternal nature and an unswerving struggle against temporal injustice are already central in his thinking. As essential as he finds it that the 'unjust distribution of goods' be abolished, he nevertheless wonders if the fulfilment of the boldest utopias would not leave the 'great torment' untouched, 'because the core of life is . . . torment and dying'.[17]

For all his Hegelianised Marxism, Horkheimer never did divorce himself from his dismal Schopenhauerian bride. The first philosophy he read was Schopenhauer's *Aphorisms on the Wisdom of Life*, after he picked up a copy in Brussels in 1911. In 1968, near the end of his life, he published an essay entitled 'Schopenhauer Today' in which he wrote: 'my relationship to Hegel and Marx and my desire to understand and change social reality have not extinguished my experience of his [Schopenhauer's] philosophy, despite the contradictions involved.'[18] Schmidt argues that all critical theory is infected, or perhaps that should be enhanced, by this contradiction: 'Conceptual motifs from Marx and Schopenhauer, the latter standing for the malum metaphysicum, metaphysical evil, the former the malum physicum, physical evil – are played out against each other on all levels of critical theory because the "just society" is also "a goal that is always implicated with guilt", not only with a scientifically controllable total process.'[19] Just as civilisation, for Benjamin, necessarily has its barbarous side, so even the utopia of a just society, for Horkheimer, is necessarily tainted with guilt.

That said, Schopenhauer's eschatology, which Horkheimer shared, is not Marx's. For Schopenhauer, there is no ultimate redemption, no punishment, no heaven, be it on or beyond Earth. There is, rather, pointlessness on a cosmic scale: 'every living thing works with the utmost exertion of its strength for something that has no value. But on closer consideration, we shall find here also that it is rather a blind urge, an impulse wholly without ground and motive.'[20] There is also, though, in his philosophy the notion of human compassion as motivating action that ameliorates suffering – a notion that Horkheimer found appealing. Schopenhauer thought compassion involved self-identification: 'To a certain extent I have identified myself with the other man, and in consequence the barrier between ego and non-ego is for the moment abolished; only then do the other man's affairs, his need, distress and suffering directly become my own.'[21]

This, in a sense, is what Horkheimer does with *Leonhard Steirer* – he creates a fictional world in which he can identify with another man, and not just any man, but a man who murders the privileged, decadent son of the father-boss, who, even worse, has tried it on with our hero's beloved. To feel compassion for someone who murders you (even if the crime involves only a simulacrum of oneself being killed off in a fictional realm) is some feat of self-identification. And yet we shouldn't doubt that, for all Horkheimer's fears of the irrationality of the underclass, his guilt about his own privilege as the son of a wealthy Stuttgart businessman combined with his desire for social change: 'I want to tear down the boundaries between countries and social classes', he wrote in his journal, 'even though I know that this struggle is insane.'[22] Guilt and identification then took Max Horkheimer to the edge of madness.

In his mature philosophy, Horkheimer went beyond such self-identification, and beyond Schopenhauerian compassion: it is, he wrote in his 1933 essay 'Materialism and Metaphysics', the existence of current shared suffering that could lead to revolutionary social change.[23] But here, sharing suffering means rather more than a boss's rich son imaginatively projecting himself into the shoes of a downtrodden worker, more than the Schopenhauerian act of identification with the suffering of the other. In any event there is something much more striking in Horkheimer's adolescent fiction than proto-Marxist social criticism and Schopenhauerian gloom. There is a scarcely sublimated Oedipal complex, in which struggles with a successful capitalist father find expression in revolution, and which connects him profoundly in his formative experiences with other leading scholars of the Frankfurt School who grew up in the same era.

In another of his novellas from this time, *Work* (1916), a young factory director, Franz Lehndorf, turns against his father who runs the firm and incites its workers to revolution because he believes 'an uprising of the people to achieve conditions of existence . . . would give them access to true culture'. That phrase 'true culture' suggests that the end of revolution is a cultural rather than material one, with culture normatively conceived by a patrician Marxist sensibility that we will encounter repeatedly as we trace the history of the Frankfurt School, especially in Adorno's essays on the culture industry: the workers, once freed of the yoke of oppression, would march to the sunlit uplands of Beethoven, rather than wallow in the sewers of Hollywood.[24]

It's very hard not to read these novellas as romans à clef. The guilt-ridden industrialist's son of *Leonhard Steirer* or the patrician revolutionary of *Work* are projections of the author, and their dramas reflections of Horkheimer's real-life troubles with his father. *Work* was dedicated to 'Maidon', the affectionate name he gave to his then lover and future wife Rose Reikehr. Rose was the love of Horkheimer's life – the couple would marry in 1926 and remain together until her death in 1969. His refusal to abandon this unsuitable lower-class gentile woman typified Horkheimer's struggle with his parents, and with his father in particular.

Horkheimer received his call-up papers in September 1916. He was spared being drafted earlier because he was working in his father's factory. Like Pollock, he would never return to work for his father: after the war, both sought intellectual training at the same three universities – Munich, Frankfurt and Freiburg. It was only in 1926, when Horkheimer completed his academic qualifications, and thus made a success of himself in a world beyond the commercial one in which his father hoped he would make his mark, that his parents were able to welcome Rose into their family. The Horkheimers' Oedipal struggle, or so it would seem, was resolved. That struggle was perhaps even an instance of a rule: 'As a rule', Hannah Arendt argues, 'these conflicts were resolved by the sons' laying claim to being geniuses, or, in the case of numerous Communists from well to do homes, to being devoted to the welfare of mankind – in any case, to aspiring to things higher than making money – and the fathers were more willing to grant that this was a valid excuse for not making a living.'[25]

The case of Walter Benjamin demonstrates this point. He repeatedly refused to take a job in the business world that had made Emil Benjamin rich, fulfilled, and respected by many. Benjamin demanded money from his parents when he was well into his thirties, and in his letters said that their insistence that he work for a living was 'unspeakable'. After the First World War, however, the Benjamin family fortunes went into rapid decline. Emil urged his son to take up a career with earning potential and agreed to support Walter's academic aspirations only if he and his young family agreed to live in an apartment in the parental home. The result was a disaster; Walter claimed that living with his parents amounted to 'a long awful period of depression'.

He, his wife Dora and their young son fled the home to live in a friend's house. On his departure he was given a one-time payment of 30,000 marks against his inheritance and a further 10,000 marks for the establishment of his own home – still not enough for them to support themselves. Through her translating work Dora became the primary breadwinner. Instead of earning a living, Benjamin behaved as if his parents owed him one and relied on a monthly stipend from Emil and Pauline while he remained functionally unemployable. It's difficult not to think of him as ludicrously mollycoddled and entitled, not least when one learns that he blamed his ostensibly overbearing mother for the fact that, aged forty, he was unable to make a cup of coffee.[26]

Benjamin's unresolved Oedipal conflict was prefigured by that of Franz Kafka. Benjamin was one of Kafka's most sensitive early readers, and his sensitivity was highly attuned to the father–son struggles in the stories, as if they were allegories of his own. Franz's father Hermann was the fourth son of a *shochet* or ritual slaughterer in a village with a large Jewish population in southern Bohemia. He had worked as a travelling sales representative, and eventually became a fancy goods and clothing retailer employing fifteen people in Prague, where he and his wife Julie had six children, of whom Franz was the eldest.

'You have often reproved me', wrote the thirty-six-year-old Franz in his famous 100-page 'Letter to his Father',

> for living in peace and quiet, warmth and abundance, lacking for nothing, thanks to your hard work. I think here of remarks that must positively have worn grooves in my brain like: 'When I was only seven I had to push the barrow from village to village.' 'We had to sleep in one

room.' 'We were glad when we got potatoes.' 'For years I had open sores on my legs from not having enough clothes to wear in the winter . . .' 'But for all that, Father was always Father to me. Ah, nobody knows what that means these days. What do these children know of these things? Nobody's been through that!'[27]

Near the end of the letter, Kafka imagines what his father would say in reply to his son's unsent evisceration of his character. 'You are unfit for life; but in order to be able to settle down in it comfortably, without worries and without self-reproaches, you prove that I have deprived you of all your fitness for life and put it into my pockets. What does it matter now if you are unfit for life, now it is my responsibility, but you calmly lay down and let yourself be hauled along through life, physically and mentally, by me.'[28] This was the abiding worry in Kafka's writings and one that Benjamin might well have found personally relevant – that in the Oedipal struggle between father and son, the son was not what he should be, while the potency of the father remained undimmed. Kafka described his father as 'a true Kafka in strength, health, appetite, loudness of voice, eloquence, self-satisfaction, worldly dominance, endurance, presence of mind, [and] knowledge of human nature.'[29] These were the kinds of virtues, if one can call them virtues, that the fathers sought to pass on to their sons; they were, though, for the most part the worldly ones that the sons either disdained or were too weak to acquire. Bookish, neurotic, ill-adapted to the Social Darwinist ethos that had made their fathers successful businessmen, sons like Franz Kafka and Walter Benjamin were unfit for life, at least for life as it needed to be lived in the modern capitalist world. Hence, in Kafka's *Metamorphosis*, Gregor Samsa, the son who turns into a giant insect who disgraces the family home and is incapable of earning a living. Hence, too, Kafka's first great short story, *The Judgment*, which drew Benjamin's critical attention, about another father–son relationship. At the end the Oedipal story is turned against the natural order as the ostensibly decrepit, toothless, senile old father hurls off his bedclothes, stands on the bed and sentences his son to death. In his 1934 essay for the *Jüdische Rundschau* commemorating the tenth anniversary of Kafka's death, Benjamin quoted this passage at length as if he was transfixed by the parallels between Kafka's drama of the avenging father punishing his ungrateful weakling of a son and his own struggles with Emil Benjamin, who had died in 1926. 'You wanted to cover me up, I know, my little scamp, but I'm not all covered up yet', says father to son. The father speaks as if the covers were the grave, and his new-found verticality expresses, albeit with the abject tragicomedy customary of Kafka, the unexpected phallic power that had been lurking, earlier, in his dressing gown. 'And even if this is all the strength I have left, it is enough for you, too much for you . . . But thank goodness a father does not need to be taught to see through his son.'[30]

One senses Benjamin both appalled and compelled as he writes about this scene: 'He has to set cosmic ages in motion in order to turn the age-old father–son relationship into a living and consequential thing. But what consequences! He sentences the son to death by drowning. The father is the one who punishes; guilt attracts him as it does the court officials.'[31] The parallel Benjamin makes here is striking: the patriarchal bureaucratic state punishes, like its prototype, the father, unfairly and incontrovertibly: against either there is no appeal. Georg flees from the room, down the stairs, jumps from a bridge and drowns himself.

The natural order, whereby father yields to son, had been overturned, the cosmic wheels set in reverse – or at least Kafka imagined as much in this disturbing, uncanny story. It is a tale for its times, a tale of vigorous, worldly fathers refusing their destinies, of hypersensitive, critically astute, dialectically imaginative sons frozen by guilt, hobbled by their powers of projection. That's the problem with sensitive geniuses: they are hardly ever men of action. The leading lights of the Frankfurt School all had this problem; a problem that, looked at another way, is part of their allure.

It's hard, though, not to be sympathetic to their excoriated, Mammon-fixated fathers. All they wanted (conceived of in one way) was the best for their precocious, privileged, one might even say bratty sons. The magnanimity of father to son often figures in the biographies of members of the Frankfurt School. Herbert Marcuse was just such a son. After military service in the First World War (captivatingly recalled by his grandson Harold[32] as involving no combat but rather, this being the pre-automobile age, 'wiping horses' asses' for the infantry in Berlin), and participating in the 1918 German Revolution, he graduated with a PhD in German literature from the University of Freiburg in 1922, and then worked for six years as a bookseller in Berlin. But what is significant is that Marcuse's father provided him with an apartment and a share in a publishing and antiquarian book business.[33]

Such paternal magnanimity and indulgence comes out most clearly in the case of Theodor Adorno. Without the materially secure family home in Frankfurt that his father provided, even as the world beyond its walls turned upside down, Teddie would most likely not have become a bracingly self-confident intellectual. Even Marcuse, with something like awe, recalled late in life (during a late 1970s TV broadcast) the way in which Adorno would speak in sentences so finished you could send them straight to the printers.[34] Adorno's father, Oscar Alexander Wiesengrund, was a Jewish wine merchant in Frankfurt who had fought his own battles against parental expectation by marrying a singer who not only had the sensational name Maria Cavelli-Adorno della Piana, but was also Catholic. Oscar disowned his Jewish identity and indeed was hostile to it, a hostility that expressed itself in his feelings towards the eastern European Jews who had fled the pogroms of Russia and Poland and settled in the eastern districts of Frankfurt. For the socially affluent, Anglophile businessman Oscar, as for Leo Löwenthal's father, these newly arrived Jews with their long beards and kaftans were an affront. As Siegfried Kracauer (1889–1966), who would become one of Theodor Adorno's intellectual mentors, put it in his novel *Ginster*: 'They were Jews who looked so authentic, you thought they must be imitations.'[35]

The snobbery in Germany among the successful, westernised Jews towards the newly immigrated *Ostjuden* was acutely recognised by Adorno who, in the Frankfurt School's key text, *Dialectic of Enlightenment*, co-authored with Max Horkheimer, wrote: 'The enlightened self-control with which the assimilated Jews managed to forget the painful domination by others (a second circumcision, so to speak) led them straight from their own, long-suffering community into the modern bourgeoisie, which was moving inexorably to cold repression and reorganisation as pure "race".[36] For Adorno and Horkheimer, writing in wartime American exile and with hindsight, the hopes of safety sought by the likes of Oscar Alexander Wiesengrund in German bourgeois society were dangerous delusions. Certainly, the newly immigrated eastern European Jews who had escaped the pogroms were a visible reminder of what Jews like Oscar Alexander wanted to forget about their ancestral sufferings.

Given this context, it is not surprising that his first son, Theodor Ludwig Wiesengrund Adorno, was not raised as a Jew but baptised a Catholic. The name evoked, argued Adorno's biographer, his twin heritages: on the one hand, 'his father's search for material security, with its reliance on the virtues of persistence and calculation; on the other hand, there was his mother's gift for empathy with its emphasis on the creativity and spontaneity of art'.[37] Indeed, Oscar's role could be readily reduced to fulfilling the function of securing the economic foundations of his family's upper-middle-class standard of living, so that the more musical and creative maternal side of family life that nourished his beloved son could flourish.

Adorno's emotional and material security was crucial for his adult personality. It is a personality that contrasts with that of his intellectual mentor, Walter Benjamin. Benjamin conceived of himself, and was thought of by others, as a bumbler, prone to bad luck and incapable of making his way in the world. 'Like Proust', wrote Arendt, 'he was wholly incapable of changing his life's conditions even when they were about to crush him.'[38] Adorno was the antithesis of a bumbler, who, if no more brilliant than Benjamin, was able to use the qualities he had acquired as a privileged child – his industry, imperiousness and self-confidence – to parlay that brilliance into getting where he wanted to go. Thus, he established himself in academia with dissertations on Husserl and Kierkegaard; thus, too, he breezed into the epicentre of musical modernism by studying composition with Alban Berg in Vienna in the 1920s.

Not all of this was due to his upbringing, but the circumstances of Adorno's secure youth were hardly incidental to either his personality or his achievements. Leo Löwenthal described the eighteen-year-old

Adorno as 'the pampered young gentleman from a well-to-do family',[39] and other friends noted that, while Germany in general and the commercial centre of Frankfurt in particular collapsed into poverty and misery during the hyperinflation of 1922, when the purchasing power of the mark was falling not just from week to week but from hour to hour, Adorno and his family could afford trips to Italy and continued to live in relatively lavish style. Much of this was due to the acumen of Oscar Wiesengrund, who invested part of his fortune in material assets and thereby avoided the bankruptcies and financial ruin that hit so many others, notably Emil Benjamin. Teddie, too, benefited from being an only son, and thus the main beneficiary of the relative prosperity of the family.

This is not to say that he didn't have his own troubles with his father. As an adolescent he regarded his father as an embodiment of bourgeois values, and saw the businessman's interest in efficiency and profit as inimical to his own concerns, but there is, nonetheless, no suggestion that he didn't respect Oscar or recognise his achievements.[40]

But arguably his primary family relationship was not with his father but with the two women who dominated his early life, his mother Maria and her younger sister Agathe, whom he spoke of as a second mother. His mother was an opera singer, his aunt a pianist. Reading his biography, one has the sense of Adorno as a child prodigy who never grew up (because he didn't need to) and, paradoxically, as a man who, unlike Benjamin, could function well in the adult world. He could establish a successful academic career, remain solvent, even reinvent himself in exile after an estrangement from his homeland and culture with a confidence inimical to the older man.

Adorno, then, did not experience as much of the bitterness of Oedipal struggle as did his future colleagues at the Institute for Social Research. Strikingly, it fell to one of those Frankfurt scholars who had been embroiled in a struggle with his own father, the psychoanalyst Erich Fromm, to rebel against Freudian orthodoxy (itself an Oedipal struggle against the authority of the father of psychoanalysis) and argue that not all human societies, and certainly not pre-capitalist ones, were quite so prone to these struggles. Fromm indeed in his formative years in Frankfurt was alienated by the commercial spirit of his native city in general and his father's work as a salesman in particular, and was drawn to the iconoclastic, spiritual and studious milieu of two early father surrogates, his uncle Emmanuel who introduced young Erich to the riches of high European culture, and great uncle Ludwig, who introduced the young boy to the joys of Talmudic study.[41]

As an adult, Fromm became steeped in the work of the nineteenth-century Swiss Lutheran jurist Johann Jacob Bachofen, whose 1861 book *Mother Right and the Origins of Religion* provided the first challenge to the prevailing orthodoxy that patriarchal society represented a natural state of affairs and thereby validated capitalism, oppression and male hegemony, as Fromm's biographer Lawrence Friedman argues. Reading Bachofen also encouraged Fromm to reflect that the mother-child bond was the root of social life and that in a matriarchal society there was no strife, conflict or even private property, reflections that were decisive for his developing socialist humanism. In Bachofen's description of matriarchal societies they functioned as what Fromm called 'primitive socialist democracies', in which sociability, generosity, tenderness, religiosity and egalitarianism prevailed.

But then something terrible happened. According to Fromm's extrapolation of Bachofen, patriarchy was unleashed by women. Women invented monogamous marriages to free themselves from the irksomeness of multiple partners and unbridled sensual demands. Soon patriarchal societies emerged in which men fought for domination over women and the needy. Where maternal love for the newborn had been free and unconditional, and thus enhanced the child's self-confidence, in patriarchy fatherly love was contingent on the fulfilment of duties, and as the child came up short in this regard, he became psychically insecure. Rationality, private property, abstract juridical concepts and the power of the state replaced matriarchal society's priorities of sensuality, emotion, pleasure and happiness. As a result, society became fraught with conflict, emotionally repressed and guilt ridden.

The German sociologist Max Weber's 1904 book *The Protestant Ethic and the Spirit of Capitalism* recapitulated much of Bachofen's perspective. For Weber, the Protestant work ethic was what made capitalism possible. For him Protestantism provided the conditions under which many in northern Europe could set up their own enterprises and accumulate wealth for investment. The result was the growth of modern capitalism and rapid industrialisation in several northern European countries. But the increasing technological developments that took place in capitalist societies alienated worker from nature and served to subjugate the weak. The guilt-hobbled son of patriarchal culture who could never quite measure up to his father's wishes became as it were emblematic of the nature of the capitalist societies that emerged in Europe – his guilt, alienation, self-alienation, propensity for conflict and emotional repression all useful fuels that ensured the efficient running of capitalism.

With patriarchy the Oedipal struggle between father and son emerged. In *The Art of Loving*, Fromm wrote: 'When private property came into existence, and when private property could be inherited by one of his sons, father began to look to that son to whom he could leave his property . . .' As a result, argued Fromm, fatherly love, unlike motherly love, is conditional – and it has a negative and a positive aspect:

> The negative aspect is the very fact that fatherly love has to be deserved, that it can be lost if one does not do what is expected. In the nature of fatherly love lies the fact that obedience becomes the main virtue, that disobedience is the main sin – and its punishment the withdrawal of fatherly love. The positive side is equally important. Since his love is conditioned, I can do something to acquire it, I can work for it; his love is not outside my control as motherly love is.[42]

But this aspect is only positive for those raised under the spirit of capitalism according to the Protestant work ethic. For them, fatherly love was a wage that could be earned through work. To refuse to work for that love was to break the contract of one's employment. To yearn instead for the paradise of unconditional motherly love was inimical to the zeitgeist, against the patriarchal law, the stuff of utopian dreaming. It's no a surprise that two members of the Frankfurt School,

Fromm and Adorno, for all their differences, dreamed of such a utopia.

Did the Oedipal struggle play out in the way Fromm describes it here in his own conflict with his father Napthali? Not quite. Fromm withdrew from a father whom he regarded as neurotic and weak. 'I suffered under the influence of a pathologically anxious father who overwhelmed me with anxiety, at the same time giving no guidelines and having no positive influence on my education.'[43] Instead, he looked elsewhere for an ego ideal, for a surrogate father. He found one such figure in his uncle Emmanuel and told his cousin Gertrud that he preferred her father to his own.

Not all the Frankfurt scholars had such struggles with their fathers. For example, the father of the Marxist economist and political leader Henryk Grossman died at the age of fifty-four when Henryk was fifteen, and one is tempted to say that any struggles he had with patriarchy took the form of youthful political action against symbolic fathers – the patriarchal Habsburg empire, and the conservative Zionist elders of his native Galicia. But then his life was different from the Frankfurt School norm. Born in the Galician city of Krakow, Grossman led an early life of political activism so racy that the first part of his biography by Rick Kuhn could easily be made into a political thriller.[44] As a young man, he organised Jewish workers' strikes, led the Jewish Social Democratic Party, boasted of having girlfriends who were gun runners for the Bolsheviks and who hid their weapons in their silk underwear, while also theorising in greater detail the Marxist shibboleth disdained by his future colleagues in Frankfurt – namely the tendency of the rate of profit to fall under capitalism.

Grossman was a tough Jew who scorned Zionism as a bourgeois distraction. He had the intellectual self-confidence of Adorno, and was willing to test his theories against the fists of other Jews affronted by his socialist principles in manner alien to other Frankfurt scholars. If capitalism was the economic manifestation of patriarchal society and the European empires (the Russian, Habsburg and German in particular) its last dismal hurrah, then Grossman was a masterless man, a fatherless revolutionary who bowed to no authority but that of Marxist theory, one refracted through the writings of Lenin and

Luckács. One incident typifies Grossman. In 1906, he went to speak at Chrnazów, a small town in what is today south-west Poland, where his Jewish Social Democratic Party sought to encourage what was then a mostly Jewish population into organising socialist associations and trade unions in the face of opposition from Khasidic bosses. It didn't go well. The middle-class law student from Krakow and his sober-suited associates stuck out in the shtetel like sore thumbs. 'Khasidic zealots', writes Kuhn, incited a large crowd to beat him up and throw him and his comrades out of town. 'The money lenders and capitalists of Chrnazów had defamed the socialists as wanting to organise pogroms, as in Russia.' And Grossman's party leaflet, distributed in town, claimed: 'We only want to improve the situation of the workers, to make them aware and educate them.'

The matter wasn't over. Grossman's party warned: 'We will see who is stronger, hundreds and thousands of organised workers or a band of cheats and money lenders.'[45] Eleven months after he was beaten up, Grossman successfully sued his attackers before a magistrate in Chrnazów. The story demonstrates that Grossman was an oddity in the Frankfurt School, an organic intellectual of the working class and one who fought for socialism on the streets and for the well-being of Jews – even if that meant taking on other Jews.

Grossman shared something of the background of Carl Grünberg (1861–1940), the Romanian-born Marxist philosopher who, as we will see in the next chapter, in 1924 became the first director of the Institute for Social Research. Both were fatherless Jewish men from the outer reaches of the Habsburg empire. Both were significantly older than their colleagues at Frankfurt who would go on to develop the multidisciplinary intellectual movement called critical theory, to which neither of these scientifically inclined Marxists were temperamentally amenable. Grünberg had converted to Catholicism in part in order to secure his post as professor of law and political science at the University of Vienna, and while Grossman never firmly repudiated his Jewish religion, both men were of a materialist outlook and hostile to spiritual beliefs. Arguably, Grünberg became a surrogate father to Grossman, and certainly an ego ideal since he was the first avowedly Marxist professor at a German-speaking university. He showed the younger man that there was a possibility of a respectable academic career. When Grünberg had been a junior professor in Vienna in 1906, the young Grossman had attended his seminars.

Later, Grünberg became Grossman's academic patron, supporting and advising him in his choice of subject for the higher doctorate or Habilitation that would provide his entrée into academia. (Even as late as 1925 when Grossman, by then a forty-four-year-old professor in Warsaw, needed to flee Poland, where he found it difficult to do academic work for fear of political persecution, it was Grünberg who arranged for him to become a research associate at the appealing-sounding Marxist-leaning institute in Frankfurt. Grünberg had become the head of the Frankfurt School the year before.)

But if Grossman's earlier street-fighting years make him sound like a hero of the revolution, what he did during the First World War undermines that story. The man with hitherto unimpeachable radical credentials became a functionary of the imperial Habsburg state. Having been trying to build his academic career in Vienna, he was conscripted into the Austrian Army's 5th Field Artillery regiment in February 1915 and was involved in fighting against Russian forces the following year. In the flat, forested, swamp-ridden region of Volhynia, now in Ukraine, his unit was involved in rebuffing the Russian offensive. Grossman's biographer reckons that the Austro-Hungarians lost one million men in that Russian campaign, but Grossman was not one of them.

Valued more for his intellectual than martial skills, he was recalled from the front line and assigned to a military think-tank in the war ministry, rising to become a lieutenant responsible for writing reports on the co-ordination of the war economy. He calculated, for instance, how much it cost for the Austro-Hungarian empire to maintain its prisoners of war and how much it cost other countries to maintain Habsburg POWs. The Marxist economist also helped prepare briefs for Count Czernin, the Habsburg imperial foreign secretary, for peace negotiations at Brest Litovsk when he faced the Bolshevik delegation led by Leon Trotsky and Karl Radek. For all his radical credentials, then, Grossman was working for the wrong side, and there is no evidence that he took part in the failed Austrian Revolution of 1918.

He returned to active communist politics only on his return to Warsaw the following year.[46]

Many other members of what within a few years would become the Frankfurt School were for the most part too young, too lucky or too canny to serve in the war in any capacity. Adorno, for instance, was only fifteen when the war ended; during it he collected models of different warships from his school's stationery shop, read the Pocket Guide to the World's Navies, and dreamt of captaining a warship. His Jewish father Oscar, by contrast, received his call-up papers and was later honoured for his war service – an honour that counted for nothing to the Nazis who drove him into exile in the 1930s.[47]

Horkheimer was exempted the draft until 1916, but even then was never sent to the front. Which is probably just as well because by that stage he was a pacifist, disabused by travel of the nationalist fervour of many of his compatriots. 'I had been in London and Paris so I could never believe that the people there were more for war than our "peace-loving" Kaiser', he wrote later. 'I could not see that they were worse human beings than I and that therefore now I have to shoot them . . . My faith in the childhood teachings of the German Reich was shaken. I had the distinct feeling that something horrible had happened to Europe and could not be reversed.' In 1914, he wrote: 'I hate the armies that are on the march to protect property . . . Bestial movies guide their arms – motives that must be overcome in our drive for enlightenment and have to be destroyed if we want to become human beings.' In a short story called *Jochai* he imagined a private running from battle: 'The deep resentment compelled him, the Jew, not to kill but to vent his desperation, the desperation of all slaves, in a piercing scream that would reach the ears of the masters and destroy their contended indifference and help to destroy the conscious-ness-betraying facade of their world; in this way he chose intellectual victory.'[48] Horkheimer never fled screaming from battle, but it is hard not to read this passage as anything but his imaginative projection of himself into the madness of a war against which he distanced himself by any means necessary.

Horkheimer's thoughts here chime with the scepticism on the German left in 1914 about the war. The German Social Democratic

Party (SPD), which was the leading force in the country's labour movement and the largest political party, organised anti-war demonstrations in the wake of the assassination of the Austrian Archduke Franz Ferdinand in July 1914. But the following month, after Germany declared war on the Russian empire, the SPD was caught up in the national enthusiasm for war. In December, Karl Liebknecht, the only deputy to oppose war bonds, was prevented from speaking in the chamber to explain his vote, so instead circulated a leaflet arguing that German soldiers should turn their weapons against their own government and overthrow it. 'It is an imperialist war', Liebknecht wrote, 'a war for capitalist control of the world market, for the political domination of huge territories and to give scope to industrial and banking capital.'[49] He was jailed for high treason as, later, was Rosa Luxemburg, the socialist with whom he would lead the failed German Revolution of 1918–19.

The twenty-three-year-old student Walter Benjamin shared Liebkneckt and Luxemburg's socialist analysis of the war and, as a result, decided dodge the draft. In October 1915, Benjamin and Gershom Scholem cemented their friendship by staying up all night drinking vast quantities of black coffee until 6 a.m. The coffee drinking, if not the conversation (which touched on the Kabbalah, Judaism and philosophy), was 'a practice then followed by many young men prior to their military physicals', Scholem wrote in his memoir, *Walter Benjamin: The Story of a Friendship.*[50] The trick was to simulate a weak heart – and it worked. Later that day Benjamin presented himself for a medical examination and his call-up was deferred.

Like Horkheimer, Benjamin could not share the nationalist mood in his homeland. Indeed, at the outset of the war, Benjamin had broken painfully with one of his first intellectual mentors, the educational reformer Gustav Wyneken, precisely because of the latter's support for war. Wyneken had taught the young Benjamin at a private progressive boarding school called Haubindia in Thuringia in 1905. There the young Walter had become captivated by Wyneken's doctrine of Youth Culture, which held that the young were morally superior to the old. From Wyneken he learned that youth, the coming humanity, could be educated as knights to protect '*geist*', the spiritual values of art. What Walter's father, presumably representing for Wyneken the old, corrupted order, thought when he had to pick up the bill for this education is not recorded, nor are his views on his son's later forays into student politics that were premised on the notion of youth as engaged in the 'holiest work of humanity'. But when the war began Benjamin quit Wyneken's Free School Association over his former teacher's essay 'War and Youth', which argued that war would afford an ethical experience to the young. Benjamin wrote to Wyneken accusing him of sacrificing youth on the altar of the state. The following year, at Scholem's instigation, he was reading the theoretical journal of Luxemburg and Liebknecht's International Group, *Die Internationale: Zeitschrift für Theorie und Praxis des Marxismus*. He was moving from being a devotee of ethical youth culture towards his mature, if eclectic, Marxist philosophy.[51]

For some of the leading lights of the Frankfurt School, then, it was as though the First World War was a storm glimpsed from a safe distance, rather in the manner that Kant described the experience of the sublime. After dodging the draft Benjamin headed for Munich. 'At my last army physical, I was given a year's deferment and, in spite of having little hope that the war will be over in a year', he wrote to Scholem in October 1915, 'I am planning to be able to work in peace, at least for a few months, in Munich.' Later he was to spend the remainder of the war in Switzerland, studying for his doctorate at the University of Bern.[52]

Contrast Benjamin's war with that of another German-speaking, Jewish philosopher of a mystical temperament. Ludwig Wittgenstein was working on his great philosophical text the *Tractatus Logico-Philosophicus* while serving as a volunteer in 1916 on the eastern front for the Austrian Army, and was thus an unwitting comrade of Henryk Grossman. As he sat in his observation post, Wittgenstein wrote that he felt 'like the prince in an enchanted castle', awaiting the night's shelling with anticipation. The following morning he reported: 'From time to time I was afraid. That is the fault of a false view of life.'[53] None of the Frankfurt School thinkers who we've been considering could have written such sentences: for most of them, the war was not an exciting adventure that would test one's resolve and personal philosophy, but a disaster to be avoided at all costs.

As for Herbert Marcuse, the future radical student hero's war experience was limited.[54] He had been conscripted into a reserve division in 1916 after finishing his last exam at gymnasium, but remained in Germany because of his poor eyesight. His duties were so light that while in the Zeppelin Reserves he was able to attend lectures. Nevertheless, he claimed to have been politically educated by his experiences in the army and during the German Revolution in 1918. Certainly in 1917 he joined the Social Democratic Party (SPD) in protest against the war – an odd decision, since in that year the Independent Social Democratic Party (USPD) had been formed precisely in opposition to the SPD's pro-war stance; nor did Marcuse think to join Luxemburg and Liebknecht's Spartacist faction.

Only late in 1918, did the young Marcuse begin to be radicalised. Germany's rapidly collapsing military situation and the growing incidence of strikes raised the possibility of a German revolution akin to the Bolshevik one of the previous autumn. In October, sailors in Kiel rebelled; a Soviet-style socialist republic was, albeit briefly, established in Bavaria which, as Rolf Wiggerhaus puts it, Horkheimer and Pollock observed 'from a rather dignified distance'.[55] The revolutionary energy spread to Berlin where Marcuse had joined a soldiers' council. In November Liebknecht and Luxemburg were released from jail and, one day later, proclaimed Berlin to be a Free Socialist Republic. Marcuse was caught up in the revolutionary fervour and became a member of the city's communist civilian defence force. One day he found himself in Alexanderplatz, charged with shooting right-wing snipers who themselves were targeting left-wing demonstrators and revolutionary agitators.

In the last days of 1918, the Spartacist League, the USPD, and the International Communists of Germany (IKD), held a congress that led to the founding of the Communist Party of Germany, on New Year's Day 1919, under Luxemburg and Liebknecht's leadership. On that day, Luxemburg said: 'Today we can seriously set about destroying capitalism once and for all. Nay, more; not merely are we today in a position to perform this task, nor merely is its performance a duty toward the proletariat, but our solution offers the only means of saving human society from destruction.'[56]

But these hopes were quickly crushed. The SPD leader Ebert called on right-wing military war veterans to destroy the revolution, and on January 15 the decisive blow was struck. Luxemburg and Liebknecht were captured and murdered. Luxemburg's body was thrown by the Freikorps into Berlin's Landwehr Canal. In his poem 'Epitaph 1919', composed a decade after her death, Brecht wrote:

> Red Rosa now has vanished too.
> Where she lies is hid from view.
> She told the poor what life is about
> And so the rich have rubbed her out.[57]

Marcuse quit the SPD after the murders. For him, as for many other left-leaning Germans at the time, the Social Democrats had betrayed socialist hopes for the new post-war Germany and instead connived with the Prussian military establishment, allowing the latter to keep its hierarchies in place under Ebert's new government. The Weimar republic, then, was born from the blood of socialist martyrs.

But what is striking about Marcuse, and his experience is emblematic of the Frankfurt School, is that following the failure of the revolution he immersed himself in books, trying to work out why the Russian Revolution that had excited him had not been repeated in Germany. Years later he was asked why he hadn't joined the Communist Party, as had fellow Marxists György Lukács and Karl Korsch. 'I don't know', he told an interviewer in 1972:

By 1919, when I went from Berlin to Freiburg [where he was to study with the future Nazi-supporting philosopher Martin Heidegger], life was completely unpolitical . . . Nevertheless I became more and more politicised during this period. It was evident that fascism was coming, and that led me to an intensive study of Marx and Hegel. Freud came somewhat later. All this I did with the aim of understanding just why, at a time when authentic conditions for revolution were present, the revolution had collapsed or been defeated, the old forces had come back to

power and the whole business was beginning all over again in degenerate form.[58]

DECADES LATER, there was to be a poignant coda to these Oedipal
struggles of the leading Frankfurt scholars. For all that many of these
men rebelled against paternal authority, they came to regret its demise
and what they saw as the destruction in totalitarian society of the
bourgeois family under the Nazis. In 1941, writing from American
exile at the moment the Nazis were at the height of their power in
Europe, Horkheimer wrote:

> During the heyday of the family, the father represented the authority of
> society to the child, and puberty was inevitable conflict between these
> two. Today, however, the child stands face to face with society and the
> conflict is resolved before it even arises. The world is so possessed by
> the power of what is and the efforts of adjustment to it, that the adoles-
> cent's rebellion, which once fought the father because his practices
> contradicted his own ideology, can no longer crop up.[59]

Viewed thus, the patriarchal father who had once been a servant of
the Protestant capitalist state, ensuring its values were instilled in the
coming generation, was no longer necessary. Father and family had
been the gatekeepers to capitalist culture, rather like the way in which
monastic scribes had power because they had a monopoly on trans-
mitting the word of God. But just as the advent of printing made the
scribes obsolete, so the rise of totalitarian society made the father's
power and the family institution redundant. Thus, the Oedipal struggles that Freud saw as natural facts about human society could be
given a use-by date. Erich Fromm had suspected that the Oedipal
struggle had a beginning, and now Horkheimer was positing its end.
'Since Freud the relation between father and son has been reversed', he
wrote. 'The child not the father stands for reality. The awe which the
Hitler youth enjoys from his parents is but the political expression of
a universal state of affairs.'[60]

These melancholy, regretful, very nearly conservative thoughts
were taken up by Adorno a few years later in *Minima Moralia*, written

to celebrate Horkeimer's fiftieth birthday on 14 February 1945, at a time when both men and the Institute for Social Research itself were in American exile. In an early section of the book, he wrote: 'Our relationship to parents is beginning to undergo a sad, shadowy transformation. Through their economic impotence they have lost their awesomeness. Once we rebelled against their insistence on the reality principle, the sobriety forever prone to become wrath against those less ready to renounce.'[61] That remark recalls the guilt of the wretched son in Kafka's *The Judgment*, hoping for his father's potency to return (if not quite recalling the Kafkaesque nightmare that ensues when his hope is fulfilled).

The reality principle invoked here by Adorno was defined by Freud in his *Civilisation and its Discontents* in opposition to the pleasure principle. The latter, Freud thought, is what guides us through childhood – we follow our id in satisfying our urges for pleasure. The reality principle is the adult corrective to this youthful indulgence, the force of the ego that ensures we behave in ways that are socially acceptable and that therefore involves the renunciation – or repression – Adorno describes. Freud envisaged civilisation involving an increasing repression from which there seems to be no escape. As we will see, Marcuse responded to this pessimism in his 1955 book *Eros and Civilisation: A Philosophical Inquiry into Freud*, arguing that liberation entailed a freeing up of the repressed pleasure principle. For Marcuse, in an analysis that married Marx and Freud, freeing up the pleasure principle meant undermining the reality principle. 'Men do not live their own lives but perform pre-established functions', he wrote. 'While they work, they do not fulfill their own needs and faculties but work in *alienation*.'[62]

But Marcuse's cocktail of Marx and Freud was for the future, as one theoretical underpinning of the libidinous sixties' radical rebellion against repressive straight society – in other words 'the Man', or the power of the symbolic Father. In the 1940s when he wrote *Minima Moralia*, Adorno was not concerned with patriarchal power so much as with parental impotence, an impotence brought about by the undermining of the social role of the family in collectivist societies in general and Nazi Germany in particular. Yes, the death of the father's patriarchal power was, or at least had once been, a consummation devoutly to be wished. But not like this. 'Even the neurotic oddities and deformities of our elders stand for character, for something humanly achieved, in comparison to pathic health, infantilism raised to the norm', wrote Adorno.[63] It's as if Adorno is here writing with the son's fond sensibility towards his beloved parents and contrasting them with what supplanted their power, namely the institutions of social control established by the Nazis.

Pathic health? Normative infantilism? It's here hard not to think of Hitler Youth in short trousers or of Leni Reifenstahl's body beautiful aesthetic fascism. By the time he wrote this, Adorno's aunt Agathe had died, but both Oscar and Maria were, thanks in no small measure to his efforts to get them out of Nazi Germany, living in New York. They were reminders of an idyllic childhood and of a world before the Nazis. The title of this section of *Minima Moralia*, 'Grassy seat', alludes to a well-known German song: 'The dearest spot I have on earth / is the grass spot by my parents' grave.' Filial piety had replaced Oedipal struggle: 'One of the Nazis' symbolic outrages', Adorno wrote, 'is the killing of the very old. Such a climate fosters a late, lucid understanding with our parents, as between the condemned, marred only by the fear that we, powerless ourselves, might now be unable to care for them as well as they cared for us when they possessed something.'[64]

In such circumstances, perhaps, we can forgive Adorno his defence of what once looked like the bastion of patriarchy, the machine for converting children into workers for capitalism, namely the family. For now, he was suggesting that the family, far from being an institution against which rebellion was necessary, was the seat of resistance to totalitarian society.

> With the family there passes away, while the system lasts, not only the most effective agency of the bourgeoisie, but also the resistance, which, though repressing the individual, also strengthened, perhaps even produced him. The end of the family paralyses the forces of opposition. The rising collectivist order is a mockery of a classless one: together with the bourgeois it liquidates the Utopia that once drew sustenance from motherly love.[65]

That invocation of motherly love is salutary. It invokes, not just the lost paradise of Adorno's childhood, but the pre-patriarchal, pre-capitalist utopia that Fromm described. Would humanity ever be able to realise such a utopia? It seemed unlikely or at least cosmically distant. Instead, life would be more difficult and the intellectual task more demanding than utopian day dreaming. As Adorno's biographer writes:

> Adorno's expectation of living in a humane world based on mutual respect and solidarity was frequently disappointed in the course of his life without his ever having armed himself against potential disillusionment. On the contrary, his thought was influenced from the outset by the perceived need to face up to reality without illusions and to anticipate its constraints.[66]

That was the task, too, of his colleagues at the Institute of Social Research. Instead of utopian dreaming, the Frankfurt School had to face up to a reality more terrible than they, as children or as young Marxists in the 1920s, could have imagined possible.

PART II:

THE 1920s

3

The World Turned Upside Down

On 22 June 1924, the Institute for Social Research opened at Victoria Allee 17 in Frankfurt am Main. It was an interesting (in the sense suggested by the Chinese curse) time and place for a group of Jewish intellectuals and businessmen to establish a Marxist research institute. Frankfurt was then home to the second-largest population of Jews in Germany and in 1924 had elected its first Jewish mayor. But it was also where the world's largest chemicals conglomerate, IG Farben, had its headquarters. In Frankfurt, they developed Zyklon B, the cyanide-based killing agent later used in the gas chambers at Auschwitz.

To get a sense of what Frankfurt's successful industry of mass murder meant for its own citizens consider these figures. In 1933, the Jewish population of Frankfurt was 26,000, but before the Second World War was over, 9,000 Jews had been deported from the city.[1] Today, in the city's Jewish Cemetery, 11,134 little metal cubes arranged in row after row on the Wand der Namen (Wall of Names) commemorate the Frankfurt citizens killed during the Holocaust. And those Frankfurt Jews who were spared deportation to death camps often came to no-less miserable ends.

The city's first Jewish mayor, Ludwig Landmann, is a case in point. On taking office in 1924, he had sought to make his city more humane with new public housing projects such as Neues Frankfurt (New Frankfurt) that resulted in the construction of 12,000 apartments to counter an acute housing shortage, and by establishing the Nassauische Heimstätte, an organisation devoted to guaranteeing every citizen had access to decent housing. Landmann, though, was removed from office by the Nazis in 1933 and eventually fled to the Netherlands where, after spending the war sheltered by friends and relatives, he died from malnutrition during the bitter winter of 1945 aged seventy-six.[2] A Frankfurt newspaper in 2015 headlined an article about Landmann as 'Der vergessene Oberbürgermeister' (The Forgotten Mayor).[3]

The Institute for Social Research was not immune to the rising anti-Semitism. When its first director, Carl Grünberg, made his inaugural speech inside the completed building on Viktoria Allee he suggested that the Institute would be an alternative to a German university system that served as a training academy for 'mandarins' who who would go on to uphold the status quo. Fine words, perhaps, but as Grünberg spoke neither he nor any of his staff, nor Herman Weil, the businessman who had funded the Institute, nor his son Felix whose idea it was, realised the truth about the building in which this intellectual revolution was to take place. It had been commissioned by Jews and built by a Nazi.

Franz Roeckle had started his career by building a rather beautiful Egyptian-Assyrian style synagogue in Frankfurt in 1908, but by 1933 he was a National Socialist party member who was jailed for his part in a pogrom, known as the Rotter Affair, in his native Liechtenstein. In 1933 Fritz and Alfred Rotter, two well-known Jewish theatre entrepreneurs in Berlin, had fled Germany to Liechtenstein in part to avoid a bankruptcy scandal which had led to them being castigated in the Hitlerite press, but mostly to escape the Nazis – propaganda minister Josef Goebbels was seeking to eliminate what he called Berlin's 'Jew-ridden amusement business'. In Liechtenstein, four Nazis including Roeckle tried to kidnap the Rotter brothers in order to take them back to Berlin where, most likely, they would have been jailed if not murdered. The brothers managed to flee their hotel, but in the resulting car chase Alfred Rotter and his wife Gertrude plunged from a cliff to their deaths, while Fritz and his companion were seriously injured.

It is not clear whether Alfred and Gertrude's deaths were accidental or if they were driven off the road by Roeckle and his associates. The four Nazis served only short jail sentences for their involvement in the deaths: indeed, Roeckle and the others were freed early after a 700-signature petition secured their parole (the tiny German-speaking Alpine principality included many enthusiastic Nazi supporters). 'It was a political assassination, perhaps not the only, but the most serious of the small country', wrote the Liechtensteiner historians Norbert Haas and Hansjörg Quaderer later.[4] If so, the Frankfurt School's architect was an anti-Semitic murderer. As the *Frankfurter Allgemeine Zeitung* put it: 'First he built for Jews, then he drove Jews to their deaths.'[5]

Nor was Frankfurt in 1924 especially amenable to Marxists. Today the city is known as Mainhattan, not just for its high-rise skyline, but also because it is a global capital of business and finance, with one of the world's largest stock exchanges and the headquarters of both the Deutsche Bundesbank (the German federal bank) and the European Central Bank. By the 1920s, it was well on its way to becoming a modern metropolis and a hub of global capital: its stock exchange opened in 1879, its central station in 1888, its university in 1914 and its first airport in 1926. Like Berlin, Germany's second city boomed in population after unification: in 1861, it stood at 71,462.[6]

Today, certainly, and in 1924, perhaps, Frankfurt looked like the least traditionally German of cities, but it had an ancient pedigree and deep symbolic links in German history and culture. For centuries it had been a Free Imperial City in which the new emperor of the Holy Roman Empire was presented on a balcony overlooking Frankfurt's central square, the Römerberg (the Roman mountain), before a celebration of ox-roasts and fireworks.[7] Even though those venerable ceremonials came to an end when Napoleon destroyed the Holy Roman Empire in 1806, after the Corsican's fall, Frankfurt rose again to become the home for the parliament of the nineteenth-century German Confederation. It was also the birthplace of Goethe, and the city Arthur Schopenhauer chose as his home since he thought it more sophisticated than Berlin: 'Healthy climate, beautiful surroundings, the amenities of large cities, the Natural History Museum, better theatre, opera, and concerts, more Englishmen, better coffee houses, no bad water . . . and a better dentist.'[8]

But in the 1920s the old ceremonial Frankfurt centring on the Römerberg, with its facades of particoloured houses that could only look more German and gingerbready if Hansel and Gretel stepped out of the fairy tale to try to eat them, was being eclipsed. Beyond the Altstadt, a different Frankfurt was rising, one of austere, streamlined, coolly functional modernist buildings demonstrating new utopian ways of living and the city's growing industrial might. The first houses built as part of Neues Frankfurt were the so-called Zigzag Hausen on the city's Bruchfeldstraße, designed by architect Ernst May for Mayor Landmann. These three-storey and terraced houses, still standing, came complete with communal play areas, gardens, and even a paddling pool; the architecture was pared-down, functionally recti-linear, parallel to the aesthetics of Walter Gropius's contemporary Bauhaus style.

And then there was the grand new dye works for Hoechst AG, built by Peter Behrens, the architect whose assistants included those titans of modernism Mies van der Rohe and Le Corbusier, which opened a fortnight before the Institute for Social Research in the summer of 1924. The swaggering brick-clad fortress-meets-Bauhaus exterior is grand enough, but inside it is something even more extraordinary and symbolic of Germany's growing worship, not of God, but of its indus-trial prowess: the cathedral-like entrance hall is five storeys high with coloured bricks evoking the dyeing process, a veritable temple to business.[9]

But even the industrial swagger of what is now known as the Peter Behrens building was eclipsed by the the most striking new development in Frankfurt in the 1920s. Built on lands formerly owned by the Jewish banking family the Rothschilds, the IG Farben headquarters, when it opened in 1930, was the largest office building in Europe and remained so until the 1950s. Inside, workers travelled between floors on a new technological marvel, paternoster lifts, that consisted of a series of linked compartments moving continuously on an endless belt.

A year before the opening of IG Farben's vast research lab, Walter Benjamin wrote a prescient little essay that put the chemical conglom-erate, and the seemingly unstoppable rise of the German military-industrial complex, in his satirical crosshairs. Entitled 'Surrealism', the essay anticipated both the horrors of the Holocaust (albeit mostly unintentionally) and the Luftwaffe's bombing raids on British cities.[10] It was as if the worship of industry, and the faith of the Germans in its technological achievements, eclipsed what a communist like Benjamin sought, namely socialist revolution. In such a context, he wrote, he resigned himself to

> pessimism all along the line ... Mistrust in the fate of literature, mistrust in the fate of freedom, mistrust in the fate of European humanity, but three times mistrust in all reconciliation: between classes, between nations, between individuals. And unlimited trust only in I.G. Farben and the peaceful perfecting of the air force. But what now, what next?[11]

These profoundly bitter, sarcastic words resonate down the decades: the scale of Benjamin's dismal prognosis is vaster than even the headquarters of IG Farben. The conditions for revolution were everywhere lacking, he concluded grimly; rather, in a fallen world in which there was no class solidarity and negligible shared human values, all that remained to command conviction was the march of technological progress by means of industry. What next? In retrospect, we can answer Benjamin's question of 1929. What came next was that Frankfurt's leading business would help Hitler commit genocide.

In such a city, a Marxist research institute – run overwhelmingly by Jews and funded by Jewish money – was wise to keep a low profile. David Ryanzov, director of the Marx-Engels Institute in Moscow, with which the Frankfurt School was closely linked in the 1920s, urged that under Grünberg the Institute should appear impeccably bourgeois, establishing for example a clear relationship with the Univeristy of Frankfurt, but inwardly it should be devoted to collective Marxist research. It was then part Marxist cuckoo in Frankfurt's capitalist nest and part monastery devoted to the study of Marxism.

The Institute's building reflected this: the Swiss architect Sascha Roessler recently described it as being a 'Festung der Wissenschaft' (Fortress of Science), one that expressed in its architecture a 'Symbolik des Ruckzügs' (symbolism of retreat).[12] The building that opened in 1924 was an austere cube with space for 75,000 books in its library, a thirty-six-seat reading room, four seminar rooms with 100 places, and sixteen small workrooms. It consisted, Roessler argued, of a 'structure of homologous oppositions' between inside and outside, visibility and invisibility, sociology and society.

The Frankfurt cultural critic Siegfried Kracauer, friend and mentor to many of the Institute's scholars, visited the newly opened building and thought the cell-like reading rooms suggested a cloistered retreat, as if the study of Marxism in Germany in the 1920s required the ancient monastic virtues of asceticism, humility and discipline. Or as if Marxism were a tender orchid that needed to be protected from the ragingly hostile environment outside. That orchid sensibility persisted for much of the Frankfurt School's history: throughout its exile years in the United States, for instance, Horkheimer insisted that the M word and the R word (Marxism and Revolution) be excised from its papers so as not to scare the Institute's American sponsors, and in the late 1950s he refused to publish a paper by the young Jürgen Habermas containing such language because he feared it would threaten the Institute's funding, not least by risking a lucrative research contract with the West German ministry of defence.

The austere cube Roeckle designed, if hardly the most revolutionary building in Weimar-era Frankfurt, was a bracing addition to the Viktoria Allee for the denizens of the upper-class villas that lined that broad boulevard. In his review, Kracauer called its architecture 'strange and unadorned'.[13] It was certainly that. Roeckle built a five-storey block in the sober Neue Sachlichkeit style. Neue Sachlichkeit is often translated into English as New Objectivity or New Sobriety, but that doesn't really get to the heart of its German sense: 'Sach' can mean thing, fact, subject or object; 'sachlich' means factual, impartial or precise; and so 'sachlichkeit' might be rendered as 'matter of factness'. This New Matter of Factness was an artistic movement that thrived in Weimar Germany as a rebuke to the perceived excesses of Expressionism. Instead of self-indulgent romantic longing, business; instead of dreams, facts; instead of the heroic hour of revolution, the 24/7 totally administered society; instead of hysteria à la Nietzsche, a techno-pragmatic sensibility melding Max Weber and William James. In part, Neue Sachlichkeit was Germany turning American.[14]

Neue Sachlichkeit, though, was hardly just American: it was also a German response to a German problem, or at least to a German aesthetic tendency. Be it the minimalism of Walter Gropius's Bauhaus or the abrasiveness of early Brecht plays such as *Baal* or *Drums in the Night*, it was a response to the perceived speciousness, self-indulgence and over-valuing of the subjective experience of Expressionist art, but also a call to order after the slaughter of the First World War. In this, to be sure, the architecture captured Grünberg's view of Marxism as scientific methodology rather than political struggle; his work was relatively indifferent to theory, and rather predicated on hard facts.[15] At the outset, Grünberg's key staff were the close friends Friedrich Pollock and Max Horkheimer, with whom he developed the idea that the Institute should be concerned with the 'knowledge and understanding of social life in its full extent'. Later they would be joined by the exiled Polish economist Henryk Grossman and the German historian and sinologist Karl August Wittfogel.

The Institute's project, Grünberg announced, involved 'a new type of scientific work organisation' that would be Marxist in that it adhered to Marxism as a scientific methodology. During its first few years, Grünberg's Institute was concerned with research into the history of socialism and economic theory and with collaborating with the Marx-Engels institute in Moscow in producing the first Marx-Engels Gesamtausgabe, or collected edition, jauntily known by its acronym MEGA. This sober, fact fixated, even bureaucratic tenor of the Frankfurt School would change after 1928 when Pollock and later Horkheimer became directors of the Institute, unleashing an era of speculative neo-Marxist theorising inimical to Grünberg and older Marxists such as Grossman; but during the 1920s the Marxist research institute seemed mired in the Neue Sachlichkeit ethos.

It was only in the 1930s that the Frankfurt School, led by Horkheimer, Pollock and Adorno, disdained the spirit that the architecture of the building they worked in expressed. For the men who more or less invented critical theory in this austere monastic building, before the Nazis forced them in 1933 to abandon Frankfurt and Germany, society and even thought were becoming more machine-like and functional under the new form of capitalism that was developing in Germany. 'Thinking objectifies itself to become an automatic, self-activating process', Adorno and Horkheimer wrote in *Dialectic of Enlightenment*; 'an impersonation of the machine that it produces itself so that ultimately the machine can replace it.'[16] From the enchantment of Expressionism, then, to what Max Weber called the disenchantment of the world – which he took to be the rationalisation of all areas of human endeavour (and which Adorno and Horkheimer took to signify humanity's domination, by means of science, over nature) – and from disenchantment to the ultimate reification: the making of thing into human and human into thing with the result that humanity, ultimately, is expendable. Neue Sachlichkeit was the spirit of this age.

There's one last thing to be said about the building's architecture. Roessler detected in it not just the spirit of Neue Sachlichkeit, but a creeping presence of the heroic style that would manifest itself in the works of Albert Speer.[17] It's an intriguing point: maybe Franz Roeckle built into the Institute for Social Research intimations of the Third Reich. Certainly, his last piece of German architecture, a 1940 monument to the businessman and patron Karl Kotzenberg with a muscle-bound superman, found in Frankfurt's cemetery, represented that fascist heroic style on steroids. But the idea that the business-friendly style of Neue Sachlichkeit expressed fascist ideas should not be a surprise. Indeed, the Frankfurt School would, as we will see, come to realise as it studied Nazism that the marriage of Hitler and business was hardly a shotgun affair – it was a love match between two compatible partners.

The austerely academic nature of this Marxist research institute and the compromises of its foundation were later waspishly ridiculed by Hanns Eisler. Over lunch one day during Hollywood exile in 1941, the composer and songwriter recounted to his friend the playwright Bertolt Brecht the plot for a planned satirical novel: 'A rich old man (Weil, the speculator in wheat) dies, disturbed at the poverty in the world. In his will, he leaves a large sum to set up an institute which will do research on the source of this poverty. Which is of course himself.'[18]

Eisler didn't want to spoil a good story with facts. In reality, Hermann Weil didn't bequeath money in his will to found the Institute (he died in 1928). Rather, he provided an initial endowment that supplied an annual income of 120,000 marks, which was later supplemented by grants from him and other sources, thus securing the independence and solvency of the Frankfurt School through financial crash, economic depression, and perilous years of exile during the thirteen years of the Third Reich, and the Holocaust. The man who made the Frankfurt School possible was, in any case, a much more interesting figure than the capitalist stooge that Eisler tried to present him as being. Hermann Weil hailed from a Jewish mercantile family in Baden[19] and had worked in the last decade of the nineteenth century for a Dutch grain company in Argentina, where in 1898 he set up his own business with his brothers. It proved so successful that, a decade later when he returned to Germany and set up home in Frankfurt, he was the world's largest grain trader.

His son Felix, like so many of the Jewish sons of businessman fathers we considered in the last chapter, turned against this ethos. The Marxist Jewish intellectual son was once more standing against the capitalistic values by means of which his businessman father had achieved material success. And yet, once more, that son was dependent on daddy's money in order for him to fulfil his manifest destiny – to castigate the economic system from which his father had prospered, and to theorise its downfall. Felix became, as he self-deprecatingly put it, a 'salon Bolshevik', one who consorted with those who wanted to destroy the capitalist system under which his father had made his fortune. Felix wrote his PhD on the practical problems of implementing socialism, which had been published by the German Marxist theoretician Karl Korsch. In the early 1920s, Felix asked his father for some money. He could have asked for anything – a yacht, a country estate, a Porsche. But instead he asked Hermann to fund a Marxist, multidisciplinary academic institute. He wanted it to be independently endowed so it was beholden to no one, least of all the rigid German university system.[20] Felix hoped that this Marxist think-tank could help explain why the revolution had failed in Germany and how, if possible, it could succeed in the future.

That Hermann agreed to his son's proposal is perhaps best explained by two factors: firstly, he was keen to use his wealth to support institutions in his adopted city (he had already made important endowments to the University); secondly, Jewish fathers of his generation very often indulged their sons' ambitions and ventures. But his agreement was still a little odd: Hermann was agreeing to loosen the family purse to pay for an institute that would help theorise the downfall of the economic system that had made him rich. The Frankfurt School was thus paid for by the economic system it was established to indict, and the businessman father who bankrolled it stood for values that his son sought to destroy. No matter: Hermann Weil's generous funding helped the Frankfurt School secure its independence and survive financial crash, exile and the Holocaust.

The Education Ministry had suggested calling it the Felix Weil Institute of Social Research, but Weil modestly demurred. The original idea of calling it the Institut für Marxismus (Institute for Marxism) was deemed too provocative. So it became known as the Institut für Sozialforschung (Institute for Social Research), and Weil invited Carl Grünberg to become its first director. Grünberg was not the first choice: Weil had originally approached a socialist economist called Kurtz Gerlach, but he died of a heart attack aged thirty-six in 1922. Grünberg was professor of law and political science at the University of Vienna with a considerable reputation as a scholar on the history of socialism and the labour movement, and mostly known for a scholarly journal called *Grünbergs Arkiv*. Grünberg set out its first research topics as: international trade unions, strikes, sabotage, revolution as wage movement, anti-Semitism as a sociological problem, the relationship between Bolshevism and Marxism, party and mass, standard of living of the population, the improvement of Germany. His opening address suggested that the Institute would be Marxist in that it adhered to Marxism as a scientific methodology; it would not be collegial, but run, as Grünberg put it, as a dictatorship.[21]

It also had no official line on whether the Soviet Union represented a betrayal of socialist hopes or its fulfilment, even as it maintained close links with its sister organisation in Moscow. For instance, when Friedrich Pollock wrote *Experiments in Economic Planning in the Soviet Union 1917–1927*, he was careful not to express support for the Soviet system. Rather, his was a more objective perspective – suggesting how the Soviet Union, with low levels of technological sophistication and without international support, had understandably struggled to achieve its revolutionary aims and economic projections.

Thus, from its inception, the Frankfurt School was riddled with paradoxes. Marxist, but not so Marxist that it would declare its philosophy in its name. Marxist, but not so Marxist that it would live up to what Marx wrote in his *Theses on Feuerbach*, words that have been deemed so key to his work that they are inscribed on his tombstone in Highgate Cemetery in London: 'The philosophers have only interpreted the world, in various ways. The point, however, is to change it.' Marxist, but bankrolled by a capitalist. Marxist, but without party affiliation. It was affiliated to the University of Frankfurt, and took students, but was still autonomous and financially independent.

Eisler's satirical suggestion, though, went to the heart of the misgivings about the foundation of the Institute and what it was for. For Brecht, in particular, the Frankfurt School perpetrated a bourgeois sleight of hand by posturing as a Marxist institute while at the same time insisting that revolution could no longer depend on insurrection by the working class, and declining to take part in the overthrow of capitalism. There were exceptions of course: in the later 1920s, the street-fighting revolutionary turned academic, Henryk Grossman, developed a Leninist-inspired economic theory of capitalism's demise, taking the line that crises in capitalism and a concomitant rise in proletarian consciousness were both necessary for the forthcoming revolution.

But he was an exception: as Grünberg's directorship gave way to that of Pollock and then Horkheimer in the late 1920s, a newer more pessimistic Marxism was taking over the Frankfurt School, one for which the revolution was not imminent, precisely because the rise in consciousness that Grossman took to be necessary for it was not possible under the new modern conditions. Under Grünberg, it seemed, the Institute became bureaucratic and agnostic; under his successors, it went into a theoretically exciting period of speculative, multi-disciplinary work inimical to the Institute's founding philosophy of scientific Marxism.

But while the Frankfurt School became increasingly clear about why the German Revolution had failed, it would never overcome its scepticism that the revolution would happen. Even though the Institute was nicknamed 'Cafe Marx', that scarcely captures its austere mood, which was better reflected in its architecture: the neo-Marxists of the Frankfurt School were modern-day monks working in retreat from a world they could not change and a politics they had no hope of influencing. As the scholar of critical theory Gillian Rose would later argue:

> Instead of politicising academia, it academicised politics. This transposition became the basis for its subsequent achievements. Yet time and time again, the history of the School reveals this tension: as institution, it reaffirmed and reinforced those aspects of German life which it criticised and aimed to change, just as it reaffirmed and reinforced those aspects of the intellectual universe which it criticised and aimed to change.[22]

If Rose is right about that, then the Frankfurt School wasn't so much a Marxist institute as an organised hypocrisy, a conservative sheep in radical wolf's clothing.

The men whom Brecht called dismissively the 'Frankfurturists' were aloof from party and had never sullied their fists in political struggle (Grossman was, Brecht might have said, the exception who proved the rule); they were men with cosy jobs who thrived in American exile. At least that is the story that Eisler and Brecht, in Californian exile, told themselves as they dabbled in satire.

THE INSTITUTE for Social Research had its roots in an event that took place in the Thuringian town of Ilmenau a year before its foundation. In the summer of 1923 a group of Marxist intellectuals had gathered for the Erste Marxistische Arbeitwoche – a week-long summer symposium organised by Felix Weil, to address the practical problems of implementing socialism. In the summer of 1923, those who gathered in Ilmenau wanted to know why the old forces had come back into power; the laws of Marxism conceived as a science of history predicted that the workers should have been more successful in overthrowing capitalism after Germany's defeat in the First World War and the hyperinflation that followed it. It was this symposium that led, a year later, to the foundation of the Institute for Social Research.

The practical problem of implementing socialism was a vexed issue. The symposium took place in the wake of the German Revolution of 1918–19 that had failed, in part, because of splits on the left. Aimed at emulating the triumph of the Bolshevik Revolution of 1917, it had been crushed by Social Democrat leaders and right-wing military war veterans called Freikorps. Felix Weil's hope for the Ilmenau symposium was that 'if afforded an opportunity of talking it out together', the intellectuals present could arrive at a true or pure Marxism.[23] A lovely if deluded hope: intellectuals hardly ever talk themselves into agreement, and, as more recent history shows, Marxism became more divided by feuding factions even than Protestantism.

Already in 1923, German Marxism resembled the Judean people's movements in *Monty Python's Life of Brian*. First and foremost, there was the so-called Pope of Marxism, Karl Kautsky, the German Social Democratic Party's leading theoretical figure. He had been a leading light of the Second International, the worldwide federation of socialist organisations that was founded in 1881 and collapsed acrimoniously in 1916 over the need for socialist revolution and differing attitudes to the First World War. It was succeeded in 1919 by the Third International, or Comintern, launched in 1919 by Lenin, which advocated world communist revolution. Kautsky, while formally stressing the need for a revolutionary overthrow of capitalism, argued that Marx had demonstrated that history was a succession of different societies and that within each society production grew until a point at which it could grow no further and then revolution took place. Revolutions, thus conceived, required the proletariat to have the patience of the bus queue. They must wait for what would, inevitably, come, and then jump on board.

Then there was Eduard Bernstein, a Reichstag deputy who had founded the Independent Social Democratic Party in 1916, set up to oppose the war that Kautsky, to his eternal disgrace in Marxist circles, had supported. Bernstein's Marxism had been akin to Kautsky's in implying the essential passivity of the proletariat in the face of economic forces that would, eventually, destroy the bourgeoisie and bring workers to power. Ultimately, Bernstein even junked the formal commitment to the violent overthrow of the bourgeois order to which Kautsky adhered, arguing that revolution was not necessary.

Then there were Rosa Luxemburg and Karl Liebknecht, the Spartacist rebels. Unfortunately for German Marxism, by 1923 they were long dead, murdered, or so it is argued, with the connivance of the SPD (as we saw in the last chapter) that Kautsky and, latterly, Bernstein supported.

But most strikingly of all, there was the figure of Lenin who, in October 1917, ousted Kerensky's social democratic provisional government in Petrograd and took Russia out of the war. Where Rosa Luxemburg took revolutionary politics to be an expression of the spontaneity of the proletariat, Lenin conceived of the party as a vanguard for the proletariat. Events had justified his theory – not only were the Bolsheviks successful in leading the Russian Revolution, they had also been so well organised during the resultant civil war as to see off a concerted international effort to oust them. In 1920, at the second conference of the Third International, Lenin threw down a challenge to other Marxists: 'The revolutionary parties must now "prove" by their practical actions that they are sufficiently intelligent and organised, are sufficiently in contact with the exploited masses, are sufficiently determined and skilful to utilise this crisis for a successful and victorious revolution.'[24]

The Marxist intellectuals at Ilmenau didn't pick up Lenin's gauntlet, nor did the Institute for Social Research. Instead of revolutionising Germany, they revolutionised Marxist theory. Two of the most eminent attendees at Ilmenau, Karl Korsch and György Lukács, were Leninists who in 1923 published books that were key to this revolution in Marxist thought. In his *Marxism and Philosophy* Korsch attacked both Kautsky and Bernstein, arguing that their scientific socialism had ceased to be a theory of social revolution. For Korsch, Marxism was a form of revolutionary action, in which theoretical discussion and practice had again to be combined. Korsch was no armchair intellectual: he had been decorated twice with the Iron Cross for acts of bravery, despite his opposition to the war and despite his claim never to have raised a sabre or rifle while in uniform. In 1919 he joined the German Communist Party and in 1923 became Minister of Justice in the coalition SPD-KPD government in Thuringia, where some hoped that this military figure might lead an insurrection on the sixth anniversary of the Soviet revolution of 1917. But the call to arms never came, and Korsch never became the Lenin of Thuringia.

Nonetheless, Korsch's Leninist perspective was echoed by Lukács whose 1922 masterpiece *History and Class Consciousness* attempted a philosophical justification of Bolshevism.[25] Lukács posited that the proletariat, once conscious of its historic role, would destroy capitalist society. Class consciousness was understood by Lukács as a result of the proletariat being the product of the contradictions of history, chief among which is the exploitation of its labour under capitalism. But then Lukács made a key distinction between the ascribed and actual consciousness of the proletariat – the higher ascribed consciousness was embodied in the revolutionary party, while actual consciousness may not be able to grasp its historic role. The party, in a sense, knows what is good for the proletariat – how it must act, and what the historic significance of its suffering under capitalism is. Into this gap between ascribed and actual consciousness, too, the Frankfurt School, as we will see, would insert itself, trying to understand what it was about capitalism's oppressed that stopped them rising up to end their bondage – to be delighted, rather, with the very chains that bound them.

Revolutionary leaders such as Lenin didn't suffer from such false consciousness – they were adepts at revolution and understood the historic role of the proletariat which, as Lukács put it in Hegelian terms, was to be the subject-object of history, by which he meant that instead of the proletariat being, as it currently was, in a mode of contemplation or passivity, it became an active subject engaged in the production of the world in which it could flourish. But why was there a gap between actual and ascribed class consciousness? Lukács's answer to that is what made his book revolutionary in Marxist theory and go on to have a profound influence on the Frankfurt School. To account for the gap, Lukács developed the notion of reification, extending Marx's analysis of the 'fetishism of the commodity form' in *Capital*. The problems of society, perhaps even the reason the German Revolution had failed, could be traced to a riddle of the commodity form that Marx wrote about at the start of his master work.

Lukács's book discussed a new form of alienation that confronted industrial workers in the 1920s. Industrial nations such as Germany, Britain and the United States were now entering what became known as the Fordist era, a period of mass production. In 1913, Henry Ford had installed the first moving assembly line for the mass production of motor cars in Detroit, reducing the time it took to build a Model T Ford from twelve hours to two and a half. Fordism's new industrial revolution changed production, consumption, culture and thereby what it was to be human. At the level of production, by training his workers to specialise in one of the eighty-four discrete steps necessary in the car production, and by deploying motion-study expert Frederick Taylor to make those jobs even more efficient, Ford raised output, enabling him to cut the prices of the finished cars and, crucially, change the relationship between workers and the product of their labour.[26] For philosophers as far back as Spinoza and, in particular, for Karl Marx, humans were productive beings, who were only alive to the extent that they grasped the world outside themselves in the act of expressing their own specific powers. Mass production, through division of labour, increasingly thwarted the possibility of such fulfilment. The idea of personally fulfilling labour, sanely remunerated and manifesting artisanal skills, was the stuff of William Morris's anti-machine-age socialist-medievalist fantasies.

Assembly lines sped up the production processes but diminished workers: they increasingly became cogs in a machine, or, worse, rendered obsolete by machines. For example, Henry Ford's car factories included machines that could stamp out parts automatically far faster than mere humans. Humans were becoming unfit for productive purpose, a fact that, for Marxists who deemed humans to be essentially productive beings, might have seemed existentially tragic were such terms part of their theoretical vocabulary. 'When I'm through', Ford said of his cars, 'about everybody will have one.'[27] Humans weren't just becoming machines or being replaced by them, but were becoming desiring machines – their identities defined through their more or less passive consumption of mass-produced goods.

At the level of culture, Fordism made the world modern. Those mass-produced goods included not just Model T Fords, but also Charlie Chaplin films. Mechanisation didn't just revolutionise industry but also industrialised art, speeding up the possibilities of production and distribution, making new art forms – cinema, photography – possible and making old ones – novels, painting, theatre – seem sluggish. Speed, economy, the ephemeral and the entertaining were the hallmarks of mass-produced culture. While Italian Futurists eulogised on the machine age's unleashing of velocity, and while, as we will see, Walter Benjamin saw revolutionary potential in new art forms, others bemoaned the pace of cultural production. 'In all the arts the output of trash is both relatively and absolutely greater than it was', wrote Aldous Huxley in 1934.[28]

But it wasn't only conservative dystopians who worried about mass-produced culture. For Frankfurt School thinkers like Horkheimer and Adorno, if not Benjamin, this output of trash had a function: to pacify the masses. Even Benjamin could write of these times: 'Experience has fallen in value. And it looks as if it is continuing to fall into a bottomless abyss.'[29] Weber's iron cage of capitalism had subdued humans during working hours; now the culture industry subdued them at their leisure – changing them increasingly from productive beings to consumers, from the Marxist dream of creatively vital humans to stupefied moviegoers all giggling at the same thing.

What it was to be human was changing radically in this Fordist modern age. Like an importunate lover, monopoly capitalism had come on too quickly in its flashy new motor promising all kinds of ruinous temptations to the masses. 'A generation that had gone to school on a horse-drawn streetcar now stood under the open sky in a countryside in which nothing remained unchanged but the clouds and beneath these clouds, in a force field of destructive torrents and explosions, was the tiny, fragile human body', wrote Benjamin.[30] To be human under such conditions was to find oneself, as Lukács put it in 1920, transcendentally homeless, longing nostalgically for what was lost. To be human involved being alienated from the machine-like, functional, replaceable thing one had become. In 1927, Brecht wrote a poem for his cycle *Reader for City Dwellers* that captured that modern sense of self-alienation and that modern fear of becoming obsolete:

> The linen hanging out to dry in the yard
> Is my linen, I know it well.
> Looking closer however I see
> Darns in it and extra patches.
> It seems
> I have moved out. Someone else
> Is living here now and
> Doing so in
> My linen.[31]

'It seems I have moved out' – here Brecht was capturing not just the uncanny modern sense of being haunted by a doppelgänger who is an upgrade of oneself, modern man undone by his undies, but also the passivity involved. Indeed, Brecht was increasingly drawn in the 1920s to representing on stage the passive types typical of the modern age who, as his biographer Stephen Parker puts it, 'adapt as best they can to the bewilderingly changing circumstances of the modern world'.[32] In *Man Equals Man*, for instance, Brecht's 1926 parable set in colonial India, he had dramatised the forcible transformation of a civilian, Galy Gay, into the perfect soldier. He envisaged personality as something that can be reassembled like a machine, a vision that prompted one critic to see *Man Equals Man* as prefiguring brainwashing techniques. The drama was in part a satire on Neue Sachlichkeit, whose functionalist ethos fitted perfectly with increased human domination by Fordist assembly lines and Weberian bureaucracy.

In *Capital* in 1867 Marx wrote about the fetishism of commodities, how human consciousness becomes reified and how the class consciousness necessary for proletarian revolution can be thwarted. The Marxists gathering at Ilmenau were living under a more advanced form of capitalism than the one Marx had described. Why was social-ist revolution increasingly unlikely in the 1920s? Because the reified structure of society, the alienation of workers and the commodity fetishism of the modern world were so complete that they militated against the class consciousness necessary for such a revolution.

But what do these terms mean? Alienation? Reification? Class consciousness? Commodity fetishism? Think of the chair you're sitting on, or the iPhone to which you're umbilically linked. A chair is a commodity – not because you can sit on it, but because it was produced by humans to be traded. It has value, that is to say, not because value is a natural property of the chair, but because each commodity has a use value, measured by its usefulness in satisfying needs and wants. This is all very sensible and straightforward, but hold on to your hat (also a commodity) because we're going into a spectral realm. Under capitalism, the things that humans make take on phantasmagoric lives of their own. Marx's *Capital* is not just a forbidding tome of philosophical and economic thought, but a racy gothic novel, a Frankenstein-like tale of how we created a monster (capitalism) from which we are alienated and which, by means of class struggle, we will slay.

The crack humans opened in the world that allowed all these monstrous things in is the gap between use value and exchange value. Through that gap came the corrupting flood of commodities. Here comes one now: it's Apple launching a fatuous new iPhone minimally different from its predecessor. When a chair or an iPhone is sold, it is exchanged for another commodity (money for instance). The exchange takes no account of the labour that went into the chair's making, still less that, for example, of Apple's overstressed and underpaid workers, some of whom have contemplated suicide in order to escape the penal servitude of manufacturing ostensibly must-have gizmos for you and me.

But that's only one part of the ghost story. The other has to do with what happens when the worker is paid wages for her labour. For Marx, the wage relationship between capitalist and worker takes no account of their respective social positions or of their social relations.[33] The labour that produced the value in the form of a coat is treated as an abstract commodity that is equivalent to any other commodity, just as the exchange value of the chair detaches the chair from its use value. This is what Marx calls commodity fetishism.

Strikingly, both Marx and later psychoanalytical thinkers derived their accounts of fetishism from nineteenth-century European attitudes to African religions.[4] Just as, in some religions, an object invested with supernatural powers becomes a fetish for those who worship it, so commodities under capitalism are accorded magical powers and illusory autonomy. The strange illusions unleashed under capitalism, for Marx, aren't just one but many: sometimes the relations between humans become a relation between things; sometimes value appears as what is not a natural property of the thing; sometimes the commodity takes on a life of its own and becomes personified.[35]

But, Lukács argued, such commodity fetishism, which existed in Marx's day, has become all-pervasive in the modern age. Under capitalism the properties of objects, subjects and social relations become reified or 'thinglike' in a particular way. According to Lukács, the mechanisation and specialisation of industrial work processes fragments human experience, leading to an attitude of 'contemplation' where one passively adapts to a law-like system of social 'second nature' and to an objectifying stance towards one's own mental states and capacities. The commodity form, he wrote:

> stamps its imprint upon the whole consciousness of man; his qualities and abilities are no longer an organic part of his personality, they are things which he can 'own' or 'dispose of' like the various objects of the external world. And there is no natural form in which human relations can be cast, no way in which man can bring his physical and psychic 'qualities' into play without their being subjected increasingly to this reifying process.[36]

Reification affects relations between persons, and even within the person: one becomes an object to oneself, self-alienated as well as alienated from other humans, particularly those with whom we should be expressing class solidarity.

This implies that objects are transformed into subjects and subjects are turned into objects, with the result that subjects are rendered passive or determined, while objects are rendered as the active, determining factor. Hypostatisation, a term that runs through Frankfurt

School writing like a thread, refers to an effect of reification which results from the fallacy of supposing that whatever can be named, or conceived abstractly, must actually exist. It's a word that crops up many, many times in the Frankfurt School's writings, as a jibe to thinkers of lesser stamp. The concept is related to, but distinct from, other terms in Marx's technical arsenal. Alienation is the general condition of human estrangement. Reification is a specific form of alienation. Commodity fetishism is a specific form of reification.[37]

The result of all this, for the Frankfurt School thinkers, is that under capitalism we don't so much inhabit a world as a phantasmagoria, a world turned upside down in which things become persons and persons things, and things (both human and non-human) take on a spectral life of their own. It was this spectral life of things that haunted the writings of Walter Benjamin. It helps explain the shift from his first attempt at memorialising his childhood in his *Berlin Chronicle* of the 1920s to the obsessively reworked *Berlin Childhood* of the 1930s. In the process, as we saw earlier, Benjamin's remembrance becomes increasingly depopulated, his attention focusing on things rather than people. But the point here is that in a phantasmagoric society dominated by commodity fetishism, things could stand in for persons and vice versa; perhaps even that things, bearing the Proustian imprint of pasts painfully recalled, could serve better as fetish guides to our lost childhoods than mere remembered humans.

But what Benjamin draws attention to again and again, particularly in his long laboured-over but at his death incomplete *Arcades Project*, is how the endless substitutability of commodities (both things and humans), and our immersion, under capitalism, in a fantasy world of material well-being, ensure that we lose sight of the class struggle that underpins this phantasmagoria. It is as though capitalism, having rubbed out the true nature of class struggle and airbrushed historical contingency, had covered up the tracks of its murder and diverted us from our detective work with the captivating allure of commodities. But that seeming heaven is exposed by Benjamin as a kind of unwitting damnation – a ring of hell in which the consumerist faithful endlessly buy and sell, eternally deluded in believing that this activity will bring fulfilment.

This was, indeed, the hell that Benjamin explored in *The Arcades Project*, a Paris that, for him, created the modern world by erasing the conditions of its existence. *The Arcades Project* is throughout bent on contrasting alluring appearance with Marxist reality. The nineteenth-century Paris he described in this book was not so much a city as a beguiling phantasmagoria akin to the one he had witnessed in the Kaiserpanorama in Berlin as a child. Paris, to Benjamin, itself a 'consequence of the reifying representation of civilisation'. What would the world be like if there wasn't commodity fetishism? If goods were made for use rather than for sale? It had become almost impossible even to imagine because capitalism had made the way in which it functioned seem natural or immutable. As Slavoj Žižek later wrote: 'the logic of exchange-value follows its own path, its own mad dance, irrespective of the real needs of real people'.[38] For Lukács, the madness was such that real people didn't know their real needs: hence the difference between actual and ascribed consciousness.

Classical economists such as Smith and Ricardo saw nothing mad in the free-market capitalist economy; rather, they treated prices, profits and rents, the law of supply and demand, as natural phenomena. Marx's incendiary point was that these were historically specific features of a particular economic system. They had not existed under feudalism; nor, moreover, would they under communism.

The Marxist article of faith, then, is that the horror story must end. Thus, for instance, in his preface to Marx and Engels' *The Communist Manifesto*, Eric Hobsbawm suggested that Marx was right to argue that the

> contradictions of a market system based on no other nexus between man and man than naked self-interest, than callous 'cash payment', a system of exploitation and of 'endless accumulation' can never be overcome: that at some point in a series of transformations and restructurings the development of this essentially destabilising system will lead to a state of affairs that can no longer be described as capitalism.[39]

But when? That is the $64,000 question. Henryk Grossman, widely held as the Frankfurt School thinker who theorised when that the mad dance would end, argued in *The Law of Accumulation and Collapse of the Capitalist System* (1929) that because capitalism increases the productivity of human labour and accelerates the production of use values, there is a tendency for the rate of profit to fall and, ultimately, for capitalism to create the conditions of its own demise.

It happens like this: what Marx calls labour power (roughly, the ability to work) yields surplus value to the capitalist over and above the costs in wages. Capitalists reduce commodity prices to undercut rivals, often by introducing new technology or machinery to increase labour productivity. But as output expands, constant capital (machinery, equipment, raw materials) expands more rapidly than variable capital (invested in wages to labour). So what? Well, as a greater share of investment goes into machinery and plant, rather than the living labour that produced surplus value, which under Marxist economics is the source of capitalist profits, the rate of profit to the total capital invested declines. If p is the rate of profit, s surplus value, c constant capital and v variable capital, Marx's formula goes like this:

$$p' = s/c+v$$

So if c gets bigger relative to v then, even if surplus value increases, the rate of profit falls. Grossman apparently used to lecture at Frankfurt wearing white gloves and carrying a cane. One can imagine him with a flourish of the cane and a magician's 'Abracadabra!' on clinching the ramifications of this equation.

But, of course, as you'll have noticed, capitalism hasn't ended. Why? Because capitalists found other means of staving off the calamitous decline of p and thereby their doom – such as exporting loan capital or the crazed speculation that Žižek mentions. Such speculations could defer capitalist oblivion to the long term, that functionally irrelevant prospect in which we are all, as John Maynard Keynes pointed out, dead. Indeed, in *The Law of Accumulation* Grossman argued against Rosa Luxemburg's account of the necessary collapse of capitalism, in which she proposed that only when there are no non-capitalist markets left to be exploited will capitalism founder.

That, he thought, could take ages. For Grossman, 'her proof of the absolute economic limits to capitalism comes close to the idea that the end of capitalism is a distant project because the capitalisation of non-capitalist countries is the work of centuries'.[40] Centuries? Only the most laid-back Marxists could wait that long.

In the same year as Henryk Grossman's masterpiece appeared, perhaps the biggest crisis for capitalism in the twentieth century occurred when the speculative bubble burst on the New York stock exchange, starting a world economic crisis and undermining what John Kenneth Galbraith called the 'faith of Americans in quick, effortless enrichment in the stock market'.[41] But capitalism didn't fall. Instead, capitalists dusted themselves down, renewed their faith in quick, effortless enrichment and started the mad dance again.

Grossman did not specify when capitalism would end. Rather, he is most bracing in *The Law of Accumulation* not for dating the revolution but for exploding the myths that suggested capitalism could carry on in principle forever and that it was not prone to crises that would ultimately destroy it – that the economic disruption was just a problem of disproportionality between different parts of the economy, or that workers' consumer spending was insufficient to buy overproduced goods. The barrier to capitalist accumulation, as Marx explained and as Grossman elaborated, was capital itself.

In such circumstances, it's a great shame that Grossman's analysis has been derided as predicting the automatic collapse of capitalism. 'The full ramifications of his argument, whose predictions have obviously failed to come true', writes Martin Jay, 'need not detain us here. Let it be said, however, that the quietistic implications of his thesis, similar to those of all Marxist interpretations that stress objective forces over subjective revolutionary praxis, were not lost on some of his contemporaries.'[42] That seems a particularly unfair charge to throw at the one Frankfurt School scholar who, unlike his colleagues philosophising from their armchairs, had seen active service in the socialist struggle. Rather, the truth of the matter is that Grossman adhered to the Leninist notion that the revolutionary process was dialectical and that capitalism's fall was one in which workers were actors in history rather than spectators observing the economic forces.

True, much of Grossman's work was directed against those who thought that the revolution could be successfully launched irrespective of the propitiousness of the circumstances. He wrote in 1928, for example, that for a revolution to break out, it is usually insufficient for the lower classes 'not to want [to live in the old way], it is also necessary that the upper classes should be unable [to live in the old way], that it becomes objectively impossible for the ruling classes to maintain their domination in unchanged form.'[43] Rather, Grossman was arguing, in a non-quietist manner, that revolution could only take place when the objective conditions could be exploited by a revolutionary party conscious of the historic role of the proletariat. The revolutionary process he envisaged was dialectical: capitalism created the working class, and the circumstances in which it was compelled to struggle against capitalism. It was during struggle that the proletariat could become aware that the destruction of capitalism was necessary for its self-liberation.

The chastening words here are 'could become', and they take us back to what worried the Marxists gathered in Ilmenau in 1923. Lukács had argued in the previous year's *History and Class Consciousness* that capitalist society is reified. It was the reification of capitalist society that shifted Marxism from the firebrand optimism of *The Communist Manifesto* to the melancholy resignation seeping through the Frankfurt School: it was as if, under the modern capitalism that confronted Marxists in 1920s Germany, the proletariat had become the gravediggers not of the bourgeoisie but of their own hopes and aspirations, so alienated from their labour and from themselves that they couldn't remember what it was they were burying.

To understand this alienation, Lukács and the Frankfurt School read Marx's early account of it in his *Economic and Philosophical Manuscripts* of 1844. There Marx draws on the notion of the 'unhappy consciousness' in Hegel's *Phenomenology of Spirit* (1807) in which an alienated soul is divided and whose aspirations to universality are thwarted. Hegel's unhappy consciousness is the 'consciousness of self as a dual natured, merely contradictory thing'.[44] For the early Marx, the worker is similarly alienated, finding not joy in her work but slavery before a commodity system that exploits and denies what labour could have been, joyful and fulfilling. This Hegelian theme of self-division and alienation was seized on by Marx's predecessor Feuerbach who, in his *Essence of Christianity*, came to the view that the Christian God was a projection of an essence otherwise denied to humanity. For Feuerbach, what we were alienated from as human beings, we turned into an object and called God. For Marx, by contrast, alienation was the necessary consequence of capitalism, distancing the worker from herself and her work. She becomes part of a system that exploits her and her fellow workers. As a result, instead of the working class being capable of changing the conditions under which it lives, it becomes passive in the face of the apparently autonomous exchanges of commodities. It becomes, in extremis, unable to create the conditions for its own self-liberation.

But if all these thoughts about alienation, commodity fetishism and reification are in Marx already, why was Lukács's *History and Class Consciousness* so influential, especially for the Frankfurt School? For one thing, the *Economic and Philosophical Manuscripts* in which Marx developed that theory of alienation were not published until the late 1920s in Moscow, so Lukács's Hegelianised Marxism of a decade earlier seemed prescient – or, rather, he had got to the same point as Marx had in his early neglected writings. Moreover, Lukács argues that the commodity fetishism Marx set out in *Capital* was, under more primitive economic systems, merely episodic. Now, by contrast, it pervades society entirely. Lukács wrote:

> With the modern 'psychological' analysis of the work-process (in Taylorism) this rational mechanisation extends right into the worker's 'soul': even his psychological attributes are separated from his total personality and placed in opposition to it so as to facilitate their integration into specialised rational systems and their reduction to statistically viable concepts.[45]

As a result, revolution was less likely than ever, especially in an advanced, rationally administered society like Germany. This, certainly, was how the Institute for Social Research saw Germany in the 1920s – not a place where revolution would be realised any time soon, but one better suited to quiet study.

No wonder then that the Soviet spy working in the library left quickly after the Institute's foundation. Richard Sorge (1895–1944) had taken part in the Ilmenau seminar and was later hired to help organise the library, while all the time reporting back to Moscow on whether the conditions were propitious for German revolution. His reports have not been published.[46] The Baku-born, Berlin-raised Sorge had won the Iron Cross while fighting for the German Army in the First World War. While convalescing from shrapnel wounds that broke both his legs and cost him three fingers, Sorge read Marx, later joining the German Communist Party and studied for a PhD in economics at Hamburg. After fleeing post-war Germany, where he had been sacked as a teacher for his political views, he went to Moscow and became a junior officer for the Comintern. This body, also known as the Third International, was set up in 1919 by delegates from around the world, including Lenin, to fight 'by all available means, including armed force, for the overthrow of the international bourgeoisie and for the creation of an international Soviet republic as a transition stage to the complete abolition of the State'. It was closed down by Stalin in 1943.

In 1921, the Comintern sent Sorge on a mission to Germany. There he worked ostensibly as a journalist but was really gathering intelligence about Frankfurt's business community. In Frankfurt, he married Christiane Gerlach, the former wife of Kurt Gerlach, and assisted for a while in the Institute's library. His views on the Marxist research institute went unrecorded; nor is it clear if his colleagues knew they had a Soviet spy working in their midst. But in any event Sorge was soon recalled to Moscow and thereafter led a life of espionage and adventure undreamt of by his armchair philosopher colleagues. In the 1930s, while still working for the Soviets, he joined the Nazi Party and managed to be sent to Japan on journalistic assignments, writing for newspapers he ideologically despised. Really, though, Sorge was dispatched to Japan to set up a network of informants from whom he could get information about Japanese foreign policy.

During the Second World War, what he gleaned proved vital to the Soviets. He informed Moscow about the German-Japanese Pact and warned of the Japanese attack on the US naval base at Pearl Harbour.

In 1941 Sorge reported to Moscow Hitler's intentions to invade the Soviet Union. Later that year, he informed the Kremlin that the Japanese had no plans to attack the Soviet Union's eastern frontier. This information allowed the Red Army commander Georgy Zhukov to redeploy eighteen divisions, 1,700 tanks, and over 1,500 aircraft from Siberia to the western front in time to resist the Nazi advance on Moscow. That redeployment proved one of the turning points in the Second World War, enabling the Red Army to break Hitler's Werhmacht that had already crushed British and French forces in western Europe. By then, though, Sorge's number may well have been up: not only had the Japanese secret service intercepted his messages to Moscow, but, it is claimed, Stalin could not afford to let it be known that he had ignored Sorge's warning over Operation Barbarossa, the Nazis' 1941 attack on the Soviet Union. So it suited him if Sorge did not live to reveal that the Soviet leader's indecision had cost so many Russian lives.

On 7 November 1944, Richard Sorge was hanged in prison in Tokyo. James Bond's creator Ian Fleming, a British intelligence officer during the Second World War, called Sorge 'the most formidable spy in history'. Sorge had to suffer the posthumous indignity of having a film made about his life by Veit Harlan, the notorious director of perhaps one of the most anti-Semitic films ever made, *Jud Suss* (1940), and one of Nazi propaganda minister Joseph Goebbels' favourite film-makers. Called *Verrat an Deutschland* (Betrayal of Germany), the 1955 film about Sorge's espionage in Japan was banned in West Germany only two days after its release. Another film *Qui êtes-vous, Monsieur Sorge?* (Who Are You, Mr Sorge?) appeared in 1961 and was seen in many countries, proving particularly popular in the Soviet Union. Only in 1964, though, did the Soviet Union officially recognise Richard Sorge's existence as a Soviet spy. He was made that year a Hero of the Soviet Union. A shame he had been dead twenty years before he was thus honoured: not many men can pin the Hero of the Soviet Union medal next to the German Imperial Iron Cross on their chest.

Sorge's life story is worth relating, not merely because this action hero's biography contrasts so markedly with those of other Frankfurt scholars (though three prominent members of the School – Franz Neumann, Herbert Marcuse and Otto Kirchheimer – worked as intelligence analysts for the Office of Strategic Services, the wartime forerunner of the CIA), but also because his politically engaged activities were inimical to the ethos of the Frankfurt School. While Sorge was slipping across borders in Europe, America and Asia, charged with helping foment world proletarian revolution by the Comintern, and tasked by the Soviet Union with assisting its resistance against Nazi invasion, the Institute remained aloof from the struggle, valuing its intellectual independence, preferring its scholars not to be members of political parties and, Grossman notwithstanding, doubting that it was worthwhile picking up the gauntlet Lenin had thrown down to Marxists around the world. The circumstances they confronted in the 1920s were very different from those that helped make the Bolshevik Revolution successful. Neue Sachlichkeit has also been translated as New Resignation, and that captures something of the mood of the Frankfurt School in this decade: it was as though the grand era of socialist revolution was over and left-leaning intellectuals would have to accommodate themselves to the Weimar Republic's social order, one that was born in the fateful compromise between the Social Democratic government and the Prussian nobility.

In 1927 Horkheimer wrote an essay called 'The Impotence of the German Working Class'. In it, this new kind of Marxist intellectual finally answered, pessimistically, the question of the practical problems of implementing socialism posed at Ilmenau four years earlier. He argued that the integration of the working class into the capitalist process of production made it unviable as an agent for socialism. The class consciousness and proletarian solidarity Lukács took to be necessary for socialist revolution was lacking in Germany. In part this was because the working class was divided between an employed, integrated working-class elite and frustrated unemployed workers. But it was also in part because the two socialist parties – the SPD and the KPD – replicated that antagonistic division at a political level. The split was tragic, since, as he wrote: 'In both parties, there exists a part of the strength on which the future of mankind depends.'[47] The lack of that unified strength not only militated against the possibility of socialist revolution in Germany, but, as the Frankfurt School would later realise, undermined resistance to Nazism.

Horkheimer argued that the prospects for reconciling the two positions were contingent 'in the last analysis on the course of economic process'. Here the barb unfairly directed at Henryk Grossman – that he took revolution to be the product of economic forces and that therefore his was essentially a politics of quietism – is better targeted at Horkheimer: it was he who cast workers as spectators observing the working out of economic forces rather than, as they were for the straightforwardly old-school Leninist Henryk Grossman, actors in history. That's not to say Horkheimer was wrong in this pessimistic view, but rather, at the very least, that it changes radically what the purpose of a Marxist think-tank such as the one he directed from 1931 was. In his history of the Frankfurt School, Rolf Wiggershaus concludes: 'None of them [the leaders of the School] put any hopes in the working class.'[48] They became, rather, virtuoso critics of a world that they could not change; the impotence of the working class that Horkheimer wrote about had its parallel in the Marxist intellectuals working at the Institute for Social Research.

4

A Bit of the Other

'What distinguishes Naples from other large cities', wrote Walter Benjamin and his Bolshevik Latvian lover Asja Lacis in their joint essay on the city in 1925, 'is something it has in common with the African kraal: each private attitude or act is permeated by streams of communal life. To exist, for the Northern European the most private of affairs, is here, as in the kraal, a collective matter.'[1]

Lexicographer Charles Pettman's 1913 book, *Africanderisms: A glossary of South African colloquial words and phrases and of place and other names*, defined kraal as: '1) An enclosure for stock. 2) A Hottentot village. 3) Any native village or collection of huts. The word seems to have been introduced by the Dutch and applied somewhat contemptuously at first to the Hottentot and Kaffir holdings and villages.'[2] But while Dutch colonists may have used kraal to suggest that Africans lived like cattle, Benjamin and Lacis used it to praise how Neapolitans lived. In particular, they were struck by how this south European city served as reproof to the lives of northern Europeans who, under capitalism, distinguished increasingly ruthlessly between private and public worlds.

Yes, the Englishman's home had long been proverbially his castle. More symptomatic of what they took to be a growing trend was that Benjamin's parents' sumptuous homes in Berlin's socially cleansed west end excluded the poor so efficiently that their son scarcely knew they existed. In *The Arcades Project*, Benjamin argued that such jealously guarded private zones first arose under the rule of the bourgeois French king Louis Philippe in the 1830s and 1840s. The result was, he thought, a growing division between private and public spaces, where the function of the former was to provide the bourgeois citizen with refuge from business and social concerns, and sustain him in his illusions. Benjamin wrote: 'From this derive the phantasmagorias the interior – which, for the private individual, represents the universe. In the interior, he brings together remote locales and memories of the past. His living room is a box in the theatre of the world.'[3] Benjamin was presciently writing before the age of television or the internet, before the assembling of the distant in space and time in the domestic interior became technologically sophisticated, before the phantasmagorias of the interior made us socially atomised spectators – or perma-gawpers in what French situationist thinker Guy Debord called the society of the spectacle.

The cities that excited Walter Benjamin as he roamed Europe in the 1920s were not like that. In Naples, Marseilles and Moscow in particular, he found private and public life thrillingly intermingled, the possibilities of transcending class apparently limitless. Each city in its different way offered him a cure for the disease of modern life in general, and of his upbringing in particular. His compatriot, the sociologist Max Weber, had written of the iron cage of capitalism inside which humans were submitted to efficiency, calculation and control. Cities were part of that system of control, which worked by keeping the poor and the rich in their proper places. The cities that turned Benjamin on were the opposite of that.

He wrote about them in a series of essays that are often erotically charged, as the privileged north European got up close with the sensual other – experiencing frottage on a crowded Moscow tram, savouring the stirring Neapolitan language of gestures, or exploring the captivatingly seamy side of Marseilles, a city then living up to its hotly contested title as the world's wickedest port.

In 1925, Benjamin left Berlin and an increasingly antipathetic Germany – one in which anti-Semitism was on the rise, and the prospect of socialist revolution receding into the distance. Benjamin's sense of Germany as an unsympathetic place was intensified by professional setback. His hopes of becoming an academic were in tatters as the University of Frankfurt had rejected his post-doctoral thesis, *The Origin of German Tragic Drama*, thus denying him the necessary qualification to be able to teach. As a result, he had to rely on money from Grub Street and the occasional commission from the Institute for Social Research; the death of his father Emil in 1926 made matters even more financially perilous.

Italy was for Benjamin, as it had been for Germans from Goethe onwards, antidote, distraction and place of erotic renewal. And so it proved when he arrived in Naples with the actress Lacis, leaving his wife Dora and seven-year-old son Stefan in Germany. What he and Lacis eulogised in Naples was a quality they called porosity. It's a term that became central to Benjamin and the Frankfurt School during the 1920s. Benjamin and Lacis defined porosity as the melting away of structural and hierarchical divisions. Instead of domestic space being ringfenced from an irksome world as it seemed to them to be in northern Europe, in Naples they found that private life was 'dispersed' and 'commingled'. They wrote: 'Just as the living room reappears on the street, with chairs, hearth, and altar, so only much more loudly the street migrates into the living room.'

The only civilised, private and ordered buildings in Naples, they thought, were the posh hotels and great warehouses; otherwise, Neapolitans demonstrated a way of urban living inimical to Benjamin's upbringing in Berlin and one piqued by poverty. 'Poverty has brought about a stretching of frontiers that mirrors the most radiant freedom of thought.' Children, he wrote with a northern European's shock, are up at all hours. 'At midday they then lie sleeping behind a shop counter or on a stairway. This sleep, which men and women also snatch in shady corners, is therefore not the protected Northern sleep. Here, too, there is interpenetration of day and night, noise and peace, outer light and inner darkness, street and home.' Of course one could dismiss this as a privileged man's poverty tourism, but what is worth preserving from his and Lacis's essay about Naples is that in their vision of it, life has become communal, space-time twisted inside-out and inwardness unthinkable. Naples wasn't just a city to Benjamin, but a Catholic carnivalesque, the realisation of utopian dreaming, and a modernist work of art.

Instead of an iron cage, Benjamin found a world of libidinal flows in Naples. For instance, he and Lacis observed the language of gestures like voyeuristic anthropologists. 'The conversation is impenetrable to anyone from outside', they wrote. 'Ears, nose, eyes, breasts, and shoulders are signalling stations activated by the fingers. These configurations return in their fastidiously specialised eroticism. Helping gestures and impatient touches attract the stranger's attention.' It's hard to tell in this passage whether Walter Benjamin is being given directions or being propositioned. Either way, he seems to like it.

In that summer of 1925, Benjamin and Lacis were joined in the Bay of Naples by other German critics and philosophers, including Siegfried Kracauer and the twenty-two-year-old composer, music critic and aspiring philosopher Theodor Adorno, who was breaking off his studies in Vienna with the composer Alban Berg. All were stimulated, not just by the city, but by its surroundings – by the idyll of Capri, by visits to Vesuvius, and, further along the coast, by the cliffs of Positano. The suggestion made in Martin Mittelmeier's book *Adorno in Naples* is that the Frankfurt scholars were schooled in Naples, that some of the most exciting ideas they developed found their inspiration there, that they were seduced like Goethe by 'das Land wo die Zitronen blühen' (the country where the lemon trees bloom). While Marxism was ossifying in Frankfurt, it was exploding into life in Naples.[4]

Between 1924 and 1926 Vesuvius was open to the public. Mittelmeier traces a distinction in Adorno's 1928 essay on Schubert, between the chthonic force of Beethoven and the fissured landscapes of Schubert, to the volcano. Mittelmeier also suggests that Adorno's repeated figure of hollow spaces or Hohlraume has a literal precursor: it is what he found on the cliffs of Positano. There, the Swiss futurist Gilbert Clavel spent much of the 1920s blowing huge holes into the rock face with dynamite. 'Whenever I create these holes', wrote Clavel in 1923, 'I always have the feeling that I am capturing air-pockets of energy, compressed spaces in which something spiritual can then explode.'[5] Mittleimeier suggests that when Adorno argues that Beethoven blows empty spaces ('Hohltstellen') in bourgeois music, that image is literally prefigured by what he saw in Positano's cliffs.

Perhaps it was at Positano that Adorno learned how to philosophise. Nietzsche philosophised with a hammer, Adorno upgraded to dynamite. Deconstructionist before the word was coined, Adorno started his writing career in the 1920s with eviscerating musical criticism, and never really ceased blowing holes in other thinkers' long-nurtured intellectual edifices. In the culmination of Adorno's mature thought, *Negative Dialectics*, for example, he blew up Hegel's philosophy of history. History for Hegel was, like a rock formation, a slow process of becoming. It was also a story with a happy ending; what's more, it was a redemptive narrative in which everything, even the dead ends of evolution, even human lives crushed on history's implacable march towards the absolute, had a meaning, a place in the story. When Hegel said 'the real is the rational' that is what he meant. When he wrote, paradoxically, that there is an 'identity of identity and non-identity', there too he was claiming that everything that comes about must contribute in some way to the workings of the absolute.

Heraclitus envisaged the world as in flux, seeing change as the truth of existence. But under Hegel's gaze, the world's Heraclitan flux congealed into something more readily comprehensible – as though instead of Vesuvian magma, it had become Positano cliff face. History became paradoxical: through a process of becoming, the laws explaining it became set in stone. Adorno, doing what Beethoven did to bourgeois music, shattered that Hegelian whole. He argued that there was a 'non-identity of identity and non-identity', by which he meant that existence is incomplete, that it has a hole in it where the whole should be, that history is not the simple unfolding of some preordained noumenal realm and that existence is therefore 'ontologically incomplete'.[6]

Adorno's takedown of western philosophy had its precursor in his writing about music in the 1920s. 'His discourse was full of melancholic allusions pointing to the crumbling of all traditional values', wrote the composer Ernst Krenek, who met the young Adorno in 1924 while the latter was a critic and tyro composer attending the rehearsals of the former's comic opera *Der Sprung uber den Schatten* (The Leap Over the Shadow). 'One of his favourite phrases was "crumbling substance", and he used it so often that we ended up joking about it.'[7]

For some, the modern and modernist art were about progress; for Adorno they were about disintegration. In the 1920s old values and aesthetics were crumbling: Schoenberg's development of twelve-tone music, abstraction in painting, Dadaism, all the new forms of artistic expression detonated traditional values. Indeed, that is why they were all loathed by the Nazis who sought to restore pre-modern artistic values. In this cultural struggle, the Frankfurt School was on the side of the modernists. When, in 1928, Adorno wrote an essay called 'On Twelve-tone Technique', an analysis of Schoenberg's atonal system, he told the history of music as a process of disintegration. The fugue and the sonata had ceased to be sacrosanct frames of musical reference. Then tonality, along with its harmonic structures and cadences, crumbled. To use such musical forms and techniques, as Stravinsky or Honegger did in their neo-classical moods, was reactionary, Adorno argued.

What crumbled most under Adorno's musical philosophising, though, was the notion that music was a neutral natural phenomenon unaffected by historical change; rather, he argued, it was moulded by the dialectics of the historical process. As a result, there could be no universally valid method of composition. Here his criticism detonated not just the bourgeois who disliked atonal music and demanded tunes, not just the neo-classicist composers, but also Krenek who argued that atonal music was primary.

If the destructive impulse Adorno discovered on his Neapolitan holiday in the 1920s was inspiring for his later writings, Benjamin's foreign wanderings during the same period fired his writings with enthusiasm. Two years after visiting Naples, Benjamin visited Moscow where Lacis, the great if unhappy love of his life, was by this time in a sanatorium after suffering a nervous breakdown. He was similarly excited by a city that, like Naples, had dispensed with the distinction between private and public lives and was embarking on a communist social experiment. While Horkheimer was bemoaning German proletarian impotence in 1927, as we saw in the last chapter, in the same year Benjamin was very nearly hyperventilating with enthusiasm over the Soviet experiment. 'Each thought, each day, each life lies here as on a laboratory table', he wrote.[8] Riding on a city tram was, for Benjamin, a miniature expression of the complete interpenetration of technological and primitive modes of life. The foreigner enjoyed the civility of the crush: 'A tenacious shoving and barging during the boarding of a vehicle usually overloaded to the point of bursting takes place without a sound and with great cordiality. (I have never heard an angry word on these occasions).' Another form of Muscovite public transport, the sleigh, captivated Benjamin even more, particularly because it annulled social distinctions.

> Where Europeans, on their rapid journeys, enjoy superiority, domi-nance over the masses, the Muscovite in the little sleigh is closely mingled with people and things. If he has a box, a child, or a basket to take with him – for all this the sleigh is the cheapest means of trans-port – he is truly wedged into the street bustle. No condescending gaze: a tender, swift brushing along stones, people, and horses. You feel like a child gliding through the house on a little chair.

How poignant, incidentally, it is that Benjamin here connects the sleigh ride with the lost innocence of his youth, finding in the Bolshevik experiment prompt for a Proustian reverie.

The essay is charged with heat, sensual excitement and political engagement. The city streets of the Soviet capital were a zone of new possibilities, junking and reappropriating old traditions, inventing new ones. This was in that brief era before the Soviet Union congealed into something monstrous – a Stalinist tyranny of gulags and show trials, where avant-garde art such as Shostakovich's *Lady Macbeth of Mtsensk* was denounced in *Pravda*, the Communist Party's official mouthpiece, in 1936 under the headline 'Muddle Not Music', as 'tick-ling the perverted taste of the bourgeoisie with its fidgety, screaming neurotic music'.[9] Benjamin's hope for modernist art – notably cinema, visual arts and the kinds of literary experiments he did in the 1920s – was that it would be part of the revolution that would liberate the minds of the oppressed.

Benjamin was rarely an excitable man. In 1921 when on a trip to Munich he bought Klee's watercolour *Angelus Novus* for 1,000 marks. His friend Charlotte Wolf then recalled how this 'gauche and inhib-ited man' had 'behaved as if something marvellous had been given to him'.[10] Something similar happened in Moscow in 1927. The Soviet

Union was a cultural experiment as invigorating to him as Kandinsky's and Klee's paintings, or the other modernist art he championed in his writings of the Weimar years – Proust's novel, Brecht's epic theatre, avant-garde cinema, surrealism and photography. But it was not just what he wrote about but the way that he wrote about it that opened a new front in the political struggle.

In the 1920s, indeed, how Benjamin wrote was his most political act. He came to prefer 'inconspicuous forms' over the 'pretentious, universal gesture of the book', and so such essays as the one he wrote on Moscow, revolutionise writing, undermine bourgeois norms and embody modernism's shock of the new. His writing is terse, dense, brief, improvised, narrative order junked in favour of writerly riffs recurring in variation, forming constellations and making meaning. It was like jazz, subversive: indeed in his Moscow essay, Benjamin noted that dancing to jazz had been banned (it represented, for the authorities, western decadence). As a result, he wrote: 'It is kept behind glass, as it were, like a brightly coloured poisonous reptile.' Benjamin's writing from this era is similarly snake like, moving unpredictably, darting through labyrinths, restlessly subverting the established literary order.

'From first to last', his biographers write of this gambler, 'Benjamin took chances in the subjects he addressed and on the form and style of his writing.'[11] The best example of this is *One-Way Street*, his 1928 collection of aphorisms, philosophical fragments and musings on modern life; the book is a jump-cut assemblage, a montage akin to what Dziga Vertov was doing in the Soviet cinema, what Weimar Dadaist artist Hannah Hoch was doing with her scissors, or what the French surrealists Benjamin admired were doing with paper scraps, portions of painted canvas, newspapers, tickets, stubs, cigarette butts, and buttons (namely creating deranging montages of found objects). His writing seemed decadent, strange, alarming to Nazis and Soviet ideologues alike. In its very structure it proselytised for a vision of art and writing inimical to the one that György Lukács agitated for in his critical eulogies to the realist novel. But for all its modernist genius, his best writing in the 1920s wasn't of the kind that would have got him tenure. Rather, in *One-Way Street* and in his deliberately fragmented impressionistic portraits of the cities that fired his imagination, he self-consciously broke out of the formats amenable to the academy and applied his techniques of criticism to phenomena that mere professors hadn't considered worthwhile – the phantasmagoria of modern urban life, and that suspicious new thing, the movies, among them.[12]

For all that, what Benjamin started in 1920s Germany – a style of writing that borrowed its form from the best journalistic vignettes (notably those composed by Benjamin's and Adorno's friend and mentor Siegfried Kracauer) and its techniques from avant-garde cinema, photography and art – would prove to be one of the most enduring literary forms for later European intellectuals (as, for example, in Roland Barthes' *Mythologies* or Gilbert Adair's *The Postmodernist Always Rings Twice*).

Despite his embrace of the modern, Benjamin was hardly an uncritical celebrant of what he found in Moscow. He was charmed but worried about where this experiment might lead. 'Bolshevism has abolished private life', he wrote. But while in Naples he savoured that abolition, in Moscow he worried about what prompted it: 'The bureaucracy, political activity, the press are so powerful that no time remains for interests that do not coincide with them.' He worried about what this nascent totalitarian society would mean for intellectual life. 'What figure does the man of letters cut in a country where his employer is the proletariat?' he asked. This, for freelance intellectuals like Benjamin as much as for Frankfurt scholars beavering away inside the sober Institute for Social Research, was a particularly vexed question. Benjamin's thought was that both kinds of intellectual were living on borrowed time:

> For sooner or later, with the middle classes who are being ground to pieces by the struggle between capital and labour, the 'freelance' writer must also disappear. In Russia the process is complete: the intellectual is above all a functionary working in the departments of censorship, justice, finance, and if he survives, participating in work – which, however, in Russia means power. He is a member of the ruling class.

He worried that all the great modernist art that he loved had been found unfit for revolutionary purpose and those who had made it either sent to the gulags or made into supine functionaries: '[T]he constructivists, suprematists, abstractionists who under wartime Communism put their graphic propaganda at the service of the Revolution have been dismissed. Today only banal clarity is demanded.' One can almost hear him shuddering here, as though he is imagining himself transported into the nightmarish bureaucratic fictions of his beloved Kafka: the freelance writer risks becoming Josef K, and (chilling phrase) 'if he survives', a functionary in a new ruling class. Banal clarity? Functionary in government? Member of the ruling class? Benjamin never returned to Moscow.

IN THE SAME year Benjamin wrote his essay about Moscow, he began the book that he described as 'the theatre of all my struggles and all my ideas' and which remained unfinished at his death thirteen years later. *The Arcades Project* was originally conceived as a newspaper article on the arcades that had begun to be constructed in Paris at the start of the nineteenth century. The project then mutated into an essay called 'Paris Arcades: a Dialectical Fairyland'. Ultimately it spiralled into a book. But why Paris? Weren't there shopping arcades in his native Berlin? In part, as its English translators write in *The Arcades Project*'s foreword, his interest in the French cultural milieu sprang from his sense of alienation from contemporary German writers.[13]

Benjamin was a longtime Francophile. His father Emil had spent several years living in Paris before moving to Berlin in the 1880s and the Benjamin household's domestic staff included a French governess. So when Walter visited Paris for the first time in 1913, he was already fluent in French, and his nascent Francophilia was piqued by the fact that the Frenchified Berlin of his childhood wanderings was trumped by his experience of the real thing. Then he felt 'almost more at home in the Louvre and on the Grand Boulevard than I am in the Kaiser Friedrich Museum or on the streets of Berlin'.[14]

No wonder: Paris was the pre-existing model of his childhood world. Later in the 1930s, in exile from Nazi Germany, Paris became his home; in a sense it had long been his spiritual home. As a result, when he wrote about the city in the book that occupied him his last years, *The Arcades Project*, Benjamin the archeologically minded critic was digging through strata of the past, and one of the layers he penetrated was his *Berlin Childhood Around 1900*.

But *The Arcades Project* was scarcely a love letter to Paris. Rather, it is the story of the birth of capitalist modernity through the figure of the iron and glass structures of the Parisian arcades. As Douglas Murphy puts it in *Last Futures: Nature, Technology and the End of Architecture*, these arcades 'created interior spaces in the city through which the new social world of modern capitalism took shape'.[15] Benjamin was sensitive, as perhaps no other writer was before, to how new spatial forms were significant for the culture of capitalism. Like the private citizen's domestic interiors, the Parisian arcades functioned for Benjamin by excluding the real world outside. 'Arcades', he wrote, 'are houses or passages having no outside – like the dream.'[16]

What's singular about Benjamin's project, though, is that he takes the arcades both as metaphors for the contradictions of capitalism but also as containing glimpses of a better world. A hopeful glimpse comes out in one of the last things he wrote, the introduction (or as he called it, exposé) to the book, in 1939: 'The century was incapable of responding to the new technological possibilities with a new social order.'[17] This was Benjamin's dialectical Marxist move – these very temples of capitalism contained intimations of capitalism's eclipse in favour of a socialism that harnessed technology for the good of the masses. Later German philosophers have been unimpressed by this gambit. Most strikingly, Peter Sloterdijk, in his 2005 book *Im Weltinnenraum* (In the World Interior of Capital), agreed with Benjamin that capitalism functions, in part, by creating exclusive spaces to keep out the undesirable and unmoneyed – be they gated estates, malls with security guards, or fortress Europe – but denied that such grand interiors of capital contained any hope for a better world. Indeed, Sloterdijk argued that another, grander capitalist temple of glass and steel, namely Joseph Paxton's Crystal Palace built to house the Great Exhibition of 1851 in London, was a better, but less hopeful, metaphor for capitalism. 'The arcades formed a canopied intermezzo between streets or squares', wrote Sloterdijk, 'the crystal palace, on the other hand invoked the idea of an enclosure so spacious that one might never have to leave it.'[18] Inside the Palace, the world's most diverting flora, fauna and industrial products were displayed under climate controlled, obligingly sanitary conditions under one roof, thus precluding the necessity for travel, while whatever remained outside (war, genocide, slavery, unpleasant tropical diseases) dwindled into irrelevance. In that respect, Crystal Palace rather than the Parisian arcade was the blueprint for how capitalism has functioned since. 'Who can deny', Sloterdijk wrote, 'that in its primary aspects, the western world – especially the European Union – embodies such a great interior today?'[19] In *The Arcades Project*, Benjamin took the bourgeois drawing room to be emblematic of private space under early capitalism, one in which the private citizen could hole up from the irksome world; under late capitalism, for Sloterdijk, the exclusion zone had expanded from drawing room to the size of a continent.

When he first considered writing about the Parisian arcades, Benjamin told his friend Gershom Scholem that he wanted to bring the collage techniques he admired in surrealism to bear on his books. He did so in his newspaper articles, the montage book *One-Way Street* and in his city vignettes, but most ambitiously in *The Arcades Project*. Instead of writing history through the study of great men, he aimed to disclose history through its refuse and detritus, studying the overlooked, the worthless, the trashy – the very things that didn't make sense to the official version but which, he maintained, encoded the dream wishes of the collective consciousness.

Benjamin's intention was to administer a kind of shock effect to awaken us from our illusions. The effect would be akin to what cinemagoers felt, or at least what Benjamin supposed they felt, when they saw a montage of images intertwining different times. Indeed, he wrote of carrying over the 'principle of montage into history'. The book grew unstoppably. After 1933, when he settled in Paris after Hitler's accession to power, he became a fixture at his desk in the Bibliothèque Nationale, filling cards with detailed notes on the the birth of capitalism. He became a ragpicker or collector stuffing his manuscript with quotations and catalogues of ephemera such as advertising posters, shop-window displays, clothing fashions. The project seemed haunted with the idea that everything carried a hidden message and it was his role to decode it. *The Arcades Project* was uncompleted at his death, but, if this was its guiding philosophy, perhaps it was uncompletable.

Some have regarded the work, published posthumously in German in 1982 and in English nearly twenty years later, as a wreck of a book. But others, notably the Italian philosopher Giorgio Agamben, believe it might have become one of the great texts of twentieth-century cultural criticism had not the Nazis, in forcing Benjamin's fateful escape, thwarted its completion.[20] What is certainly true is that the book with which he sought to awaken us from the dream of capitalism never achieved what he hoped for it.

In writing *The Arcades Project*, though, Benjamin had a grand political ambition: he was striving to recast Marxism for a new consumerist era in which we were in thrall to commodities in a way even Marx had not imagined. The latter described the fetishism of the commodity as a reintroduction of pre-modern religious consciousness into the modern, into the very nature of capitalism. In order to understand the fetish power of commodities, then, Marx suggested: 'we must take flight into the misty realm of religion. There the products of the human brain appear as autonomous figures endowed with a life of their own, which enter into relations both with each other and with the human race. So it is in the world of commodities with the products of men's hands.'[21] Through the alienation of free labour came the unconscious reactivation of a kind of collective religious consciousness or, to put it another way, mass delusion. This, Marx thought, was necessary to make alienation seem natural and inevitable.

Commodities, for Marx, were both economic and symbolic forms which he conceived of primarily as manufacturing goods and raw materials. Benjamin's twist on Marx's fetishism of commodities was to focus on objects of consumption rather than production. 'One could say that Marx grasped the theological complexity of the commodity', argued the Benjamin scholar Max Pensky, 'but not the commodity's status as a phantasmagoria; that is, as a delusional expression of collective utopian fantasies and longings, whose very mode of expression itself, as delusional, ensures that those same longings remain mere utopian fantasies.'[22]

Benjamin, like Marx, took flight into the misty realm of religion, imagining that the modern world was a kind of hell. 'The "modern", the time of Hell', he wrote in *The Arcades Project*. By investigating obsolete pieces of historical detritus such as the Kaiserpanorama or the Parisian arcades, Benjamin found not just hopes and dreams, but the dashing of those hopes and dreams. He invited us to realise that the consumer goods, gizmos and technological innovations that bewitch us today will become passé, leaving us trapped in the Sisyphean quest of acquiring something else new to satisfy our degraded longings. Such was the hellish fate of capitalism's victims. He urged us also to realise that past collective hopes were dashed, and through their contemplation, invited us to realise that the ones we hold now will similarly be unfulfilled in the future. Max Pensky wrote of what Benjamin sought to achieve: 'The fantasy world of material well-being promised by every commodity now is revealed as a Hell of unfulfilment; the promise of eternal newness and unlimited progress encoded in the imperatives of technological change and the cycles of consumption now appear as their opposite, as primal history, the mythic compulsion toward endless repetition.'[23]

The device by which Benjamin sought to awaken us from our dreams in *The Arcades Project* was what he called the dialectical image. This was a key notion in his developing philosophy during the 1930s. In the following passage, he tried (and for many readers, failed) to explain successfully what a dialectical image is:

> It's not that what is past casts its light on what is present, or what is present its light on the past; rather, image is that wherein what has been comes together in a flash with the now to form a constellation. In other words, image is dialectics at a standstill. For while the relation of the present to the past is a purely temporal, continuous one, the relation of what-has-been to the now is dialectical: is not progression but image, suddenly emergent. Only dialectical images are genuine images (that is, not archaic); and the place where one encounters them is language.[24]

This esoteric notion has baffled Benjamin scholars. Pensky, for instance, wryly wrote that the '"lightning flash" of the dialectical image has, to this day, remained far more a dark star, indeed a kind of theoretical and methodological black hole, a "singularity" following its own extraordinary laws and capable, apparently, of absorbing any number of attempts at critical illumination.[25] Even the term 'dialectical image' sounds like an oxymoron: 'dialectical' usually describes the relationship of concepts or arguments to each other; images, by contrast are normally singular and immediate. It is tempting to despair of understanding Benjamin here. But despair is not an option, as Pensky rightly realised, if we want to do justice to the central thought at the heart of the mature Marxist philosophy of arguably the most original thinker associated with the Frankfurt School.

For Benjamin, it was the aborted attempts and abject failures erased from the narratives of progress that drew his critic's attention and by means of which he represented hell. Blasting such historical objects out of their usual context (i.e. becoming part of the triumphalist narrative of progress or being disappeared from it) was to be a kind of Marxist shock therapy aimed at reforming consciousness. In 1843, Marx described the reform of consciousness as consisting in 'making the world aware of its own consciousness, in awakening it out of its dream about itself, in *explaining* to it the meaning of its own actions'.[26] Benjamin's notion of the dialectical object was Marxist in that sense: it involved ripping objects from their context, reconfiguring them with others from different times and setting them in a different context or what he called a constellation. The idea then was that each would illuminate the other and expose the lie-dream of capitalism in a sudden, shocking image.

This elusive thing, the dialectical image, then, is not so much an image that can be seen, but something that can only be represented in language and yet connects past and present in dialectical relationship. Benjamin wrote: 'The new, dialectical method of doing history presents itself as the art of experiencing the present as waking world, a world to which that dream which we name the past refers in truth.'[27] For this method, the present is haunted by the ruins of the past, by the very detritus capitalism sought to airbrush from its history. It was this method, however esoteric, that was to possess the philosophy of Theodor Adorno in the 1930s, and become an important sideline of critical theory, if not a cul-de-sac. Benjamin scarcely wrote in Freudian terms of the return of the repressed, but that is what his project sets in motion.

In this sense, Benjamin sought to be a redeemer, freeing capitalism's victims from hell. And the dialectical image was supposed to help in that liberation. But the reception has been mixed; Pensky worried that perhaps nobody other than Benjamin can find or make dialectical images. Other critics wondered if there is such a thing at all.[28] Most likely, the term dialectical image obscures the simpler truth Benjamin was trying to convey. Under capitalism, he thought, we fetishise consumer goods – imagining that they can fulfil our hopes for happiness and realise our dreams. By considering old fetishes for now obsolete products or innovations, we might liberate ourselves from our current fetishes and so from our delusive belief that capitalism can provide us with fulfilment or happiness. By meditating on past disappointments, we might free ourselves from future disappointment. That liberation would have involved the reform of consciousness that Marx sought. But Benjamin, in part because his writings in the 1930s got sucked into a terminological black hole, never succeeded in it. This exemplifies a more general truth: Walter Benjamin and the Frankfurt School never freed capitalism's victims from hell, but rather became increasingly caustic and elegant critics of it.

TWO YEARS AFTER starting *The Arcades Project*, Benjamin was in Marseilles, and there wrote about a city that – like Naples and Moscow – was an antidote to his Berlin home.[29] 'Marseille – the yellow studded maw of a seal with salt water coming out between the teeth', he wrote savouringly. 'When this gullet opens to catch the black and brown proletarian bodies thrown to it by ship's companies according to their timetables, it exhales a stink of oil, urine and printer's ink . . .' Benjamin wrote these words for a newspaper article in the same same year as *From Deauville to Monte Carlo: A Guide to the Gay World of France* excoriated Marseilles. Its author Basil Woon warned respectable readers that, whatever they do, they should on no account visit France's second city. 'Thieves, cut-throats and other undesirables throng the narrow alleys and sisters of scarlet sit in the doorways of their places of business, catching you by the sleeve as you pass by. The dregs of the world are here unsifted . . . Marseille is the world's wickedest port.'[30]

Unlike Woon, Benjamin revelled in the city – precisely because it was wicked, clamorous, poor, sexy and dirty. Another French city, Toulouse, called itself *la ville rose*, the pink city, but for Benjamin, pink was more truly the colour of Marseilles. 'The palate itself is pink, which is the colour of shame here, of poverty. Hunchbacks wear it, and beggarwomen. And the discoloured women of Rue Bouterie are given their only tint by the sole pieces of clothing they wear: pink shifts.'

Much has changed since 1929. Today gay doesn't mean what it used to mean. Marseilles isn't the world's wickedest port, but subject to one of Europe's biggest architectural makeover projects. It has become respectable enough to serve as European Capital of Culture in 2013. Its port has been sandblasted and civilised. Throughout the city there are new trams, designer hotels, luxury flats and high-rise developments. The blurb for the new Eurostar service from London seems to suggest that Marseilles has been, if not ethnically, then symbolically cleansed in preparation for visitors. 'Famous for its soap factories', went the blurb, 'the second largest city in France enjoys an average of 300 days of sunshine a year, making Marseilles a pleasant (as well as sweet-smelling) place to be all year round.'[31] It risks becoming as amiably polite, as fragrant, as everywhere else. Benjamin, the safe money says, would have hated it.

Benjamin's enthusiasm for dirty, sexy, wicked cities like Marseilles is, nearly 100 years on, contagious. Particularly as so many of the world's leading metropolises have turned sclerotic – socially stratified cages to keep the riff-raff out and the rest of us polishing our must-have Nespresso machines. In Paris, the poor are banished beyond the *périphérique* so that when they revolt, they destroy their own *banlieues* rather than the French capital's fussily maintained environment. London's key workers strap-hang on laughable trains from distant commuter towns to serve the wealthy before being returned to their flats in time for the de facto curfew each day. Manhattan island is today a pristine vitrine on which the lower orders don't even get to leave their mucky paw prints, but inside which the rich get to fulfil with unparalleled freedom their uninteresting desires. I'm exaggerating in each case, but not much. Many of the world's leading cities are becoming like the Berlin that Benjamin called a prison, and from which he escaped whenever possible. What he wrote about cities in newspaper essays in the 1920s and early 1930s, as well as in *The Arcades Project*, remains fascinating and instructive, and not just because he was one of the first thinkers to suggest that cities became zones of segregation, exclusion and control. His writing is even more compelling because he also found the opposite – flashes of the utopian in the abject – and suggested that cities as a result could provide solutions to, as well as be the causes of, alienation.

Especially if, as Benjamin sometimes did, you experienced a city such as Marseilles after taking hashish. 'Events took place in such a way that the appearance of things touched me with a magic wand, and I sank into a dream of them', he wrote in 'Hashish in Marseilles'. 'People and things behave at such hours like those little stage sets and people made of elder pith in the glass tin-foil box, which, when the glass is rubbed, are electrified and fall at every moment into the most unusual relationships.' Benjamin found here what his beloved Baudelaire found when taking hashish in Paris nearly seventy years earlier – an artificial paradise. He felt, he recalled in 'Hashish in Marseilles', as joyful as Ariadne unwinding her thread:

> And this joy is related to the joy of trance, as to the joy of creation. We go forward; but in so doing we not only discover the twists and turns of the cave, but also enjoy the pleasure of discovery against the background of the other, rhythmical bliss of unwinding the thread. The certainty of unrolling an artfully wound skein – is that not the joy of all productivity, at least in prose? And under hashish we are enraptured prose-beings in the highest power.[32]

Even in drug-induced reverie, Benjamin was dreaming like a Marxist, putting the joy of productivity and the dignity of labour at the heart of his vision. The trance-like work of unwinding the thread resembles D. H. Lawrence's very nearly contemporary poems of the late 1920s.

There is no point in work
unless it absorbs you
like an absorbing game.
If it doesn't absorb you
if it's never any fun,
don't do it.

When a man goes out to work
he is alive like a tree in spring,
he is living, not merely working.[33]

The kind of work Benjamin and Lawrence blissfully celebrate here is precisely the kind of work denied in machine-age capitalism, wherein the worker is alienated from her labour, what she produces, and therefore from herself. This kind of work, too, is an antidote to passive consumerism, to what Adorno and Horkheimer would later call the culture industry.

In the late 1920s, there was a thread binding Benjamin and Lawrence. The latter wrote:

Whatever man makes and makes it live
lives because of the life put into it.
A yard of India muslin is alive with Hindu life.
And a Navajo woman, weaving her rug in the pattern of her dream
must run the pattern out in a little break at the end
so that her soul can come out, back to her.

Benjamin wrote in *One-Way Street* that 'Work on good prose has three steps: a musical stage when it is composed, an architectonic one when it is built and a textile one when it is woven.'[34] For both writers the joyful absorption in work is dialectical, a self-actualising process through which one weaves into being, not just text or textile, but oneself.

The thought that Benjamin unravels here – that one realises oneself through creative productive labour – was especially pertinent as Taylorite production processes and capitalist dreams of endless technological progress seemed to thwart such self-realisation. At the time the question of what work was became immensely controversial.

But at the same time as work under capitalism offered less opportunity for self-fulfilment, a gimcrack alternative – call it consumption of consumer goods, call it shopping – was being born. If we couldn't realise ourselves through the self-actualising process of work, perhaps we could do it through shopping? That was the possibility, as we will see in the next chapter, that Benjamin's friend Bertolt Brecht explored in his and Kurt Weill's opera *Mahoganny*. Capitalist society, then, seemed to be at a pivotal moment during the late 1920s and 1930s in terms of how human beings might fulfil themselves and realise their potentialities. Writers as varied as D. H. Lawrence and Simone Weill meditated on what work could and should mean in an era when it seemed to be, increasingly, a brain-numbing, spirit-crushing, soul-destroying nightmare, and the only alternative to the Marxist cogito (I work therefore I am) was the consumerist one (I shop therefore I am).

Marx's concept of work was to prove particularly controversial for the Frankfurt School. His suggestion was that man and woman need to work to flourish and achieve dignity. Even in a communist paradise, we must work. On the face of it, what Benjamin wrote in 'Hashish in Marseille' and *One-Way Street* about work was in line with this Marxist orthodoxy that humans defined themselves through work; the problem was that the increasingly mechanised, routine and exploitative nature of work under capitalism thwarted any possibility of fulfilment.

But scepticism about humans defining and liberating themselves through work was to become a hallmark of critical theory as it evolved from the 1930s onwards. The Frankfurt School has been called neo-Marxist, but in this area at least it might more accurately be called anti-Marxist. Indeed, the man who would take the Frankfurt School on a new intellectual trajectory in the 1930s baulked at this Marxist perspective. Max Horkheimer wrote in *Dämmerung*, a book of aphorisms published not long after Benjamin's description of his drug-fuelled ramble around Marseilles: 'To make labour into a transcendent category of human activity is an ascetic ideology . . . Because socialists hold to this general concept, they make themselves into carriers of capitalist propaganda.'[35] For Horkheimer, who when *Dämmerung* was published was the director of the Frankfurt School and its primary intellectual influence, Marx fetishised labour as a category.

If that was true, then Marx was following in a venerable tradition in German thought. As Erich Fromm wrote in his 1961 book *Marx's Concept of Man*, Spinoza, Hegel and Goethe all held that, as he put it,

> man is alive only inasmuch as he is productive, inasmuch as he grasps the world outside of himself in the act of expressing his own specific human powers, and of grasping the world with these powers. Inasmuch as man is not productive, inasmuch as he is receptive and passive, he is nothing, he is dead. In this productive process, man realises his own essence, he returns to his own essence, which in theological language is nothing other than his return to God.[36]

Hegel wrote in *The Phenomenology of Spirit* that the productive man makes the world his own by grasping it productively, by 'translating itself from the night of possibility into the day of actuality'.[37] The work of unravelling the thread, similarly, helps lead one from the cave to the daylight – to actualise oneself, rather than being like the deluded prisoners in Plato's cave or the Niebelungen of Wagner's Ring Cycle mining for gold in an endless subterranean night. Under Horkheimer, the Frankfurt School rebelled against this orthodox German view of the value of work and in particular against the Marxist credo that we fulfil ourselves through labour. For the likes of Horkheimer and Adorno, if not for Fromm who remained more faithful to Marx than his colleagues, labour is not the basic category of human realisation.

Indeed, when Horkheimer read Marx's recently published *Economic and Philosophic Manuscripts* in the early 1930s, in which this orthodoxy about work is expressed, he detected in it something that made him queasy. Even Benjamin, who eulogised creative productive labour, found a presentiment of the Nazi jackboot in it. The vulgar Marxist conception of labour, he wrote, 'already displays the technocratic features later encountered in Fascism . . . The new conception of labour amounts to the exploitation of nature which with naive complacency is contrasted with the exploitation of the proletariat.'[38] That wasn't the kind of creative productive labour that he eulogised in *One-Way Street* or 'Hashish in Marseille'; it was just the socialist flip side of the capitalist coin. This queasiness before the ruination of nature in what Benjamin called vulgar Marxist thought was to become an increasing concern of the Frankfurt School. Indeed, as late as 1969, Adorno told an interviewer that Marx wanted to convert the world into a gigantic workhouse.[39]

Perhaps, though, that's unfair. Read sympathetically, Marx's notion of productive humans didn't entail the ruination of nature, but rather the mastery, through creative work, of oneself. And yet the Frankfurt School repeatedly disavowed this aspect of their Marxist heritage. Two decades after Horkheimer accused Marx of fetishising labour, Herbert Marcuse elaborated the accusation in his 1955 book *Eros and Civilisation: A Philosophical Inquiry Into Freud*. Marcuse used the stand-in of Marx's favourite cultural hero Prometheus for a coded attack: 'Prometheus is the culture-hero of toil, productivity and progress through repression', he wrote, 'the trickster and (suffering) rebel against the gods, who creates culture at the price of perpetual pain. He symbolises productiveness, the unceasing effort to master life . . . Prometheus is the archetypal hero of the performance principle.'[40]

The performance principle was a special version of Freud's reality principle, whereby one repressed one's pleasures in order to function better in civilisation. But there were other principles, and other heroes, Marcuse suggested. Against Prometheus, he pitted different Greek heroes – Orpheus, Narcissus and Dionysius: 'they stand for a very different reality . . . Theirs is the image of joy and fulfilment, the voice that does not command but sings, the deed that is peace and that ends the labour of conquest: the liberty from time that unites man with god, man with nature . . . the redemption of pleasure, the halt of time, the absorption of death: silence, sleep, night, paradise – the Nirvana-principle not as death but life.'[41] Marcuse's utopian suggestion contradicted not just the German philosophical tradition that embraced Hegel, Marx and Schopenhauer, but also Freud. It was

Freud who posited the Nirvana principle as an innate psychic drive or death instinct that aims to end life's inevitable tension. We all yearn to leave the treadmill of labour, perhaps, but our fate as humans is to remain on it until we die: Thanatos and Eros are, for Freud, contrary to one another. Marcuse refused to accept that.

But were Horkheimer, Adorno and Marcuse right to suggest that Marx fetishised labour? It could be argued that he fetishised not labour but human development, and it is precisely that fetish that Fromm, in *Marx's Concept of Man*, shares and that Marcuse seeks to overcome through, somehow, realising the Nirvana principle in life. Indeed, the very idea of a communist society is one that, for Marx, involves the 'withering away' of the state since it is no longer necessary; in fact its continued existence would hamper the free development of the productive forces of society. But that society, as Hannah Arendt argued, was one of individuals freely fulfilling themselves: this doesn't sound like a communist society premised on solidarity and shared activities, but a prelapsarian paradise wherein material needs are satisfied.

What then is the paradise to which Marx thought proletarian revolution paves the way? The American Marxist critic Marshall Berman argued: 'Marx wants to embrace Prometheus and Orpheus: he considers communism worth fighting for because for the first time in history it could enable men to have both. He might also argue that it is only against a background of Promethean striving that Orphic rapture gains moral or psychic value: "luxe, calme et volupté" by themselves are merely boring, as Baudelaire knew well.'[42] And who would want a revolution if it resulted only in an eternity of boredom? But that seems precisely the boring paradise Marcuse invoked in *Eros and Civilisation* when he suggested that the Nirvana principle can be realised in human lives. More charitably, perhaps, we can interpret Marcuse as arguing for a work–life balance by means of shortening the working day to give opportunity for, if not Orphic rapture, then the redemption of pleasure and the halt of time.

Marx's suggestion, nonetheless, was that to be free involves being free to do work that is not alienating, by means of which one becomes what he thought was increasingly unlikely under capitalism, a self-actualising subject. The French philosopher Simone Weil (no relation to the founders of the Frankfurt School) argued that there must be more to human liberation than this in her essay *Oppression and Liberty*,[43] published in the same year, 1934, as Horkheimer published *Dämmerung*, in which he attacked Marx's conception of labour.

For Simone Weil, human relations must not be conflated with labour and work: the latter are merely instrumental since they involve relations of a subject to an object. For her, human interactions need to be revolutionised as much as productive forces and production relations if humans are truly to be free. Weil's thoughts were to prove important to one later Frankfurt School thinker, Jürgen Habermas, who wrote: 'Liberation from hunger and misery does not necessarily converge with liberation from servitude and degradation; there is no automatic developmental relation between labour and interaction.'[44] That distinction between work and interaction runs through Habermas's monumental 1981 book *The Theory of Communicative Action*, in which he systematically argues for liberation from servitude and degradation not through revolutionising productive labour, but through interaction.

Axel Honneth, who was to succeed Habermas as director of the Institute, argued that the degradation of work in Taylorite production processes prompted the Frankfurt School thinkers to abandon the Marxist notion of work as self-fulfilment. But they replaced it with something else: arguably, rather than making a fetish of industrial labour, one might expect the Frankfurt School to fetishise communication, which could be construed not as an alternative to productive labour but as the form of productive labour to which they were temperamentally suited. As William Outhwaite notes in his book about Habermas, 'this might seem a welcome exercise in demythologisation on the part of people whose preferred form of work involves reading and, from time to time, speaking and writing'[45] – people, no doubt, such as armchair Marxist philosophers and social theorists. For them, and indeed for many of us now in the overwhelmingly post-industrial west, work is interaction, and one of the pleasures of being human as well as one of the conditions of human dignity is that we can freely converse. (The other alternative is that communicative action is a professor's dream of what revolutionising degraded humanity involves, and one that not many outside the academy share.) The Taylorised form of labour the Frankfurt School excoriated has been massively outsourced to other parts of the world where workers can be more readily exploited – a fact that, as Henryk Grossman would have pointed out were he still alive, helps capitalism to defer its demise.

Habermas's utopia, wherein human relations are revolutionised through uncoerced reasoned discussion, is akin to the delight Adam takes in 'Reason in the Garden of Eden' imagined by Milton:

> Yet not so strictly hath our Lord impos'd
> Labour, as to debarr us when we need
> Refreshment, whether food, or talk between,
> Food of the mind, or this sweet intercourse
> Of looks and smiles, for smiles from Reason flow,
> To brute deni'd, and are of Love the food,
> Love not the lowest end of human life.
> For not to irksom toile, but to delight
> He made us, and delight to Reason joyn'd.[46]

Paradise on Earth. But, instead of paradise, at the end of the 1920s western industrial societies were in hell. Walter Benjamin thought as much when he sat at his desk in the Bibliothèque Nationale working on *The Arcades Project*; so too did his friend Bertolt Brecht as he wrote a Marxist opera with Kurt Weill. As we will see in the next chapter, what Brecht and Weill dramatised on stage was not the traditional Marxist hell of exploitative production relations, but one of unfettered consumerism. Instead of a gigantic workhouse, capitalism seemed to be reconfiguring the world as a gigantic shopping mall, where every taste, no matter how base or grubby, could be fulfilled – if you could afford the price.

At the start of the 1930s, Brecht's vision of that hell was to prove influential to the Frankfurt School as they diagnosed what had gone wrong with modern society, and why the revolution had not happened.

PART III:

THE 1930s

5

Show Us the Way to the
Next Whiskey Bar

In 1930, Adorno wrote a little review of a new opera.[1] It was a work the Nazis branded as an embodiment of the 'Jewish-Bolshevik threat' and demanded be banned. And indeed, before the decade was out, that demand would be met: all public performances were prohibited and in 1938 the work was confined to a shadow existence as part of an exhibition of degenerate music. The opera was Brecht and Weill's *The Rise and Fall of the City of Mahoganny*, whose premiere at the Neues Theater in Leipzig on 4 March 1930 that year was marked by Nazi brownshirts demonstrating outside, audience members trading punches, and a tumult in the third act so noisy that the conductor could scarcely hear the musicians.[2] Adorno, for his part, was intrigued by the work. 'Just as in Kafka's novels', he wrote, 'the commonplace bourgeois world appears absurd . . . The present system, with its mores, rights and order, is exposed as anarchy; we ourselves live in Mahoganny, where everything is permitted save one thing: having no money.'

In those respects, *Mahoganny* was nothing if not topical: the opera was performed in Leipzig at a time when Germany was on the brink of anarchy, when the Weimar Republic had committed the ultimate capitalist crime of running out of cash. On Friday October 29 of the previous year, the financial markets in New York had collapsed, provoking a global economic meltdown that was felt most strongly in Germany. In spring 1929, the American-led Young Plan to allow Germany to pay its debt of 112 billion gold marks over fifty-nine years seemed to offer a lifeline to an economy already ailing owing to the punitive First World War reparations demanded by the allied victors, but after the Wall Street Crash the following autumn, the plan was scrapped and American banks started recalling money and cancelling credit. Germany was economically bankrupt and thrown into political chaos, ruled by emergency presidential decree since feuding parties could not form a ruling coalition.

Only one group seemed able to capitalise on capitalism's crisis: the National Socialist Party, which increased its number of seats in the Reichstag from twelve to 207 in the general election of September 1930. Disastrously for the future of Germany, the two leading left-wing parties – the Social Democrat SPD and the Communist KPD – could not form an alliance to combat the rise of the Nazis. In *The Impotence of the German Working Class*, published in 1932, Horkeimer argued that the schism between the two workers' parties was deepened because skilled employed workers voted SPD and unemployed workers KPD. The split in the proletariat seemed to confound Marx's thoughts about its growing unity.

There was even less likelihood of a successful proletarian revolution in Germany than there had been in 1919 – working-class and lower-middle-class Germans were increasingly drawn to the dictatorship promised by Adolf Hitler as an alternative to weak democratic government. In 1929 Horkheimer and Fromm launched a project to carry out empirical research aimed at identifying the conscious and unconscious attitudes of the German working class towards authoritarian figures. Though the study was never completed, this psychoanalytically conceived research concluded that German workers unconsciously desired their own domination.[3] They were getting ready, not for socialist revolution, but for the Third Reich.

It was in this situation that Brecht and Weill staged their opera, set in a fictitious city in the American West presented as a modern Sodom and Gomorrah, destroyed by its worship of graft and fraud, whiskey and dollars. Many Weimar artists were fascinated by America and what it signified as a creative symbol, and Adorno himself wrote an uncompleted opera in the early 1930s called *The Treasure of Indian Joe*, drawing on Mark Twain's novel *The Adventures of Tom Sawyer*.

Mahoganny starts with three crooks on the run. When their lorry breaks down, they decide to establish Mahoganny – a city of pleasure, whoring, gambling and whiskey. One of its founders, Ladybird Begbick, a madam, sets out the city's business model:

> Everywhere men must labour and sorrow
> Only here it is fun.
> For the deepest craving of man is
> Not to suffer but to do as he pleases.

Forget the Marxist-Lawrentian notion of defining yourself through productive labour; forget the misery of the nine to five; indeed, forget production. Savour instead the pleasures of consumption. In Mahoganny, it wasn't so much I think therefore I am, still less I work therefore I am, but rather I consume therefore I am. Among the punters lured into town is Jimmy, a lumberjack, who believes he can do whatever he wants there – have sex with prostitutes, go on drinking binges and gamble. When he loses all his money on a boxing match wager and so cannot pay his bar tab, he is arrested and sentenced to death by electric chair. Being broke – a new experience that people from Oklahoma to Oldenburg were getting used to in the Great Depression that followed the Wall Street Crash – was unacceptable. Mahoganny descends into chaos as demonstrators parade Jimmy's corpse around town, with slogans displaying contradictory demands – 'For the natural order of things', 'For the natural disorder of things', 'For the unjust division of earthly goods', 'For the just division of earthly goods'. Brecht hoped this vision of anarchy would help catalyse socialist revolution. His hopes were dashed, at least in Germany, within two years. Instead, and much more in keeping with the vitalist heroes of his 1920s dramas such as *Baal*, a strong man, the authoritarian figure unconsciously desired by German workers, one with the violent temperament of Wagner's Siegfried and the body of Charlie Chaplin, would eliminate the contradictions of German society.

At the Leipzig premiere, the drama spilled from stage to auditorium, as the fourth wall in Brechtian theatre was broken, not for the last time. As brownshirts brawled with their opponents in the Neues

Theater, on stage there was a funeral procession with the chorus singing first 'Nothing can be done to help a dead man!', and then the final,
dismal words of the opera: 'Nothing can be done to help the living.'
Like the Weimar Republic (we realise with hindsight), Mahoganny
was doomed.

'The city of Mahoganny is a representation of the social world in
which we live, projected from the bird's-eye perspective of an already
liberated society', wrote Adorno. 'Mahoganny does not present a class-
less society as a positive standard against which to compare the
depraved present; instead, from time to time this society shimmers
through just barely – as unclear as a movie projection over which
another has been superimposed.'

The opera is important in the history of critical theory because it
showed the world as the Frankfurt School saw it, in a high definition
that brought the hell of the present into extreme focus. Violence,
whose (mostly) unspoken threat is the foundation of capitalism's
order, was omnipresent in *Mahoganny*. Everyone could be bought and
sold and prostitution provided the model for human interaction,
while, as Adorno sourly noted, 'whatever love may exist here can only
burst forth from the smoking rubble of adolescent fantasies of sexual
power'. It's hard not to read Adorno's review without thinking that we
still live in Mahoganny today, no longer just a city but a global economy where in principle anything can be had for money and in practice
everything is. 'The anarchy of commodity production which Marxism
has analysed is projected as the anarchy of consumption, abbreviated
to the point of a crass horror which could not be rendered by an
economic analysis', he added. This shift in focus from production to
consumption was to prove central in the Frankfurt School's reconfig-
uration of Marxist theory for a new era of monopoly capitalism. In
Mahoganny, the pleasure seekers are trapped on a wheel of Ixion on
which one desire leads to another in a degrading, neurotic repetition
echoed in Brecht's lyrics:

> Oh, show us the way to the next whiskey bar
> Oh don't ask why!
> Oh don't ask why

> For we must find the next whiskey bar
> For if we don't find the next whiskey bar,
> I tell you we must die!
> I tell you we must die.
> I tell you. I tell you. I tell you we must die!

And every commodity is substitutable for another – whiskey, dollars, little girls – the fulfilment of the logic of Marx's exchange principle.

In the same year *Mahoganny* was premiered, Samuel Beckett published an essay about Proust in which he wrote: 'Habit is the ballast that chains the dog to his vomit.'[4] It's as if in 1930 Brecht and Beckett were realising how wrong Rousseau was: it's not that man is born free but is everywhere in chains, as the philosopher claimed in *The Social Contract*; rather, man is born chained, remains chained and is everywhere in chains.

Adorno took *Mahoganny* to be an exemplar of what modernist art should be. Art shouldn't play footsie with capitalism, but assault it. Brecht certainly intended the work as an assault. 'One of its functions is to change society', he wrote in an essay accompanying the first performance. 'It brings the culinary principle under discussion.' By 'culinary' he meant that the opera of the day sated jaded bourgeois palates with narcotising entertainment. 'An opera is appreciated by its audience', Brecht wrote, 'precisely because opera is antiquated.'[5] In noting this hunger for past musical forms as an escape from the modern, from the rationalised, administered, unheroic, functional present, Brecht and Adorno were singing from the same hymn sheet. In his musicological writings of the 1930s for the Institute's journal, Adorno attacked classical music audiences for seeking music that detached them from real social conditions and offered a phoney reconciliation between their cultural education and their property. But as Adorno had argued in his post-doctoral thesis *Kierkegaard: Construction of the Aesthetic*, written in the early 1930s, the quest for such inwardness was chimerical, though comprehensible as a reaction among the rich and privileged to an intolerable Neue Sachlichkeit world of machines and functional humans.

In T. S. Eliot's 1915 poem *A Portrait of a Lady*, the lady, whom the callous narrator seeks to reveal in her false inwardness, argues that communion with the nineteenth-century artistic soul needs to take place in the drawing room rather than the concert hall, so fragile is this precious commodity.[6] Classical concertgoers, Adorno argued, sought that 'soul' in the concert hall, especially in the figure of the conductor whose imperious gestures were taken as a performance of that soul but really, in their absence of genuine spontaneity, were the musical equivalent of the authoritarian dictator. It's as though, for Adorno, the conductor on the early 1930s concert podium was a prototype for the Führer at the Nuremberg rallies later in the decade.

Marcuse, who also thought about the great soul of twentieth-century culture, distinguished in his essay 'The Affirmative Character of Culture' between the universal man of the Renaissance who sought happiness in worldly action, questing for power and sensuality, and the spiritualised personality of bourgeois culture.[7] The latter, Marcuse argued, sought higher experience in withdrawing from the world into a more refined spiritual milieu of rarified aesthetic experience. It was as if bourgeois culture had kept the nineteenth-century 'great soul' on life support into the twentieth century, since its continued deployment helped obscure society's antagonisms and contradictions. The great soul, perfumed handkerchief to its nose to repel the stench of the poor, oblivious to the racket of machines and Nazi jackboots, transported itself with Chopin.

But not for long. Monopoly capitalism and the fascist state could not tolerate this autonomous sphere of life that represented a potential threat to the existing order, so they did to rarefied bourgeois culture what they did to the family – invaded it, obliterated its autonomy and co-opted any lingering power it had to uphold the current social order. Such, Marcuse argued, was the 'total mobilisation' through which the individual must be, in all areas of his existence, submitted to the discipline of the authoritarian state.[8]

Adorno was attracted to *Mahoganny* because it displayed society's contradictions. Art that aspired to cheerful harmony or resurrected the great soul of nineteenth-century bourgeois culture was delusive entertainment that failed to do what art should do: expose the lie at the heart of capitalism, namely that this economic system could deliver freedom and happiness. In 'The Social Situation of Music', an essay he wrote for the Institute's journal in 1932, Adorno opposed two contemporary composers, Schoenberg and Stravinsky, taking them as opposite poles of what music should and shouldn't be under monopoly capitalism.[9] His bracing notion was that music, purportedly the most abstract and therefore the least socially grounded, most autonomous art form, actually contained social contradictions in its own structure. Schoenberg, in whose second Vienna school's ethos Adorno had been trained while working with the great composer's disciple Alban Berg in the mid 1920s, had evolved during the early years of the twentieth century. He moved from being a composer of expressionist music to one who wrote music that eschewed harmonic resolutions, still less offered hummable tunes, but rather involved a musical twelve-tone system, whereby the repetition of any note in a twelve-tone row was prohibited until all of them had been sounded. The harmonic resolution of, say, Schoenberg's 1899 string sextet *Verklärte Nacht* (Transfigured Night), was unthinkable for a composer who, in the early 1930s, was so bewitched by the aesthetic purity and logic of his twelve-tone method that for the title of his uncompleted operatic masterpiece *Moses Und Aron* of 1932 he dropped one of the As from Aaron's name so that it would have twelve rather than thirteen letters.

Stravinsky, for his part, in the ten years between the premiere of one of the founding texts of musical modernism, *Le Sacre Du Printemps*, to the premiere of his opera *Pulcinella*, had mutated from musical revolutionary to conservative revivalist of old forms. In the 1920s Stravinsky disinterred old musical forms – the concerto grosso, the fugue, the symphony – for a new era. Just as Brecht excoriated opera as culinary – a mouthwatering diversion from the realities of modern life – so Adorno accused Stravinsky of composing music that offered false reconciliations, redeploying old forms that served to satisfy his audience's degraded need for escape into a chimerical past. He also detected a connection between Stravinsky's neo-classicism and fascism: the irrationality of the composer's system, Adorno argued, was of a piece with the arbitrary control of a Führer. He was stretching the point, perhaps, but then Adorno was apt to see Nazism in nearly everything he disliked – understandable given what it was about to do to him, his colleagues and his family.

At the time, Adorno took Schoenberg – a Jew who like Adorno would be compelled to flee Europe with the rise of Hitler, and who would become a neighbour in Los Angeles in the 1940s – to represent all that was progressive in music. Schoenberg's music was, he noted with approval, not seduction by harmony and melody but 'the conglomeration of broken shards'. But there was, he realised later, a problem with his idol's musical system: its absorbing logic, like that of a game of chess, detached Schoenberg from the social situation for which it provided a fitting soundtrack. Worse, Schoenberg's twelve-tone system became, Adorno later realised, hypostatised – the revolutionary form of composition became the only game in town for avant-garde composers and therefore, paradoxically, conservative. A system that had seemed to promise a breakout from bourgeois music was reified in its turn.

How did Weill's music for *Mahoganny* map on to this musical taxonomy? Weill once said he would be happy if every taxi driver could whistle his melodies. One might have thought Adorno would have damned Weill's music as part of the culture industry that helped capitalism run more smoothly, but in fact he enjoyed Weill's music for *Mahoganny*. He saw in it what Benjamin loved in surreal-ist art, which often involved creating montages of historical detritus and thereby producing potentially liberating 'constellations'. Adorno called *Mahoganny* the first surrealist opera. 'This music,' he wrote of the score, 'pieced together from triads and off notes with the good beat of old music hall songs which we hardly recognise anymore but are nonetheless remembered as an heirloom, is hammered and glued together with the fetid mucilage of a soggy potpourri of operas. This music, made up of the debris of past music, is completely contemporary.'

Brecht's libretto, too, sought to make it clear that the bourgeois world was absurd and anarchic. 'In order to represent this convinc-ingly', wrote Adorno of the dramatisation of the bourgeois world as absurd and anarchic, 'it is necessary to transcend the closed world of bourgeois consciousness which considers bourgeois social reality to be immutable. Outside of this framework, however, there is no posi-tion to take – at least for the German consciousness, there is no site which is non-capitalist.' This was to become one great theme of crit-ical theory: there is no outside, not in today's utterly rationalised, totally reified, commodity-fetishising world. When Marx wrote *Capital* in the mid nineteenth century, the more primitive capitalist system he was diagnosing made commodity fetishism merely episodic; now it was everywhere, poisoning everything. 'Paradoxically, therefore', Adorno added, 'transcendence must take place within the framework of that which is.' Brecht's assault on capitalist society in *Mahoganny* was then paradoxically both from within and from without at the same time, both immanent and transcendent.

In this, it bore similarities to how Adorno conceived of the role of a serious music critic. In his 1929 essay 'Motifs', he wrote that in order for criticism not to collapse into a middlebrow alliance between dilettantism and smug, Olympian expertise, it is 'essential for the critic to extend his immanent listening as far as possible, while at the same time approaching music radically from the outside. To think about twelve-note technique at the same time as of that childhood experience of *Madama Butterfly* on the gramophone – that is the task of every serious attempt to understand music today.'[10] And what Adorno counselled for music criticism was true too of the critical theory that was being born in Frankfurt as Brecht and Weill's opera was being attacked by Nazis: it was to be practised by those who real-ised that there was no non-capitalist perspective from which to critique capitalism and that its practitioners were implicated in what they critiqued.

Brecht and Weill's opera, similarly, was an inside job, drawing attention to the art form's self-contradictory nature. 'The opera *Mahagonny* pays tribute to the senselessness of the operatic form', wrote Brecht. In this, its techniques parallel those deployed by the Frankfurt School during the 1930s as it developed critical theory in response to a clutch of -isms Horkheimer would lump together under the heading of traditional theory – positivism, vulgar Marxism, among others. For Horkheimer each of these disciplines was

insufficiently dialectical, and their followers made the error of imagining that there was a transcendental position from which they could
observe and analyse an objective world of facts. There was no such
position, and so in a sense the critical theorist risked the kind of
absurdity Brecht happily embraced in writing *Mahoganny*. 'It still
perches on happily on the same old bough, perhaps', he wrote in his
notes to the opera, 'but it has started (out of absent mindedness or bad
conscience) to saw it through.'

You can almost hear Brecht cackling manically as the branch on
which he's sitting plummets to the ground; but there was nothing
absent-minded about where he had decided to place his bottom. He
wanted musicians, singers and audience to realise that they were part
of the culture industry, that the first two groups were pandering to
prevailing economic interests and deluding themselves by thinking
they were making art that floated free, unsullied by capitalism's
dictates; they were supplying to the latter group, at a price, opera
which obeyed laws of commodity fetishism. He even, incredibly,
attacked his musical partner Kurt Weill for posturing as an avant-
garde composer who naively thought he was above being in thrall to
economic interests. Through attacking the established 'dramatic' form
of theatre, Brecht hoped to transform its sated spectators into observ-
ers hungering for political and social engagement.

Adorno, though he never became close to Brecht, was a kindred
spirit, an Agent Orange-style critic scorching all and sundry.
Sometimes even himself. But the philosopher never shared the dram-
atist's agitprop hopes. Brecht hoped that there would be an abrasion
between the grandeur of the opera house and the harsh message.
Instead, it became another culinary treat in the operatic repertory,
aberrantly decoded by its audiences and then happily consumed like
whiskey. Thus when *Mahoganny* was staged in Covent Garden in
2015, the British novelist Will Self wrote:

> This museum piece – a sort of diorama of failed utopianism – has
> nothing to teach us. We can enjoy the lushness of Weill's through-
> composed score; we can thrill to the unvarnished portrayal of human
> cupidity; we can admire the repurposing of Brecht's epic theatre as

entertainment. But to expect us to be moved to a critical engagement with the fundamental terms of our social being would be – frankly and idiomatically – a bit much.[11]

SOMETHING SIMILAR may be said of the Institute for Social Research as it evolved in the 1930s. It was Brechtian in its inverse relationship between scabrous critique and changing that which it critiqued. Like Brecht's theatre, critical theory arguably postured otherwise but became another fetishised commodity – the philosophical equivalent of a titillatingly 'shocking' night at the opera, made all the more exciting by its brush with fascism, a more or less harmless diversion for the chattering classes. Lukács, in his damning 1962 critique of the German intelligentsia in general and the Frankfurt School in particular, suggested that, like operagoers in the posh seats watching *Mahoganny*, thinkers like Adorno had taken up comfortable residence in the Grand Hotel Abyss.[12] Brecht even had a name for the residents of the Hotel. He called them Tuis (an acronym deriving from a scrambling of the German word for intellectual, i.e. Tellekt-Ual-In). The Tuis were partisan but not members of a party, independent of official institutions yet experienced in surviving within institutions. Such Tuis, among whom Brecht included the Frankfurt School, could have helped overthrow capitalism by instructing the masses in Marxist doctrine. Instead, by failing to do so they effectively contributed to the collapse of the Weimar Republic and the rise of Hitler. For Brecht, the Frankfurt School were traitors to the revolution they affected to espouse.[13] Adorno and Horkheimer returned the abuse: they regarded Brecht as a petit-bourgeois poseur and apologist for Stalinism. One might argue there was something of the Tui about Brecht too: his theatre, like the Frankfurt School's writings, thrived creatively during the escalation of capitalism's contradictions; instead of destroying the bourgeois art form of opera, he extended its lifespan.

While Brecht during the 1930s brought together material for a Tui novel that he never completed but which was conceived as a satire on intellectuals in the German Empire and Weimar Republic, it was during his Californian exile that he adopted the term Tuismus as his name for the Frankfurt School. By then, he regarded the Frankfurt scholars as something worse than traitors to the revolution. They had become, he charged, prostitutes in their quest for foundation support during their American exile, selling their skills and opinions as commodities in order to support the dominant ideology of oppressive US society.

6

The Power of Negative Thinking

The year after *Mahoganny*'s premiere, Max Horkheimer became director of the Institute for Social Research. Carl Grünberg had retired after suffering a stroke in January 1928 to be replaced by Friedrich Pollock. In 1931, Horkheimer replaced his friend, Pollock, who would go on to do much of the largely unsung, administrative work necessary to safeguard the finances and organisation of the Institute in its exile years. It was Pollock, for instance, who had used used his contacts in the International Labour Organisation to establish a branch of the Institute in Geneva, to which he and Horkheimer moved after the Nazi seizure of power in 1933.

Horkheimer changed the direction of the Institute radically. No longer would it be, as it had been under Grünberg, essentially a Marxist research institute studying the history of socialism and the workers' movement, still less one that took economics to be the key determinant in the fate of capitalism. To account for the failure of revolution in Germany and for the rise of fascism, it was necessary to reconfigure Marxism. 'When Marx undertook his critique of the capitalist mode of production', wrote Walter Benjamin in his 1936 essay 'The Work of Art in the Age of Mechanical Production',

this mode was in its infancy. He went back to the basic conditions underlying capitalistic production and through his presentation showed what could be expected of capitalism in the future. The result was that one could expect it not only to exploit the proletariat with increasing intensity but ultimately to create conditions which would make it possible to abolish capitalism itself.[1]

But capitalism was no longer in self-destruct mode: the rest of Benjamin's essay was about a capitalist mode of production no longer in its infancy, but one that dominated the whole of society, and where one key front in the struggle between capitalism and socialism was art and culture.

Capitalism had become not just a mode of production but a system that, through mass culture and communication, technology and various forms of social control, masked the intensity of the exploitation of the proletariat. In 1931, capitalism seemed able to defer its abolition, perhaps even indefinitely. In such circumstances, Horkheimer argued, the Institute must consider not only the economic basis of society but its superstructure. It must develop a critique of the ideological control mechanisms that held capitalism in place. While Lukács, in his 1922 *History and Class Consciousness*, had insisted on the importance of proletarian consciousness for revolution, it seemed to Horkheimer that the chasm Lukács had identified between ascribed and actual consciousness could not be closed – at least not by the proletariat. 'The members of the Frankfurt School grew to see themselves as the only revolutionary subject', wrote Thomas Wheatland, 'because only they had achieved a state of self-conscious reflection that transcended the reified world of the totally administered society.'[2] It was as if the proletariat had been found wanting and so had to be replaced as revolutionary agent by critical theorists.

Adorno, at least, appreciated the paradox of being an ideology critic while defining ideology as socially necessary false consciousness. He knew that the Frankfurt School, like Brecht, was sitting on the bough even as they sawed through it. In *Minima Moralia*, he wrote of the critical theorist's paradox:

> By allowing themselves to still think at all vis-a-vis the naked reproduction of existence, they behave as the privileged; by leaving things in thought, they declare the nullity of their privilege . . . There is no exit from the entanglement. The only responsible option is to deny oneself

the ideological misuse of one's own existence, and as for the rest, to behave in private as modestly, inconspicuously and unpretentiously as required, not for reasons of good upbringing, but because of the shame that when one is in hell, there is still air to breathe.[3]

Under Horkheimer and Adorno, the Frankfurt School turned its attention to critical theory calibrated to understand the hell in which they lived. To do so, they had to move beyond the kind of Marxist theory that fetishised economics. In his inaugural lecture, 'The Present Position of Social Philosophy and the Tasks Facing an Institute for Social Research', Horkheimer said that the Institute must address the 'question of the connection between the economic life of society, the psychological development of individuals and challenges in the realm of culture in the narrower sense (to which belong not only the so-called intellectual elements such as science, art and religion, but also law, customs, fashion, public opinion, sports, leisure activities, lifestyle, etc).' Under Horkheimer, the Institute went interdisciplinary. It would, he said, 'organise research projects stimulated by philosophical problems, in which philosophers, sociologists, economists, historians and psychologists were brought together in permanent collaboration.'[4]

The interdisciplinary trend was demonstrated by the new intellectuals who arrived at the Institute: Leo Löwenthal arrived as a literary scholar, Erich Fromm as an analytical social psychologist, Herbert Marcuse was hired as a political philosopher, and Theodor Adorno as a lecturer and writer on philosophy and music. Those thinkers on the fringes of the school – Walter Benjamin, Ernst Bloch, Siegfried Kracauer and Wilhelm Reich – encouraged the Institute to do things it would never have done under Grünberg's leadership, such as to consider, for instance, not just the economic and political basis of fascism, but its psychopathology and its aestheticisation of politics.

The Frankfurt School therefore decided to remove the white gloves in which Marxist economist Henryk Grossman delivered his lectures and get its hands dirty. It would study horoscopes, movies, jazz, sexual repression, sadomasochism, the disgusting manifestations of unconscious sexual impulses, take critical notes at the trough of mass culture, and explore the shabby metaphysical foundations in the basements of rival philosophies. Horkheimer's vision in his inaugural lecture was that philosophy should open up a synoptic, critical view of human life that empirical research and interdisciplinary work might fill in. Critical theory, Martin Jay argues, placed emphasis on the totality of dialectical mediations which had to be grasped in the process of analysing society.

Karl Korsch argued in *Marxism and History* that Marx's successors had betrayed his vision. 'Later Marxists', wrote Korsch,

> came to regard scientific socialism more and more as a set of purely scientific observations, without any immediate connection to the political or other practices of class struggle . . . A unified general theory of social revolution was changed into criticisms of the bourgeois economic order, of the bourgeois state, of the bourgeois state of education, of bourgeois religion, art, science and culture.[5]

Marxism, that is to say, had become subject to the prevailing division of labour and that undermined its critical power. In order to recover that critical power, the Frankfurt School needed to restore the totalising Marxist vision and become multidisciplinary. In doing so, incidentally, it served as a standing rebuke to the evolution of universities in the twentieth century. Universities were becoming latter-day towers of Babel, divided increasingly into specialist faculties populated by experts scarcely even speaking the same language.

Almost instantly, however, in a presentiment of the tensions that were to come in the Frankfurt School, Adorno went off message. A couple of weeks after Horkheimer's inaugural address, he argued in his first lecture as Privatdozent that this commitment to interdisciplinarity was a waste of time. Although he was as sceptical as his director about the revolutionary potential of the workers' movement in Germany, Adorno thought it futile to strive towards the goal of what Horkheimer called 'a theory of the whole' or the 'totality of the real', given that the social world had collapsed in ruins. Adorno's inaugural lecture thus sounded like a raspberry to his boss's vision of the Institute's research programme.

But what was Adorno's alternative vision? Although to come to a diagnosis of what had gone wrong in society required one to 'construct keys to unlock reality', he didn't accept that philosophy 'is capable', as Horkheimer put it, 'of giving particular studies animating impulses'. Instead, Adorno thought, philosophy risked becoming merely purely speculative unless individual disciplines (including presumably philosophy) were in what he called 'dialectical communication'. He argued that thought alone would not enable one to grasp the whole of reality; indeed, he argued that reality itself was an enigma. But it's not clear how one is to understand an enigma. Adorno developed a dialectical method of knowledge that many in his audience found obscure. He argued that 'the function of riddle solving . . . is to illuminate the puzzle in a flash'. Here one thinks of Proust at the start of *À la recherche du temps perdu*, tasting the madeleine and in so doing bringing his whole childhood to life. Adorno, similarly, was envisaging an interpretative mind with an exact imagination because, as his biographer puts it, 'the questions arising in response to the riddles are gradually surrounded by possible answers that propose tentative solutions'. Adorno's theory of knowledge involved models of philosophical interpretations being brought into changing constellations whose truth content emerges in a flash, illuminating what had previously been thought. The truth emerges in evanescent flashes. Baffling, perhaps, but it was a theory of knowledge that set Adorno alongside Benjamin and Proust, and a model to which he would remain faithful.[6]

On the train home after Adorno's lecture, Horkheimer was asked what he thought of what he'd heard. 'His reaction to Adorno's views was: what's the point?' reported Institute assistant Willy Strzelewicz.[7] Horkheimer carried on regardless. In taking this multidisciplinary turn, he was self-consciously moving his Institute back to the Hegelian roots of Marxism, and away from the kind of scientific Marxism that took proletarian revolution to be inevitable according to iron laws of historical progress. In doing so, he was inspired by reading Marx's recently released *Economic and Philosophic Manuscripts* of 1844, which had served to confirm what Lukács had written in 1922: yes, worker alienation could produce a revolutionary sense of class consciousness, but it could also produce worker disenchantment and resignation.

This new direction also gave the Frankfurt School the intellectual armoury to attack positivism, which Horkheimer took to be one of the intellectual evils of the age. The true materialism of Marx, he argued, was dialectical, which meant there was an ongoing interaction between subject and object. Everywhere he looked, Horkheimer saw dialectical processes in action. Instead of seeing a world of facts which it was the job of social theory to mirror (this is what he called the positivist illusion), he saw interplay. For instance, while some vulgar Marxists reductively derived superstructural phenomena such as culture and politics from the economic basis of society, Horkheimer argued for the crucial importance of mediation to any social theory that sought the transformation of society. In this he was following Lukács, who wrote: 'Thus the category of mediation is a lever with which to overcome the mere immediacy of the social world.' For Lukács the objects of the empirical world were to be understood in Hegelian terms as the objects of a totality, i.e. 'as the objects of a total historical situation caught up in the process of historical change'.[8] Politics and culture were not simply expressions of class interests or phenomena that could be read off from the socio-economic basis of a society. Rather, they were in multidimensional relations to the material substructure of society, reflecting and contradicting class interests, expressing and contracting that substructure. Think of Balzac: Engels praised this political reactionary of a novelist precisely because his novels portrayed the concrete reality of nineteenth-century France in all its contradictions. His novels didn't just express the author's class interests; indeed, one thing that made them valuable to the left is that they described how those interests were in self-contradiction.

But what did the term dialectic mean to the Frankfurt School? To understand this, we need to go back to Hegel. Hegel's classic example of the dialectical process in *The Phenomenology of Spirit* is the relationship between master and slave. The master seems to have everything, the slave nothing; but the master does lack something – the fulfilment of his need for acknowledgment. The acknowledgment of the slave is not enough since the slave is merely a thing to the master, not an independent consciousness at all. Nor does the slave receive acknowledgment from the master because the former is a thing to the latter. But here's the twist. The slave works, while the master receives the temporary pleasures of consumption. But in working, the slave shapes and fashions material objects and in the process becomes aware of his own consciousness, since he sees it as something objective, namely, as the fruit of his labours.

Clearly, this connects with the Marxist notion of man as essentially a producer, one who defines himself or rises to self-consciousness, even personal fulfilment, through meaningful work. For the slave, Hegel thought, labour, even at the direction of a slave master, makes him realise he has a mind of his own and means that the situation is not stable: its tensions generate a dialectical movement that leads to a higher synthesis. That synthesis leads to another dialectical tension, to another synthesis, and so on, at least in Hegel's conception of history. Forty years after Hegel set out this dialectical process, Marx argued that if the object produced through labour is owned by another (be that other a slave-owner or a capitalist), the worker has lost his own objectified essence. Such is alienated labour.

Hegel took history to be an unfolding of such dialectical processes towards the self-knowledge of what he called the Absolute Spirit. Dispensing with Hegel's mysticism and progressive developmental logic, Horkheimer took up the Hegelian dialectic and pitted it against what he considered to be the baleful, conservative influence of positivism. It was to be an abiding intellectual commitment of the Frankfurt School. Thirty years later, Marcuse would write in the 1960 Preface to his *Reason and Revolution: Hegel and the Rise of Social Theory*:

> Dialectic thought . . . becomes negative in itself. Its function is to break down the self-assurance and self-contentment, to undermine the sinister confidence in the power and language of facts, to demonstrate that unfreedom is so much at the core of things that the development of their internal contradictions leads necessarily to qualitative change: the explosion and catastrophe of the established state of affairs.[9]

In his inaugural lecture, Horkheimer opposed positivism because it 'sees only the particular, in the realm of society it sees only the individual and the relations between individuals; for positivism, everything is exhausted in mere facts'.[10] Positivism, an approach to social theory devised in the nineteenth century by the French philosopher Auguste Comte, held that society, like the physical world, operates according to laws. In philosophy, logical positivism holds that all we can reasonably claim to know is based on reports of sensory experience, along with logical and mathematical operations. Propositions not based on such reports or operations are metaphysical and hence nonsense, and even aesthetic or moral judgements, rightly understood, are not genuine judgements but more or less sophisticated grunts of approval or disapproval.

Such a philosophy was developed almost contemporaneously with the Frankfurt School. The so-called Vienna Circle of logical positivism, founded by Moritz Schlick in 1922, consisted of a group of philosophers and scientists who met until 1936 at the University of Vienna. Some former members of the Circle went into exile from Austria around the time of the Nazi Anschluss of 1938, and the Circle went on to greatly influence philosophy departments in Britain and the United States, in part because their intellectual trajectory (they took most of Hegel to be metaphysical and therefore nonsense) was more amenable to the Anglophone universities.

Horkheimer, for his part, argued that behind positivist social theory's ostensible focus on neutral facts, behind the law's apparent working through of formal procedures, beyond the apparently neutral operations of formal logic, there was another story: while positivists had once been progressive they now upheld the hellish status quo. For instance, Kant's founding of his ethical system on the categorical imperative (the principle that one should 'Act only according to that maxim whereby you can, at the same time, will that it should become a universal law'), at the birth of the Enlightenment, had developed a disinterested, individualist morality that challenged the *ancien régime*'s *droit de seigneur*. Now though, Kantian ethics served to uphold the status quo by means of making bourgeois morality seem not just natural but eternal. Similarly, the German *Rechtstaat* or rule of law was premised on judicial universality without relating the law's political origins in the defence of private property, and it airbrushed its current function as upholder of the existing capitalist system and structures of ownership. This wide-ranging attack on positivism would become a lifelong preoccupation for Horkheimer and his colleagues, culminating in the Positivism Dispute that embroiled the Frankfurt School in the the 1960s.

Dialectical thinking, by contrast, dynamited this order. Where Hegel offered a vision of historical change consisting of dialectical movement, an endlessly shifting interplay of forces and constellations, the positivists – at least those whom Horkheimer characterised thus – suspended facts in aspic and falsely eternalised the status quo. In reality there was, for the Frankfurt School, no end to the eternal process of becoming, no cessation to the wheel of Ixion – Horkheimer had read enough Schopenhauer to realise that metaphysical truth. But the other impulse of positivism was, the Frankfurt School crucially believed, political: in reducing the world to hypostatised facts, positivism served to conceal an authoritarian, dominating social order. In his 1937 essay 'The Latest Attack on Metaphysics', Horkheimer argued that logical positivism 'holds only to what is, to the guarantee of facts' and thereby serves as a handmaiden to capitalism, since it tries to insulate the individual sciences from broader interpretation.[11] This had long been Horkheimer's contention: as early as his 1930 thesis *The Origins of the Bourgeois Philosophy of History*, he had connected the Renaissance view of science and technology to social and political domination.[12]

Throughout the 1930s Horkheimer honed this perspective, formulating it most clearly in his 1937 essay 'Traditional and Critical Theory'.[13] By traditional, Horkheimer meant those -isms the Frankfurt School disdained – positivism, behaviourism, empiricism and pragmatism. He even gave the traditional theorist a derisive name, the Savant, designating one who does not recognise that the economic (and thus currently capitalist) structure of society shapes scientific work. He attacked this figure of the Savant for their presumptuousness in imagining they had an objective stance before a world of facts: 'bringing hypotheses to bear on facts is an activity that goes on, ultimately, not in the savant's head but in industry', he wrote. The Savant fails to realise that he or she is not a free-floating intellectual but a lackey of capitalism, complicit, albeit often unwittingly, in the suffering caused by its exploitative nature. Against traditional theory Horkeimer pitted critical theory: the latter, he thought, understood that no facet of social reality could be considered by the observer as final or complete in itself.

The Cartesian cogito (I think therefore I am) was an exemplar, for Horkheimer, of traditional theory's missteps: it seemed fact-based, sensible, self-evident, but was anything but since it smuggled in all kinds of philosophical assumptions. It assumed, for instance, that there is something that can be called 'I' and that it endures in space and time. Worse, Descartes' method took the subject out of any kind of social determination, rendering it a passive observer of reality, rather than one involved (ideally dialectically) in reality's construction.

The return to Hegel and the dialectical method involved, for the Frankfurt School, an escape from the intellectual shackles of a scientific Marxism of the kind that one of its number, Henryk Grossman, endorsed but which other members, Horkheimer especially, thought inadequate to the modern era. Appropriating Hegel and the early, Hegelian Marx allowed them to think about alienation, consciousness, reification and how those factors thwarted revolution in late capitalist society. Doing so also pushed them to revive Hegel's emphasis on reason. German idealists had distinguished between *Vernunft* (critical reason) and *Verstand* (instrumental reason), and the suggestion in both Kant and Hegel is that *Vernunft* goes beyond mere appearances to the reality beneath. *Vernunft* penetrates to the dialectical relations beneath, while *Verstand*, by contrast, involves structuring the phenomenal world according to common sense. *Vernunft* is concerned with ends, *Verstand* merely with means. For the Frankfurt School's most Hegelian devotee, Herbert Marcuse, *Verstand* had become the tool of capitalism, *Vernunft* the means by which we challenge it.[14]

IN THIS HEGELIAN turn taken by the Frankfurt School, the appointment of Marcuse was key. It was Marcuse who realised and theorised, even before Adorno, the power of negative thinking. He contrasted such negative thinking, not just with positivism, but with a tradition of empiricist thought which he took to dominate the English-speaking world in which the Frankfurt School sought refuge after fleeing the Nazis. Empiricism naively accepted things as they are, bent the knee to the existing order of facts and values. Marcuse's Hegelian notion was that critical reason realises the essence of entities. 'Essence' here is a technical philosophical term by which Marcuse meant the fully realised potentiality of an entity. If a society, for instance, lacked the freedom, material well-being and justice that would allow it to fulfil its potential, then the job of the critical theorist, applying his or her critical reason, was to condemn that society as a 'bad form of reality, a realm of limitation and bondage'.[15] Empiricism as a philosophical programme was unable to do this.

What is a little odd is that the Hegelian idealism that Marcuse took to be critical and revolutionary was originally the philosophy of a thinker who was an apologist for the status quo in Prussia. Meanwhile, it was the leading lights of empiricism who were in some respects social radicals. John Locke, for instance, contested the divine right of kings, while David Hume's sceptical assessment of religious faith involved anything but accepting the existing social order. Intriguing too was the fact that empiricism thrived in Britain and America, the very countries where so many German exiles, such as Marcuse, sought refuge from Nazism. This fact made Marcuse's attempt, in *Reason and Revolution*, to rescue Hegel from his unfair reputation in those countries as the progenitor of fascism, to put it mildly, interesting reading.

Marcuse was an expert in Hegel who contributed to the German idealist philosopher's renaissance in Europe during the thirties – his post-doctoral thesis *Hegel's Ontology and Theory of Historicity* was published in 1932. Equally importantly, he published one of the first studies of Marx's rediscovered *Economic and Philosophic Manuscripts* which, as we have seen, reclaimed from obscurity a Hegelian early Marx for whom alienation, commodity fetishism and reification are important and the necessary collapse of capitalism is not yet proposed according to scientific laws. Marcuse came to the Institute, in part, because he knew that his job prospects were otherwise limited. 'Because of the political situation, I desperately wanted to join the Institute. At the end of 1932, it was perfectly clear that I would never be able to qualify for a professorship under the Nazi regime'.[16] By the time he started work for the Institute, they had relocated to Geneva in order to elude the Nazi threat to their work and lives.

Marcuse had spent the 1920s studying with Heidegger and was profoundly influenced by his teacher's critique of western philosophy and his attempt to reconfigure it in a world in which technological rationality was taking over everyday life, stripping individuals of freedom. But to develop a critique of this totally administered society he saw arising everywhere, Marcuse turned from Heidegger to Hegel. Heidegger, in any case became a member of the Nazi party in 1933, and so was ill-suited to serve as an intellectual mentor to a socialist thinker like Marcuse. Hegel was more promising. Marcuse took him not to be a conservative philosopher, but rather one who developed a critique of irrational forms of social life. Following Hegel, he took his intellectual role to involve, as Douglas Kellner put it, postulating 'norms of criticism, based on rational potentials for human happiness and freedom, which are used to negate existing states of affairs that oppress individuals and restrict human freedom and well-being'.[17]

But what happens, Marcuse worried in a 1937 essay 'Philosophy and Critical Theory', 'if the development outlined by the theory does not occur? What if the forces that were to bring about the transformation are suppressed and appear to be defeated?'[18] Very reasonable questions, given that the Frankfurt School was in that year exiled to the other side of the world, the forces of Nazism seemed unstoppable, and Soviet Marxism was in the process of degenerating into Stalinist show trials and gulags. Perhaps surprisingly, Marcuse did not retreat into pessimism.

DURING THE 1930s, though, some of Marcuse's Frankfurt School colleagues lost faith in the power of critical thinking to transform society. Horkheimer, in particular, moved from hope to despair. At one point early in the decade he wrote, 'it is the task of the critical theoretician to reduce the tension between his own insight and oppressed humanity in whose service he thinks'.[19] The problem was that he couldn't reduce that tension, and so couldn't think in such a way as to serve oppressed humanity. By 1937, Horkheimer had come to the despairing thought that the 'commodity economy' might usher in a period of progress until, 'after an enormous extension of human control over nature, it finally hinders further development and drives humanity into a new barbarism'.[20]

What the worries of Horkheimer and Marcuse brought into question was the point of intellectuals like those of the Frankfurt School at a time when socialist revolution had stalled and fascism was on the march. In his *Ideology and Utopia*, Karl Mannheim, a sociologist working at the University of Frankfurt but not a member of the Insitute for Social Research, put forward the notion of the 'free-floating intellectual', arguing that a socially unattached intelligentsia was suited to providing a leadership role. His intellectual was the 'watchman in what otherwise would be a pitch-black night', aloof from the practical concerns of society and so capable of access to a broader perspective on life.[21] Brecht and Benjamin opposed Mannheim's vision, arguing that material interests decisively shaped the intelligentsia all the way down the line, not just in what, say, a social scientist chose to research but also in how they researched it. The intellectual was either propping up capitalism or detonating its foundations – there was no neutral observer's position on this battlefield.

Earlier Marxists had already effectively exploded the idea that intellectuals were in a class of their own. In the 1920s, the Italian thinker Antonio Gramsci, for instance, distinguished between traditional intellectuals who tend to conceive of themselves as an autonomous group very much in the manner of Mannheim's free-floating intellectuals, and organic intellectuals who are defined by their rootedness in a particular social group, giving them experiences which enable them to express the group's collective will and fight for its interests. Henryk Grossman, when he was fighting on the streets for the Jewish Social Democratic Party of Galicia, might well be taken as an exemplar of a Gramscian organic intellectual; it would be harder to find anyone else among the leading lights of the Frankfurt School who might be so described.

Mannheim was a Jew who in 1933 was ousted from his professorship and fled to Britain, where he was appointed as a sociology lecturer at the London School of Economics. Like his fellow Jewish intellectuals at the Institute for Social Research, Mannheim was blown away by a storm, like them hurled into exile. 'The angel would like to stay, awaken the dead and make whole what has been smashed', wrote Walter Benjamin in his 'Theses in the Philosophy of History', which he completed in the spring of 1940. 'But a storm is blowing from Paradise; it has got caught in his wings with such violence that he can no longer close them. This storm irresistibly propels him into the future to which his back is turned, while the pile of debris before him grows skyward. This storm is what we call progress.'[22]

Citing Benjamin's famous words here may seem strange: Mannheim was a sociologist of knowledge not an angel of history, and the storm Benjamin writes about was not merely the Third Reich. Moreover, Mannheim was temperamentally different from Benjamin's angel: he turned round and dared to look into the future, and imagined that it would contain a utopia. The power to change present conditions by means of imagining utopias was for him the driving force of history and essential for the well-being of society.

This, in a sense, was not very Jewish. Marxism, a political philosophy devised by a Jew, is notoriously bad at imagining the communist future for which the proletariat is ostensibly striving. Perhaps that failure in imagination, if that's what it is, has ancient origins. 'We know that the Jews were prohibited from investigating the future', wrote Benjamin a few pages on from his description of the angel. 'The Torah and the prayers instruct them in remembrance, however. This stripped the future of its magic, to which all those succumb who turn to the soothsayers for enlightenment.' Benjamin's Marxism lent a new twist to the traditional Jewish rituals of mourning and the remembrance of ancestral suffering. That was not all his Marxism amounted to, though: 'This does not imply, however, that for the Jews the future turned into homogeneous, empty time. For every second of time was the strait gate through which the Messiah might enter.'

For Mannheim, the task of the intellectual was to project into that homogeneous, empty time an inspiring hope, to imagine utopia and thereby take a step towards its realisation. The Frankfurt School, in sharp contrast, disdained that role and, during the 1930s and 1940s, turned away from any idea it may have earlier had about transforming society. Horkheimer and Adorno devoted themselves increasingly to the philosophical and cultural critique of western civilisation (which would express itself in their book *Dialectic of Enlightenment*) rather than imagining social transformation. Even Marcuse – when he wrote *One-Dimensional Man*, the critique of advanced industrial society that would make him the darling of the New Left in the 1960s – drew back from imagining utopia. 'The critical theory of society possesses no concepts which could bridge the gap between the present and its future; holding no promise and showing no success, it remains negative.' But pessimism isn't the same thing as hopelessness. The last words of *One-Dimensional Man* are a quotation from Walter Benjamin: 'It is only for the sake of those without hope that hope is given to us.'[23]

THE OTHER key figure in the development of the Frankfurt School in the 1930s was Erich Fromm, a young psychoanalyst who had trained as a sociologist. Horkheimer appointed Fromm in part because he was attracted to his unified social theory which blended Freud's account of psychosexual development and Marx's insistence that economic and technological developments shaped the individual. Typical in this respect is Fromm's 1930 essay 'The Dogma of Christ', which challenged the account of Theodore Reik, one of his teachers at the Berlin Psychoanalytic Institute, who had produced a straightforward Freudian account whereby the dogma of the crucified Jesus was rooted in Oedipal hatred for the father.

In contrast, Fromm argued that this Oedipal conflict was also linked to the underlying economic situation: the lower classes turned Jesus into a revolutionary who could bring them justice. But then, Fromm noted, the counter-revolution in Christianity began – the rich and educated took over the Christian church, deferred the Day of Judgment almost indefinitely, and insisted that Christ's sacrifice on the cross, because it had already taken place, meant that the social transformation for which the downtrodden earlier Christian believers yearned was unnecessary. Fromm wrote: 'The change in the economic situation and in the social composition of the Christian community altered the psychic attitude of the believers.'[24] The downtrodden lost hope in the possibility of the social change they hoped Christ the

Messiah would bring them. Instead, they turned their emotional aggression against themselves.

Fromm, whom Horkheimer promoted to a tenured post soon after the publication of this paper, went on to write other articles melding Marx and Freud in the early 1930s. In two papers on the criminal justice system, he argued that the state presented itself subconsciously as a father and therefore ruled through the fear of paternal punishment; he also contended that it had a class bias and that, by focusing on crime and punishment rather than tackling the oppressive social conditions that led some to commit crime, criminals became the scapegoats for society's unfairness and economic inequality. The image of the punishing father was now projected into the authority of the state. Fromm even contended that the criminal justice system did not reduce the crime rate; rather, its function was to intensify oppression and crush opposition. These thoughts are echoed in our time by the American activist and professor Angela Davis, a one-time student of Marcuse. What she and other leftist intellectuals call the 'prison-industrial complex', a tawdry if tacit alliance between capitalism and a structurally racist state, results not in a reduction in the crime rate but in profits for business and a withdrawal of democratic rights for the US's overwhelmingly black and hispanic inmates. She told me in 2014: 'The massive over-incarceration of people of colour in general in the US leads to lack of access to democratic practices and liberties. Because prisoners are not able to vote, former prisoners in so many states are not able to vote, people are barred from jobs if they have a history of prison.'[25] For Davis, the prison-industrial complex is not just a racist American money-making machine, but a means to criminalise, demonise and profit from the world's most powerless people. Fromm, writing in 1931, had seen the criminal justice system of his native land in structurally similar terms.

The shotgun marriage between Freud and Marx over which Horkheimer and Fromm ostensibly officiated was scandalous to orthodox Marxists in general, and inimical to the Comintern in particular, while for orthodox Freudians the hopes Marxists placed in revolution for the transformation of society were delusive. For instance, in 1930 Freud published *Civilisation and Its Discontents*, pessimistically arguing that a non-repressive society was impossible. Untrammelled sexual gratification was incompatible with what civilisation and progress demanded, namely discipline and renunciation. Work, monogamous reproduction, moral rectitude and social restraint entailed the sacrifice of pleasure and repressing one's uncivilised impulses. Only in 1955, when Marcuse wrote *Eros and Civilisation: A Philosophical Inquiry into Freud*, would a Frankfurt scholar challenge this Freudian pessimism, without abandoning Freud's insights or Marx's faith in the attainability of an unrepressed communist society.

Fromm was less Freudian than the foregoing might suggest. For all that Horkheimer cultivated good relations with Freud, Fromm's developing social psychology junked much of the Freudian orthodoxy to which other members of the Institute, in particular Horkheimer and Adorno, adhered. What appeared to be a melding of Freud and Marx – and one that was amenable to Horkheimer as he recast Marxism to account for subjective factors rather than relying solely on objective economic laws – was something stranger. Fromm wasn't uniting Marx and Freud; rather, he was uniting Marx with his own developing psychosocial account of those subjective factors, one that outraged both Freudian orthodoxy and, increasingly, his colleagues at the Frankfurt School. Thus Fromm was doubly heretical. First, he dared to sully Marxism with psychoanalysis. Second, he challenged Freud's view that that libidinal drives were all-important and that individual neuroses were rooted in early childhood experience. In a 1931 paper for the Institute's journal called 'The Method and Function of an Analytic Social Psychology', he wrote that the human instinctual apparatus (including the libidinal structure that was the focus of the Freudian account of psychosexual development) was 'to a high degree modifiable; the economic conditions are the primary modifying factors'. Once modified by the economy these libidinal forces 'cease, as it were, to be cement and instead become dynamite'. Libidinal forces and social forces were not set in stone, not eternal truths, but in a dialectical relationship.[26]

Consider, for instance, anal eroticism. In the Middle Ages, so Fromm argued in a 1931 paper called 'Psychoanalytic Characterology', people enjoyed the worldly pleasures to be derived from feast days, costumes, paintings, beautiful buildings and art.[27] Then came the Reformation, Calvinism and capitalism. Pleasures in the here and now were increasingly deferred, or so Fromm argued, in favour of thrift, discipline, devotion to work and duty; kindness, sensuality, empathetic unconditional sharing became expendable, even socially questionable, traits.

It's easy to parody Fromm's historical account (you can almost imagine the people removing the bells from their boots and their fancy dress feast-day costumes, before entering the iron cage of capitalism, locking the door and obligingly presenting the key to their masters through the bars), but his point was that an anal social character, one who repressed their feelings, saved rather than spent, and denied themselves pleasure, was useful as a productive force to help sustain capitalism. At this stage in his intellectual development, Fromm wasn't yet clear about the extent to which that valuable anal social character was an adaptation to the requirements of the capitalism, and the extent to which an underlying anal eroticism served as a productive force in the development of the capitalist economy. But what is clear is that he was moving away from the Freudian orthodoxy of libidinal drives whose sublimation provided the key to an individual's psychic development, towards a notion of social character types that changed according to historical circumstance – and, also, changed historical circumstances.

Later in his intellectual distancing from Freud, Fromm argued that the socialisation of character began at infancy but was not so much rooted in instincts as in interpersonal relationships. By the time he came to write *Escape from Freedom* in 1941, he thought that instincts were shaped less by the sublimations Freud posited than by social conditions. Initially, Horkheimer took Fromm to be an intellectual ally in his shifting of Marxism from focusing on impersonal economic forces to a negative critique of the culture of modern monopoly capitalism. It was only later in the 1930s that Horkheimer and indeed Adorno would become queasy about Fromm's anti-Freudianism. Earlier in the decade, though, Fromm was important to Horkheimer not only because he brought psychoanalysis into the Marxist academy, but also because he had trained as a sociologist. As a result,

Horkheimer entrusted the young psychoanalyst with the task of investigating the attitudes of German workers since 1918 to work out whether they could be relied on to fight against Hitler.[28]

The idea for this originated from Felix Weil, who had written to the German Ministry of Science, Art and Education seeking to conduct an empirical investigation into the thoughts and conditions of German workers. Fromm's work on the study actually began in 1929, when the hope was that the questionnaire-based survey would serve to answer positively the burning question as to whether German workers be counted on to resist the rise of Nazism. Much of the inspiration for the survey came from a similar study undertaken in 1912 by the sociologist Adolf Levenstein who, as a former industrial worker, suspected that monotonous industrial labour increases the psychological impoverishment of the workers' sensibilities and capacity for autonomous action. Levenstein devised three psychological types for the workers surveyed – revolutionary, ambivalent and conservative-deferential. Fromm wanted to find out what correlations there were between these psychological types and their capacity for resisting fascism.

Fromm and his team of field staff sent out 3,300 questionnaires, mostly to workers. They consisted of 271 open-ended questions asking respondents for their views on such issues as the education of children, the likelihood of avoiding a new war, and the rationalisation of industry. By 1931 about 1,100 completed replies had been received. Fromm and his team carried on working on the results even when all hope was lost that the German workers would rise up and destroy fascism. Some 82 per cent of respondents associated themselves with the Social Democrats and the Communists, but only 15 per cent of them possessed the anti-authoritarian character or psychological type, while 25 per cent were either ambiguously or consistently authoritarian. Writing in the late 1930s after the Nazis had come to power, Fromm argued that the results demonstrated a 'discrepancy between leftist conscious political opinions and the underlying personality structure; a discrepancy which may [have been] responsible for the [subsequent] collapse of the German workers' parties'. For him, only 15 per cent of German workers had 'the courage, readiness for sacrifice and spontaneity needed to rouse the less active and overcome the enemy'. He argued that better leadership from the two leftist parties could have provided stronger resistance to Hitler.[29]

Fromm's study was never published by the Institute, although some of its findings appeared in his 1941 book *Escape from Freedom*. It was, rather confusingly, also plundered for the Institute's huge study of authority and the family, which engaged all the leading Frankfurt scholars except Grossman and Adorno for much of the 1930s after their exile from Germany. In it, they reflected on what had happened to the institution of the family as capitalism mutated from the early form analysed by Marx and Engels into the monopoly form that confronted the Frankfurt School.

The question of whether the family was a site of resistance to the powers that be or a zone in which capitalist values could be instilled intrigued the Frankfurt School. For Hegel, the family was the society's central ethical unit and a site of resistance against dehumanisation. For Marx and Engels in *The Communist Manifesto*, the family was a tool of capitalist oppression, and needed to be abolished. 'Even the most radical flare up at this infamous proposal of the Communists', wrote Marx and Engels wryly. But they were undaunted:

> On what foundation is the present family, the bourgeois family, based? On capital, on private gain . . . But this state of things finds its comple- ment in the practical absence of the family among the proletarians, and in public prostitution. The bourgeois family will vanish as a matter of course when its complement vanishes, and both will vanish with the vanishing of capital.[30]

For the Frankfurt School, the bourgeois family hadn't vanished, but its power in general and the authority of the father in particular was in free fall. It had been the key social institution mediating between material base and ideological superstructure but it was heading towards impotence – not for the revolutionary reasons that Marx and Engels had yearned to see realised, but because other institutions could socialise the populations of capitalist societies more effectively.

Horkheimer noted in an essay for *Studies on Authority and Family* that it was chiefly in the era of early capitalism (or bourgeois liberalism) that paternal power was at its height in the family. That made sense because in Hegelian terms the father was, thanks to his greater physical size and his role as economic provider, the rational head of the household. That paternal power had declined under monopoly capitalism, not to be replaced by what Fromm sought for – a concomitant rise in the traditional maternal ethic of warmth, acceptance and love. Not that Horkheimer was celebrating this transformation.

Rather, the leading members of the Frankfurt School chose solidarity with their parents at the moment of the latters' greatest impotence. Adorno, in *Minima Moralia*, spoke of a 'sad, shadowy transformation' in his generation's relationship with their parents.[31] He was writing not just about the decline of the family under monopoly capitalism, but of something much more specific: what the Nazis in their shamelessness did to the parents of these German Jewish intellectuals. Adorno certainly tried to care for his parents when they, roughed up and financially ruined by the Nazis in Frankfurt, fled to join him in his American exile at the start of the 1940s. The Frankfurt School, spurred by Hitler, turned away from Marx's contempt for the family towards a bitterly won Hegelian, post-Oedipal conception of that derided institution as a site of resistance to, and mutual consolation amid, what Adorno called the 'rising collectivist order' that the School took to be visible not just in Berlin and Moscow, but in Paris, London and New York.

What the Frankfurt scholars lamented was that as the family weakened alternative agents of socialisation took over its role; and those agents (meaning everything from the Nazi party to the culture industry) were instrumental in creating what Fromm would call the authoritarian personality. The social institutions of late capitalism manufactured such personalities like human equivalents of Model T Fords. They were identikit, fearful, passive, and unable to construct their own identities.

Fromm took the authoritarian personality, in the 1957 book of that name, to describe both ruler and ruled under this collectivist order. Both had this much in common, he wrote: 'the inability to rely on one's self, to be independent, to put it in other words: to endure freedom . . . He needs to feel a bond, which requires neither love nor reason – and he finds it in the symbiotic relationship, in feeling-one with others; not by reserving his own identity, but rather by fusing, by destroying his own identity.' Fromm pitted the authoritarian person-ality against the mature personality which he described as one 'who does not need to cling to others because he actively embraces and grasps the world, the people, and the things around him'.[32]

The active embrace of the world, the ability to rely on oneself and thereby endure freedom – these were precisely the character traits that were eliminated under the collectivist order the Frankfurt School saw rising all around them.

7

In the Crocodile's Jaws

When, in the summer of 1932, Walter Benjamin reached the Tuscan seaside resort of Poveromo, he was the personification of the name of his destination: Poveromo means poor man in Italian.[1] His marriage was over, two subsequent love affairs had ended, his best work remained unpublished, and, in the twilight before Nazism spread its darkness across Europe, his hopes of making a living from literary criticism had dwindled to nothing. Broke and miserable, he bummed cigarette money from his friend Wilhelm Speyer and relied on credit from the proprietors of the Villa Irene for his accommodation. It was unclear how he could repay his hosts.

But, lest we get too caught up in sympathy for this poor man, we should reflect that Benjamin had been born into a wealthy family and had spent much of the 1920s travelling, gambling, collecting, and neglecting his wife Dora and son Stefan. After his rancorous divorce from Dora in 1930, the court decided to award her the lion's share of his inheritance as a lump sum in compensation for his mistreatment of her – a ruling that accounted for much of the penury that was to be Benjamin's lot until his death a decade later.

In the summer of 1932, he was roaming Europe as he had done the previous decade, but with much less money. He had deferred his return to Germany in order, as he wrote to his friend the Jewish mystic and Zionist intellectual Gershom Scholem, to avoid 'the opening ceremonies of the Third Reich'.[2] In the German capital that summer, Hitler's obliging predecessor as chancellor, Franz von Papen, had deposed the Social Democrat-led Prussian government in what

Scholem called 'a sort of coup d'état', and on June 2 had formed a reactionary cabinet. Von Papen revoked the ban on the Sturmabteilung, the Nazis' paramilitary wing, and thereby unleashed a wave of political violence and terror, targeted overwhelmingly at Jews and communists, as well as intellectual repression, thus paving the way for Hitler's assumption of power a year later.

That July Benjamin learned that the directors of the radio stations in Berlin and Frankfurt for whom he had made eighty radio broadcasts from 1927 onwards had been dismissed. This was the result of government policy to bring radio into line with other media, rendering them mouthpieces of right-wing propaganda. Benjamin had depended on these broadcasts for much of his income. They included plays, funny little sketches advising listeners on how to get a pay rise, and even – most improbably – a how-to-guide for aspiring comedy writers from one of Germany's most difficult thinkers.[3] Many of these broadcasts had been written for children and devised to equip his young listeners with the critical faculties that the rise of fascism would henceforth strive to deny them. No recordings of these broadcasts were made, so we will never hear what Walter Benjamin sounded like when he spoke on the radio. But the scripts for them were among the papers the Gestapo found during the Second World War when they raided his last apartment in Paris. In 2014, some of those scripts were read by the actor Henry Goodman as part of a BBC programme, *The Benjamin Broadcasts*, made by the children's writer Michael Rosen.[4]

Today, Benjamin's scripts for broadcasts on such subjects as witch-hunts, Berlin's demonic side, successful swindles and human disasters read as allegories of National Socialism, warnings of what was to come. The last time Benjamin broadcast on German radio was on 29 January 1933; the following day, Hitler was appointed chancellor and a Nazi torchlight parade supplied the material for the very first nationwide radio broadcast.

These were indeed the opening ceremonies of the Third Reich. The Weimar Republic that had emerged from the rubble of the First World War and the collapse of the German Empire had, through its Bill of Rights, guaranteed every German citizen freedom of speech and religion, and equality under the law; its elected Reichstag appointed the government. But Weimar's tentative democratic flowering was readily crushed in part, to get dialectical for a moment, by the very structure of its foundation. Weimar's system of proportional representation under which electors voted for parties rather than individual elected representatives resulted in tiny parties with no party strong enough to get a majority and no effective government that could ensure the passage of laws in the Reichstag; worse, the constitution's article 48 allowed the president to rule by decree in case of emergency, though – fatally – left the definition of what constituted an emergency unclear, a fact that allowed Hitler to take power by the back door legally.

In *Poems of the Crisis Years 1929–33*, Brecht meditated on the disaster for Marxists such as himself of German workers fighting for fascists against communists rather than finding common cause. His poem 'Article One of the Weimar Constitution' (which stated: 'From the People proceeds the power of the state') conceives of the power of the Weimar State as a force marching through the city streets, wheeling to the right, outraged at those who dare to question its power.[5] The poem ends with a murder: a shot rings out and the 'power of the State' looks down to identify the corpse:

> What's lying in the shit?
> Something's lying in the shit
> – The People, why, that's it.

Hardly one of Brecht's greatest poems, but it does vividly imagine the perversion of this presumed power of the People. And, as we will see, for the Frankfurt School, the people's seduction by National Socialism. The avowedly Marxist and overwhelmingly Jewish thinkers of the Frankfurt School now had a new task: not just to work out why the German Revolution had failed, but to understand why the people could be seduced by an ideology that favoured, among other things, murdering Marxists and Jews. In books that appeared over the next decade, such as Fromm's *Escape from Freedom*, *Behemoth: The Structure and Practice of National Socialism* by the political theorist

Franz Neumann, and Marcuse's *A Study on Authority*, the Frankfurt scholars tried to work out why the German people desired their own domination.

One hope of those who supported the Nazis was for a restoration of the old German values that Weimar had challenged, for an end to the derangement by sex, jazz, democracy and modernism. Influenced by the brief cultural explosion in the Soviet Union that Benjamin had witnessed first hand when he visited Moscow in 1927, Weimar's literature, cinema, theatre and music entered a phase of great modernist creativity against which the fascists pitted themselves. For the Nazis, the flourishing cabaret and jazz scenes of the leading German cities were barbaric, typified by the performances of the American dancer Josephine Baker that were greeted with euphoria in Berlin; expressionist painting was loathsome, and in the case of artist George Grosz intolerably defamatory of the military; the new type of architecture taught at the Bauhaus school was ugly, Jewish and communist. The Third Reich spelled the end for these decadent, degraded, communistic, Jewish-inflected and above all foreign (i.e. American, Soviet and French) types of cultural expression.

Josef von Sternberg's 1930 film *The Blue Angel*, starring Marlene Dietrich as the beautiful, seductively untrustworthy cabaret dancer Lola Lola, captured the erotic allure and uncertainties of Weimar. The film ends with the eminent professor Immanuel Rath, who has fallen in love with Dietrich's dancer, humiliated in front of his former colleagues after his erotic folly, clinging to the desk that had represented his eminence and learnedness as to a shipwreck on stormy waters.[6] Germany, perhaps, was atoning for its Weimar folly by sadomasochistically surrendering to fascism.

But the opening ceremonies of the Third Reich also heralded its death. In *Minima Moralia: Reflections from Damaged Life*, written in American exile, Adorno, that virtuoso of immanent critique, wrote: 'No one who observed the first months of National Socialism could fail to perceive the moment of mortal sadness, of half-knowing surrender to perdition, that accompanied the manipulated intoxication, the torchlight processions and the drum-beating.'[7] This leitmotif – sadness in intoxication, catastrophe foreshadowed in the very moment of exultation, death figured in birth pangs – is, for Adorno, utterly German, and it had an historic parallel. In 1870, he notes, as the German Empire was born in victorious military campaign, Wagner wrote *Götterdämmerung*, 'that inflamed spirit of the nation's own doom . . . In the same spirit, two years before the Second World War, the German people were shown on film the crash of their Zeppelin at Lakehurst. Calmly, unerringly, the ship went on its way, then suddenly dropped like a stone.'[8] Like Benjamin, Adorno reimagined history as breaking through what the former called empty, homogeneous time, establishing resonant constellations of disasters or hopes, assembling them into allegories of their own demise. Not that such thoughts were a consolation for those in Berlin in 1933.

The death of the Weimar Republic certainly affected Benjamin personally. It didn't just hit him in the pocket, but effectively silenced him. The *Frankfurter Zeitung*, on which Benjamin had relied for publication of some of his finest short essays, stopped answering his letters and manuscript submissions – a sign of things to come. As the 1930s wore on, his work would only rarely be printed in German, and then mostly under a pseudonym. His 1936 book *Deutsche Menschen*, for example, was published under the pseudonym Detlev Holz, and even then only because its theme could be twisted to serve the patriotic agenda of the Nazis (it consisted of twenty-seven letters between Germans including Hölderlin, Kant, the Grimm brothers, Schlegel and Schleiermacher in the hundred years after 1783, with commentaries by Benjamin). In 1938, though, even that book was put on the censor's list of banned German books.

From Berlin, as Benjamin languished in Italy, came news that he would have to give up his apartment, where his library was housed, because of 'code violations' (the sub-letter's nightmare). He was being airbrushed from his homeland. Although Benjamin returned to Berlin in November, it was only a brief stay: the following March he would leave Berlin for good, becoming an exile living mostly in Paris. Before he left the city of his birth on 17 March 1933, the citizens of Berlin bore witness to the burning of the Reichstag on February 27 and its use by Hitler as a pretext to justify the murder of communist and other political enemies. Benjamin had left Berlin though before the symbolic death of the Weimar Republic and the birth of the Third Reich on March 23, when the Enabling Act became law giving Hitler absolute power to rule and to pass any law without parliamentary approval. On 10 May 1933, books were burned in most German university cities and the minister of propaganda Joseph Goebbels announced the end of the age of 'overblown Jewish intellectualism'.[9]

Across the decades, then, a very particular tragedy resonates in the midst of a much bigger one: the tragedy that the greatest German critic of the twentieth century, because of anti-Jewish proscriptions, was systematically deprived of the opportunity to share his thoughts in his native language about the culture in which he was steeped just as his critical powers reached their maturity. But there is another element to Walter Benjamin's tragedy, beyond the frustrations of love and the rise of Nazism. In his 1997 novel, *Benjamin's Crossing*, Jay Parini imagined Gershom Scholem standing at his friend's grave ten years after Benjamin's death. 'The death of Benjamin was, for me, the death of the European mind, the end of a way of life', says Scholem in the novel.[10] This fictionalised tribute chimes with what Brecht wrote of his dead friend:

> So the future lies in darkness and the forces of right
> Are weak. That was plain to you
> When you destroyed a torturable body.[11]

The idea that Benjamin's tragedy represented the death of the European mind may initially seem to be a pardonable exaggeration, born of love and respect, but there is more to it than that, for what it gets near to is the distinction identified by Hannah Arendt in her introduction to *Illuminations*, a collection of Benjamin's essays.[12] Benjamin was not just a freelance intellectual effectively precluded from making a living in 1930s' Europe: he dreamed of being and nearly realised his wish of becoming an *homme de lettres*. But what does that term signify? Arendt (the twentieth century's most astute observer of, as well as best-connected participant in, German Jewish intellectual life) noted that an *homme de lettres* was very different from an intellectual. The former had its origins in pre-revolutionary France, among the landed, leisured and intellectually voracious; the latter was, at least as Arendt describes it, handmaiden to the technocratic state. 'Unlike the class of intellectuals', she wrote,

> who offer their services either to the state as experts, specialists, and officials, or to society for diversion and instruction, the homme de lettres always strove to keep aloof from both the state and society. Their material existence was based on income without work, and their intellectual attitude rested upon their resolute refusal to be integrated politically or socially. On the basis of this dual independence they could afford that attitude of superior disdain which gave rise to La Rochefoucauld's contemptuous insights into human behaviour, the worldly wisdom of Montaigne, the aphoristic trenchancy of Pascal's thought, the boldness and open-mindedness of Montesquieu's political reflections.[13]

Aloof from state and society. Resolute refusal to be integrated politically or socially. Attitude of superior disdain. Aphoristic trenchancy. As one reads this passage's most colourful phrases, it's hard not to be struck by how well they pertain not just to pre-revolutionary French writers, but also to the leaders of the Frankfurt School, and to Walter Benjamin. He dreamed of being 'neither obliged nor willing to write and read professionally, in order to earn a living',[14] as Arendt put it.

If Arendt is right, Benjamin's dreams of becoming an *homme de lettres* unencumbered by professional duty were catalysed in and constrained by the anti-Semitic nature of the Wilhelmine Germany in which he grew up. In that pre-First World War society, unbaptised Jews were barred from university careers: they could only hold the rank of an unpaid Extraordinarius. As Arendt puts it: 'it was a career which presupposed rather than provided an assured income'.[15] So instead of futilely dreaming of what couldn't happen, suggests Arendt convincingly, he dreamed of the best that could be realised: of becoming an independent private scholar – what was at the time called a Privatgelehrter, a scholarly German figure which the Francophile Benjamin gave a Gallic spin. He wanted to be an *homme de lettres*, subsidised and independent, free to pursue his own eclectic interests.

What's striking about Benjamin in this context is that he didn't redraft his wishes in the face of changed political realities. In the Weimar Republic, thanks to its Bill of Rights, university careers were open to everyone including unbaptised Jews. True, this door, once opened, was fast closing: in April 1933 Hitler issued the Law for the Restoration of the Civil Service, requiring the dismissal of Jews and 'politically unreliable persons' (a law that meant the dismissal, for instance, of Arnold Schoenberg by the Prussian Academy of Art, as well as painters like Klee, Dix and Beckmann from other German art academies). But in the Weimar Republic, it was for a moment possible for Jews to dream of university careers. Why then did Benjamin not seek out a career in academia? Arendt's theory is that he had decided what he wanted to be before the war and then strived increasingly hopelessly to realise that dream. The disastrous tensions with his father after the First World War are mostly due to the fact that daddy would not bankroll his son to follow a profession that was premised on not making a living. As his biographers put it: 'His parents pushed for a career with some earning potential and steadfastly refused the kind of support that would enable Benjamin to live independently while continuing to live and write as he wished.'[16] Their son was temperamentally incapable of pursuing a career with earning potential: he was too astute a reader of Kafka for that. Kafka had bent the knee to his father's desires and taken a job in an insurance office. The novelist described what that work meant: 'You have to earn your grave.'[17] Benjamin was not temperamentally capable of following Kafka's abasement.

What's significant for us is how his aspiration was emblematic of the Frankfurt School's determination to remain independent from university system or political party. Partly this was an insistence on intellectual autonomy – rather than becoming what Arendt describes pejoratively as intellectuals, they would live and write independently, pursing their Marxist analysis of society with the financial backing of the Marxist son of a successful and unimpeachably capitalist Argentine grain trader. Partly it was because they were Jews, understandably suspicious of casting their lot into a university system that had only just allowed Jews to make their careers. Certainly, when Benjamin tried and failed to gain his Habilitation, the German post-doctoral qualification usually sought after because it leads to a university career, he did so only to impress his father into loosening the purse strings so that he could carry on his work independently.

He also had a disdain for the work for which he was paid. For instance, he dismissed his radio broadcasts that provided the bulk of his income for the years 1927 to 1932 as unimportant, as if they were hack work (we need not agree – they are preludes to such texts as 'The Work of Art in the Age of Mechanical Reproduction' or his 'Theses on the Philosophy of History'; moreover, they're impressive in their own right, fulfilments of what public radio could become but so often hasn't been since). But the fact remains: he was a miniaturist when miniatures didn't pay, and a toiler in Grub Street who regarded hack work as beneath contempt even before his editors started failing to reply to his correspondence. Arendt wrote:

> It was as though shortly before its disappearance the figure of the *homme de lettres* was destined to show itself once more in the fullness of its possibilities, although – or possibly because – it had lost its material basis in such a catastrophic way, so that the purely intellectual passion which makes this figure so loveable might unfold in all its most telling and impressive possibilities.[18]

This is the tragedy: that Benjamin's writings over the eight years from destitution in Poveromo to death in Port Bou show the fullness of possibilities rather than the fullness of realisation. What he wrote of Kafka – 'an understanding [of Kafka's] production involves, among other things, the simple recognition that he was a failure'[19] – is true too of what Benjamin understood about himself.

In the dying of that European type, then, there was a brief, intense flash of light – the writings of Walter Benjamin. If the Frankfurt School was the last hurrah of German romanticism, then Benjamin was its emblem, revealing the group in all its contradictions – Marxists without party, socialists dependent on capitalist money, beneficiaries of a society they sniffily disdained and without which they would have had nothing to write about.

As he wandered fugitive around the Mediterranean in that summer of 1932, Benjamin was suicidal. Only a month before his arrival in Poveromo, he had stayed in a hotel room in Nice where he had drawn up his will, written farewell notes and planned to take his own life. 'Dear Jula', he wrote to Jula Radt, the sculptor with whom he had an affair both before and during his marriage to Dora Pollak, 'You know that I once loved you very much. And now that I am about to die, my life has no greater gifts in its possession than those conferred on it by moments of suffering over you. So this greeting shall suffice. Yours Walter.'[20]

According to his friend Gershom Scholem, the immediate reason Benjamin felt impelled to draw up suicide plans was due to the failure of another relationship. Earlier that summer, on Ibiza, he had proposed to Olga Parem, a Russian-German woman he had met in 1928 and who had come to the Mediterranean island to visit him. Parem was charmed by Benjamin: 'He had an enchanting laugh; when he laughed, a whole world opened up', while Scholem reported that she was 'very attractive and vivacious'.[21] What Benjamin thought of her is unrecorded, though Parem was one of many women with whom Benjamin had fallen hopelessly in love during and after his thirteen-year marriage. As his biographers suggest, he was drawn into love triangles – especially those in which the two other parties were attached. Such erotic geometry is what makes, for instance, his long, intimate correspondence with Gretel Karplus, wife of his great critic and champion Adorno, so compelling, so tantalising for Benjamin and yet, ultimately, conventionally minded persons would have thought, so unsatisfactory for all concerned. Dora wrote to Scholem when her ex-husband sought to marry Asja Lacis:

> He is altogether under Asja's influence and does things which I can scarcely bring myself to write about – things which make it unlikely that I shall ever again exchange a word with him in this lifetime. All he is at this point is brains and sex; everything else has ceased to function. And you know or can well imagine that in such cases it's not long before the brains abdicate.[22]

Although the arousing (for Benjamin) triangulation of love and jealousy did not apply in the case of Olga Parem, her response to his proposal on Ibiza was certainly unsatisfactory. She rejected him and so, days later, when Benjamin celebrated his fortieth birthday he could well imagine himself loveless, jobless and very nearly hopeless.

For all the gloom of these months spent wandering impecuniously around the Mediterranean deferring the return to Berlin, and the seeming imminence of death, Benjamin was able to write about one incident that summer with the delicate wit that friends emphasised but that all-too-rarely emerges in his writings. Picture the scene: Benjamin is leaving Ibiza, his luggage stowed on the boat that will bear him to Majorca. It is midnight as he arrives at the quay with friends, and he notices that not only has the gangplank been removed but the boat is already moving. You don't have to imagine how much the great German Jewish intellectual could resemble, in certain photographs, Groucho Marx or Charlie Chaplin to enjoy the next sentence, but it might help. 'After calmly shaking hands with my companions', he wrote to Scholem, 'I began to scale the hull of the moving vessel and, aided by curious Ibizans, managed to clamber over the railing successfully.'[23] Benjamin was many things but not a comic writer, though the superb punctiliousness and sang froid of 'calmly' and the understatement of 'curious' make one wonder if he could have had another vocation.

From Majorca he travelled to Nice, checked into a hotel and started dividing up his possessions in preparation for his looming death. He bequeathed his library to his son Stefan, another bequest was made to Dora, while he left precious objects and paintings to friends and former lovers including Jula Radt-Cohn, Asja Lacis and Gretel Karplus. There is a clue to the mood of this man who frequently contemplated taking his own life and would ultimately succeed in doing so in his aphoristic essay 'The Destructive Character', published in the *Frankfurter Zeitung* the previous November:

> The destructive character has the consciousness of historical man, whose deepest emotion is an insuperable mistrust of the course of things and a readiness at all times to recognise that everything can go wrong . . .

The destructive character sees nothing permanent. But for this very reason he sees ways everywhere. Where others encounter walls or mountains, there, too, he sees a way. But because he sees a way everywhere, he has to clear things from it everywhere. Not always by brute force; sometimes by the most refined. Because he sees ways everywhere, he always stands at a crossroads. No moment can know what the next will bring. What exists he reduces to rubble – not for the sake of rubble, but for that of the way leading through it.

The destructive character lives from the feeling not that life is worth living, but that suicide is not worth the trouble.[24]

Benjamin's writings in the last eight years of his life were examples of Joseph Schumpeter's notion of creative destruction, reducing history to rubble the better to find a path through its ruins. What he wrote of Baudelaire, his beloved nineteenth-century French poet – 'To interrupt the course of the world – that was Baudelaire's deepest intention' – was also true of the basis of his own messianic Marxism, that seeming oxymoron. That deep, destructive intention made his philosophy heretical to the communist party line, certainly if that party line saw history as necessarily unfolding towards the realisation of a communist utopia. When Scholem described Benjamin's writings as 'counter revolutionary', the latter wrote back saying the description was quite correct.[25]

This eviscerating tendency of Benjamin's, as we will see, extends through his criticism and his messianic vision of revolutionary politics. It was this tendency then, paradoxically, that made him decide against suicide – at least until that moment in 1940 when he could resist its dismal overtures no longer. But if Benjamin was a destructive character was he, too, a self-destructive character? What he had written for the *Frankfurter Zeitung* only refers to suicide to dismiss it sarcastically as not worth the trouble, which in itself is a double shrug at traditional mores – one shrug against a tradition that excoriated suicide; the other at the transgressive counter-tradition that found suicide seductive. Certainly suicide has a lively history in Germany. In his essay 'On Suicide', Schopenhauer wrote: 'As far as I can see, it is only the monotheistic, that is to say Jewish religions whose members regard self-destruction as a crime.'[26] Quite so, but to name something as a crime is not just to announce its prohibition, but to confer on that act a libidinal cathexis: transgression is sexy.

In Goethe's Sturm und Drang novel *The Sorrows of the Younger Werther*, first published in 1787, the hero reasons that one member of the love triangle in which he is embroiled must take their own life and so, because he is incapable of committing murder, but feels he must act, he shoots himself in the head and dies twelve hours later. Goethe's novel led to a spate of copycat suicides among young people in Germany after it's publication. In 1903 the twenty-three-year-old Austrian philosopher Otto Weininger shot himself in the chest in the same room in which Beethoven had died seventy-six years earlier. 'There are three possibilities for me', he had declared. 'The gallows, suicide, or a future so brilliant that I don't dare to think of it.'[27] The third of those possibilities, thanks to the cool critical reception of his recently published book *Sex and Character*, seemed unlikely to be realised.

So what prompted Benjamin to contemplate suicide in 1932? The Werther effect borne of a love triangle? The sense that his genius was going unrecognised? Certainly, his biographers suggest, thoughts of suicide had been often on his mind for the best part of two decades, ever since in fact the outbreak of the First World War. In 1914, one of his closest friends, the poet Fritz Heinle along with Rika Seligson had committed suicide. One morning, Benjamin was awoken by the arrival of an express letter that read: 'You will find us lying in the Meeting House.'[28] It was there that the couple had gassed themselves. Their tragic end was depicted in the newspapers as the outcome of doomed love, but their friends thought it a protest against war.

For Benjamin, Heinle's suicide was a shadow that extended over the rest of his life. He wrote a cycle of fifty sonnets over the years that followed his friend's death, and read Heinle's poems to friends during the 1920s. The suicide figures in his writings of that decade: 'How much more easily the leave taker is loved!' he wrote in his 1928 book *One-Way Street*. 'For the flame burns more purely for those burning in the distance, fuelled by the fleeting scrap of material waving from the ship or railway window. Separation penetrates the disappearing person like a pigment and steeps him in gentle radiance.'[29] Perhaps Benjamin imagined himself steeped in such radiance as he went through the formalities of separating himself from friends and lovers in the summer of 1932, but he could not then commit the act that would make the separation final.

Suicide, then, was a spectre that stalked Benjamin's adult life. But, for all that, he wrote with terrible beauty about what death means to those who remain. In *One-Way Street*, for instance, he wrote: 'If a person very close to us is dying, there is something in the months to come that we dimly apprehend – much has we should have liked to share it with him – could only happen through his absence. We greet him at last in a language that he no longer understands.'[30]

The fact remains that in 1932 he didn't commit suicide. Why? Perhaps because there was work that remained to be done. 'The only cogent moral argument against suicide is that it is opposed to the achievement of the highest moral goal, inasmuch as it substitutes for a true redemption of this world of misery a merely apparent one.'[31] It may seem obtuse to quote Schopenhauer here – Benjamin was hardly an avid reader of his writings – but Schopenhauer's mention of the word 'redemption' seems relevant. Adorno wrote at the conclusion of *Minima Moralia*: 'The only philosophy which can be responsibly practiced in the face of despair is the attempt to contemplate all things as they would present themselves from the standpoint of redemption. Knowledge has no light but that shed on the world by redemption: all else is reconstruction, mere technique. Perspectives must be fashioned that displace and estrange the world, reveal it to be, with its rifts and crevices, as indigent and distorted as it will appear one day in the messianic light.'[32]

In thesis IX of his 'Theses on the Philosophy of History', quoted earlier, Benjamin imagined precisely such a standpoint of redemption, and how perilous it was to occupy it. He did so by contemplating an image that he took from the painting *Angelus Novus* by Paul Klee:

> This is how one pictures the angel of history. His face is turned toward the past. Where we perceive a chain of events, he sees one single catastrophe which keeps piling wreckage upon wreckage and hurls it in

front of his feet. The angel would like to stay, awaken the dead, and make whole what has been smashed. But a storm is blowing from Paradise; it has got caught in his wings with such violence that the angel can no longer close them. The storm irresistibly propels him into the future to which his back is turned, while the pile of debris before him grows skyward. The storm is what we call progress.[33]

But if the storm is what we call progress, the angel might be seen as a likeness or symbol of Walter Benjamin in that summer of 1932 in Poveromo, as he tried, through the remembrance of writing, to redeem the past, to make whole what had been smashed. The storm was blowing, the wreckage growing, but Benjamin was attempting to stand his ground by doing the only thing he could: writing. Certainly, he had been captivated by Klee's *Angelus Novus* since he first saw the Swiss artist's small watercolour at a Berlin exhibition in 1920. He bought it for 1,000 marks and hung it in every apartment he lived in (today, after a torrid history, it hangs in the Israel Museum in Jerusalem), almost like a lucky charm. In 1921, he edited a journal he named *Angelus Novus*, 'in part because of the attempt to draw a connection between the artistic avant-garde of the period and the Talmudic legend about angels who are being constantly created and find an abode in the fragments of the present'.[34] He also cited the painting in his 1931 essay on the Austrian writer and satirist Karl Kraus, according to which the painting makes it possible 'to understand a humanity that proves itself by destruction'.[35] And in 1933, the year in which the Nazis came to power and he fled Berlin for the last time, he left the painting behind and wrote in an autobiographical essay called 'Agesilaus Santander' while in exile on Ibiza: 'The angel, however, resembles all from which I had to part: persons and above all things.'[36]

In his essay, 'Walter Benjamin and His Angel', Scholem noted that at the time Benjamin saw in the painting a parallel to his tangled relations with Jula Cohn and Asja Lacis.[37] But the angel of history had more than just personal resonances. The insistence that the past can be transformed remains, for Marxists and others, one of Benjamin's most appealing ideas. The critic Terry Eagleton, for instance, wrote: 'In one of his shrewdest sayings, Benjamin remarked that what drives men and women to revolt against injustice is not dreams of liberated grandchildren, but memories of enslaved ancestors. It is by turning our gaze to the horrors of the past, in the hope that we will not thereby be turned to stone, that we are impelled to move forward.'[38] Thus, the enigmatic figure of the Angelus Novus, so captivating to Benjamin, has become an iconic emblem for the left; whether he would have recognised it quite that way is another question.

In any event, by the time he got to Poveromo, Benjamin may not have been convinced that life is worth living, but certainly that it was to be lived – even though, for him, its circumstances were increasingly terrible. A year after he wrote the consoling memoir of his Berlin childhood in the Tuscan seaside resort, he was forced to leave the city of his birth forever to evade the Nazis. He spent the last eight years of his life in perilous exile, wandering an increasingly inhospitable Europe, like so many other Jews and communists of the time. In 1938, he described himself in a letter as 'something like a man who has made his home in a crocodile's jaws, which he keeps prised open with iron braces'.[39] That, perhaps, was how he lived in his final decade – until the lonely moment in a Spanish hotel room when he decided to take his own life rather than risk being murdered.

It was in those years, though, that Benjamin wrote some of his best work, including, as we will see in the next chapter, a still-great essay on the revolutionary possibilities of art, one filled with hope amid the hopelessness of the times. His friend and fellow exile Theodor Adorno knew that well when he wrote: 'For a man who no longer has a homeland, writing becomes a place to live.'[40]

8

Modernism and All That Jazz

Throughout the 1930s, the Frankfurt School was engaged with working out why socialist revolution had not happened and why Hitler had come to power. Nonetheless, some of its most virtuosic work concerned culture – that new front in the neo-Marxist struggle. In 1936, for instance, the Institute's journal published two essays to do with modern art. One of them, by Walter Benjamin, has become a classic of twentieth-century writing, endlessly reproduced, mimeographed, downloaded, cited, cut and pasted until its aura suffuses nearly every text written on the theory of art since it appeared. The other, by Theodor Adorno, has become intellectual kryptonite, disdained even by many of his most ardent admirers for its ostensible racism and for its diagnosis of the art form under discussion as both a kind of premature ejaculation and a more or less sadomasochistic repressive desublimation that was emblematic of the perverse weakness and passivity into which it cast its practitioners and audiences.

There are other differences. Benjamin's 'The Work of Art in the Age of Mechanical Reproduction' is almost crazily hopeful for the revolutionary potential of new mass art forms, particularly cinema.[1] Adorno's 'On Jazz', written under the pseudonym Hektor Rottweiler, is a vicious savaging of a new kind of music whose social impact he loathed and which he took to be representative of the disaster of commodified art under capitalism.[2]

But both essays are neo-Marxist critiques of mass culture, and so antidotes to the snobbish conservative jeremiads that prevailed then as now. Both men were cultural iconoclasts by upbringing and temperament, but you'd be hard pushed to find anything of the snob-bery of Proust, the contempt for mass cultural production of Huxley or the disdain for popular entertainment of D. H. Lawrence in either of these essays. Neither sees in the new art forms they are writing about cause for a Spenglerian lament over the decline of the west. Neither seeks to damn the barbarisms of the present by juxtaposition with the glories of the past.

Both essays were written in the limbo of exile – Benjamin was in Paris, Adorno in his third year at Oxford, and the future of both seemed bound up with leaving Europe. As a result, fascism haunted both texts. Adorno's critique of jazz was deranged by hearing mili-tary marches in its syncopated rhythms; while for Benjamin, fascism was an urgent threat to which communism responds by politicising art. Benjamin seems to realise that the luxury of despair over the diminishing of human experience by mass culture is improper at a time when fascism needs to be attacked. The despair he expressed in his essay 'Eduard Fuchs, Collector and Historian' about how human experience was diminished by our 'bungled reception of technology' was set aside in favour of a hopeful reflection on how new techno-logical art forms, in particular cinema, might revolutionise human sensibilities, and perhaps even make them more resistant to fascism. His dreams for cinema were not quite crushed by the onrushing Hollywood machine. He worried about how the cult of the movie star involved the phoney spell of personality and commodity fetish-ism, but almost parenthetically: most of the rest of his most famous essay ran excitingly against the grain of the proverbial negativity of the Frankfurt School. 'The Work of Art in the Age of Mechanical Reproduction' opens with the idea that, at the end of the nineteenth century, there was a tipping point in art's relationship with technology:

Around 1900 technical reproduction had reached a standard that not only permitted it to reproduce all transmitted works of art and thus to cause the most profound change in their impact on the public; it had also captured a place of its own among the artistic processes. For the study of this standard nothing is more revealing than the nature of

these repercussions that these two different manifestations – the reproduction of works of art and the art of the film – have had on its
traditional form.

Where Huxley, in words that Benjamin quoted in a footnote, had
taken this change as facilitating 'vulgarity' and the 'output of trash',
Benjamin imagined its liberating potential. Not that he was naive
enough to argue that the output of trash had not also increased
thanks to technological change. For him, the new standard of technical reproduction was what alcohol was for fellow dialectician Homer
Simpson – the cause of, and remedy for, the impoverishment of
human experience.

It's easy to imagine what this impoverishment looks like: D. H.
Lawrence imagined it when he wrote about humans

> sitting with our tails curled
> while the machine amuses us, the radio or film or gramophone.
> Monkeys with a bland grin on our faces[3]

What's much harder to do is what Benjamin did in this essay: to
imagine how the changes in mechanical reproduction might liberate
us. Benjamin hoped that photography and cinema would blast open
the cultural tradition, liquidate the power that the ruling class has
exerted over the masses by means of the aura of authenticity, authority and permanence of works of art. His writings around this time
were marked by violent images – as if the coming war had begun for
him already.

'The ideologies of the rulers are by their nature more changeable
than the ideas of the oppressed', wrote Benjamin in *The Arcades
Project* around the time of this essay. 'For not only must they, like the
ideas of the latter, adapt each time to the situation of social conflict,
but they must glorify that situation as fundamentally harmonious.'[4]
The ideologies of the rulers, then, are like what evolutionary biologist
Richard Dawkins would four decades later call memes – units for
carrying ideas and practices that mutate and respond to adaptive
pressures. Benjamin's hope was to disrupt that viral spread of the

ruling class's memes. Works of art weren't just beautiful autonomous expressions of human creative impulses, but rather had an instrumental role in maintaining the ruling class's power. By being situated in a cultural tradition that conferred status on them and the tradition, works of art became fetishes and served the same mystifying purposes as the commodities Marx wrote about: they airbrushed the bloody social conflict and glorified a disharmonious situation as fundamentally harmonious. Benjamin wanted to reduce that whole tradition to rubble.

Robespierre had reappropriated ancient Rome for the French Revolution and thereby had, as Benjamin put it in his 'Theses', blasted open the continuum of history. Benjamin wanted to blast open the continuum of cultural heritage, so that the oppressed could see the circumstances in which they were living, reveal the barbarism that underlay the beauty, shake the masses from their slumbers. What seems normal must be exposed as perverse and oppressive. Benjamin thought he could see how this could be done. 'Mechanical reproduction emancipates the work of art from its parasitical dependence on ritual', he wrote. The force of this gnomic remark may be difficult to grasp, since we don't immediately think of the work of art as being involved in ritual. But that's precisely what Benjamin thought had been the function of the work of art. 'As we know', he wrote, 'the earliest artworks originated in the service of rituals.' No doubt, but the leap from that to this next sentence was at least counterintuitive. 'In other words: the unique value of the "authentic" work of art always has its basis in ritual.' But that is far from obvious. Perhaps we might see ritual in the ancient Greeks' veneration of a statue of Venus, but not in a trip to the Louvre to see the Venus de Milo. Benjamin's point, his biographers argued, is that if a work of art is reproduced mechanically, the viewer or listener doesn't have to receive it in the space consecrated to its cult, such as a museum, concert hall, or church. But, one might retort, surely sitting in a cinema or listening to a record is as much (or as little) about cultic practices and rituals as experiencing arts that are not reproduced mechanically.

Benjamin's suggestion – and it's a suggestion that has to be constructed from the rubble of his thoughts, since the essay is written in a manner parallel to the montage techniques that he admired – is that art's ritual basis is maintained even when, as it did during the Renaissance, it steps down from the sacred altar and joins the profane cult of beauty. The picture gallery and the concert hall are temples that don't declare themselves as such. Even in an age when God is dead and beauty secularised (roughly, the era from the Renaissance to the start of the twentieth century in Benjamin's view), the work of art still has its basis in ritual.

But then something remarkable happens. Photography is born. Around the same time and, Benjamin implied, not coincidentally, socialism is too. The former, for Benjamin, is the first truly revolutionary means of reproduction; the latter the politics that will destroy the ruling class and all its works. Together they will liquidate art's dependence on ritual. Only one problem: art refuses to be recast in a political role on the world stage of history. Instead, art spends the nineteenth century dressing itself up and pretending to be that which, for Benjamin, it is not: it denies itself any social function. The work of art affects to be intrinsically valuable, not valuable in part because it helps uphold the status quo. Thus, perhaps, the insistence in Kant's *Critique of Judgment* that the aesthetic judgement is necessarily disinterested. Hence the nineteenth-century aesthetic movement that called for art for art's sake. In this aesthetic movement, art was making a last stand, asserting its autonomy and purity when, if Benjamin was right, its destiny was political. Photography, Benjamin argued, separated art from its basis in cult and its autonomy disappeared forever. Instead of art for art's sake, the twentieth century would see art for politics' sake.

And when art became political in the age of mechanical reproduction, that involved two things: first revolutionising the sensory apparatuses of the masses so that they could see for the first time how they have become the handmaidens to the powers that be; and destroying the aura of the work of art itself.

The aura is a mystifying phenomenon. Benjamin wrote: 'that which withers in the age of mechanical reproduction is the aura of the work of art', defining it in terms of nature: 'If, while resting on a summer afternoon, you follow with your eyes a mountain range on the horizon or a branch which casts its shadow over you, you experience the aura of those mountains, of that branch.' Aura then involved distance; mechanical reproduction, he suggested, involved abolishing that distance. But the distance to which Benjamin referred in his essay need not be physical: rather it's the psychological distance, or authority, that gives the work of art its aura. That distance may involve a ritualised peek-a-boo with the spectator. 'Certain sculptures in cathedrals', noted Benjamin, 'are invisible to the spectator on ground level.' Some sculptures of the Madonna are covered nearly all year round. Some statues of gods were available to be seen only to the priests in the inner chamber of Greek and Roman temples.

Thus, in various ways, the aura of the work of art is inapproachable: the riff-raff are often held at a distance in something like awe, admitted on special occasions with timed tickets; meanwhile, the initiates have access all areas, confirming their status and the power of the work of art. Of course, all this is equally true of the class-stratified demographics of today's rock festivals or opera houses. At the former, the unfortunates risk trench foot in muddy fields, while the elite have backstage passes and helicopters to whisk them from the horrors of the campsite to their boutique hotels. At the latter, the unfortunates either don't have what it takes to buy tickets or get vertigo in the Gods, while the privileged few recline in the dress circle plush with enviable views of the action on stage and the prospect of liquid treats in the crush bar at the interval. All of which only goes to show how mechanical reproduction didn't eliminate the cultural heritage of auratic art as Benjamin had hoped. The secular ritual – think Glastonbury, think Bayreuth – survived the liquidation Benjamin yearned for.

The work of art in the age of mechanical reproduction, Benjamin thought, abolished this privileged access, and detonated cultural heritage. He saw cultural heritage as the debased glorification of a site of bloody conflict, and that which preened and postured as beautiful wasn't much to be trusted either. But, you might object, surely reproduction has been commonplace in art and literature for centuries and has repeatedly revolutionised not just art and culture, but human society – albeit not in the ways Benjamin wanted? For example, think of scribes. These men laboriously copied by hand the wisdom of the ages from fragile and decaying manuscripts. For generations they were indispensable in refreshing cultural memory, until in the mid fifteenth century Gutenberg's invention of movable type not only made their skills obsolete, but facilitated the Protestant Reformation. In 1492, the Abbot of Sponheim wrote a tract called *In Defence of Scribes* urging that the scribal tradition be maintained because the very act of handcopying sacred texts brought spiritual enlightenment. One problem: the abbot had his book set in movable type so his argument could be spread quickly and cheaply.

Benjamin didn't deny any of this. He noted that any work of art is in principle reproducible: since time immemorial, pupils would copy masters' work for practice, and for financial gain. The Greeks knew only two ways of technically reproducing works of art – stamping and founding, so their reproductions were confined to bronzes, terracottas and coins. Only with the woodcut would graphic art become reproducible; then during the Middle Ages etching and engraving were added. But, Benjamin argued, it was only with lithography that the reproduction of graphic art caught up with the Gutenberg revolution in printing. But lithography was soon surpassed by photography which, for Benjamin, was the revolutionary form of technological reproduction par excellence, since it 'freed the hand of the most important artistic functions which henceforth devolved only upon the eye looking into the lens'.

What was the significance of that? In the past the presence of the original was the prerequisite for the concept of authenticity. The manual reproduction of a work of art confirms the authority of the original; by contrast, mechanical reproduction may subvert that authority – indeed, in some circumstances, it may even mean it doesn't make any sense to speak of an original. 'From a photographic negative, for example, one can make any number of prints; to ask for the "authentic" print makes no sense', wrote Benjamin. Is there an original print of *Porky's 3*? It's not impossible, but even if there is, it won't stand in the same relation to its reproductions as the original of the *Mona Lisa* stands to any of the billions of reproductions of Da Vinci's painting. There is no original work of art imperiously conferring legitimacy on copies and withholding it from forgers – the king is dead, long live the democracy of things.

But Benjamin couched this death of distance in odd terms, arguing that the 'contemporary masses' desired to bring things ' "closer" spatially and humanly, which is just as ardent as their bent toward overcoming the uniqueness of every reality by accepting its reproduction'. But where did this desire come from? Here Benjamin, and it was a charge that Adorno laid at his door more than once during the 1930s, was insufficiently dialectical. More plausibly, we might argue, improvements in reproduction technologies change what it is possible for capitalists to sell to those whom Benjamin calls the 'masses'. Desires, that is to say, don't spring from nowhere. They can be constructed. They are, perhaps, even in dialectical relationship with technology. Technology changes not only what humans can do; it changes humans, makes them desire things they didn't know existed before. Benjamin realised this, writing: 'One of the foremost tasks of art has always been the creation of a demand that could only be satisfied later.'

Cinema, radio, TV, recorded music, the internet and social media all involve technological innovations that enable capitalists to provide products that change our desires and so change us. Consider the internet. 'The development of the internet has more to do with human beings becoming a reflection of their technologies', the German post-structuralist philosopher and media theorist Friedrich Kittler once argued. 'After all, it is we who adapt to the machine. The machine does not adapt to us'. Kittler was countering the benign vision of the Canadian media theorist Marshall McLuhan, who took technological innovations to be human prostheses (hence the subtitle to McLuhan's book *Understanding Media: The Extensions of Man*). On the contrary, Kittler argued, 'media are not pseudopods for extending the human body. They follow the logic of escalation that leaves us and written history behind it.'[5]

As for Benjamin, he certainly envisaged technology as prosthetic. He noted that a photograph may capture what the eye can't see. As a result, the original would not be a point of comparison, through which we judge the success of the photo as a reproduction. It would make no sense in such a case to speak of a forgery. Benjamin also argued that technical reproduction can put the copy into situations impossible for the original: 'The cathedral leaves its locale to be studied in the studio of a lover of art; the choral production, performed in an auditorium or in the open air, resounds in the drawing room.' He was considering, in the case of the former, a photograph; in the case of the latter, a phonograph.

But, if photography and other art forms of the era of mechanical reproduction extend human perceptual powers, Benjamin imagined that these arts have a political purpose, namely to bring the nature of reality into high definition.

> Our taverns and our metropolitan streets, our offices and furnished rooms, our railway stations and our factories appeared to have locked us up hopelessly. Then came the film and burst this prison asunder by the dynamite of the tenth of a second, so that now, in the midst of its far-flung ruins and debris, we calmly and adventurously go travelling. With the close-up, space expands; with slow motion, movement is extended . . . The camera introduces us to unconscious optics as does psychoanalysis to unconscious impulses.

Many years later, in 1962, Alfred Hitchcock, whose films have the logic of dreams as if they are realisations on celluloid of unconscious impulses, echoed Benjamin's insights here when he told François Truffaut what cinema was for: it was, he said, to contract time and to extend it.

Just as Freud placed his hand gently on the back of his patients' heads and pushed them into their dirty linen, acquainting them with the dark forces that underlay their rational selves, so the camera exposes the brutal dissonances of modern life. And just as there is work for the analysand to do, so there is work for the moviegoer too, Benjamin suggested. But the work doesn't involve long periods of concentration of the kind that was characteristic of standing before a painting in a picture gallery and taken to heroic extremes by the philosopher of art Richard Wollheim, who wrote: 'I spent long hours in the Church of San Salvatore in Venice, in the Louvre, in the Guggenheim Museum, coaxing a picture into life. I noticed that I became an object of suspicion to passers-by, and so did the picture that I was looking at.'[6] Instead, Benjamin called for 'reception in distraction'. He imagined such reception as a revolutionary form of perception – an incendiary notion, especially for us to read about in hindsight. Today distraction is more vice than virtue. Indeed, it's why you can't get anything done. Technological innovation keeps us leaping from one pointless task after the other, replying to emails, updating Facebook status, tweeting, texting, always working at our screens, like victims of a cyberspace Sisyphean curse. This distracted way of living runs counter to the popular theory of the Hungarian psychologist Mihaly Csíkszentmihályi that people are happiest when they are in a state of flow.[7] But then Benjamin was not a poet hymning work, or a philosopher of happiness. More likely, he would have regarded happiness, flow, absorption and the cult of fulfilling labour as fatuous quests for wholeness, delusions that stop us realising we are in a broken world, knee deep in accumulated rubble, downtrodden and exploited.

Absorption and flow are characteristic of the creation and reception of auratic art. The kind of art Benjamin prized and took to have revolutionary potential was otherwise: it involved disruption and estrangement, bursting open the smooth surface of reality. Instead of meditation on delusive harmonies, it meant being discombobulated by dissonances, jump-cuts, deranging montages. Absent-mindedness was very nearly a virtue for Benjamin. You might say that cinema, for him, was a Brechtian alienation technique with better technology. Film, as he put it, isn't so much an art form that soothes as one that trains its viewers 'in the vast apparatus whose role in their lives is expanding almost daily'. Here apparatus means the phantasmagoric world of urban commodity capitalism that we take to be real, natural and given, and so accept fatalistically.

But there is more. Think of Greta Garbo or, if you prefer, George Clooney. Movie stars seem to be auratic, that is to say, their worship appears to be like that of Greek statues. As a result, the cinema appears to be another temple for the enactment of rituals. Benjamin had an incendiary idea about this which subverts the thought that Garbo and Clooney are akin to gods. Film acting, he maintained, is different from earlier forms of acting in that every film performance is a composition of separate takes, each of which has been assembled not by the actor, but by the director, cinematographer, lighting designer, executive producer, lighting designer. So the actor's performance is broken up and edited back together. As Benjamin's biographers argued:

> this disjunctive, testable nature of the performance before the apparatus [i.e. camera, editing studio, cinema projection] makes visible something otherwise hidden: the self-alienation of the modern, technologised subject, the susceptibility to measurement and control. The actor thus places the apparatus in the services of a triumph over the apparatus, a triumph of humanity.[8]

Benjamin thought that the cinema held up to us a mirror of our condition – we too are technologised subjects, broken up, studied, reified in the same way actors' performances are. For him, the new technology of mechanical reproduction meant that the actor's performance was 'detachable from the person mirrored'. While earlier forms of acting, particularly in the theatre, involved performances that were not detachable and so had about them an aura, film acting was different The film star's performance was 'transportable and subject to a different control – that of the viewers, who confront it en masse'. As a result, we could break up the cult of the movie star by reflecting on how his or her performance has been mechanically assembled. 'During long periods of human history, the mode of human sense perception changes with humanity's entire mode of existence', wrote Benjamin, and his hope was that since our mode of sense perception changes thanks to technological innovation, from the enhanced perception that cinema allows us we can see that we have become things.

Benjamin's technological utopianism is beguiling, and one can understand his hopes for it under fascism, but one could also argue the opposite: instead of making self-alienation visible, cinema can erase it. Instead of annulling approachability, cinema can extend auratic distance. The technology may, but needn't, help us realise our alienation. And the training that Benjamin recommended in order to hone the new sensory powers cinema offers us is one that few have undertaken. What he seemed to be arguing for here is a kind of aberrant decoding. But the hope for such decoding involves an active, informed, politicised role for the cinema audience that, we realise with hindsight, it didn't have, and is incredibly rare. Cinema, certainly in the hands of the Hollywood culture industry that Adorno and Horkheimer would excoriate in *Dialectic of Enlightenment*, has been an ideological tool for the domination of the masses rather than revealing to them their plight under monopoly capitalism. What Benjamin hoped would be consciousness raising has, quite often, been merely brain numbing.

'Mechanical reproduction emancipates the work of art from its parasitical dependence on ritual', wrote Benjamin. Again, one could just as well argue the opposite: that it tightens the bonds with more sophisticated technology. Our film stars are subjects of cultic veneration. The Italian devotee of Walter Benjamin, Roberto Calasso, wrote in *The Ruin of Kasch* that 'every movie star is a constellation, incorporated into the heavens after being devoured by the gods'.[9] The movie star is thus both a god and a sacrifice to the gods. More precisely, we might say that the movie star becomes a god only after being sacrificed. And what is true of movie stars is true of all celebrities: the culture industry produces gods and sacrificial victims by means of the same technology; indeed, it erases the distinction between them.

WALTER BENJAMIN had a blind spot about music. If he hadn't, he might have written about jazz in the same utopian spirit in which he wrote about cinema. One could map his optimism about cinema's revolutionary potential onto jazz, which, like cinema but more so, liquidates tradition, fractures, telescopes, alters our staid perceptions and has a subversive political potential, challenges ruling-class orthodoxy, and subverts affirmative culture. If the camera introduces us to an optical unconscious so perhaps jazz introduces us to an aural one.

Adorno argued that jazz does the opposite of all of these things. For him it has no revolutionary potential. What he attempts to do in 'On Jazz' is tear off the mask of this music to reveal what lies beneath. Jazz adds improvisation and syncopation to the standardised character of popular music in order to veil its own commodity character. What jazz lovers prize in jazz, then, is the fig leaf that conceals what it is: a mass commodity. 'Jazz wants to improve its marketability and veil its own commodity character which, in keeping with one of the funda-mental contradictions of the system, would jeopardise its own success if it were to appear on the market undisguised.'[10] This imputation of cynicism seems laughably unfair. Did Miles Davis really veil his music's commodity character? Were John Coltrane's improvised sax solos disguised expressions of ruling-class orthodoxy? If you gotta ask, as Louis Armstrong once put it, you ain't never gonna know. Where one might take jazz as a site of resistance, and in particular African-American resistance, to the culture industry, to the ideologi-cal apparatus, to white domination, Adorno saw nothing of the kind.

But these objections are themselves misplaced. Adorno was writ-ing, not about African-American jazz (indeed there is no indication that he had heard it before his immigration to the United States), but about what he heard in Germany. But even before he heard the music, he was revolted by what he mistakenly thought the word connoted: 'I remember clearly that I was horrified when I read the word jazz for the first time. It is plausible that my negative association came from the German word Hatz [a pack of hounds], which evoked blood-hounds chasing after something slower.'[11] Later, when he heard the jazz of the Weimar Republic in the 1920s, his revulsion didn't dimin-ish. The jazz he heard was upper-class entertainment for Germans rather than African-American art form. It was a combination of salon music and march music. 'The former represents an individuality which in truth is none at all, but merely the socially produced illusion of it; the latter is an equally fictive community which formed from nothing other than the alignment of atoms under the force that is exerted upon them.'

The black American roots of jazz served, he thought, as factors that made jazz more appealing to its privileged, white European audiences. 'The skin of the Negro as well as the silver of the saxophone was a coloristic effect.' But he heard something else: he heard, in so far as jazz was the authentic African-American expression, not so much rebellion against slavery as resentful submission to it. Jazz, as Adorno understood it, was sadomasochistic. He thought it was suitable for fascism, not just because it mobilised military marches and acted through its collective characters as a corrective to 'the bourgeois isolation of autonomous art', but also because 'its rebellious gestures are accompanied by the tendency to blind obeisance, much like the sadomasochistic type described by analytic psychology'.

Jazz also suggested premature ejaculation. Its syncopation was, for Adorno, very different from Beethoven's. While the latter involved 'the expression of subjective force which directed itself against authority', that of jazz led nowhere. 'It is plainly a "coming-too-early", just as anxiety leads to premature orgasm, just as impotence expresses itself through premature and incomplete orgasm.' Later, in *Dialectic of Enlightenment*, Adorno and Horkheimer would find in Hollywood cinema a similar kind of sexual disappointment: the culture industry, they wrote, 'endlessly cheats customers out of what it endlessly promises, especially in terms of sexual pleasure. In erotic films, for instance, everything revolves around coitus because it does not take place.'[12] Jazz, similarly, seemed to promise liberation but only delivered ascetic denial.

Jazz, as a result, involved symbolic castration. The weak modern male as performed by Harold Lloyd and Charlie Chaplin, who followed 'too weakly the standard of the collective which has been unproblematically set', found his counterpart in jazz: the ego of the 'hot' variety of jazz, he thought, expresses its impotence, perhaps even revels in it. By playing, listening or dancing to hot jazz, he argued, one submitted sadomasochistically to an authority while affecting to do the opposite – it was a form of self-alienation masking itself as rebellion.

> The decisive intervention of jazz lies in the fact that this subject of weakness takes pleasure precisely in its own weakness . . . By learning to fear social authority and experiencing it as a threat of castration – and immediately as fear of impotence – it identifies itself with precisely that authority of which it is afraid . . . the sex appeal of jazz is a command: obey and then you will be allowed to take part. And the dream thought, as contradictory as reality, in which it is dreamt: I will only be potent once I have allowed myself to be castrated.

For Adorno, then, jazz involved a perversion typical of the whole of the culture industry. In embryo in this essay of Adorno's is all that

Marcuse would write about repressive desublimation thirty years later.

When Adorno got to the US he could have immersed himself in American jazz. There is no suggestion, though, that he did go to the jazz clubs on Central Avenue in Los Angeles, the heart of the West Coast jazz scene in the 1940s, where he might have heard jazz beyond the cynical philosophy he imputed to it. He might have heard, say, Charlie Parker, Lionel Hampton, Eric Dolphy, Art Pepper and Charles Mingus. He not only didn't, but continued to write anti-jazz jeremiads during his American exile and after. His 1955 book *Prisms* included an essay called 'Perennial Fashions – Jazz', in which he wrote: 'Considered as a whole, the perennial sameness of jazz consists not in a basic organisation of the material within which the imagination can roam freely and without inhabitation, as within an articulate language, but rather in the utilisation of certain well-defined tricks, formulas, and clichés to the exclusion of everything else.'[13]

The deluded technological utopianism of Benjamin's essay on the work of art in the age of mechanical reproduction finds its opposite in Adorno's essay on jazz. One could substitute the word 'cinema' for 'jazz' in the above quotation and use it to summarise what Hollywood did to Benjamin's hopes for art. Jazz, for Adorno, despite its musical montages, its shock, its technological reproducibility, was a 'phantasmagoria of modernity' and provided only 'counterfeit freedom'. Arguably cinema, on which Benjamin had pinned revolutionary hopes, had become like the image of jazz that Adorno calumnised.

If Walter Benjamin had managed to cross the Atlantic and join the Frankfurt School and his friend Brecht in American exile, it's possible he would have been disabused of his revolutionary hopes for cinema. He might have embraced America with the gusto of Fromm. He might have become a hero to the New Left of the 1960s like Marcuse. He might have got high with Charlie Parker and dug bebop. Charlie Chaplin might have played him in a Benjamin-scripted biopic. He might have been brought before the House UnAmerican Activities Committee and there outwitted Richard Nixon and lived to a ripe old age as emeritus professor at Harvard. All the lovely American possibilities we can imagine for the Frankfurt School's greatest critic exist only in a redemptive vision in which what has been smashed is made whole. In reality, a storm was blowing through Europe and Benjamin was about to become one of its millions of victims.

9

A New World

On 13 March 1933, the swastika flag was raised over Frankfurt town hall. On the same day police closed down the Institute for Social Research. Only two years after Horkheimer's inaugural lecture, which set out the multidisciplinary nature of the Institute's research that would become critical theory, he and his Frankfurt School colleagues were compelled to go into exile. Franz Röckle's Neue Sachlichkeit fortress, once known as Café Marx, became first offices for the state police, then a university building used by National Socialist students. In 1944, it was destroyed by Allied bombs.[1] Fromm's research into the German working class had been proved correct: German workers could not be counted on to resist the rise of Hitler.

Why had fascism triumphed in Germany? There was no shortage of theories and indeed the question was to divide the Frankfurt School bitterly, as we will see later. For Fromm, there were two key factors: German economic backwardness and sadomasochism. Fromm argued that, as Germany had shifted from early to monopoly capitalism, the social character of the lower middle class persisted, outliving its economic function. This class, which was central to the earlier form of capitalism of the nineteenth century, about which Marx had written, should have become economically and politically powerless, and thus obsolete, under monopoly capitalism. But in Germany this had not happened. Even though this class's parsimonious, duty-bound character traits were incompatible with modern forms of capitalist production, they survived in considerable number in Germany. And this German petit bourgeois class proved to be the keenest supporters of Hitler because, as Fromm put it, 'the desire for authority is chan-nelled towards the strong leader, while other specific father figures become the objects of the rebellion'.[2]

That the supporters of Nazism were sadomasochists bewitched by authoritarian father figures was a view that many in the Frankfurt School shared. Marcuse in his 1934 essay 'The Struggle Against Liberalism in the Totalitarian View of the State' argued that in fetishis-ing blood, soil, racial purity, homeland and the Führer, the Nazis ingeniously urged their sadomasochistic followers to submit to poverty and death for their country as the highest duties. Marcuse had been catalysed to write this paper by a two-and-a-half-hour speech Hitler gave to an industrial club in Düsseldorf in 1932. Marcuse argued that the speech highlighted how monopoly capitalism was entering a new era, one wherein the totalitarian state and its ideological apparatus would provide a defence of capitalism against the crises to which it had been prone, not least during the German hyperinflation of the 1920s and the global deflationary effects of the 1929 Wall Street Crash.

During the speech in a hotel ballroom to 650 business leaders, Hitler strove to convince his audience that the Nazis were not, as they had feared, socialist and anti-capitalist. He insisted that only he could defend German businesses from capitalist crisis and from the socialist threat of working-class parties; only he could free Germany from the yoke of war reparations that were stopping Germans from benefitting from the success of its native industry. He refrained from making anti-Semitic remarks. He told them:

> The labour resources of our people, the capacities, we have them already: no one can deny that we are industrious. But we must first refashion the political preconditions: without that, industry and capac-ity, diligence and economy are in the last resort of no avail; an oppressed nation will not be able to spend on its own welfare even the fruits of its own economy but must sacrifice them on the altar of exactions and of tribute.[3]

Hitler kept up the charm offensive by suggesting that the noisy rallies and marches by Nazis that may have kept business leaders awake at night involved the kind of sacrifice necessary for Germany to be great again. He went on:

> Remember that it means sacrifice when today many hundreds of thousands of SA and SS men of the National Socialist movement have every day to mount on their lorries, protect meetings, undertake marches, sacrifice themselves night after night and then come back in the grey dawn to workshop and factory, or as unemployed to take the pittance of the dole: it means sacrifice when from the little they possess they have further to buy their uniforms, their shirts, their badges, yes and even pay their own fares. Believe me, there is already in all this the force of an ideal – a great ideal!

The speech ended with long and tumultuous applause – Hitler had convinced many of those present he was good for business.

Here, then, in Hitler's words, was the kind of sadmasochism that the Frankfurt School thought Nazism involved – a perversion that was useful to help capitalism function better. 'This ideology', wrote Marcuse, 'exhibits the status quo, but with a radical transvaluation of values: unhappiness is turned into grace, misery into blessing, poverty into destiny'.[4] Happily for Hitler, duty-bound, pleasure-denying Nazis were temperamentally well suited to bend the knee to that transvaluation.

For Marcuse fascism was not a break with the past, but a continuation of tendencies within liberalism that supported the capitalist economic system. This was the Frankfurt School orthodoxy – fascism wasn't an abolition of capitalism, rather a means of ensuring its continued existence. Horkheimer once wrote 'he who does not wish to speak of capitalism, should also be silent about fascism'.[5] Perhaps one needed to be German to bow before that injunction. What has long shocked some readers of the Frankfurt School is the apparent blitheness with which they elided Hitlerian fascism, Stalinist communism and Roosevelt's America. But what was most personally important about Hitlerian fascism to the Frankfurt School in 1933 was not so much how it played footsie with business leaders as how it made life impossible for Jewish Marxist intellectuals. Adorno, for instance, was given an uncomfortable lesson on the impossibility of being a Jewish German intellectual in the 1930s when the president of the Reich Chamber of Literature, to which he needed to belong if he were to teach non-Aryan pupils, rejected his membership application in 1933 on the grounds that it was restricted to 'reliable members of the Volk', by which was meant 'persons who belong to the German nation by profound ties of character and blood. As a non-Aryan you are unable to feel and appreciate such an obligation.'[6]

Adorno, like Horkheimer and Pollock, had his home searched by Nazi paramilitaries. He feared he was being spied on. He wrote from Frankfurt to his friend, the great composer and his former teacher, Alban Berg on 9 September 1933 that he had not been able to give planned lectures the previous semester at Frankfurt University;[7] nor, he feared, would he be able to do so again. His fears were justified: three days later on his thirtieth birthday, September 11, the Nazis withdrew his licence to teach. Life in Germany was becoming impossible and so he, like his Frankfurt School colleagues, was forced to leave.

It's difficult to overstate the pain for these men, not just of exile but of the particular suffering entailed by being uprooted from German intellectual culture and cast into an intellectual milieu where few spoke German, shared their philosophical heritage or cared about their work. Adorno fled first to Oxford where he would spend four years from 1934 to 1938 as an advanced student at Merton College – a demotion from his position as lecturer at Frankfurt. There were worse slights to his self-esteem: at Merton, he was obliged to dine communally. This was 'like having to return to school', he wrote, adding, with pardonable exaggeration, 'in short, an extension of the Third Reich'.[8] It was there that he composed music, wrote his brilliant essay on Hitler's favourite composer 'In Search of Wagner', and his critique of Husserl's epistemological system, without attracting one invitation to speak at Oxford's intellectual clubs.[9] Throughout those years he was an outsider whose work was not appreciated. A. J. Ayer, the British exponent of Viennese logical positivism at Oxford, and thus not one sympathetic to Adorno's dialectical thinking, recalled in his autobiography that no one in Oxford took him seriously but regarded him as a dandy.[10] Deracinated, lonely, struggling to make his philosophy understood in a language that he was just mastering, Adorno took succour in occasional trips to visit Gretel Karplus, whom he would marry in 1937, and Walter Benjamin, who had settled in Paris.

Just possibly, Adorno took succour, too, from the fact that that other great Jewish German-speaking philosopher, Ludwig Wittgenstein, found English academia out of his depth. In 1929, after defending his thesis before Bertrand Russell and G. E. Moore, as a result of which he became a fellow at Trinity College, Cambridge, Wittgenstein clapped the two examiners on the shoulders and said, 'Don't worry, I know you'll never understand it.'[11] Adorno did not meet Wittgenstein during his English exile years. A great shame: they had so much in common – their negative philosophical sensibilities, cultural iconoclasm and pessimism. What's more, given Wittgenstein's temper and Adorno's waspishness, the former's lack of interest in dialectical method and the latter's scorn for what he took as English philosophy's positivism, the results of any meeting between the two would probably not have been pretty. Wittgenstein was charged with having attacked Karl Popper with a poker during a meeting at the Cambridge Moral Sciences Club;[12] what he would have done to Adorno is anybody's guess.

Horkheimer fled first to Geneva. Aided by Friedrich Pollock, he had made preparations to leave Germany soon after the first Nazis took up their seats in the Reichstag, first by transferring assets to Holland and then by establishing a branch office called the Societé Internationale de Recherches Sociales in the Swiss city, as well as research centres in Paris, London and New York. It was to Geneva that Horkheimer, Löwenthal, Fromm and Marcuse moved in 1933 to carry on their work. But it became clear that it could only be a temporary home – only Horkheimer had a Swiss residency permit, while his colleagues had to keep renewing their tourist visas. The Frankfurt School considered Paris or London as possible permanent homes, but Horkheimer believed neither was safe from fascism.

New York looked like a more promising refuge. During 1933 and 1934, Erich Fromm and Julian Gumperz, an American-born sociologist who had studied in Germany and had become a colleague of Pollock and Horkheimer, negotiated with Columbia University over the possibility of accommodating the exiled Frankfurt School in New York.[13] Its president, Nicholas Murray Butler, as well as sociologists Robert S. Lund and Robert MacIver, were impressed with the Institute's research projects and agreed to loan offices at 429 West 117th Street, not far from the Columbia campus. Horkheimer and his colleagues moved in towards the end of 1934.

But wasn't an American university thereby opening its doors to the red menace? Was Columbia suckered into supplying the building for a new branch of the Café Marx franchise? Was the International Institute of Social Research (as the Frankfurt School was called in New York) really a crypto-Marxist entryist outfit that had successfully infiltrated a leading university for nefarious, communistic purposes, while concealing its true identity in order to avoid political scrutiny and, quite possibly, expulsion from the United States? All these questions can be answered positively if you believe the theory rehearsed in 1980 by the American sociologist Lewis Feuer, who pointed out that Horkheimer and his colleagues were happy to criticise bourgeois culture and society, but were suspiciously silent about Stalinist excesses like liquidations, show trials and gulags.[14] Perhaps, Feuer inferred, their silence about Stalin's Soviet Union spoke volumes – the Frankfurt scholars were really a bunch of communist infiltrators.

Horkheimer and Pollock, though, hardly had the same genius for duping intellectuals as the Bolshevik Comintern spymaster, Willi Münzenberg, who targeted left-leaning liberal intellectuals (including Ernest Hemingway, Lillian Hellman, André Malraux and André Gide) to run communist front organisations and attempted to seduce them into supporting various causes of the Soviet Union.[15] Feuer's suggestion that Columbia University's negotiators with the Frankfurt School were dupes is implausible. The School, by this time in its evolution, had no party affiliation, still less any solidarity with the Soviet Union. Their brand of multidisciplinary neo-Marxism was heretical to the Kremlin and, unless their development of critical theory was an elaborate smokescreen, its thinkers were unlikely foot soldiers for Stalin.

What the Frankfurt School did have, though, was a long-term commitment to Aesopian language, that is, words or phrases that convey an innocent meaning to an outsider but a hidden meaning to those in the know. Quite possibly it was that commitment that duped Feuer into believing the Frankfurt scholars were a bunch of reds who had infiltrated New York academia. In 1923, for instance, the founders of the School had abandoned the idea of calling themselves the Institut für Marxismus (Institute for Marxism) because it was too provocative, and chose, as Martin Jay put it, a more Aesopian alternative.[16] During the 1930s, many of the Frankfurt School members felt compelled to use pseudonyms so that they could write without attracting persecution by Nazis or, at least, express themselves with a waspishness inimical to their scholarly identities. Hence, Horkheimer published as Heinrich Regius, Adorno as Hektor Rottweiler and Benjamin as Detlev Holz. In American exile, Horkheimer ensured that the Frankfurt scholars remained aloof from the society in which they lived. The decision to publish in German precluded the School from having much influence on an overwhelmingly monoglot English-speaking country. Such decisions prevented the Frankfurt School's integration into American society, certainly, but they also gave it the kind of intellectual independence it had sought from its inception. As, it must be said, did the fact that it had an independent income (albeit one that was drastically reduced by financial speculations in the US).

During American exile, Horkheimer was also scrupulous in ensuring that the School's journal, the *Zeitschrift für Sozialforschung*, where possible, used euphemisms for words that might be read as demonstrating the Institute's political sympathies and result in political harassment by his American hosts.[17] When the *Zeitschrift* published Walter Benjamin's 1936 paper 'The Work of Art in the Age of Mechanical Reproduction', for instance, it changed the final sentences, which might otherwise have been read as a call to communist-supporting artists to resist fascism in their work. Benjamin had written: 'This is the situation which Fascism is rendering aesthetic. Communism responds by politicising art.' In the *Zeitschrift* version, though, 'the totalitarian doctrine' was substituted for 'Fascism' and 'the constructive forces of mankind' for 'communism'. Thus, even right-wing

Americans, if they penetrated the German in which Benjamin's essay was published, might be reassured into believing that he was not eulogising communistic art's political role, but the role of any non-fascist art. This may be read as a grotesque misrepresentation of Benjamin, and it was, but it was one that had the pragmatic purpose of helping the Frankfurt School in the 1930s avoid persecution by American anti-communists. Whether that pragmatism was justified is a different matter. This wasn't yet the time of McCarthyite witchhunts against suspected communists, but Horkheimer wasn't going to take any risks. The pragmatic imperative became more important once, as a result of the financial difficulties the School suffered following disastrous speculation in the US stock market and property, Horkheimer and his colleagues sought research contracts and so needed to promote themselves as sober scholars rather than crypto-Stalinist henchmen.

What is clear is that these German Jewish exiles were uneasy. Given what they had just experienced in the old world, perhaps their compunction about disclosing their identities too much in the new world is understandable. It's striking, for instance, that when, after his four years in Oxford, Adorno joined his Frankfurt School colleagues in New York, he dropped Wiesengrund from his name at Pollock's suggestion because there were too many Jewish-sounding intellectuals on the Institute's roster. If this sounds ridiculous – after all, the United States was a country of exile for many Jews who would otherwise have been murdered in Nazi Germany – consider the remark of Leo Löwenthal: he told Martin Jay that many in the Frankfurt School thought the Germans less anti-Semitic than the Americans they knew during their exile years.[18]

It's a remark that needs to be taken with a pinch of salt, since whatever anti-Semitism these exiled Jews experienced in the United States, it didn't involve house searches by paramilitaries, revoked teaching licences and the looming threat of the death camps. Rather, they were welcomed to New York and there given the opportunity to think, write, publish and research as they wished. It's significant that when Adorno gave his first impressions of his new home, he stressed how familiar it seemed. 'As we both expected', he wrote to Benjamin after sailing to New York with his wife Gretel, 'we are not finding it difficult to adapt to the living conditions here. It is *sérieusement* much more European here than in London, and 7th Avenue, which is close to us, is as peacefully reminiscent of the boulevard Montparnasse as Greenwich village.'[19] True, he was trying in this passage to convince Benjamin, the irredeemable Francophile, to emigrate to New York by stressing its similarities to the Parisian neighbourhood in the 15th arrondissement where Benjamin was then living. But he was also making the city seem less alien and more sympathetic.

Compare Adorno's first impressions with those of his wife in a letter to Benjamin from the same time: 'What amazes me most is the fact that things here are by no means all as new and advanced as one would really think; on the contrary: one can observe the contrast between the most modern and the most shabby things wherever one goes. There is no need to search for the surreal here, for one stumbles over it at every step.'[20] Here, Gretel Adorno was jettisoning the stereotypical European idea of America as land of endless newness, but holding on to the sense of its (not necessarily unpleasant) strangeness that her husband couldn't, or didn't want, to feel. He, and indeed the rest of the Frankfurt School, didn't adapt to America, but tried to make it adapt to them – and those aspects of American life that they instinctively disliked, as we will see, they treated with contempt and ruthlessly rejected, almost as if they were trying to inoculate themselves against infection by a lower life form.

But the old world iconoclasm of the Frankfurt School hardly went unchallenged in New York. Not long after settling at the Columbia University campus on Morningside Heights, overlooking Harlem, Horkheimer and his colleagues found the basis of critical theory challenged by a group called the New York Intellectuals. The Intellectuals dissented from two of the Frankfurt School's articles of faith, namely that the dialectical method was essential in the would-be Marxist's conceptual toolkit and that those who were insufficiently dialectical were doomed to uphold the status quo. At two charged meetings in 1936 and 1937, Horkheimer and his colleagues were confronted by another group of (broadly) Jewish and/or Marxist thinkers who thought that the dialectical method explained little and that the Hegelian distinction between *Vernunft* and *Verstand* was metaphysical obfuscation.[21] The New York Intellectuals were headed by Sidney Hook, a ferociously argumentative man, heretical Marxist and devotee of American pragmatism, nicknamed John Dewey's Pitbull. He was joined by the Trotskyist art historian Meyer Schapiro, and two men who, intellectually at least, represented much that the Frankfurt School despised, the logical positivist philosophers Ernest Nagel and Otto Neurath.

Neurath, in particular, is worth remarking on because he, in both the mathematical cast of his philosophy and the committed application of his logical thinking to real-world problems, was so inimical to the Frankfurt School's brand of speculative, often armchair philosophising. He was an exiled member of the Vienna Circle of logical positivists, as well as an economist and sociologist. Before his untimely death aged sixty-three in 1945, Neurath would establish the Isotype Institute in Oxford, devoted to his symbolic way of representing quantitative information which he was to deploy to help with slum clearance planning in the English West Midlands. That was one of the rare moments, with all due respect to the philosophical discipline, in which a logician's skills have helped improve the living conditions of those suffering under capitalism. If Neurath's Isotope Institute was *Verstand* in action, then perhaps it could be usefully construed as a counter to Horkheimer and Marcuse's insistence that formal logic was a tool of oppression.

But what was most striking about the meetings between the two schools was not so much the conflict between Frankfurt and Vienna, between dialectical method and logical positivism, but rather the clash of two Marxist heresies – both disdained as perversions of the true creed by the international Comintern. Horkheimer and Hook were Marxists, perhaps, but not as Stalin understood the term.

Hook is an intriguing figure, who in the 1920s had studied with Karl Korsch in Berlin and at the Marx-Engels Institute in Moscow, but by 1985 had changed his political views so markedly in light of Stalin, the Cold War and Vietnam, that he was able to accept the presidential medal of freedom from President Ronald Reagan. By the mid 1930s Hook had broken with the Comintern and, while studying with the great American philosopher John Dewey at Columbia, had developed an intellectual synthesis of Marxism and pragmatism. That synthesis was prompted by the same motives that drove Horkheimer to reconfigure Marxism and develop interdisciplinary critical theory: the revolution hadn't happened and it was imperative to work out why. Both the Frankfurt School and the New York Intellectuals led by Hook were opposed to the orthodox Marxist belief in historical determinism. Hook saw pragmatism as offering an intellectually respectable Marxism that dispensed with the determinism and fitted better with American sensibilities.

Professor Ned Rescher in the *Oxford Companion to Philosophy* describes pragmatism's characteristic idea as being 'that efficacy in practical application – "What works most effectively in practice" – somehow provides a standard for the determination of truth in the case of statements, rightness in the case of actions and value in the case of appraisals'.[22] Pragmatism is not, as the Frankfurt School charged positivism and empiricism with being, value-free – a fact that Marcuse conceded in his 1941 review of Dewey's *Theory of Valuation*.[23] Rather, value is built into pragmatism's insistence on efficacy in practical application. As a philosophy, pragmatism has a long tradition in the United States, and it's tempting to suggest its very practical turn made it temperamentally appealing to can-do Americans, certainly if the alternative was the proverbial abstruseness of German idealism.

Annoyingly, matters aren't that simple. In fact, pragmatism, as theorised by Dewey, borrowed from German idealism, in particular from Hegel. Dewey was attracted by Hegel's notion of an active mind able to construct reality – a notion that had influenced American Transcendentalists in the nineteenth century. As we saw earlier, the Hegelian notion of self-actualisation, which Marx had recast in material terms so that for him to be free was to realise one's identity through non-exploited labour, was controversial to the Frankfurt School. And yet Dewey took up this Hegelian heritage and applied it, pragmatically, to science: science was seen as a tool to help humans realise their potential and thus create utopias. Though Dewey was no Marxist (Hook would describe him in his autobiography as an 'honest liberal'), this pragmatic twist to what science might be harnessed to achieve was attractive to Hook. It fitted with his view of Marx as a scientist-activist and it made him sceptical of the Hegelianised Marxism of the Frankfurt School. He suspected this effectively returned German philosophy to conservatism, authoritarianism and obscurantism, and argued that his pragmatic Marxism avoided these elitist pitfalls. As Thomas Wheatland in his history of the Frankfurt School's exile years argues, both Hook and Dewey were influenced by the egalitarian ideas of the greatest pragmatist philosopher C. S. Peirce, who blew a breath of fresh, democratic air through science and philosophy. Wheatland writes of Peirce's vision of intellectual endeavour: 'Any person, like any scientist, was capable of generating new and creative ideas about the world that could be tested and evaluated according to practical experience. Knowledge and reason could then be refined as the discoveries were shared by this scientific community and consensus began to take shape.'[24]

Hook thought Marxism could be revived through a similar pragmatic turn – freely arrived at consensus could prompt collective action that had a democratic course. This pragmatist vision of unconstrained, consensus-oriented democratic collective action was hardly appealing to Horkheimer or the rest of the first generation of the Frankfurt School, but it was to prove inspiring to the second generation, in particular to Jürgen Habermas whose development of the notion of communicative action relied to a considerable extent on his readings of American pragmatists, in particular George Herbert Mead.

This championing of science as a tool for liberation rather than a tool of oppression was inimical to Horkheimer and the rest of the Frankfurt School. For them, Hook was insufficiently dialectical. Hook retorted to these charges by sarcastically asking Horkheimer and Marcuse what doctrines are dialectically true but scientifically false or scientifically true yet dialectically false. For Hook, the Frankfurt School's dystopian perspective on science was unwarranted. We don't have the Frankfurt scholars' replies to Hook's disdainful challenge, but what we do know is that, even after these conversations with the New York Intellectuals, Horkheimer carried on loathing pragmatism. He took it as a form of positivism that, like empiricism, facilitated capitalism rather than, as the Hegelianised critical theory he was developing did, critiqued it. In a 1943 letter to Pollock he wrote that 'pragmatism and empiricism and the lack of genuine philosophy are some of the foremost reasons which are responsible for the crisis which civilisation would have faced even if the war had not come'.[25] America was hobbled, he thought, by its lack of a dialectical philosophical heritage, by its dearth of critical thinking.

As for Hook, he carried on thinking that the Frankfurt School was hobbled by its commitment to fruitless dialectical thinking that didn't lead to practical results.

ADORNO DIDN'T TAKE part in these charged debates between the Frankfurt School and the New York Intellectuals. At the time he was still in Oxford, only arriving in New York in 1938. But once he arrived, his first work for the School involved a clash with the new world that was even more bruising than the one Horkheimer had endured with John Dewey's Pitbull. It was a confrontation that would serve to deepen his old world iconoclasm and his scepticism about American mass culture, and lead to many of the devastating criticisms of what he and Horkheimer later called the culture industry in *Dialectic of Enlightenment*.

His first job in America began in 1938 when he joined the Princeton Radio Research Project. This was a project to study the effects that new forms of mass media could have on American society, made possible by a grant from the Rockefeller Foundation to Princeton University. It was led by the exiled Viennese sociologist Paul Lazarsfeld, who years before had worked as a research associate for the Frankfurt School in its studies on authority and family.[26] Before Adorno got involved, Lazarsfeld's researchers had studied the social effects of Orson Welles's notorious radio adaptation of H. G. Wells's *War of the Worlds*, which was broadcast on CBS Radio to six million listeners on Halloween 1938. The broadcast was taken by many listeners as suggesting that a Martian invasion was currently in progress and, so legend has it, spread panic across the United States. But while Welles's broadcast is often cited as an example of the power of new forms of mass media and the gullibility of the public, it also serves to demonstrate how supposedly passive consumers of mass media are aberrant decoders of its messages. Indeed, according to *Invasion from Mars: A*

Study in the Psychology of Panic, by Lazarsfeld's researchers, a quarter of those who heard the show did not realise it was a drama (even though the broadcast had been prefaced with an announcement telling listeners it was indeed a dramatic adaptation), and a majority of those reported that they did not think it was an invasion from Mars, but an attack from Germany – a deluded belief possibly explained by the Munich Crisis over Hitler's annexation of parts of Czechoslovakia the previous month.[27]

Adorno was hired by Lazarsfeld as the project's musical director because he was thought to have a stimulating mind and because his musicological expertise might be useful. But once inside the disused brewery building in Newark, New Jersey, where the project had its headquarters, Adorno was in an alien intellectual environment, one involving empirical research he had never done before and using an analytical framework that he distrusted. He was doubtful that measuring an audience's likes or dislikes of programme material would get to the heart of why they listened to particular broadcasts. He wrote to Lazarsfeld: 'You may be able to measure in percentage terms how many listeners like classical music, how many classical or romantic music and how many prefer verismo opera and so on. But if you wish to include the *reasons* they give for their preferences, it would most likely turn out to be incapable of quantification.'[28] He was especially scandalised by a device called the programme analyser that Lazarsfeld developed with psychologist Frank Stanton. This was a kind of forerunner of the Nielsen audiometer used by TV and radio networks today. Listeners studied by the project were supposed to use it to register their likes or dislikes by pressing a button. 'I reflected that culture was simply the condition that precluded a mentality that tried to measure it', Adorno recalled.[29] It's just as well, you might think, that he didn't live to see how Facebook users are encouraged to like things – be they each others' cakes or Beethoven symphonies – thereby submitting everything to the same scale of judgement.

Adorno's alienation from the project stemmed in part from his insistence on asking interpretive questions beyond the remit of its empirical study. What's more, he baulked at sociological work being useful for commercial purposes, in this case by supplying data that helped programme makers decide what kinds of shows would maximise ratings. This kind of capitalistic spirit was inimical to Adorno's Marxist-inflected sensibility. Instead, he wrote four papers for the project that underlined his distance from Lazarsfeld's conception of social research and of how sociology could function as handmaiden to business. In his long essay 'Music in Radio', for example, he developed a concept he called fetish making in music. He wrote: 'By musical fetish making, we mean that, instead of any direct relationship between the listener and the music itself, there exists only a relationship between the listener and some sort of social or economic value which has been attributed either to the music or to the performers.'[30] In short, music had become a commodity and/or a means of encouraging the purchase of other commodities.

Lazarsfeld, when he read this 160-page paper, furiously annotated it with marginal comments like 'idiotic', 'you never know what he's talking about' and – in words that might have struck a chord with Sidney Hook – 'Dialectics as excuse not to have to think in a disciplined way.' Lazarsfeld also wrote directly to Adorno, damning his essay: 'You pride yourself in attacking other people because they are neurotic and fetishists, but it doesn't occur to you how open you are yourself to such attacks . . . Don't you think it is a perfect fetishism the way you used Latin words all through your text?'[31]

Adorno carried on writing for Lazarsfeld's project regardless, developing his ideas about music as fetishism and about listening to music on the radio as a pseudo-activity, before quitting the project in 1941. He regarded American commercial radio as akin to the totalitarian radio he had heard in Nazi Germany, which, he reflected, had been assigned the task 'of providing good entertainment and diversion' to control the masses. He came to believe that the function of American commercial radio was to distract listeners from political reality while making them passive consumers who chose what was offered to them.

In his 1939 essay 'Plugging Study', for instance, Adorno suggested that music was used in jingles and standardised hit parade tunes in order to produce an emotional reaction in what he called 'the victim'.

'Like the sound of dropping dog food in a bowl, the dog comes running.' Such music wasn't music any more but a formulaic system of sounds that achieved its effect on the listener by devices such as climaxes and repetition. This was a devastating critique not only of how popular music was written, but of the way music was used to sell products. 'Once a formula was successful, the industry plugged the same thing over and over again. The result was to make music into a kind of social cement operating through distraction, displaced wish-fulfillment, and the intensification of passivity.'[32] In this, you might well think, Adorno was prescient: he recognised early the developments that would dominate television, film, commercial theatre, book publishing and the internet in the twentieth and twenty-first centuries, how the endless repetition of successful formulas, such as in sequels or online retailer recommendations based on past consumption patterns, keeps us in a kind of Sisyphean hell, buying and consuming minimally different cultural products.

His biographer Stefan Müller-Doohm suggests that by the end of his association with the project, Adorno had become convinced that the stereotypical production mechanisms of popular culture moulded the expectations of consumers to maximise profits for its shareholders. There was what he called a pre-established harmony between the culture industry and its audiences, such that the latter demand what they are given. True, that pre-established harmony helped capitalism function more efficiently, but the price was that its victims, as Adorno called them, were locked into a degrading relationship of dependency with commodities, consuming things that they did not need, becoming passive, stupid and – no small matter this to the German composer – increasingly unable to properly hear music deserving of the name.[33]

Such was Adorno's first gift to his American hosts – an eviscerating attack on the capitalistic values and the commodified, customised culture he took to dominate the new world in which he lived. More incendiary yet was his suggestion that the United States was not dissimilar in its techniques of mass control to the Germany he had fled into exile to avoid. The idea that there was a parallel between the mass media of Roosevelt's America and Hitler's Germany may have seemed scandalous at the time and may seem so now, but the Frankfurt School was not to abandon that conviction during its exile years in the United States. On the contrary, it was to deepen once they experienced more of the new world.

PART IV:

THE 1940s

10

The Road to Port Bou

'My dears', wrote Adorno to his parents on 13 January 1940. 'We were overjoyed to hear from Leo Frenkel, who called us last night, that you have landed – and immigrated! – successfully. We send you our warmest welcome to the land that may be ugly, and inhabited by drugstores, hot dogs and cars, but is at least safe to some extent at the moment!'[1] Maria and Oscar had arrived in the United States after initially sailing from Hamburg to Cuba. At the time, their son was in New York, serving as Horkheimer's deputy while the director was travelling on the West Coast and planning to work on a project that would trace the psychology and typology of present-day anti-Semitism. Given what had happened to Adorno's parents, the project had personal resonance. Since 1938, the Nazis had stepped up their policy of compelling Jews to emigrate and on November 9 and 10 of that year, had unleashed Kristallnacht, in which Jewish homes, hospitals, synagogues and schools were destroyed, hundreds of Jews killed and tens of thousands arrested to be imprisoned in concentration camps. This rise of Nazi violence against Jews would soon lead to what became known as the Final Solution. In Frankfurt, Adorno's father, nearly seventy, was injured during the ransacking of his office. He and Maria were then arrested and spent several weeks in jail, and his right to dispose of his property was withdrawn. Suffering physical and emotional after-effects, Oscar contracted pneumonia so that the couple could not immediately use their travel permit to sail to Havana; when they did arrive there they were obliged to wait several months before being able to travel to the United States.

Throughout these terrible times, Adorno kept up a charmingly infantile correspondence with his parents, often signing off 'your old child Teddie', before, presumably, returning to his work on the fetish character of music and the study of anti-Semitism. He begins one postcard to his mother 'My dear, faithful Wondrous Hippo Cow . . . may you continue to live with the same contentment, the same security, and the same stubborn superiority as the hippo cow overleaf.'[2] Overleaf was a photograph of Rose the hippopotamus in New York City Zoo. He and his wife Gretel ended their letters to his parents: 'Heartiest kisses from your two horses, Hottilein and Rossilein' or 'Heartiest kisses from Your old Hippo King and his dear Giraffe Gazelle.' It's especially lovely to stumble across such sentimental endearments in Adorno's letters, not just because they're an antidote to the customary asperities of his grown-up writings, but also because they stem from real affection – they are not what one might have expected, the desperately cheery mask of one who can see the abyss opening behind his parents as they travel towards him. 'It seems to me', Adorno wrote to Horkheimer, whose parents Moritz and Babette similarly scrambled to flee anti-Semitic Germany, 'as if all the suffering we are accustomed to thinking of in connection with the proletariat has now been transferred to the Jews in horribly concentrated form.'[3] A decisive moment for critical theory – the suffering of the proletariat, which was ostensibly the purpose behind the foundation of the Institute for Social Research – was being superseded as an object of the Frankfurt School's attentions. Indeed, Adorno and Horkheimer's *Dialectic of Enlightenment* – to which they added the final chapter on anti-Semitism in 1947 – scarcely mentions the proletariat during their analysis of 'why mankind, instead of entering into a truly human condition, is sinking into a new kind of barbarism'.[4]

The safe arrival of Oscar and Maria in the United States was a solace to Adorno, especially as the position of German refugees became more difficult once the Second World War began in September 1939. In France, for instance, German speaking émigrés who lived in Paris were rounded up and interned in a football stadium called Yves du Manoir in Colombes. Walter Benjamin, who had been living in materially perilous exile in the French capital since fleeing Berlin in

1933, was among them. He was not German enough to live in Germany (the Nazis had stripped German Jews of their citizenship), but German enough for the French to incarcerate him for three months in a prison camp near Nevers in Burgundy. On his return to his apartment at 10, Rue Dombasle, Benjamin wrote what turned out to be his last essay, 'Theses on the Philosophy of History', which includes the following words: 'The tradition of the oppressed teaches us that the "state of emergency" in which we live is not the exception but the rule. We must attain to a conception of history that is in keeping with this insight. Then we shall clearly realise that it is our task to bring about a real state of emergency, and this will improve our position in the struggle against Fascism.'[5]

On 13 June 1940, the day before the Germans entered Paris, he and his sister Dora, who had just been freed from an internment camp, fled for Lourdes in unoccupied France.[6] Benjamin had cleared his flat of his most important papers – including the 1938 version of *Berlin Childhood Around 1900*, a version of 'The Work of Art in the Age of Mechanical Reproduction', and his copy of 'Theses on the Philosophy of History' – and entrusted them to Georges Bataille, the writer and librarian at the Bibliothèque Nationale. The remainder were confiscated from his flat by the Gestapo, who had orders to arrest him.

There was no doubt he was in great danger. A few days before, the French Republic had been dissolved and in the ensuing armistice between the Third Reich and Marshal Pétain's collaborationist Vichy Regime, refugees from Hitler's Germany were in danger of being shipped back to Germany. The United States had distributed some emergency visas through its consulates in unoccupied France to save Nazis' political opponents – a category of refugee at particular risk if they were returned to their homeland. Benjamin's fellow German Jewish intellectual Hannah Arendt, at the time also on the run from the Nazis and their French lackeys, would later write that this category of refugees 'never included the mass of unpolitical Jews who later turned out to be the most endangered of all'. Benjamin was equivocal about taking up one of these visas. 'How was he to live without a library, how could he earn a living without the extensive collection of quotations and excerpts among his manuscripts?' Arendt wrote.

'Besides, nothing drew him to America where, as he used to say, people would probably find no other use for him than to cart him up and down the country to exhibit him as the "last European".'[7]

In Lourdes, a market town in the foothills of the Pyrenees that has become the centre for Roman Catholic pilgrimage and miraculous cures ever since Bernadette Soubirous saw visions of the Virgin Mary in 1858, Dora and Walter suffered. She was enduring ankylosing spondylitis and advanced arteriosclerosis, while his heart condition was made worse by the elevation and, doubtless, by the threat of falling into the hands of the Nazis. It was a very justifiable fear, we realise with hindsight: their brother Georg was killed at the Mauthausen-Gusen concentration camp in 1942. Walter's chief consolation during those two months in Lourdes was reading Stendhal's *The Red and the Black*.

Benjamin knew little of the work that the exiled Frankfurt scholars in New York were doing to try to bring him to safety in America; nor were they sure of his whereabouts – letters and postcards from them arrived at his flat in Paris after the Gestapo had raided it. But they tried to make arrangements for him on the other side of the Atlantic. At one point, thanks to Horkheimer's efforts, Benjamin was to become a professor at the university in Havana, loaned there by the Institute.

After two months in Lourdes, Benjamin learned that the Institute had secured a visa for him to enter the United States. It was to be issued to him at the US consulate in Marseilles. He headed off, leaving his sister in Lourdes and to her fate (she was later to hole up in a farm and the following year made it to neutral Switzerland). In Marseilles, he returned in horrible circumstances to a city that, like Naples or Moscow, he loved for its collectivist chutzpah, its very unGerman vibrancy. At the start of the 1930s, he had published two essays hymning the city, one entitled 'Marsellies'[8] and the other, 'Hashish in Marseilles', an endearingly crazed description of a happy crawl through its bars and cafés 'in the ecstasy of trance'.[9]

But the Marseilles he encountered in August 1940 was very different, teeming with refugees terrified of falling into the Gestapo's clutches, and his experiences there were anything but ecstatic. At the US consulate, he was issued with an entry visa for the US and transit visas for Spain and Portugal. He plunged into depression, contemplating all kinds of mad schemes to get out of Europe – one of which involved him and a friend bribing their way onto a freighter bound for Ceylon disguised as French sailors.

In mid September he and two refugee acquaintances from Marseilles decided, because they had no prospect of leaving France legally, to travel to the French countryside near the Spanish border and try to cross the Pyrenees on foot. His plan was to go through the ostensibly neutral, though fascist Spain to Lisbon and sail from the Portuguese capital to the US. In New York, in expectation of his arrival, Theodor and Gretel Adorno were looking for a place for Benjamin to live. Meanwhile, the odds of him and the other refugees even reaching Spain had diminished because Vichy officials were closely guarding a direct route to their Spanish destination, Port Bou. So, on September 25, a little group of refugees including Benjamin, started over the mountains following a rugged, remote trail. One of the group, the political activist Lisa Fittko, was worried that the poor state of Benjamin's heart would make it a risky crossing, but he insisted on coming along. Throughout the journey, he would walk for ten minutes, and stop for one minute to catch his breath – all the time clutching a black attaché case that, he told Fittko, contained a new manuscript that was 'more important than I am'.[10] But that wasn't all he was carrying: the writer and fellow refugee Arthur Koestler remembered that Benjamin had left Marseilles with enough morphine to 'kill a horse' (indeed, Koestler himself tried and failed to take his own life with morphine around this time). When, on a hot September day they were in sight of Port Bou, one member of Benjamin's party noted that he looked on the point of having a heart attack. 'We ran in all directions in search of water to help the sick man', recalled Carina Birman.[11]

Worse was to come. When the refugees reached Port Bou and reported to the customs office to get their papers stamped to travel across Spain, they were told that the Spanish government had recently closed the border to illegal refugees from France. As a result, the party faced being returned to French soil – probably to face internment then transportation to, and murder in, a German concentration camp. They were put under guard at a hotel, where Benjamin, in despair, wrote a suicide note that he gave to one of his fellow refugees, Henny Gurland. Gurland said later that she thought it necessary to destroy the note, but reconstructed it from memory: 'In a situation presenting no way out, I have no other choice but to make an end of it. It is in a small village in the Pyrenees, where no one knows me, that my life will come to a close.'[12] Later that night he is believed to have taken the morphine he had brought from Marseilles. His death certificate, though, says that his cause of death was a cerebral haemorrhage – perhaps, Benjamin's biographers speculate, the Spanish doctor was bribed by the other refugees to say that in order to spare them a scandal that would have made their return to France more likely. The date on the certificate is September 26. The following day the border reopened. Had he not taken the morphine, he would have been allowed safe transit across Spain and thence to America.

When they heard the news of Benjamin's death, Theodor and Gretel Adorno were plunged into despair over what they took to be their friend's suicide. If only, Adorno wrote to Gershom Scholem, Benjamin could have held out for twelve more hours he would have been saved. 'It is completely incomprehensible – as if he had been gripped by a stupor and wished to obliterate himself even though he had already been rescued.'[13]

Daring theories have, since Benjamin's death, rushed in to fill that gap in comprehensibility. Among them is one that suggests Stalin's henchmen killed Benjamin. In *The Mysterious Death of Walter Benjamin*, Stephen Schwartz, a Montenegro-based journalist, wrote that Stalinist agents were operating in the south of France and northern Spain during the early years of the war, when the Nazi–Soviet pact was still in operation. The result was that two of the most powerful secret police forces in Europe were working in close co-operation. 'Unquestionably the Soviet secret police was operating a chokepoint in southern France – sifting through the wave of fleeing exiles for targets of liquidation', wrote Schwartz. 'Walter Benjamin walked straight into this maelstrom of evil. And, although his acolytes have chosen to ignore it, he was eminently qualified to appear on a Soviet hit list.' Others whom Schwartz reckoned fell prey to what he calls the Stalinist 'killerati' included the German communist Willi Münzenberg, that former spy for Stalin, who in Paris had become a leader of the German émigré anti-fascist and anti-Stalinist community until forced, like Benjamin, to flee the Nazi advance. But Münzenberg was arrested and imprisoned at an internment camp. He was later freed but found hanging from a tree near Grenoble, murdered, Schwartz claims, by a Soviet agent masquerading as a fellow jailed socialist. Schwartz argues that the man who knew most about Russian disinformation operations was airbrushed from history.[14]

But why would Benjamin attract similar attentions from Stalin's henchmen? Schwartz notes that a few months before he died, Benjamin wrote his 'Theses on the Philosophy of History', one of the most insightful analyses of the failure of Marxism ever produced. He died at a time when many former Soviet loyalists were becoming disillusioned with Moscow because of the Hitler–Stalin pact. In response Stalinist agents, often recruited from socialist intellectuals, were carrying out assassinations. Benjamin had, perhaps unwittingly, associated with Comintern agents. Schwartz wrote: 'Benjamin was part of a subculture honeycombed with dangerous people – it was known not to be safe.' In the late thirties, argues Schwartz, Stalinist agents in Spain were assigned to track down German-speaking anti-Stalinists and torture them into making false confessions. 'Moscow wanted a parallel, outside Soviet borders, to the infamous purge trials.' Perhaps, but Walter Benjamin was hardly a threat to Soviet communist orthodoxy akin to Leon Trotsky, murdered in Mexican exile one month before Benjamin's death. Unlike other victims of Stalin's killerati, Benjamin was never a member of the Communist Party. Nor was his eccentric brand of theologically and mystically infused Marxism (which even his friend Brecht called 'ghastly') a real and present threat to Stalin. Moreover, Schwartz offers no compelling account of precisely how Stalin's henchmen were supposed to have murdered him.

But if the murder theory seems dubious, so, argues Schwartz, is the suicide theory. Documentation by a Spanish judge shows no evidence of the presence of drugs. It is by no means certain that the doctor's report that a cerebral haemorrhage, perhaps aggravated by the exertion of crossing the Pyrenees, killed him, is false. One more mystery surrounding Walter Benjamin's death remains. What was in the black attaché case and what happened to it? One story is that the case was entrusted to a fellow refugee who lost it on a train from Barcelona to Madrid. But what was the manuscript? A completed version of *The Arcades Project*? A new version of the book on Baudelaire? His biographers discount these possibilities, arguing that his health was so bad he worked only sporadically in the last year of his life so such huge literary tasks would have been beyond him. Or perhaps it was a refined version of his last essay, 'Theses on the Philosophy of History'. Again, his biographers Eiland and Jennings doubt this, arguing that Benjamin would not have attributed such significance to a new version unless it differed markedly from the copies he'd entrusted to Hannah Arendt in Marseilles. Of course, that is hardly a decisive argument; perhaps it was precisely that: a revision made on the run of an essay already shot through with hopes for redemption. But even if so, we will most likely never know what it contained.

Instead, we have the version of the essay that Hannah Arendt, luckier than Benjamin, was able to give to Adorno in New York and which was published in 1942 by the Institute. That version had an electrifying effect on Adorno and Horkheimer. For Adorno it chimed with his own way of thinking, 'above all to the idea of history as a permanent catastrophe, the criticism of progress, the domination of nature and the attitude to culture'.[15] It's worth pointing out, though, that the essay has also been taken to be a rejection of history as a process of continuous progress, and in particular a gnomic critique of Benjamin's contemporaries, the vulgar Marxist ideologues of the Second and Third Internationals. They, Benjamin may well have been suggesting, albeit obliquely, took historical materialism as asserting that there is continuum of progress towards a benign resolution, namely a communist utopia. Certainly, the angel of history whom Benjamin invokes in thesis IX is a figure who inverts such crude historical materialism: for the angel, the past is not a chain of events but a single catastrophe and the task of any justifiable historical materialism is not to predict revolutionary future or communist utopia, but to attend to and thereby redeem the sufferings of the past.

Dialectic of Enlightenment, the great book that Adorno and Horkheimer would write in their Californian exile, could be read as an extrapolation of the eighteen theses Benjamin proposed in this essay, his intellectual testament. Today, written in both Catalan and German on his tombstone in Port Bou is a quotation from thesis VII of that essay: 'There is no document of civilisation which is not at the same time a document of barbarism.'[16]

11

In League with the Devil

Max Horkheimer moved from New York to California in April 1941 on the advice of his doctor who recommended a more temperate climate to improve his heart condition. In November that year, Adorno followed him to the West Coast. Max and his wife Maidon had enough money to build a bungalow in Pacific Palisades in the affluent westside of Los Angeles. It was spacious enough also to accommodate Max's childhood friend (and later the dedicatee of *Dialectic of Enlightenment*) Friedrich Pollock, while Theodor and Gretel Adorno moved into a rented duplex in the similarly prosperous Brentwood that was large enough to house them and Adorno's grand piano.

They were joining a growing German exile community whose other members included Thomas Mann, Bertolt Brecht, Arnold Schoenberg, Fritz Lang and Hanns Eisler, an outpost of German civilisation on the other side of the world from their then barbarous homeland. Brecht, for his part, wrote poetry describing his new home as hell:

> On thinking about hell, I gather
> My brother Shelley found it was a place
> Much like the city of London. I
> Who live in Los Angeles and not in London
> Find, on thinking about hell, that it must be
> Still more like Los Angeles.

In this Californian hell, Brecht reflected, the luxuriant gardens withered if not nourished with expensive water, the fruit had no odour or flavour, and the houses were built for happy people, 'therefore standing empty / even when lived in'.

> The houses in Hell, too, are not all ugly.
> But the fear of being thrown on the street
> Wears down the inhabitants of the villas no less
> than
> The inhabitants of shanty towns.[1]

Through the kind of modernist disruption that Adorno and Horkheimer liked, Brecht's poems translated the utopian images of the city of angels and thereby produced an allegory of a modernist city that was ugly and uncharitable.[2] This kind of disruptive perspective was a feature of modernist art, as the critic Raymond Williams pointed out in his essay 'When Was Modernism?' The international anti-bourgeois modernist artists (Apollinaire, Beckett, Joyce, Ionescu, for example) who thrived in London, Paris, Berlin, Vienna and New York, now thrived in Los Angeles. Brecht would write that 'emigration is the best school of dialectics':[3] it certainly catalysed his art, and the writings of Adorno and Horkheimer.

In this city, though, Brecht was obliged, or so he suggested, to prostitute himself, as perhaps did other German exiles who worked for Hollywood's culture industry:

> Every morning, to earn my bread,
> I go to the market where lies are bought.
> Hopefully I take my place among the sellers.[4]

It was in this putative marketplace for lies, this supposed hell where everyone was compelled to be in league with the devil, that Brecht was to write his great play *Galileo*, Stravinsky wrote *The Rake's Progress*, Thomas Mann completed *Doctor Faustus*, and where Orson Welles made *Citizen Kane*.

Los Angeles became the Frankfurt School emigrants' last, distant refuge from Nazi persecution. And yet they couldn't help comparing the Third Reich to that other oppressive empire on their doorsteps,

Hollywood. In this, they were with ruthless consistency following Walter Benjamin's dictum about civilisation. In 1941, arguably, there were some similarities between the Third Reich and what the historian of Hollywood Otto Friedrich called that 'great empire built out of dreams of glamour, dreams of beauty, wealth, and success'.[5] By this time, each was at the summit of its influence and self-regard, and few in that year would have dared to predict either's decline and fall.

The Third Reich had continental Europe pinned under its jackboot, while Britain had been effectively marginalised, and the Soviet Red Army apparently neutralised as a result of the Nazis' Operation Barbarossa, launched in June 1941. By December Japan had entered the war as Hitler's ally, while Roosevelt's United States was still three years away from putting boots on the ground in Europe. In such circumstances, the Nazis imagined themselves invincible conquering heroes. 'It is no exaggeration to say that the Russian campaign has been won in fourteen days', wrote General Franz Halder, chief of the Oberkommando des Heeres, or supreme high command of the German Army, in his diary on July 3.[6] When Japan allied itself with Nazi Germany in December 1941, Hitler waved the communique bringing this news in his bunker and dared to suppose that the Third Reich was unvanquishable. 'Now it is impossible for us to lose the war', he said, 'for we have an ally who has not been vanquished for 3,000 years.'[7] The decisive blow against Hitler, struck at the battle of Stalingrad, did not come until the winter of 1942–43.

Otto Friedrich argued that the leading Hollywood moviemakers in this era, similarly, 'could with some justification regard themselves as conquering heroes'.[8] By 1939, Hollywood was America's eleventh-largest business, producing 400 movies a year, drawing 50 million Americans to cinemas each week, and grossing nearly $700 million annually. It was the golden age of Hollywood thanks to movies such as *Gone with the Wind*, *Ninotchka*, *Wuthering Heights*, *The Wizard of Oz*, *The Maltese Falcon* and *Citizen Kane*, as well as stars and directors like Bogart, Bacall, Bergman, Hitchcock and Welles. But, like the Third Reich after Stalingrad, Hollywood was living on borrowed time. 'Hollywood's like Egypt. Full of crumbling pyramids. It'll never come back', said David O. Selznick, the producer of *Gone with the*

Wind and *Rebecca*, which won best picture Oscars in 1939 and 1940 respectively. 'It'll just keep on crumbling until finally the wind blows the last studio prop across the sands.'[9] Not quite: while the Third Reich collapsed in 1945, Hollywood has teetered on. But a decade after 1941, its studios were losing money, many of its celebrities were accused of being communists during McCarthyite witchhunts that also embroiled German exiles like Brecht, and its audiences were turning to television.

It was Hollywood's values, as much as Hitler's, that the Frankfurt School challenged in their Californian exile. But isn't it ludicrous to compare the Third Reich to Hollywood? Even if one could argue that that German civilisation had led to the barbarism that was the Third Reich, it seems obscene to suggest that every civilisation has the stamp of the jackboot on its face, and intellectual barbarism to suggest that the evils of Hitler's Germany had their parallels in Roosevelt's America. And yet, once Horkheimer and Adorno settled near Hollywood, this was their suggestion. They started writing *Dialectic of Enlightenment* in 1941 in a spirit of iconoclasm rather than the pragmatic prostitution Brecht satirised. They knew that hardly anybody was listening to their messages.[10] That iconoclasm was intensified by the disappointment of the Frankfurt School's plans for an alliance with West Coast academia. Horkheimer's hope had been to find a university in California with which the Institute for Social Research could have an affiliation in the same way it had with Columbia University in New York. Horkheimer suggested that this western branch of the Institute could offer lectures and seminars on philosophy and on the history of sociology since Comte, and offered $8,000 to support the venture. But Robert G. Sproul, president of the University of California, turned down the idea, because Horkheimer sought more autonomy than Sproul was prepared to tolerate. Some other members of the Frankfurt School including Löwenthal, Marcuse and Pollock nonetheless joined Horkheimer and Adorno in California.

This rejection made the Frankfurt School feel more isolated in exile. It may well also have sharpened their disdain for the American culture in which they lived and deepened their attachment to the European one they had lost. Adorno, for instance, had been having a recurring dream throughout his emigration years. He was sitting at his mother's desk in the living room in the family home in Oberrad, a suburb of Frankfurt, looking out into the garden – in some variations of the dream, after Hitler had come to power. He wrote: 'Autumn, overcast with tragic clouds, an unending melancholy, but a pervasive scent over everything. Everywhere vases with autumn flowers.'[11] He dreamed he was writing the 1932 essay 'On the Social Situation of Music', but during the dream that manuscript mutated into the one he was writing in Los Angeles, *The Philosophy of Modern Music*. He was clear what the dream meant: 'Its true meaning is evidently the retrieval of the European life that has been lost.' Adorno, like other German exiles in this wartime Los Angeles colony that has been called Weimar on the Pacific (Thomas Mann in particular, as we will see), longed for that European life even as it was dying. Their homesickness was most intense because there seemed to be no direction home.

In *Dialectic of Enlightenment*, Adorno and Horkheimer dared to make breathtakingly explicit parallels between Hollywood and Hitler's Germany. They described a scene at the end of Charlie Chaplin's 1940 satire on Hitler, *The Great Dictator*. 'The ears of corn blowing in the wind at the end . . . give the lie to the anti-Fascist plea for freedom. They are like the blond hair of the girl whose camp life is photographed by the Nazi film company in the summer breeze.'[12] Given that Chaplin had paid for the film himself, since in 1939 Hollywood studios were worried about the costs of provoking a German boycott, this might seem an unfair comparison. And in any case, if the message of Chaplin's film was anti-fascist and the Nazi one pro-fascist, what was the force of dwelling on the alleged similarities of imagery? But Horkheimer and Adorno were making a more profound point: 'Nature is viewed by the mechanism of social domination as a healthy contrast to society, and is therefore denatured. Pictures showing green trees, a blue sky and moving clouds make these aspects of nature into so many cryptograms for factory chimneys and service stations.'[13]

The writing here is somewhat cryptic, but the suggestion is that both UFA, the Nazi film studio, and Hollywood studios, used images of nature along with other stereotypical images of human life to propagandise for the status quo – be that the Third Reich or American capitalism. Hence the invocation of natural, repetitive cycles that seem eternal, and the use of stereotypical imagery: 'What repeats itself is healthy, like the natural or industrial cycle. The same babies grin eternally out of the magazines; the jazz machine will pound away for ever . . . This serves to confirm the immutability of circumstances.'[14] Such natural cycles and such stereotypes of good health needed to be invoked in Hollywood cinema in order to make the very thing that was unnatural – the existing system of monopoly capitalism in the US, with all its manifold means of domination and cruelty – seem not just appealing, but precisely what it was not: natural (and therefore unobjectionable, eternal).

Consider, for instance, Donald Duck. Once, such cartoon characters were 'exponents of fantasy as opposed to rationalism', wrote Adorno and Horkheimer. Now they had become instruments of social domination. 'They hammer into every brain the old lesson that continuous friction, the breaking down of all individual resistance, is the condition of life in this society. Donald Duck in the cartoons and the unfortunate in real life get their thrashing so that the audience can learn to take their own punishment.'[15] They reproduce the cruelty of real life so that we can adjust to it. But, one might object, while Disney's Donald Duck (and presumably Warner Brothers' Daffy Duck – there's probably a doctoral thesis on why Hollywood had a thing about hurting ducks) may serve such a purpose, surely the drama of MGM's Tom and Jerry, or Roadrunner's desert contests with Wile E. Coyote, do not. Surely they involve not just the little guy standing up heroically to an oppressive tyrant, but a reversal of the pecking order of nature, turning hunter into hunted, predator into road kill. Perhaps such cartoons are emblematic of the Hegelian master–slave dialectic, and suggest the instability of the existing power relations rather than confirming them. But Horkheimer and Adorno didn't write about those cartoons: most likely they would have seen them as fantastical projections of the downtrodden and dispossessed who could not realise those fantasies in real life.

Or consider laughter. The ideological function of laughter is like the function of all entertainment, Horkheimer and Adorno argued, namely to produce agreement.

Fun is a medicinal bath. The pleasure industry never fails to prescribe it. It makes laughter the instrument of the fraud practised on happiness. Moments of happiness are without laughter; only operettas and films portray sex to the accompaniment of resounding laughter. In the false society laughter is a disease which has attacked happiness and is drawing it into its worthless totality.[16]

And what is that totality? A fiendish audience of individuals sitting in the movie house, laughing at the comedies of Preston Sturges, Howard Hawks and the Marx Brothers, in a form of barbaric self-assertion. They wrote: 'Such a laughing audience is a parody of humanity. Its members are all moods, all dedicated to the pleasure of being ready for anything at the expense of everyone else. Their harmony is a caricature of solidarity.' The laughter induced by the culture industry was a Schadenfreude that takes pleasure in and only in others' misfortunes. Its hateful noise was a parody of another kind of laughter that was programmatically silenced in these circumstances, a better laughter, better because it was conciliatory. The next time I laugh at that scene in the Marx Brothers' 1939 film *At the Circus*, in which the unfortunate, plump dowager howls 'Get me out of this cannon!' and Harpo futilely rushes to her aid yelling 'I'm coming Mrs Dukesberry!' (for what is my laughter but sadomasochism? And what is the cannon but an allegory of repressive desublimation, and what is Mrs Dukesberry's fate but emblematic of the premature ejaculations that Adorno and Horkheimer found elsewhere in the culture industry?), I will know that I am part of the problem, that I'm enjoying the wrong kind of Marxism.

And yet Adorno and Horkheimer had a point: the screwball comedy of, say, Howard Hawks' 1940 film *His Girl Friday*, with its machine-gun repartee between editor Cary Grant and hot-shot hack Rosalind Russell, is nothing if not unremitting, while outside the hysteria of their jailhouse press room is the prison yard, where they're building a scaffold for a hanging. It's as if Hawks dare not let the laughter stop, for if he did, we would drop into the abyss. Adorno, in the kind of chiasmus he was fond of (in *Minima Moralia*, which he wrote mostly in American exile, he has a section called 'The Health Unto

Death', inverting the title of Kierkegaard's *The Sickness Unto Death*), would probably have called the film *The Laughter Unto Death*. If Horkheimer and Adorno had programmed a movie season called 'Barbaric Laughter', *His Girl Friday* would have been on it.

Given Horkheimer and Adorno's evisceration of Hollywood and the culture industry, it is surprising to discover that in exile they did not associate just with German exiles but with the very targets of their attacks. Adorno, for instance, became acquainted with Charlie Chaplin, though it isn't clear whether the latter ever read Adorno and Horkheimer's disobliging remarks about his film *The Great Dictator* in *Dialectic of Enlightenment*. In 1947, Adorno and Gretel attended a private screening of Chaplin's new film *Monsieur Verdoux*, and, following dinner, Adorno played selections from Verdi, Mozart and Wagner operas while Chaplin parodically interpreted the music. At another party, in a Malibu villa at which he and Chaplin were guests, Adorno tried to shake hands with the actor Harold Russell, who played a wounded veteran in the 1946 film *The Best Years of Our Lives*. Russell had lost his hand in the war and had it replaced with what Adorno described as an 'artificial claw'. 'When I shook his right hand and it responded to the pressure', Adorno recalled, 'I was very taken aback, but realising at once that I should not let Russell see my reaction under any circumstances, I instantly transformed the shocked expression on my face into a winning grimace which must have looked even more shocking.' As soon as Russell left the party, Chaplin started mimicking the scene. 'So close to horror is the laughter that he provoked', wrote Adorno, 'and only from close up can it acquire its legitimacy and its salutary aspect.'[17] It's not clear from this whether the laughter Chaplin provoked was the bad, derisive kind Adorno and Horkheimer excoriated in *Dialectic of Enlightenment*, or the good, conciliatory sort. Let's hope the latter.

But Adorno and Horkheimer's point remains. Nazi propaganda minister Josef Goebbels was at least explicit about what he was doing in propagandising for the Third Reich. So was Andrei Zhdanov, Stalin's one-time cultural commissar, whose 1946 doctrine known as *zhdanovshchina* required that Soviet artists and writers conform to the party line or risk persecution. In the absence of any explicit acknowledgement on the part of Hollywood and the rest of the American culture industry that they were instruments of domination, it fell to the Frankfurt School to expose them. Perhaps it's unfortunate that Chaplin's anti-fascist propaganda movie got caught in the same crosshairs as Leni Riefenstahl's films at this historical juncture, but no one could doubt their close reading of the movies.

It's unfair, though, to treat the exiled Frankfurt scholars as European snobs who came to America and merely loathed what they saw and heard. Certainly, they shared the perspective of fellow Marxist heretic Ernst Bloch who called America 'a cul-de-sac lit by neon lights'.[18] They argued that US society was hideously bent on the pursuit of individualised happiness – and the result was the epitome of shallow and inauthentic surfaces and insincerity. But their critique of that society and the culture industry they argued served to uphold it was not based on a defence of European civilisation against American barbarism, or a championing of high art over low culture, for all that their occasionally glib dismissals of the products of the latter may have made it seem that way. Rather, what they hated about putatively popular culture was that it was not democratic and that its subliminal message was one of conformism and repression.

At the end of the eighteenth century, Kant had argued that art exhibited 'purposiveness without purpose'. In the mid twentieth century, Adorno and Horkheimer proposed that popular culture involved 'purposelessness for a purpose' and suggested that that purpose was dictated by the market. Mass culture seemed to promise liberation, but the seeming spontaneity of jazz or the peek-a-boo sexual display of movie stars, for Horkheimer and Adorno, concealed its opposite. Marcuse would later use the phrase 'repressive desublimation' to account for the seeming liberation in sexual attitudes, fashions and music in the purportedly swinging sixties. The germ of that idea was already in *Dialectic of Enlightenment*. What Malcolm X would say of African-Americans being duped by the American Democratic Party – 'I say you've been misled, you've been had, you've been took' – was what Adorno and Horkheimer took to be the true impact of popular music and movies on their consumers. And the cultural changes that took place later in the century as popular art,

TV, music and cinema took a greater hold on the masses might well seem to bear out their arguments. In his 1957 book *The Uses of Literacy*, for instance, the English cultural studies theorist Richard Hoggart wrote that in Britain during the 1950s, the traditional working-class culture he discerned in popular fiction, songs and newspapers that he thought was supportive, neighbourly and sentimental, was being eroded. Thanks to affluence, it was being replaced, Hoggart argued, by gangster fiction and sex-and-violence novels that fostered moral emptiness, and glossy magazines and pop songs that lured consumers into 'a candyfloss world'.[19]

Adorno and Horkheimer would have recognised Hoggart's description of this candyfloss world, seeing in it the extension of the culture industry's remit; they might well too have seen that the eroded working-class culture had represented an intolerable threat to an authoritarian society that replaced spontaneous popular culture with mass culture organised from above. If they had lived to see *X Factor* or read *Grazia* magazine, they would have seen its stranglehold intensifying even further.

The Frankfurt School's attack on popular culture, then, was from a radical rather than a conservative position. Benjamin had already distanced himself from writers like Aldous Huxley for their reactionary jeremiads against popular culture. That said, they were nostalgic for pre-fascist Germany and its cultural products, which Horkheimer and Adorno took to have 'a degree of independence from the power of the market', an independence increasingly absent in what they called the more advanced industrial nations, preeminently the United States.[20] Nor were they straightforwardly defending a civilised high art canon against its barbarous popular opposite. Marcuse, in his 1937 essay 'The Affirmative Character of Culture', had argued that bourgeois culture in the nineteenth century had sought higher experience in withdrawing from the world into a more refined spiritual world. But segregating cultural life from its material base, he thought, served to reconcile its consumers to the inequalities in the latter. Adorno and Horkheimer shared Marcuse's contempt for what he had called 'affirmative culture'. What they championed was neither high art nor low culture, but art that exposed the contradictions of capitalist society rather than smoothing them over – in short, modernist art. That is why, for instance, Adorno attacked Stravinsky's neoclassical period in his 1949 book *Philosophy of Modern Music* as 'universal necrophilia'. He argued that in such works as *Oedipus Rex* and the *Symphony of Psalms*, Stravinsky's incessant quotation of earlier music 'is the very essence of everything approved and certified in the two hundred years of bourgeois music . . . The authoritarian character of today is, without exception, conformist; likewise the authoritarian claim of Stravinsky's music is extended totally and completely to conformism.'[21] In that book, Adorno once more championed Schoenberg over Stravinsky (both of whom were at this time his neighbours in Los Angeles) for moving on from his twelve-tone system, which had become a cage from which Schoenberg exploded, like Beethoven, into a late style.

This championing of modernist art has looked to Adorno and Horkheimer's later critics like elitism. As J. M. Bernstein points out in his introduction to Adorno's *The Culture Industry*, it looked as though they were defending an esoteric modernist art against a culture available to all.[22] Thirty years later, the new cultural theorists of postmodernism disdained what they took to be the elitism of modernists such as Adorno and Horkheimer. But what they had defended was not elitist art per se, but art that refused to be affirmative – as Adorno would put it in his posthumously published book *Aesthetic Theory* – the idea of art as the only remaining medium expressing the truth of suffering 'in an age of indescribable horror'. What some called esoteric modernist art was for them the only art that could express that suffering, could dare to be negative. It was defined in opposition to what is, to the powers that be: it was, as Adorno put it, a *promesse du bonheur*, a vision of something other than the affirmative culture.

What the Frankfurt School did not have the temperament to do was consider popular culture as a site of resistance against affirmative culture. In Frankfurt's twin city of Birmingham, though, another group of left-wing intellectuals, including Richard Hoggart and Stuart Hall, would do just that. The Birmingham Centre of Cultural Studies, established in 1964, while following the Frankfurt School in recognising that culture was a key instrument of political and social control, appreciated how the culture industry could be aberrantly, even rebelliously, decoded by its mass consumers and that popular sub-cultures might subvert the culture industry in a form of immanent critique. Adorno could not hear in jazz the truth of suffering, nor (one suspects) would he have enjoyed punk rock or hip hop – but in those forms of music and other kinds of popular culture, Birmingham's cultural studies scholars found a critical negation of the existing social order. Indeed, the modernist canon became an esoteric retreat for a cultural elite and thus akin to bourgeois high art – the opposite of what Adorno had hoped for it. The Sex Pistols' 'God Save the Queen', Public Enemy's 'Fight the Power', NWA's 'Fuck tha Police' or Sleaford Mods' 'Jolly Fucker' more effectively dared to negate what Chuck D called the powers that be.

IN CALIFORNIA, Adorno and Horkheimer had more than Hollywood and the culture industry in their sights. *Dialectic of Enlightenment* turned the Hegelian and Marxist notion of history as the unfolding of human freedom on its head. For Adorno and Horkheimer, Enlightenment values themselves had become a prison rather than a means of escaping prison. They were not automatically progressive but were undermined by our enslavement within the totality of capitalist social relations. This was what was incendiary about their book: while eighteenth-century Enlightenment thinkers such as Rousseau, Voltaire, Diderot and Kant took the process of enlightenment to involve liberating mankind from nature and thereby led to human freedom and flourishing (Kant defined enlightenment as 'the human being's emergence from self-incurred immaturity'), Horkheimer and Adorno took it to be a process that imprisons mankind – as reason is used instrumentally to create ever more pervasive networks of administrative discipline and control. For them, the founding father of the scientific mindset was Francis Bacon, the seventeenth-century English thinker, who argued that technological innovations had made man 'master of nature'. It was Bacon, they argued, who eulogised what Max Weber would later call the 'disenchantment of the world'. Bacon cited the printing press, artillery and the compass as the key innovations that changed the world – the first changed learning, the second changed war, the third made possible oceanic travel and so man's domination of the globe.

Mankind sundered itself from nature in order to dominate it – to make it and other men calculable, substitutable and, above all, exploit-able. Putatively value-free science and capitalism walk hand in hand, calculating the world the better to exploit both it and humans. In the process nature is denatured and we are dehumanised. 'Nature becomes', Adorno and Horkheimer wrote, 'what can be registered mathematically; even what cannot be assimilated, the insoluble and irrational, is fenced in by mathematical theorems. In the pre-emptive identification of the thoroughly mathematised world with truth, enlightenment believes itself safe from the return of the mythical. It equates thought with mathematics.'[23] The philosophical villains of this piece are Parmenides and Bertrand Russell, since both the pre-So-cratic philosopher and the father of contemporary logical analysis were fixated on reducing everything to abstract quantities and ulti-mately to the One – a fixation that seems rational but that could equally well be called utterly irrational. Just as bourgeois society is ruled by equivalence, and capitalism unthinkable without the exchange principle that strips human labour and the fruits of that labour of anything but its equivalence to other commodities, so Parmenides and Russell render everything that cannot be reduced to numbers as illusion, to be written off as mere literature. 'The destruc-tion of gods and qualities alike is insisted upon.'[24]

It's a shame that Russell came under fire here, not least because the Englishman, who had taught at the University of California from 1939 to 1940 and who was barred from teaching at the College of the City of New York in 1941 because of his radical views on women and the family, presumably didn't think the values for which he had fought – such as pacifism, women's suffrage, or, later, nuclear disar-mament – could be written off as mere literature.[25] At a moment when some in New York were calling for Russell to be 'tarred and feathered and thrown out of our country', merely because he had dared years before to suggest that adultery may not always be a bad thing, he might have warranted a more sympathetic approach from two philosophers who spent much of their book bemoaning the dearth of human solidarity. Certainly Russell's commitment to formal logic and the power of logical analysis was inimical to the German dialecticians, but to take him and his philosophy as upholders of scientific orthodoxy and therefore social oppression seems unfair.

The anthropocentric hubris and urge to dominate, though, that Adorno and Horkheimer took to be characteristic of the Enlightenment involved self-alienation. Consider, by way of analogy, they suggested, what happened to Odysseus and his men when they tried to avoid the lure of the Sirens and not fall prey to their lethal song.[26] They took this incident in Canto 12 of Homer's *Odyssey* to be filled with symbolic meaning, and one can understand why it was so resonant for them – like Odysseus' sailors they were wanderers encountering strange lands miles and years from home. The sailors stop their ears with wax so they can continue the work of rowing their ship, just as modern labourers discipline themselves, repressing their sensuality and desire for gratification in order to keep working. As for their master, he can hear the songs of the Sirens but has been tied to the mast, so he cannot respond to temptation. Adorno and Horkheimer argued that this attempt to break the feared power of nature (symbolised here by the Sirens) led thought 'all the more deeply into enslavement. Hence the course of European civilisation.' Both the sailors and Odysseus have liberated themselves from the constraints of nature through self-discipline, and in so doing have used human reason instrumentally to break the coercive power of nature and thus dominate it. But the human subject was thereby reduced 'to the nodal point of conventional responses and modes of operation expected of him'. The process of individuation took place therefore 'at the expense of individuality'. They took this mythical incident dramatised by Homer in the eighth century BC as an allegory of how the bourgeois subject of the Enlightenment domesticated, not just nature, but itself. Odysseus is the first bourgeois hero – one whose treacherous journey involves risks that justify profits, one who uses reason, trickery, self-renunciation and self-discipline to survive. What Odysseus started, the technological innovations eulogised by Francis Bacon continued in the seventeenth century – namely, the domination of nature and the self-alienation of the human subject.

In another excursus in *Dialectic of Enlightenment* called 'Juliette: or Enlightenment and Morals', Adorno and Horkheimer argue that a completely secularised scientific knowledge refuses to recognise any moral limits.[27] This is the terrifying thought that haunted writers like Nietzsche and de Sade. For Nietzsche, if God was dead anything was permitted; for de Sade, the cruel subjugation of women, the denial of their subjectivity, their reduction to sex objects, was the perverse corollary of the Enlightenment's mastery of nature. Adorno and Horkheimer argued that Kant's attempt to ground morality in practical rationality, the application of reason, served to extend the calculating, instrumental, formal rationality that involves the domination of nature and mankind. De Sade, then, is the barbarous dark side to Kant's civilised project of enlightenment.

The historian of the Frankfurt School Martin Jay contended that this instrumental rationality led to the horrors of the twentieth century. 'In fact', he argued, 'the Enlightenment's sadism towards the "weaker sex" anticipated the later destruction of the Jews – both women and Jews were identified with nature as objects of domination.'[28] But while the Frankfurt School, understandably, spent a lot of time writing and thinking about the oppression of Jews, they spent hardly any on the oppression of women. In part that's because there were no eminent women in the Frankfurt School – odd for a putatively radical group of thinkers in the twentieth century. Contrast critical theory at this point with the new and related psychoanalytical theory, where women such as Melanie Klein and Anna Freud made substantial and distinctive contributions. That's not to say that the Frankfurt School was ignorant about the oppression of women. In *Minima Moralia*, for instance, Adorno wrote a single paragraph unpicking the notion of the 'feminine character', arguing that it is the product of masculine society. Women, like nature, are dominated and mutilated as part of the Enlightenment project. In our civilisation, he argued, nature and the feminine character have this much in common: they seem natural, but bear the scars of domination. 'If the psychoanalytical theory is correct that women experience their physical constitution as a consequence of castration', wrote Adorno mordantly (and the implication is he didn't accept this theory), 'their neurosis gives them an inkling of the truth. The woman who feels herself a wound knows more about herself than the one who imagines herself a flower because that suits her husband.'[29] Women are oppressed and no more so, Adorno thought, than in being reduced to, and compelled to perform, the role of the feminine character.

What's more, some later feminists have found critical theory, and Adorno in particular, inspiring for their work. In *Dialectic of Enlightenment* he and Horkheimer exposed instrumental reason as a new mythology, a justificatory lie to obscure the oppression, domination and cruelty beneath the smooth workings of bourgeois society. 'That which appeared as rational order in bourgeois society was shown by Adorno to be irrational chaos', wrote Susan Borck-Morss, 'but where reality was posited as anarchic and irrational, Adorno exposed the class order which lay beneath this appearance.'[30] This perspective, Renée Heberle notes in her introduction to *Feminist Interpretations of Theodor Adorno*, is echoed in feminism. 'Where some feminists have shown the historicity of presumably natural qualities of sexed existence, others have shown the irrational, mythic, naturalising force of historically constituted notions of masculinity and femininity.'[31] Indeed, Adorno was sensitive to how male philosophers used these historically constituted notions of masculinity and femininity to oppress women. Nietzsche once wrote: 'Thou goest to woman? Forget not thy whip.' Adorno, in *Minima Moralia*, noted that Nietzsche had conflated 'woman with the unverified image of the feminine from Christian civilisation that he otherwise so thoroughly mistrusted'. Women weren't all feminine characters, but it suited Nietzsche to imagine so. In other words, Nietzsche's advice was worthless since, as Adorno wrote: 'Femininity is already the effect of the whip'.[32]

Domination, cruelty and barbarism were, for Adorno and Horkheimer, the repressed truths of the Enlightenment. Not that the two men were, as is sometimes portrayed, anti-Enlightenment. They were, rather, sons of the Enlightenment, beneficiaries of its heritage as much as its victims and, moreover, compelled to use its tools to critique their intellectual inheritance. There was no transcendent position from which to perform that task: like Brecht on his bough, they were obliged to saw through the branch on which they sat. Their book was, among other things, a virtuoso performance of immanent critique, one that used reason to critique the categorical reason of the Enlightenment.

In sum, *Dialectic of Enlightenment* traced how mankind started its descent with Francis Bacon, continued it with Immanuel Kant and culminated in Hitler. The catalyst for their thought was that Nazism had radically problematised the mythic narrative of the Enlightenment as the unfolding of human maturity, freedom and autonomy. Instead of moral progress, they argued, the Enlightenment had produced a regression to barbarism, intolerance and violence. But that couldn't be the whole story. Yes, National Socialism might be accounted for by such a dialectically unfolding narrative, but surely not the forces that were fighting fascism in Europe and elsewhere as the two Frankfurt scholars wrote *Dialectic of Enlightenment* in California? On the contrary, relentless in their application of Benjamin's dictum about civilisation, Adorno and Horkheimer argued that the Enlightenment had postured as freeing mankind from myth and delusion, but even in the countries that were currently fighting Nazism it had degenerated into barbarism – the culture industry, science and technology as tools of ideology and domination, the destruction of the individual, and the administered society. Implicitly, they took Marxism – certainly in its current Soviet perversion – as a new instrument for domination. Later they would describe their work as 'an assessment of the transition to the world of the administered life', and the barbarism that entailed was to be found as much in New York, Paris, London, or Moscow as in Berlin. *Dialectic of Enlightenment* underlined the Frankfurt School's abandonment of its previous commitments to Marxism, as well as its collapse into despair.

IN 1943, THOMAS MANN invited Adorno to his home in San Remo Drive in Pacific Palisades to read to him from the manuscript of the Nobel laureate's last great novel *Doctor Faustus: The Life of the German Composer Adrian Leverkühn as Told by a Friend.* The sixty-eight-year-old Mann sought from Adorno, twenty-eight years his junior, expert musical advice that he could incorporate into the novel, an updating of the Faust legend. Mann wrote to Adorno: 'Would you be willing to think through with me how the work – I mean Leverkühn's work – might look; how you would do it if you were in league with the devil?'[33] That Faustian pact was irresistibly tempting to Adorno – even if it seemed to involve Mann as Mephistopheles draining Adorno of his musical expertise, just as Mann's diabolical hero in the novel, Adrian Leverkühn, drained his teacher of knowledge.[34] As a result of the collaboration Adorno was given not just a chance to work with the German language's most eminent man of letters, but also an outlet for expressing the ideas he was working on about music and philosophy, as well as an opportunity to produce sketches for music in the manner of his late master, Alban Berg.

Mann was a writer whose understandings of Nazism and of exile chimed in some important respects with Adorno's own. True, there were some who doubted the exiled German's literary merits. 'Who's the most boring German writer? My father in law', the English poet W. H. Auden was fond of joking.[35] (Auden had agreed to a marriage of convenience with Mann's daughter Erika in 1936 to help her escape from the Nazis by making her eligible for a British passport.[36]) There is nothing to suggest that Adorno felt that way. Rather, as George Steiner noted, 'Adorno had been a lifelong, if at times uneasy, admirer of Thomas Mann's genius.'[37] Mann was also, and this was perhaps no small issue for Adorno as he contemplated collaborating with the Nobel laureate, one who had overcome anti-Jewish sentiments in some of his writings. As late as April 1933, as Hitler took power, Mann could write in his diary: 'But for all that, might not something deeply significant and revolutionary be taking place in Germany? The Jews: it is no calamity after all . . . that the domination of the legal system by the Jews has been ended.'[38] By 1936, though, Mann had allied himself with persecuted Jews, particularly exiled ones. Dr Eduard Korrodi, a literary critic and an editor at the *Neue Zürcher Zeitung*, had attacked German writers living in exile, claiming they represented the international Jewish influence in German letters, with which the fatherland could easily dispense.[39] In an open letter published in the *Neue Zürcher Zeitung*, Mann retorted that the Jewish influence was not dominant among exiled novelists but rather (as a writer for the *New Republic* put it in an article praising Mann in 1936 for standing up to anti-Semites) 'that the international or European spirit, shared equally by Jewish and gentile writers, has helped to raise Germany from barbarism'. Mann added that the anti-Semitic campaign of the present German rulers 'is aimed, essentially, not at the Jews at all, or not at them exclusively. It is aimed at Europe and at the real spirit of Germany'. That real spirit of Germany, if there was one, was the one that he, Adorno and Horkheimer, among others, felt they were guarding in their exile. Mann added: 'The deep conviction . . . that nothing good for Germany or the world can come out of the present German regime, has made me avoid the country in whose spiritual tradition I am more deeply rooted than are those who for three years have been trying to find courage enough to declare before the world that I am not a German.'[40]

Such convictions were, for Mann, hard won. His temperament was initially unpolitical, and the idea of expressing solidarity with anyone, Jews especially, unappealing. In 1918 he had written *Reflections of an Unpolitical Man*, in which he tried to justify the authoritarian state against democracy and inward culture over moralistic civilisation. His most celebrated novel, *The Magic Mountain*, published in 1924, was a radical inversion of that philosophy. Its hero, the engineer Hans Castorp, is seduced, while visiting a cousin at a sanatorium in Davos, by the temptations of disease, inwardness and death, but ultimately decides for a life of service. The denouement represented, Mann argued, 'a leave-taking from many a perilous sympathy, enchantment, and temptation, to which the European soul had been inclined'.[41]

By 1930, Mann was able to write against one particular European enchantment, that of Nazism. In a speech in Berlin that year entitled 'Ein Appell an die Vernunft' (An Appeal to Reason), he called for the formation of a common front of the cultured bourgeoisie and the socialist working class to resist Nazism. The speech at least served to make him a prominent enemy of the National Socialists: indeed, in 1933 when Hitler came to power, Mann was on holiday in Switzerland and was advised by his son and daughter not to return to Germany. There began his exile years of foreign vagabondage which he would share with Jewish intellectuals such as Adorno.

The updating of the Faust legend that Mann wrote in LA, dedicated to his desk every day between 9 a.m. and noon, was ambitious in that he sought to intertwine the current tragedy of Germany with the history of the tragic life of a modern composer. Mann thought that a pact with the devil, 'the Satanic covenant, to win all power on Earth for a time at the cost of the soul's salvation', was, for him, 'something exceedingly typical of German nature'.[42] The novel was narrated by the composer Leverkühn's friend Serenus Zeitblom from his wartime exile and included Zeitblom's commentaries on the unfolding war. These commentaries are hard not to read as evocations of Mann's thoughts as news came from Europe during the last years of the Second World War. Indeed, the book can be read as a history of the Weimar Republic and of the Second World War, with Leverkühn's pact with the devil juxtaposed with the German people's no-less diabolical pact with National Socialism. At one point, Zeitblom speaks of how the citizens of Weimar walk past Buchenwald's crematoria going about their business and trying 'to know nothing, though at times the wind blew the stench of burned human flesh up their noses'.[43]

It's striking, though, that although Zeitblom doesn't name the victims of Buchenwald as Jews, Mann was certainly aware as he wrote that this was an overwhelmingly Jewish tragedy since he had spoken of it in radio broadcasts that he recorded at NBC's studios in Los Angeles and that were transmitted by the BBC to Germany. But the published novel portrays a Germany without anti-Semitism. It also includes two characters portrayed in an anti-Semitic light. One, a concert agent called Saul Fitelberg who tries to lure Leverkühn to become an international conductor and pianist, was kept for comic relief, despite warnings from Mann's family.[44] 'We Jews had everything to fear from the German character, *qui est essentiellement anti-semi-tique*', Mann has Fitelberg say at one point, 'and that is reason enough, of course, for us to plump for the worldly side and arrange sensational entertainments'.[45] This passage, certainly, doesn't bear the hallmarks of collaboration with Adorno as much of the rest of the book did.

Mann realised if he was to write about music convincingly in the novel, in particular about Germany's self-image as world capital of music and Leverkühn's avant-garde musical contribution to it, he would need help. Fortunately, in July 1943, while he was in the early stages of writing *Faustus*, Mann read Adorno's manuscript 'Schoenberg and Progress', which was to become the first part of *Philosophy of New Music*. Schoenberg had been much in Mann's mind as he thought about his novel; indeed, he was friendly with the great, exiled Viennese composer and dined at the latter's Brentwood home. Mann also read the composer's textbook on harmony which he found to be 'the strangest mingling of piety toward tradition and revolution'.[46] Adorno's writing about Schoenberg was more to his taste; moreover, it provided an intellectual framework his novel otherwise lacked. 'I encountered an artistic and sociological critique of our current situation of the most subtle, progressive and profound kind and one which displayed a striking affinity to the central conception of my own work.' He thought to himself: 'This is my man.'[47]

And so, after writing for three hours on the novel each morning, in the afternoons Mann received Adorno who delivered musicological lectures to the great novelist, explaining the intricacies of Schoenberg's twelve-tone system and performing at the piano. Mann liked to call Adorno his 'privy counsellor' (in the German: Wirklicher Geheimer Rat). One afternoon, Adorno played him Beethoven's last piano sonata, Opus 111, and then lectured the novelist on its significance, and in particular how Beethoven's late style dialectically marries subjectivity and objectivity. This prompted Mann to rewrite chapter eight of *Doctor Faustus*, about a lecture on the composer's late works by Leverkühn's music teacher Wendell Kretzschmar. It's hard to read this without imagining that Mann has put Adorno's words in Kretzschmar's mouth, hard not to read such superb passages as the following as Mann's notes from a lost lecture by Adorno:

> Beethoven's art had outgrown itself, risen out of the habitable regions of tradition, even before the startled gaze of human eyes, into spheres of the entirely and utterly and nothing-but personal – an ego painfully isolated in the absolute, isolated too from sense by the loss of his hearing; lonely prince of a realm of spirits, from whom now only a chilling breath issued to terrify his most willing contemporaries.[48]

Or again: 'Where greatness and death meet, there arises a sovereign objectivity amenable to convention and leaving arrogant subjectivity behind, because the merely personal . . . supersedes itself again; it enters collective and mythical ghostlike and gloriously.[49]

If Mann plundered Adorno's thoughts about Beethoven's late style, he did slip into the chapter coded gratitude for the material, albeit in a clumsy compliment: in chapter eight, Kretzschmar illustrates his lecture on the sonata by singing the word 'Wiesengrund' (which translates as meadowland). This, of course, was Adorno's patronym, though he had suppressed it in the United States.[50]

These eulogies in the novel to Beethoven's late style – whether they be Adorno's, Kretzschmar's or Mann's – importantly echo what Adorno was writing at the time about his exiled Hollywood neighbour Schoenberg's own late style: how it, like Beethoven's, represented a dialectical culmination of the composer's work. Thus, Adorno had criticised Schoenberg's atonal music of around 1910 for its free expression, criticised too his twelve-tone musical style from 1923 onwards for its absorption in the musical material and elimination of the subjective elements. Only with his late style did Schoenberg, according to Adorno in *Philosophy of New Music*, marry extreme calculation and subjective expression to achieve a 'new sovereignty' akin to Beethoven's.[51] This dialectical movement from aesthetic failures to the new sovereignty of a late style became the story of Adrian Leverkühn's musical evolution too.

No wonder then that when German exiles read the completed novel in 1947, some took Leverkühn as Schoenberg's fictional doppelgänger. Schoenberg, though he declared his eyes were too weak to read the book, was furious at the reports about it that reached him. That's perhaps understandable. Not many people would like to see themselves depicted as someone who agrees to a diabolical pact that involves renouncing love in favour of twenty-four years' of life as a musical genius. Schoenberg was upset not least because Mann had plundered a dinner conversation in which the composer had described using his experiences of illness and medical treatment in a new trio for a chapter on Leverkühn's chamber music. But his ire was increased by what he heard from Alma Mahler Werfel (illustrious former wife of both the composer Gustav Mahler and the architect Walter Gropius, and recently widowed following the death of her third husband the novelist Franz Werfel in 1945). 'She loved to start gossip, and it was she who got Arnold Schoenberg going on the business of the twelve-tone system, telling him that Thomas Mann had stolen his theory', wrote Mann's wife.[52]

Schoenberg, feeling betrayed by his celebrated neighbour, asked Werfel to persuade Mann to put a note into copies of the novel stating that the twelve-tone system was actually Arnold Schoenberg's invention. Mann initially refused. With superb arrogance, he imagined that the twelve-tone system that appeared in *Doctor Faustus* was his. 'Within the sphere of the book . . . the idea of the twelve-tone technique assumes a coloration and a colour which it does not possess in its own right and which – is it not so? – in a sense make it really my property.'[53]

There is a third possibility: that the twelve-tone system as it appears in *Doctor Faustus* should be attributed not to Schoenberg or to Mann but to Theodor Adorno. It was he, after all, who came up with the leading musical ideas that were deployed in Mann's fiction. Adorno sketched versions of Leverkühn's final compositions which Mann, as he put it, 'versified'. For Adorno, this part of the collaboration had something of the realisation of his hitherto largely frustrated dreams of being a composer. He recalled in a letter to Mann's daughter in 1962: 'I thought about the problems exactly as I would have done as a composer actually confronted with the task of writing such works, just as someone, like Berg for example, would generally prepare before setting to work.' He then went on to elaborate these musical ideas 'as if they were not merely preparatory outlines, but descriptions of real pieces of music'.[54]

One of these elaborations by Adorno was the *Lamentation of Doctor Faustus*, Leverkühn's last work. Its central idea is one that borrows from Adorno's melancholy philosophy, namely the identity of the non-identical – a notion exemplified by Walter Benjamin's dictum about the inseparability of civilisation and barbarism that proved so influential to the Frankfurt School. There is a 'substantial identity of the most blessed and the most heinous, the inner identity of the chorus of angelic children and hell's laughter', says the novel's narrator Zeitblom, when describing an earlier oratorio by Leverkühn.[55]

That identity between the blessed and the most heinous becomes the guiding principle of Leverkühn's final work.[56] Bahr argues that hell's laughter is expressed by musical chirps representing screams from the 'torture cellars of the Gestapo'. This integration of heaven and hell, civilisation and barbarism, was essential, as Adorno would explain in his posthumously published *Aesthetic Theory*, if art was to be authentic – if, that is, it was to serve as a memory of suffering, to function as critique rather than be merely affirmative. In the novel, Zeitblom describes Leverkühn's final work as the inverse of Beethoven's 'Lied an die Freude' (Ode to Joy) from his ninth symphony. It is, rather, a 'Lied an die Trauer' (Ode to Sorrow), and in this sense it attempts to do justice to suffering. The Gestapo torture cellar is the non-art that the modern work of art needs to identify in order to oppose it.[57]

Arguably, the finished novel reflects Adorno's melancholic philosophy more profoundly than Mann's. This is not to suggest plagiarism: as Adorno wrote in 1957, the insinuation that Mann made illegitimate use of his 'intellectual property' is absurd.[58] The underlying aesthetic philosophy of the novel goes beyond the binary opposition between the Apollonian and Dionysian, between the orderly and the ecstatic, that Nietzsche set out in *The Birth of Tragedy* and to which Mann repeatedly appealed in his fiction. Indeed, Mann originally conceived *Doctor Faustus* as representing the escape from 'everything bourgeois, moderate, classical, Apollonian, sober, industrious, and dependable into a world of drunken release, a life of bold Dionysian genius, beyond the bourgeois class, indeed superhuman'.[59] During the collaboration with Adorno, however, Mann set aside his original, Dionysian conception of the composer and as a result Leverkühn became something much more interesting – a figure who dramatised something of the Frankfurt School's, and in particular Adorno's, distinctive contribution to the philosophy of art. Early in the novel, Leverkühn worries that his work as an artist has become a game for producing beautiful illusions. But he wonders 'whether all illusion, even the most beautiful, especially the most beautiful, has not become a lie today'. This chimes with Marcuse's 1937 essay on the affirmative character of bourgeois art, how it functions as an alibi for an oppressive order rather than in opposition to it. It also fits with Adorno's thought that dissonance is the truth of harmony, that the production of beautiful and harmonious works of art is an ugly and barbaric lie in the face of such horrors as the Holocaust.

What was needed, Adorno thought, was art that set aside its mask of self-satisfaction and did justice to suffering, and in particular to the horrors of the death camps. Antagonism, contradiction and disharmony were the truths about social relations under capitalism and art must reflect those. 'The self-satisfied illusion of music itself has become impossible and no longer tenable', declares Leverkühn. They are words that could have been, perhaps even were, Adorno's. What's more, they were implicitly critical of Mann's aesthetics in his earlier books. In his 1912 novella *Death in Venice* the writer Aschenbach masters his Dionysian reverie on the beach and produces an Apollonian work of art. Aschenbach's work of art thereby entails the erasure of the agony, the suffering, that made it possible. Leverkühn's last musical work, by contrast, sketched by Adorno and the application of his aesthetic philosophy, for all that it is described in a novel authored by Thomas Mann, involves no such mastery by objective technique of subjective emotion, and no erasure of the suffering that made the work possible.

There was, nonetheless, a temptation for Mann to create a beautiful illusion or resolution at the end of *Doctor Faustus*. Adorno worried that it would be 'as if the archsinner already has salvation in his pocket' and urged Mann to resist it.[60] One might think that Leverkühn redeems himself from his diabolical pact by producing a work of art that does justice to human suffering, one that shows that he has not, as he promised as a condition of being a genius, renounced love. Adorno advised Mann against such a trite denouement: it was enough that Leverkühn's last music provided a memory of suffering.

Instead of being redeemed, Leverkühn is punished. He spends the last decade of his life raddled by brain disease, his years of musical genius finished. But even before that collapse, he is tormented by the death of his beloved nephew Echo, whom he believes dies as a result of the composer's pact with the devil. Over champagne at a party to celebrate the novel's publication in 1947, Mann read from a section in which Leverkühn gazes with love at Echo, a character modelled on

Mann's beloved grandson Fridolin. For that look of love, which breaches the diabolical contract, Leverkühn in punished – Echo falls sick and dies even as the composer's mighty final work takes shape in his mind. Mann considered that section the most poetic passage in the novel. After he finished reading, more champagne was served. It's hard not to feel queasy about this glorying in the poetic expression of suffering – as if Mann the creative artist, even as he gestured towards human suffering, remained ruthlessly, narcissistically fixated on his own creative achievement. No matter: the novel became a bestseller in America – the first edition of 25,000 copies rapidly sold out and the reviews were overwhelmingly positive.

As for the novel itself, Mann ended it with a wail for post-war Germany. 'Today, clung round by demons, a hand over one eye, with the other staring into horrors, down she flings from despair to despair. When will she reach the bottom of the abyss? When, out of uttermost hopelessness – a miracle beyond the power of belief – will the light of hope begin to dawn?'[61] It's interesting, to put it mildly, to compare this assessment with what Adorno found when he returned to Frankfurt in 1949. Instead of a Germany staring with one eye into the horrors, he found it, as we will see, with both eyes shut.

Arnold Schoenberg was not the only one to worry that he had a disobligingly fictional doppelgänger in Mann's novel. Adorno himself wrote to Mann in 1950 worrying if, as one literary critic had charged, the devil depicted in chapter twenty-five as a pimp turned music scholar with horn-rimmed spectacles on his hooked nose was Adorno. Mann replied: 'the idea that the Devil in his role as a music scholar was modelled on your appearance was quite absurd. Do you in fact wear horn-rimmed spectacles?'[62] Adorno's biographer suggests that Mann was probably astonished that Adorno didn't solve the riddle – the devil was not Adorno but, rather, bore remarkable similarity to Gustav Mahler.

But Adorno could not quite elude association with the diabolical whiff of sulphur. In 1974, the postmodern philosopher Jean-François Lyotard wrote an essay called 'Adorno as the Devil'. For Lyotard, Adorno pessimistically lamented the decline from a position of privilege. 'The diabolical figure is not just dialectical', wrote Lyotard with characteristic lucidity, 'it is expressly the failure of dialectics in dialectics, the negative in the heart of negativity, the suspended moment or momentaneous suspension.'[63] Adorno's brand of critical theory, that is to say, was impotently mired in negativity, incapable of offering the promise of a better future that readers found in Marx.

Certainly, Adorno opposed the Marxist notion, extolled by György Lukács, that avant-garde intellectual artists were valuable to the extent that they drew attention in their works to the contradictions in social reality of which their readers or hearers would not otherwise have been conscious – and thereby helped transform that reality for the better. Adorno dismissed Lukács's perspective as a 'vulgar materialist shibboleth' and 'Soviet claptrap' in an essay entitled 'Reconciliation under Duress'.[64] But if it is not useful for catalysing revolution, what is the point of bearing witness to suffering in art as Adorno sought? James Hellings captures well Adorno's vision of what art should be when he writes: 'Art does not copy or imitate, depict or reflect objective reality – limping after it impotently à la Lukács – but rather art recollects, reproduces and redeems what is beyond objective reality (the incommensurable, the Other, something more).'[65] Art had, as Adorno would later put it, a dual essence of 'autonomy and *fait social*'.[66] Art could not be affirmative; it could not be deployed either to uphold or overturn the status quo. And yet it was only art that could express the truth of suffering, only art that did not yield to the temptation to use suffering for other ends.

This was what the autonomy of art, for Adorno, amounted to. That said, he also held to the idea that art worthy of the name depicted an irksome social reality (that's what he means by art as essentially involving a 'fait social' – or social fact) without aspiring to change it. Art could only negate an existing state of affairs. This unremitting negativity in Adorno's philosophy of art was what led Karl Popper to argue that it was 'vacuous and irresponsible'.[67] Or, as Lyotard put it, diabolical. Adorno, perhaps, was in league with one kind of devil: the Mephistopheles of Goethe's *Faust* who says 'I am the spirit that negates.'

12

The Fight Against Fascism

While Adorno and Horkheimer remained in California during the Second World War, several other members of the Frankfurt School went to work for the US government in Washington to help with its anti-war effort. The Institute for Social Research could as a result cut its wage bill. Viewed from the other side of the Cold War, it may seem surprising that a group of apparently neo-Marxist revolutionaries was invited into the heart of the American government. But Leo Löwenthal, Franz Neumann, Herbert Marcuse, Otto Kirchheimer and Friedrich Pollock were all hired because, as recent Jewish exiles from Germany, they knew the enemy intimately and so could help in the fight against fascism. Within a decade, the McCarthyite witchhunts against suspected communists in the US would begin in earnest. In 1942, though, the reds weren't under the bed, but invited between its sheets.

But what did fascism mean to the Frankfurt School? A decade earlier, Wilhelm Reich, in his 1933 book *The Mass Psychology of Fascism*, ascribed its rise to sexual repression. He wrote:

> Suppression of the natural sexuality in the child, particularly of its genital sexuality, makes the child apprehensive, shy, obedient, afraid of authority, good and adjusted in the authoritarian sense; it paralyses the rebellious forces because any rebellion is laden with anxiety; it produces, by inhibiting sexual curiosity and sexual thinking in the child, a general inhibition of thinking and of critical faculties.[1]

The family was not for Reich, as it had been for Hegel, an autonomous zone that offered resistance to the state, but rather an authoritarian miniature state that prepared the child for later subordination.

The Frankfurt School's leading psychoanalytical thinker Erich Fromm agreed with much of Reich's analysis, though worried it had too little empirical confirmation and focused too much on genital sexuality. He contended that the rise of fascism was to do with sado-masochism. In his essay 'Social-Psychological Aspects', he distinguished the 'revolutionary' character from the 'masochist'.[2] The former had ego strength and sought to change his destiny, the latter submitted to his fate, turning over his destiny to a higher power. Fromm followed Freud in taking sadism to be of the same coin as masochism: the sadist turned himself against those who showed signs of weakness. The sadomasochistic social character was essential for authoritarian society, involving as it did deference to those above and contempt for those below. For Fromm, the sadomasochist was charac-terised by anal strivings for order, punctuality and frugality: this was the kind of social character a fascist would want in spades if he wanted to make the trains run on time or murder Jews on an industrial scale.

But all this said little about why fascism arose in Germany in particular. During the 1930s, Fromm developed an account of what happened that enriched his 1941 book *Escape from Freedom*, published after he had left the Institute. Fromm argued that, as Germany shifted from early to monopoly capitalism, the social character of the lower middle class persisted. The petit bourgeoisie, who were the icons of early capitalism, owning and managing their own businesses, became anomalies under corporate forms of capitalism. This class had been the unwitting heroes of the story Max Weber's *The Protestant Ethic and the Spirit of Capitalism*: it was the parsimonious, pleasure-deny-ing, duty-bound characters who predominated under early capitalism. Now they were politically powerless, economically crushed and spirit-ually alienated in the Weimar Republic. Sadomasochistically, they yearned not to change their own destiny but to yield to the authority that would do that for them. 'The desire for authority is channelled towards the strong leader, while other specific father figures become the objects of the rebellion', wrote Fromm in 'Psychoanalytic

Characterology and its Relevance for Social Psychology' in 1932.[3] By 1941, when he came to write *Escape from Freedom*, Fromm was to cast this sadomasochistic yearning on the part of the German petit bourgeois for a strong leader as part of a grand historical dialectical process. The process of becoming freed from authority (whether the authority of God or of social convention) resulted, Fromm argued, in a kind of anguish or hopelessness akin to what infants feel during child development.

He thought that freedom from authority can be experienced as crushing and terrifying. Fromm distinguished between negative and positive freedom – freedom from and freedom to. The responsibility conferred on humans by having freedom from authority can be unbearable unless we are able to exercise our positive freedom creatively. Fromm's thought connected with the near-contemporaneous account of the anguish of freedom as experienced in the existentialist philosopher Jean-Paul Sartre's 1938 novel *Nausea*. But while Sartre took the nauseating experience of freedom to be a human fact, Fromm set it in a historical, dialectical context. But taking the responsibility to exercise positive freedom creatively was precisely what the weak, ego-depleted social character was incapable of doing. Instead, in order to achieve spiritual security and escape from the unbearable burden of freedom, the frightened individual replaced one form of authority with another.

Fromm wrote: 'The frightened individual seeks for somebody or something to tie his self to; he cannot bear to be his own individual self any longer, and he tries frantically to get rid of it and to feel security again by the elimination of this burden: the self.'[4] Hence Hitler: the Führer's authoritarian personality not only made him want to rule over Germany in the name of a higher if fictional authority (the German master race) but also made him appealing for an insecure middle class. Fromm argued that this fear of freedom was not a peculiarly fascist one, but threatened the basis of democracy in every modern state. Indeed, at the outset of *Escape from Freedom*, he quoted with approval the words of the American pragmatist philosopher John Dewey. 'The serious threat to our democracy is not the existence of foreign totalitarian states. It is the existence within our own personal attitudes and within our own institutions of conditions which have given a victory to external authority, discipline, uniformity and dependence upon The Leader in foreign countries. The battlefield is also accordingly here – within ourselves and our institutions.'[5]

Fromm's view of fascism as premised on the sadomasochism of its supporters became Frankfurt School orthodoxy. 'This ideology', wrote Marcuse in his 1934 essay 'The Struggle Against Liberalism in the Totalitarian View of the State', 'exhibits the status quo, but with a radical transvaluation of values: unhappiness is turned into grace, misery into blessing, poverty into destiny.'[6]

The German Marxist philosopher Ernst Bloch, writing in exile in Zurich, dissented from this Frankfurt School orthodoxy, which took Nazism to be a symptom of a desire for an authority figure. In his 1935 book *Heritage of Our Times*, Bloch instead argued that fascism was a perverted religious movement that won people over with anachronistic kitsch and quasi-utopian ideas about the wonders of a future Reich.[7] Fascism was, as a result, a paradox, being both ancient and modern: more precisely it was a system that used a tradition hostile to capitalism for the preservation of capitalism. For Bloch, as for Walter Benjamin, fascism was a cultural synthesis that contained both anti-capitalist and utopian aspects. The Frankfurt School failed to emphasise in its analysis of fascism what Benjamin called the 'aestheticisation of politics'. It fell to Benjamin, Bloch and Siegfried Kracauer to reflect on the Nazi deployment of myths, symbols, parades and demonstrations to command support. Benjamin wrote in 1936 that mankind's self-alienation had 'reached such a degree that it can contemplate its own destruction as an aesthetic pleasure of the first order.'[8] By mankind, he meant that part of it that had succumbed to the delusive dreams of the Italian futurist poet and fascist Filippo Marinetti who saw war as beautiful.

These conflicting ideas fed into a dispute between two of the leading Frankfurt School theorists of fascism, Friedrich Pollock and Franz Neumann.[9] Pollock had long argued that there was such a thing as state capitalism, and that both Nazi Germany and the Soviet Union had not abolished capitalism, but rather, by means of state planning, the encouragement of technological innovation, and the boost to industry from increased military spending, had made it possible to defer its contradictions. Perhaps, hypothesised Pollock pessimistically, Hitler and Stalin had made the capitalist system invulnerable even during the Great Depression of the 1930s. This in itself was heretical: it certainly flew in the face of Henryk Grossman's account wherein capitalism was destined to founder on its own contradictions. Neumann demurred. For him 'state capitalism' was a contradiction in terms. If the state became the sole owner of the means of production it stopped capitalism functioning properly. Rather, Neumann believed that what was happening in Germany under Nazi rule was 'that the antagonisms of capitalism are operating at a higher and, therefore, more dangerous level, even if these antagonisms are covered by bureaucratic apparatus and by the ideology of the people's community'.[10] What Neumann called Hitler's totalitarian monopoly capitalism was perhaps even more prone to crisis than liberal monopoly capitalism.

But even Neumann, who was not especially amenable to psycho-social or aesthetic explanations of Hitler's success, still less to the idea that sadomasochism supposedly characterized his key supporters, could write in his 1942 book *Behemoth: The Structure and Practice of National Socialism*: 'Charismatic rule has long been neglected and ridiculed, but apparently it has deep roots and becomes a powerful stimulus once the proper psychological and social conditions are set. The leader's charismatic power is not a mere phantasm – none can doubt that millions believe in it.'[11] But what proved disastrous for the Nazis was that they made the error of believing their own publicity. Adorno recognised as much when he wrote this passage of *Minima Moralia* during the last days of the Second World War:

They [the Nazi leaders] saw nothing before them except cheering assemblies and frightened negotiators: this blocked their view of the objective power of a greater mass of capital. It was immanent revenge on Hitler that he, the executioner of liberal society, was yet in his own state of consciousness too 'liberal' to perceive how industrial potential outside Germany was establishing, under the veil of liberalism, its irresistible domination.[12]

For Adorno, Germany was defeated by a more advanced form of capitalism. Indeed, in a letter to Horkheimer, he wrote that 'the forces of production of more progressive countries have been proved to be the stronger after all . . . the war has been won by industry against the military'.[13] There is something in this, though it does leave out the role of the Soviet Union, that non-liberal polity, whose defeat of Hitler's forces at Stalingrad in 1943 was decisive in the course of the European conflict. It was Soviet totalitarianism that delivered the crucial blow to Nazi totalitarianism, not liberal capitalism.

ONE QUESTION remained about fascism, namely its connection with anti-Semitism. In the final section of *Dialectic of Enlightenment*, 'Elements of Anti-Semitism', written after the war and first published in 1947, Adorno and Horkheimer argued that Jews served as a necessary outlet for frustrations and aggressions in society. But that necessity they ascribed to the capitalist system rather than, specifically, to fascism in Germany. The frustrations and aggressions of workers were offloaded on to another group. 'The productive work of the capitalist, whether he justifies his profit by means of gross returns as under liberalism, or by his director's salary as today, is an ideology cloaking the real nature of the labour contract and the grasping character of the economic system', they wrote. 'And so people shout "Stop thief!" – but point at the Jews. They are the scapegoats not only for individual manoeuvres and machinations, but in a broader sense, inasmuch as the injustice of the whole class is attributed to them.'[14]

But why were the Jews the scapegoats? Because, Adorno and Horkheimer suggested, the image of the Jew was the false projection of things that were unbearable about non-Jewish society. Jews were hated because they were, unfairly, taken as being what non-Jews wanted to be.

> No matter what the Jews as such may be like, their image, as that of the defeated people, has the features to which totalitarian domination must be completely hostile: happiness without power, wages without work, a home without frontiers, religion without myth. These features are hated

by the rulers because the ruled secretly long to possess them. The rulers are only safe so long as the people they rule turn their longed-for goals into hated forms of evil.[15]

And Jews could readily serve as those hated forms – the image of the wandering Jew, Adorno wrote in his 1940 'Note on Anti-Semitism', 'represents a condition of mankind which did not know labour, and all later attacks against the parasitic, consumptive character of Jews are simply rationalisations'.[16]

Löwenthal, Marcuse, Kircheimer, Neumann and Pollock helped to defeat the fascism that the Frankfurt School had described by working for the American government. Pollock worked for the anti-trust division of the Department of Justice, Löwenthal with the Office of War Information. Meanwhile, William Donovan, aka 'Wild Bill', head of the Office of Strategic Services (OSS), the US's wartime intelligence agency established by President Roosevelt in 1941, recruited the three other members of the Frankfurt School – Neumann, Marcuse and Kirchheimer – to work as intelligence analysts.

Marcuse said he went to Washington 'to do everything that was in my power to help defeat the Nazi regime'. After the war, Marcuse's communist critics chided him for working for what was the forerunner of the CIA. 'If critics reproach me for that', he said in a later interview, 'it only shows the ignorance of these people who seem to have forgotten that the war then was a war against fascism and that, consequently, I haven't the slightest reason for being ashamed of having assisted in it.'[17]

As German exiles, these three men had profound knowledge of the Americans' enemy. In particular, Neumann had just published *Behemoth*, the fruit of detailed scholarly research into the workings of the Nazi system, albeit one written from a neo-Marxist perspective. In his Foreword to *Secret Reports on Nazi Germany: The Frankfurt School Contribution to the War Effort*, the Cambridge philosopher Raymond Geuss suggested that such 'toleration of intellectual deviancy', in which the ideas of Marxism could be harnessed in the defeat of fascism, contrasts with the 'politics of myopic intellectual conformism' of the Anglo-American world in the twenty-first century.[18] What

Geuss had in mind is that Neumann, Marcuse and Kirchheimer were recruited because they offered profound insight into the enemy's political culture – which was, you might think, precisely the type of insight that might have served a purpose during the invasion of Iraq in 2003. But Bush and Blair didn't allow such knowledgeable dissident voices to inform their 'war on terror'. In sharp contrast, the Frankfurt scholars brought a refreshing challenge to established opinions about Nazism. They doubted, for instance, Churchill's notion that either 'Prussian militarism' or the 'Teutonic urge for domination' could explain the rise of Hitler, instead ascribing it to something more modern, namely a series of pacts between the industrial bourgeoisie and the regime.

They doubted, too, the Allied strategy of bombing the Germans into submission. In June 1944, Neumann wrote a paper criticising the bombing of German cities, not because it was inhumane, but because it was counterproductive. 'Manifold as the effects of the air raids on the German population may be, they have one common characteristic', he wrote, 'they tend to absorb all political issues into personal issues, on the national as well as the individual level.'[19] This was, effectively, a Marxist analysis of the utility of bombing: Neumann was arguing that bombed-out German civilians would put their immediate survival above their class interests or the imperative to topple Nazism. Bombing German cities risked extending the Third Reich's lifespan rather than killing it off. Only many decades later with books such as Jörg Friedrich's *The Fire: The Bombing of Germany 1940–45* and W. G. Sebald's *On the Natural History of Destruction*, that broke the near silence about how 635,000 Germans, mostly civilians, died and 7.5 million were made homeless when British and US bombs were dropped on 131 cities and towns, might one realise the prescience of Neumann's argument – how, in the rubble of Hamburg or Dresden, it was scarcely possible to think about organising resistance to Nazism.

Neumann is the most intriguing of the Frankfurt scholars who helped Uncle Sam, and not just because during the war he supplied information to Soviet spies who knew him by the code name Ruff. Born in 1900 in Katowice, Poland, Neumann had as a student supported the failed German Revolution of 1918;[20] later he trained as a labour lawyer, represented trade unions and eventually became the lead attorney for the German Social Democratic Party. In 1933, fearing arrest from the Nazis, he fled to Britain, where he studied at the London School of Economics with, among others, Karl Mannheim. In 1936, he joined the Institute in New York on the recommendation of the LSE's Harold Laski. While working for the Institute he not only wrote *Behemoth* but helped secure the backing of the American Jewish Committee for the Frankfurt School's study of anti-Semitism.

As deputy head of the Central European Section of the Research and Analysis Branch of the OSS, Neumann had access to secret information from American ambassadors that he obligingly passed on to Elizabeth Zarubina, a Soviet spy working in the US whom he met through his friends Paul Massing (a sociologist with connections to the Institute) and his wife Hede, both of whom had worked for and still had links to the NKVD, the Soviet secret service. Once he became a naturalised American citizen in 1943, though, the Massings worried that he would stop sending the Soviets information out of a new-found patriotic duty. Neumann wrote back saying he still saw his prime duty to be the defeat of Nazism and so, 'If there is something really important, I will inform you without hesitation.'[21]

It has been suggested that Neumann may have been a Soviet spy mentioned in the the top secret Venona Papers. Declassified only in 1995, these papers disclosed the workings of a counter-intelligence programme run by the US Army Signal Intelligence Service, the forerunner of the National Security Agency, from 1944 to 1980. It was the Venona Project that uncovered a Soviet spy ring targeting the Manhattan Project that was developing nuclear weapons, and later exposed Ethel and Julius Rosenberg for passing information about the atomic bomb to Moscow, leading to their executions in 1953. But the suggestion that Neumann, for all his Marxist credentials, was a traitor like them seems fanciful: he was hardly a double agent but rather saw it as his wartime duty to help the Allies, one of which was the Soviet Union, to defeat Nazism. For him, at least, there was no conflict of interests. That said, as the US government increasingly focused on resisting the spread of Soviet communism across Europe in the aftermath of Hitler's defeat, his Washington bosses might have had other ideas. After the war, Neumann became professor of political science at Columbia University in New York and helped establish the Free University of Berlin. The latter, founded in the early Cold War in West Berlin, had a symbolic name: unlike the communist-controlled Humboldt University in East Berlin, it was part of what Americans liked to call the free world. Of course, sceptics might argue, these activities would be a good cover for a really cunning Soviet double agent, particularly one who wanted to avoid being executed like the Rosenbergs or forced into glum Muscovite exile like some of the Cambridge network of spies who betrayed secrets to the Kremlin. None of this, though, should be taken as indicating that Franz Neumann was one of their number.

All three men – Marcuse, Kirchheimer and Neumann – worked for the OSS as political analysts, helping to identify both the Nazis who were to be held accountable for war crimes and the anti-Nazis who could be relied upon to help in the post-war reconstruction. Jürgen Habermas once asked Marcuse if their resultant suggestions were of any consequence. 'On the contrary', came the reply. 'Those whom we had listed as "economic war criminals" were very quickly back in the decisive positions of responsibility in the German economy.'[22]

After the defeat of the Nazis, Neumann continued to work for the OSS and the Nuremberg War Crimes Tribunal under its chief prosecutor Robert H. Jackson. He wrote analyses of twenty-two Nazi defendants, including Hermann Göring who had been Hitler's designated successor, that were central to the indictments against them. He was also asked by Donovan to investigate the purpose of the Nazi's persecution of the Christian church. He and his team concluded that the power of the church over the people, and young people in particular, was broken because it represented a site of resistance to the ideology of National Socialism. 'They avowed their aim to eliminate the Christian Churches in Germany and sought to substitute therefore Nazi institutions and Nazi beliefs and pursued a programme of persecution of priests, clergy and members of monastic orders whom they deemed opposed to their purposes and confiscated Church property.'[23]

What's striking is that Donovan did not instruct Neumann and his team to investigate the other, more devastating form of Nazi religious persecution – one that led to the destruction of 267 synagogues across Germany during Kristallnacht in November 1938 – still less the persecution that led to the murder of six million Jews.

ON 9 JULY 1946, Adorno wrote to his mother after receiving a telegram informing him of his father's death. Oscar Wiesengrund died aged seventy-seven after a long illness:

> There are two thoughts I cannot shake off. The first: that I find death in exile, even though it was certainly a blessing compared to an existence over there, particularly dreadful – that the continuity of a person's life is senselessly broken in two, that he cannot live his own life to its natural conclusion as it were, but instead ultimately has the entirely external category of the 'emigrant' forced upon him, a representative of a category rather than an individual . . . The other thought: that when one's father dies, one's own life feels like theft, an outrage, something that has been taken away from the older person – the injustice of continuing to live, as if one were cheating the dead man of his light and breath. The sense of this guilt is ineffably strong in me.[24]

But the guilt of the survivor had another cause. Adorno had survived the Holocaust. In August 1945, as two atomic bombs were detonated over Hiroshima and Nagasaki to end the Second World War, the industrial-scale murder of Jews at Auschwitz, Treblinka, Bergen-Belsen, Sobibor, Majdanek and other camps was being revealed to the world.

In *Minima Moralia*, which Adorno was composing at the time, he saw the death camps as a kind of perverted expression of Marx's exchange principle, involving a Freudian projection onto the other of what was most intolerable about oneself, both a culmination and a denial of the Enlightenment's values. 'The technique of the concentration camp is to make the prisoners resemble their guards, the murdered, murderers. The racial difference is raised to an absolute so that it can be abolished absolutely, if only in the sense that nothing different survives.'[25] For Adorno, Auschwitz was nonetheless a horror incomparable with earlier horrors. 'Auschwitz cannot be brought into analogy with the destruction of the Greek city-states as a mere gradual increase in horror, before which one can preserve tranquility of mind. Certainly, the unprecedented torture and humiliation of those abducted in cattle trucks does shed a deathly livid light on the most distant past.'[26]

Thinking could not go on as it had before. In 1949, deranged by Auschwitz, feeling not just the guilt but the responsibility of the survivor, Adorno returned from California to Frankfurt where he, along with Horkheimer, would philosophise in different circumstances – in the rubble of western civilisation.

PART V:

THE 1950s

13

The Ghost Sonata

In the autumn of 1949, Adorno sailed across the Atlantic on the Queen Elizabeth back to Europe. He was on his way to the city of his birth, Frankfurt, after fifteen years of exile, to start teaching again. Horkheimer, who had been offered a professorship at Frankfurt University, was too sick to travel. In Paris, Adorno broke off his journey and from there wrote to Horkheimer:

> The return to Europe gripped me with such force that words fail me. And the beauty of Paris shines more beautifully than ever through the rags of poverty ... What survives here may well be condemned by history and it certainly bears the marks of this clearly enough, but the fact *that it*, the essence of untimeliness, still exists, is part of the historical picture and permits the feeble hope that something humane survives, despite everything.[1]

The gravitational pull of Europe didn't work on many other of his exiled colleagues with such force. Other former members of the Institute – Marcuse, Fromm, Löwenthal, Kirchheimer and Neumann – all remained in the United States although they would occasionally visit their homeland. On the other hand, Henryk Grossman, who had spent his American exile years semi-detached from the Institute, was happy to leave the United States for Germany's Soviet-occupied zone. During the war, he had been suspected by the FBI of being a German spy, and during the first years of the Cold War his communist affiliations made him fear being targeted by the House of UnAmerican

Activities Committee. 'Marxism is designated a crime', he wrote to a friend, 'and one can only make a career if one writes against Marx.'[2] So in 1948, he accepted a lump sum pay-off from the Institute arranged by Friedrich Pollock and took up an invitation to become professor of economics at the University of Leipzig, then in the Soviet-occupied zone, and from 7 October 1949 part of East Germany.

Grossman no longer had any immediate family: his wife, Jana, and his son, Jan, had been murdered in Auschwitz in 1943 and his second son Stanislaw, apparently, had died before them. Grossman and the likes of Ernst Bloch, Hanns Eisler and Bertolt Brecht were major successes for East Germany in their Cold War competition with West Germany to attract eminent intellectual anti-Nazi exiles. In March 1950, Grossman was nominated by the city of Leipzig for the National Prize 'for the totality of his scientific achievements in the area of scientific socialism', but didn't win. Possibly his achievements were insufficiently pure in doctrinal terms for the Berlin authorities.

He joined the Victims of Fascism organisation after his arrival and was recognised as a 'fighter against fascism'. Strikingly, for official purposes he described himself as 'without religion', rather than as Jewish. His biographer Rick Kuhn reckons this was because he was 'unable to conceive that anti-Semitism would be tolerated in "socialist" East Germany'. Grossman thought he needn't express solidarity with other Jews, but could reveal his secular beliefs instead.[3]

Despite being ill, he gave every sign of enjoying his new berth in a new, purportedly socialist state. He lectured and enjoyed socialising with committed communists from the first intake of students who came from peasant and working-class backgrounds and who graduated in 1949. In November 1950, though, he died after suffering from prostate problems and Parkinson's Disease. His biographer concluded: 'Grossman had gone to Leipzig with high expectations and large illusions about the regime in east Germany. He seems to have died with those illusions intact. They concealed the distance between his Marxist belief in the capacity of the working class to usher in a radically democratic socialism and the realities of the dictatorial state capitalist regime.'[4]

Other Frankfurt School intellectuals had fewer illusions. Adorno chose capitalist West Germany over Marxist East Germany as his base when he returned from exile. So did Horkheimer when he finally arrived in Frankfurt. 'We are unable to see anything in the practice of military dictatorships disguised as people's democracies other than a new form of repression and, in what people over there are accustomed to call "ideology", we see only what was originally intended by that word: the lie that justifies an untrue condition of society', wrote Adorno.[5] The bigger question was why Adorno as well as Horkheimer and Pollock returned to Europe at all. Didn't they realise that Europe was no longer the centre of western civilisation? 'America is no longer the raw and unformed land of promise from which men of superior gifts like James, Santayana and Eliot departed, seeking in Europe what they found lacking in America', wrote the art critic Harold Rosenberg in the *Partisan Review* in 1940, claiming that America's century-long cultural dependence on Europe was over. 'The wheel has come full circle and now America has become the protector of Western civilisation, at least in a military and economic sense.'[6] Since the war, that nascent swagger had developed and something new asserted itself, America's proud insistence on its cultural virility over European decadence.

When, for instance, the young Saul Bellow visited Paris in 1948, the year before Adorno's visit, the young American novelist felt like Dostoevsky a century earlier. 'I, too, was a foreigner and a barbarian from a vast and backward land', Bellow wrote.[7] Or at least he was treated as such. He went home to write his 1953 novel *The Adventures of Augie March*, which begins: 'I am an American, Chicago born' – as if in self-assertive rebuke to culturally dead old Europe.[8] Europeans had no business in taking American civilisation to be an oxymoron when theirs had revealed its dark side during the Third Reich.

Adorno was travelling into the centre of that barbarism, into the heart of European darkness, only to find that, five years after the war had ended, his countrymen were carrying on as though the Third Reich had never happened. He didn't deny feeling homesick, but he stressed another factor – the German language, which, he suggested in an essay called 'On the Question "What is German?"', had a 'special affinity with philosophy', and was able 'to express something in the phenomena that is not exhausted in their mere thus-ness, their positivity and givenness'.[9] A bracing idea – as though, for example, English speakers were doomed to the philosophies he and the Frankfurt School excoriated by dint of the structure of their language; as if in the rubble of Germany, there was a priceless jewel that could be rescued.

Adorno was hardly eulogising German culture at this, to put it mildly, unpropitious moment in history. In fact, such was his ambivalent sense of belonging to a German tradition, that in the same paper he was able to reflect that the idea of national identity was a product of the reified thinking that critical theory opposed. 'The fabrication of national collectivities, however – the common practice in the abominable jargon of war which speaks of the Russian, the American and certainly also of the German – is the mark of a reified consciousness hardly capable of experience. Such fabrication remains precisely within those stereotypes which it is the task of thinking to dissolve.'[10] But here's the paradox: if there was thinking to be done in order to dissolve reified consciousness, that thinking was best done – perhaps could only be done in Adorno's view – in German. But such thinking in German, and the critical philosophical heritage in which Adorno, for all his exile wanderings, felt at home was now viewed with suspicion. Jürgen Habermas, the former Hitler Youth who in a few years would become Adorno's first research assistant, would later say that he could only identify his own intellectual traditions at a distance which enabled him to 'continue them in a self-critical spirit with the scepticism and the clear-sightedness of the man who has already once been fooled'.[11]

Adorno was returning to a city from which nearly everything had been erased. German troops had destroyed all but one of the bridges across the river Main in the last days of the war. Allied bombings had destroyed 177,000 houses, leaving only 45,000 still standing in 1945. One ghostly memory of his family remained: on the parquet floor of the only habitable room left in his father's bombed-out house on Seeheim Street, he could discern the imprints left by his mother's piano. It was from this city that he had been forced to flee into exile, leaving behind his ageing parents who had been roughed up and jailed by the Nazis and compelled to sell their properties at well below market rate, before scrambling into exile so as not to be murdered in the death camps. No wonder he struggled to keep his feelings in check. Only once, he reckoned, did he fail to do so, when he confronted the son of the owner of another of his father's houses in the Schöne Aussicht: 'I called him a Nazi and a murderer, although I am not sure that I found the guilty party. But that is how things go – it's always the wrong ones who get caught and the villains are always so experienced and able to cope with the real situations that they get by.'[12]

That was one of the problems with the Germany to which he and Horkheimer returned: there were no Nazis any more. The returning exiles found their homeland in a state of mass denial. When Horkheimer visited Frankfurt in 1948 to discuss with the university authorities the possibility of re-establishing the Institute for Social Research, he found his former colleagues 'as sweet as pie, smooth as eels and hypocritical . . . I attended a faculty meeting yesterday and found it too friendly by half and enough to make you want to throw up. All these people sit there as they did before the Third Reich . . . just as if nothing had happened . . . they are acting out a Ghost Sonata that leaves Strindberg standing.'[13]

That meeting was emblematic of much of the spectral new Federal Republic of Germany that Adorno and Horkheimer uncovered on their return. A few weeks before Adorno arrived in Frankfurt, Germany had been divided into two states: the German Democratic Republic, which had been the Soviet zone of the post-war occupation, and the German Federal Republic, made up of the French, British and American zones. Delegates to the People's Congress of the GDR were elected from a single list of Communist Party candidates; the first elections to West Germany's Bundestag resulted in the conservative Konrad Adenauer becoming the Federal Republic's first Chancellor. In his first speech as chancellor Adenauer did not refer to German responsibility for the murder of Jews – underlining how the new republic was to refuse to acknowledge Germany's shame during the Second World War. Worse yet, the West German government hired many individuals who had served as civil servants and lawyers under the Nazis; responsibility for the country's economy was taken over by those whom Marcuse and his team at the OSS had called economic war criminals.

The Federal Republic refused to acknowledge or definitively break with Germany's recent past. For the Frankfurt School, the emblematic figure in this respect was Martin Heidegger, the great German philosopher and Nazi Party member, who had never disavowed publicly the speeches that made him, in many eyes, one of Nazism's strongest intellectual proponents. In the spring of 1947, while in Germany as part of his work for the OSS, Marcuse visited his former teacher in his hut at Todtnauberg in the Black Forest. Heidegger told Marcuse that he had fully dissociated himself from the Nazi regime as of 1934 and that in his subsequent lectures he had made extremely critical remarks. But that wasn't enough for Marcuse, who wrote to Heidegger later that year:

> Many us have long awaited a statement from you, a statement that would clearly and finally free you from such identification, a statement that honestly expresses your current attitude about the events that have occurred. But you have never uttered such a statement . . . A philosopher can be deceived regarding political matters; in which case he will openly acknowledge his error. But he cannot be deceived about a regime that has killed millions of Jews – merely because they were Jews – that made terror into an everyday phenomenon, and that turned everything that pertains to the ideas of spirit, freedom and truth into its bloody opposite. A regime that in every respect imaginable was the deadly caricature of the Western tradition that you yourself so forcefully explicated and justified . . . Is this really the way you would like to be remembered in the history of ideas?

In reply, Heidegger wrote that, when the Nazis came to power in 1933, he had 'expected from National Socialism a spiritual renewal of life in its entirety, a reconciliation of social antagonisms and a deliverance of western Dasein from the dangers of communism'.[14] Indeed, he had said as much in his notorious rector's address at the University of Freiburg. The following year, he had realised his 'political error' and resigned his rectorship. But why had he never publicly retracted or condemned those words after 1934? He wrote to Marcuse: 'it would have been the end of both me and my family . . . An avowal after 1945 was for me impossible: the Nazi supporters announced their change of allegiance in the most loathsome way; I, however, had nothing in common with them.'[15]

This sounded slippery enough. But in 1953, the twenty-four-year-old Jürgen Habermas pointed out something that made Heidegger's story about his change of heart over the Nazis seem even more dubious. Habermas publicly challenged Heidegger to explain what he meant in his 1935 book *Introduction to Metaphysics* by the 'inner truth and greatness' of National Socialism. Hadn't Heidegger claimed to Marcuse that his endorsement of National Socialism had ceased a year earlier? How could Heidegger have allowed the republication in 1953 of these lectures without any revisions or commentary? 'What was really offensive', wrote Habermas in *Between Naturalism and Religion*, 'was the Nazi philosopher's denial of moral and political responsibility for the consequences of the mass criminality about which almost no one talked any more eight years after the war.'[16]

For the young Habermas, this was not only his first intervention in public life but a key moment in his intellectual and moral development. Born in 1929, Habermas had been one of the 'Flaghelfer generation' (anti-aircraft generation) of post-war intellectuals like the novelist Günter Grass and the sociologists Ralf Dahrendorf and Niklas Luhmann, who had, as teenagers, helped to defend Hitler. At fifteen, Habermas was, like most of his contemporaries, a member of the Hitler Youth. Too young to fight and too old to be exempted from any war service, he was sent to the western front to man anti-aircraft defences in rear-guard action against the Allied advance. He later described his father, director of the local seminary, as a 'passive sympathiser' with the Nazis and admitted that as a youth he had shared that mindset. But he was shaken out of his and his family's complacency by the Nuremberg trials and documentaries about the Nazi concentration camps. 'All at once we saw that we had been living in a politically criminal system', he later said. His horrified reaction to what he called his fellow Germans' 'collectively realised inhumanity' constituted what he described as 'that first rupture, which still gapes.'[17]

After the war, Habermas enrolled at the University of Bonn, later also studying philosophy at Göttingen and Zurich. Between 1949 and

1953, he spent four years studying Heidegger, so his letter to the philosopher was freighted with symbolic resonances. A young intellectual was calling out his older mentor, demanding that he not hide in silence but rather explain how he could have eulogised a politically criminal system. A new German generation was calling on an older one to account for itself, and perhaps atone for its sins.

In his mature writings, Habermas would hypothesise that there was something called communicative reason that had emancipatory power. In what he called an 'ideal speech situation', citizens would be able to raise moral and political concerns and the ensuing discourse would unfold in an orderly, conflict-free manner. It was a utopian hope that grew from the rubble of Germany, the philosophy of one who yearned for a human society that engaged in the free and rational discourse that was the good legacy of the Enlightenment. For Habermas, the inherent aim or telos of language was to reach understanding and bring about consensus. He argued that such rationally achieved consensus was both necessary and possible for human flourishing post-Auschwitz. The barriers preventing the exercise of reason and mutual understanding could be identified, comprehended and reduced.

Perhaps he was hoping for something like that in his exchange with Heidegger, but it didn't happen; Heidegger didn't reply. That silence confirmed for the young Habermas that German philosophy had failed in its moment of reckoning. Heidegger's failure seemed to him symptomatic of the repressive, silencing anti-discourse prevalent in the new Federal Republic. Just as Heidegger refused to publicly acknowledge his support for the Nazis, so Konrad Adenauer's government, mired in anti-communist jeremiads against its East German neighbour, refused to acknowledge or definitively break with Germany's recent past.

If the Frankfurt School was to have a role in post-war Germany, it was to disrupt this ghost sonata, to challenge the culture of silence and denial. Adorno and Horkheimer were at least temperamentally suited to that task, since they were, as the latter put it to the former, 'at right angles to reality'.[18] When the Institute reopened in August 1950, with Horkheimer and Adorno as co-directors, some of its offices were in the bombed-out ruins of Franz Röckle's Neue Sachlichkeit building. The following year they would move into Alois Geifer's similarly spare, functionalist new building. Perhaps, once more, the Institute had committed an architectural blunder: in 1923 its architecture seemed to collude with the prevailing Weimar ethos of functionalism, managerial efficiency and positivism. Nearly three decades later, the pale ghost of that deluded design was rising from Frankfurt's rubble, suggesting perhaps that the Institute wasn't quite as oppositional to the powers that be as it postured. Architectural history was repeating itself, not quite as farce, but certainly as disappointment. Striking too was that what had, before 1933, been known as Café Marx, in 1951 became known as Café Max, after Horkheimer. Marx, the philosopher whose name the Institute astutely airbrushed from their papers during their American exile so as not to offend their hosts, was now sidelined in the Frankfurt School's second European incarnation too.

Café Max opened for business. The newly reformed Institute started a new sociological project to investigate the conspiracy of silence that had descended on Germany. 'The obviousness of disaster becomes an asset to its apologists', wrote Adorno in *Minima Moralia*. 'What everyone knows no one need say and under cover of silence is allowed to proceed unopposed.'[19] The so-called 'Group Experiment' bore similarities to an earlier sociological project called the 'Authoritarian Project' which Adorno had worked on in Berkeley during his Californian exile. The Group Experiment too relied on psychoanalytical concepts to investigate the complex of guilt and defensiveness, which Adorno thought especially necessary because subjective opinion differed so sharply from objective fact – there was a need to dig behind the manifest content of what people said to explore what Adorno and his researchers took to be the collective psychopathology beneath.

The experiment involved about 1,800 participants taking part in 120 discussions between groups of fifteen to twenty. Though not representative of the German people, participants included former soldiers, fashion students, homeless people and even an ex-SS officer. Adorno found that participants were more likely to be defensive the more they were conscious of the enormity of Nazi crimes. They were likely, too, to identify with the new Germany despite those crimes. As a result, Germany seemed to be founded on a mass bad conscience, a collective psychopathology of denial. Of course it wasn't as simple as that. Some respondents admitted guilt, but attempted to convert it into a private matter, a subject for self-pity. Others projected the guilt on to Nazi leaders as if to suggest that they were helpless in the face of the power of Hitler and his clique. Indeed, about half of those who took part in the group discussions rejected the suggestion of their guilt for the crimes of the Nazis. A few were able to confront their guilt, and it was in those that Adorno placed some hope: 'It is the people who do not repress their consciousness of guilt and have no desperate need to adopt defensive attitudes who are free to speak the truth that not all Germans are anti-Semites.'[20]

Transcripts of interviews conducted for the Group Experiment included evidence of continued anti-Semitic and nationalist attitudes, which were sometimes combined with democratic views. Adorno identified a strange syndrome whereby people:

> appeal to democracy in order to argue against the Jews . . . their reaction is: we have nothing against the Jews, we have no wish to persecute them, but they should not do things that conflict with an interest – wholly undefined and arbitrarily selected – of the nation. In particular, they should not have an over-representative share of highly paid and influential jobs. This kind of thinking . . . provides a way out for people caught in a conflict between bad conscience and defensiveness.[21]

Adorno concluded that in the post-war Federal Republic authoritarian attitudes and a general tendency to conform continued. When the Group Experiment was published in 1955, Adorno was attacked for his interpretation of the results. Its authors wanted to force the entire nation to repent, argued Hamburg social psychologist Peter Hofstätter in a review. 'But how far can we assume that the majority of the members of a "nation" can be responsible for self-accusation for years on end?'[22] But Adorno argued that it was the victims who had to bear the burden of the horrors of the Nazi regime, not a German people in denial. He saw that the Group Experiment would be resented for disrupting the ghost sonata. Or as he put it: 'In the house of the hangman you should not speak of the rope; otherwise you will open yourself to the suspicion that you are rancorous person.'[23]

In the house of the hangman, Adorno kept speaking of taboo subjects. His essay 'Culture Critique and Society', when published in *Prisms* in 1955, proved incendiary to German and, more widely, European cultural life. He wrote:

> Cultural criticism finds itself today faced with the final state of the dialectic of culture and barbarism. To write poetry after Auschwitz is barbaric. And this corrodes even the knowledge of why it has become impossible to write poetry today. Absolute reification, which presupposed intellectual progress as one of its elements, is now preparing to absorb the mind entirely. Critical intelligence cannot be equal to this challenge as long as it confines itself to self-satisfied contemplation.[24]

What Adorno had in mind, in part, was that culture served as an alibi, a zone of escape from political realities rather than painful confrontation with them. Culture, that is to say, was like Heidegger retreating into his Black Forest hut for spiritual contemplation when his proper task was to confront his past – an unjustifiable distraction. In his book of aphorisms, *Minima Moralia: Notes on Damaged Life*, which he had brought in manuscript in his suitcase from California and published to great acclaim in 1951, Adorno wrote: 'That culture has so far failed is no justification for furthering its failure, by strewing the store of good flour on the spilt beer like the girl in the fairy-tale.'[25]

Thus far the revolutionary potential of works of art in the age of mechanical production in which Walter Benjamin had placed so much hope had not been realised: culture had become impotent to change oppressive social reality; worse, it helped hold that oppressive order in place. Marcuse, in his 1937 essay 'The Affirmative Character of Culture', had argued that culture separates itself from society or civilisation and creates the space for critical thought and social change. But instead of fulfilling any emancipatory role it had become an autonomous zone, a place of retreat from social reality. In this zone,

Marcuse argued, the demand for happiness in the real world is abandoned for an internal form of happiness, the happiness of the soul. Bourgeois culture creates an interior of the human being where the highest ideals of culture can be realised. This inner transformation does not demand an external transformation of the real world and its material conditions. Such is affirmative culture: the horrors of the everyday can be dissipated by attending to the beauties of Chopin.

But that failure of culture to perform its critical social role effectively was a prelude to an even greater obscenity. In his memoir *If This Is a Man*, Primo Levi described hearing the musical reveille every morning from his infirmary bed in Auschwitz. 'We all feel that this music is infernal', he wrote. 'When this music plays, we know that our comrades, out in the fog, are marching like automatons; their souls are dead and the music drives them, like the wind drives dead leaves, and takes the place of their wills.'[26] What was the point of culture when it had failed in its critical role, and when it did little more than supply a soundtrack to mass murder? And yet, philosophers, artists and writers railed against Adorno's stricture. The Auschwitz survivor and philosopher Jean Améry accused Adorno of using a language intoxicated by itself in which he had exploited Auschwitz for his metaphysical phantom of 'absolute negativity'. The author and playwright Wolfgang Hildesheimer argued in his poetics lectures in 1967 that poetry was the only possible literary option after Auschwitz. For him, such poems as Paul Celan's *Todesfuge* and Ingeborg Bachman's *Früher Mittag* 'were flight and flashes of insight into the terrifying instability of the world, the absurd'.[27] Bachman's poem, for instance, written seven years after the Second World War ended, begins with a description of lush summer, a verdant lime tree and gushing fountains, and then, in its second stanza, abruptly shifts mood:

> Where Germany's sky blackens the earth
> Its beheaded angel seeks a grave for hate
> And offers you the bowl of the heart[28]

Bachman's partner, the Swiss playwright and novelist, Max Frisch once argued that culture could serve as an alibi; Bachman's poem does the opposite. It tells us that it is no longer possible to remember Germany's lyrical poetic heritage without also remembering its crimes. It is a poem that displaces and estranges the world – the task that, in *Minima Moralia*, Adorno had insisted was necessary for philosophy but which poetry such as Bachman's could do just as well.

The Austrian poet and Adorno became friendly, particularly after she gave poetry lectures in Frankfurt in 1959. By 1966, in *Negative Dialectics*, Adorno would revise his opinion of a decade earlier:

> Perennial suffering has as much right to expression as a tortured man has to scream; hence it may have been wrong to say that after Auschwitz you could no longer write poems. But it is not wrong to raise the less cultural question whether after Auschwitz you can go on living – especially whether one who escaped by accident, one who by rights should have been killed, may go on living. His mere survival calls for the coldness, the basic principle of bourgeois subjectivity, without which there could have been no Auschwitz; this is the drastic guilt put on him who was spared.[29]

In *Negative Dialectics*, too, Adorno expressed better what human duty was in the wake of Auschwitz than he had a decade earlier. 'A new categorical imperative has been imposed by Hitler upon unfree mankind: to arrange their thoughts and actions so that Auschwitz will not repeat itself, so that nothing similar will happen.'[30]

AS HE SURVEYED his native land on his return, Adorno saw little that made him think that the German part of unfree mankind was capable of acting in line with that categorical imperative. Not only were the new bosses silent about, or former allies of, Hitler, but the rest of Germany still bent the knee to power. He wrote to Thomas Mann in June 1950:

> The inarticulate character of apolitical conviction, the readiness to submit to every manifestation of actual powers, the instant accommodation to whatever new situation emerges, all this is merely an aspect of the same regression. If it is true that the manipulative control of the

masses always brings about a regressive formation of humanity, and if Hitler's drive for power essentially involved the relationship of this development 'at a single stroke', we can only say that he, and the collapse that followed, has succeeded in producing the required infantilisation.[31]

Fascism had been overthrown in Germany but the personality type that supported it had survived. The notion that those likely to be seduced by fascist leaders were infantile was a long-running theme of Adorno's work before he returned to Germany. But another important theme of the Frankfurt School after the war, and one that scandalised in particular those who had fought for the Allies against the Nazis, was that there were parallels between how the National Socialists controlled the German people and how the seemingly free citizens of putatively liberal democratic states such as the United States were robbed of what they took to be their collective birthrights, freedom and autonomy.

At a symposium of psychoanalysts and sociologists in San Francisco in 1944, before he returned to Europe, Adorno had accounted for the success of fascist propaganda by saying that 'it simply takes people for what they are: genuine children of today's standardised mass culture who have been robbed to a great extent of their autonomy and spontaneity'.[32] There were similarities, he argued, between Nazi propaganda and the radio broadcasts by Californian preachers whom he called 'would-be Hitlers'. Both tried to gain authority over their audiences by a two-stage rhetorical process – first, professing their own weakness and thus identifying with the weak recipients of that message; second, stressing their status as one of the chosen few whom their listeners could join if they would only submit to their authority. To be a successful Führer or an effective charismatic radio preacher, Adorno argued, one must be what he called the 'great little man', enough like the follower to appeal to those elements of narcissism which remain attached to the follower's own ego, and yet also embody their collective hopes and even virtues. Hitler's genius, Adorno suggested, was that he 'posed as a composite of King Kong and the suburban barber'.[33]

This symposium led to Adorno's work in the development of what became known as the Californian F-scale, a personality test he developed in 1947 with researchers working at the University of California at Berkeley, that was published in 1950 in a book called *The Authoritarian Personality* in the Studies in Prejudice series sponsored by the American Jewish Committee. F stands for fascist, and the idea worked from the hypothesis Erich Fromm had similarly sought to test in his study of German workers nearly two decades earlier, that to investigate the character types most likely to succumb to fascism, researchers would have to penetrate the manifest dimensions of personality to get to the latent structures beneath. Like Fromm's study, the Berkeley project involved a Freudian developmental model: the authoritarian personality was unable to confront their harsh and punitive parents, and instead identified with authority figures. More dubiously, the authoritarian personality was linked to the suppressed homosexuality taken to be common to sadomasochists. 'The forbidden action which is converted into aggression is generally homosexual in nature', wrote Adorno and Horkheimer in *Dialectic of Enlightenment*. 'Through fear of castration, obedience to the father is taken to the extreme of an anticipation of castration in conscious emotional approximation to the nature of a small girl, and actual hatred to the father is suppressed.'[34]

But while Fromm's worker study was initiated to investigate the likely strength of German workers in resisting fascism and their amenability to revolutionary socialist ideas, the Berkeley study investigated the personality types that were likely to succumb to anti-democratic ideas and those that were not. One reason for this change was that, as we have seen, while in America the Institute dared not use the M word (Marxism) in its essays or research, for fear of alienating potential sponsors. As a result, ironically, the values and behaviours that had been associated with successful revolutionary Marxism in Fromm's study were now associated with support for democracy in the Berkeley study.

But there is more to this shift in taxonomy than self-censorship – the disappearance of the language of Marxism from the Institute indicated the Frankfurt School's declining faith in the proletariat and in revolution. Lukács had written in *History and Class Consciousness*: 'The fate of the revolution (and with it the fate of mankind) will depend on the ideological maturity of the proletariat, i.e. on its class consciousness.'[35] The Frankfurt School didn't believe in revolution any more, precisely because the proletariat was unlikely to come to ideological maturity. As Fromm put it in his 1956 book *The Sane Society*: 'The world is one great object for our appetite, a big apple, a big bottle, a big breast; we are the sucklers, the eternally expectant ones – and the eternally disappointed ones.'[36] Ideological maturity was unlikely in such a world. The manipulative control of the masses always brings about a regressive formation of humanity, wrote Adorno in a 1950 letter to Thomas Mann.[37] He was writing about Hitler's impact, but the Frankfurt School's growing belief was that such control and regression were features of the societies that had only recently allied against Hitler.

The F-scale was devised as part of a research project to explore what Adorno and his team called a 'new anthropological type', the authoritarian personality. It involved a set of questions designed to measure fascist potential, by means of testing nine personality variables as set out in *The Authoritarian Personality*, which Adorno described as follows:

Conventionalism: Rigid adherence to conventional, middle-class values. Authoritarian Submission: Submissive, uncritical attitude toward idealised moral authorities of the ingroup. Anti-intraception: Opposition to the subjective, the imaginative, the tender-minded. Authoritarian Aggression: Tendency to be on the lookout for, and to condemn, reject, and punish people who violate conventional values. Superstition and Stereotypy: The belief in mystical determinants of the individual's fate; the disposition to think in rigid categories. Power and 'Toughness': Preoccupation with the dominance-submission, strong-weak, leader-follower dimension; identification with power figures; overemphasis upon the conventionalised attributes of the ego; exaggerated assertion of strength and toughness. Destructiveness and Cynicism: Generalised hostility, vilification of the human. Projectivity: The disposition to believe that wild and dangerous things go on in the world; the projection outwards of unconscious emotional impulses. Sex: Exaggerated concern with sexual 'goings-on'.[38]

The questionnaires invited respondents to state the extent to which they agreed with such statements as:

- Obedience and respect for authority are the most important virtues children should learn.
- What this country needs most, more than laws and political programs, is a few courageous, tireless, devoted leaders in whom the people can put their faith.
- What the youth needs most is strict discipline, rugged determination, and the will to work and fight for family and country.
- There is hardly anything lower than a person who does not feel a great love, gratitude, and respect for his parents.
- Sex crimes, such as rape and attacks on children, deserve more than mere imprisonment; such criminals ought to be publicly whipped, or worse.
- The true American way of life is disappearing so fast that force may be necessary to preserve it.[39]

Respondents were allowed to make graduated agreement or disagreement with these and other statements and the responses entered on a scale that went from +3 to -3. From the 2,099 people – all white, gentile, middle-class Americans – who filled in the questionnaires, those who scored high or low on the F-scale were invited to take part in longer evaluative interviews. Adorno used information from these interviews to draw up a list of six types of authoritarian personality, and five types of non-authoritarian personality.

Authoritarian personality types included the 'tough guy' (whose 'repressed id tendencies gain the upper hand, but in a stunted form' according to Adorno) and the 'crank' and 'manipulative' types (both of whom, Adorno thought, 'seem to have resolved the Oedipus complex through a narcissistic withdrawal into their inner selves'). Adorno also devised a typology for respondents who scored low on the F-scale. Non-fascist types included the 'protesting' type (whose 'undercurrent of hostility against the father, leads to the conscientious rejection of heteronomous authority instead of its acceptance. The decisive feature is opposition to whatever appears to be tyranny') and the 'genuine liberal' (who 'may be conceived in terms of that balance between superego, ego, and id which Freud deemed ideal').[40]

Adorno didn't specify which type he belonged to, but the safe money says he would have described himself as a genuine liberal.[41]

When *The Authoritarian Personality* was published in 1950, the F-scale was criticised for many things, not least for its assumption that conservatism and authoritarianism were related. It was also attacked because clever people could second guess the significance of the questions, react in a more suitable manner and skew the results. The University of Chicago sociologist Edward Shils wondered why authoritarianism was linked to fascism rather than communism in Adorno and his team's work. Would a C-scale be very different from an F-scale? Surely in 1950 the real opposition was between liberal democracies and totalitarianism, be that fascist or communist? The Cold War had begun and so what was needed was not to understand the personality types that supported Hitler, but the personality types that supported Stalin and his successors and, quite possibly, to weed out those with communistic tendencies. Retooled, the F-scale could become the R-scale (R standing for Red); and another scale could be calibrated to investigate the desirable types who would resist the Red menace. The idea may have been to pit the unfortunate sadomasochistic hordes of the Soviet bloc against the free, virile individual personality types who thrived in the free west, but Adorno and the rest of the Frankfurt School refused to contrast Soviet totalitarianism with the individualist non-ideological libertarian west. They saw domination everywhere – in fascist, socialist and liberal capitalist polities.

Indeed, in *The Authoritarian Personality*, Adorno went so far as to suggest that the rhetoric of individualism, deployed during the Cold War against Soviet collectivism, was itself a tool of domination. 'Individualism, opposed to inhuman pigeonholing, may ultimately become a mere ideological veil in a society which actually is inhuman and whose intrinsic tendency towards the "subsumption" of everything shows itself by the classification of people themselves.' Adorno bracingly argued that humans were little more than instances of types in class-ridden society. 'In other words', he wrote, 'large numbers of people are no longer, or rather never were, "individuals" in the sense of traditional nineteenth-century philosophy . . . [O]verpowering social processes . . . leave to the "individual" but little freedom for action and true individuation.'[42]

14

The Liberation of Eros

In 1950 and 1951, Herbert Marcuse gave a series of lectures at the Washington School of Psychiatry. This was his return to philosophy and writing after a lengthy period working for the American government in its fight against Nazism. The lectures marked the moment that critical theory started to divide between Horkheimer and Adorno's pessimistic Frankfurt version and the more hopeful American mutations of Marcuse and Fromm, who both remained on the other side of the Atlantic.

For Horkheimer and Adorno, *The Authoritarian Personality* and the Group Experiment served as empirical justifications for their gloominess about the chances of realising the practical goal for critical theory – the radical transformation of society. Marcuse's lectures proposed that such transformation was possible. He didn't quite contradict the dismal diagnosis of *Dialectic of Enlightenment* that 'mankind, instead of entering into a truly human condition, is sinking into a new kind of barbarism', but he did suggest something in these lectures that seemed beyond Horkheimer and Adorno's philosophy – the subversive potential of sexual desire. The lectures formed the basis of Marcuse's 1955 book *Eros and Civilisation: A Philosophical Inquiry Into Freud*, dedicated to his first wife, the mathematician and statistician Sophie Wertheim, who died of cancer in 1951. In 1955, Marcuse married Inge Neumann. She was the widow of his friend Franz Neumann, who had died in a car crash in Switzerland in 1954. During this time Marcuse was teaching as a political philosopher, first at Columbia University, then at Harvard.

The subversive potential of sexual desire was not a new theme. In his 1938 essay 'On Hedonism', Marcuse had written:

> The unpurified, unrationalised release of sexual relationships would be the strongest release of enjoyment as such and the total devaluation of labour for its own sake . . . The dreariness and injustice of work conditions would penetrate explosively the consciousness of individuals and make impossible their peaceful subordination to the social system of the bourgeois world.[1]

These ideas were a challenge to Freudian orthodoxy, as well as a rebuke to classical Marxism that never imagined sexual liberation could shake the social system of the bourgeois world. In *Eros and Civilisation*, though, Marcuse went further. He specifically took on one of Freud's most bleak and pessimistic books, *Civilisation and Its Discontents*, and used its leading ideas to argue for the most liberating and hopeful conclusions. It was a resonant moment in which to address the possibilities of sexual liberation. Post-war America was preoccupied with sex. Alfred Kinsey had founded the Institute for Sex Research at Indiana University in 1947, and became renowned for his two books *Sexual Behaviour in the Human Male* (1948) and *Sexual Behaviour in the Human Female* (1953). In the late 1940s, too, the Austrian-born maverick Marxist psychoanalytical theorist Wilhelm Reich had become famous in America as a prophet of sexual liberation. 'A sexual revolution is in progress', he wrote in *The Invasion of Compulsory Sex-Morality*, 'and no power on earth will stop it.'[2]

During the 1930s, members of the Frankfurt School including Marcuse and Fromm had read Reich's writings and, indeed, the school's account of fascism was influenced by his book *The Mass Psychology of Fascism*. Reich had been exiled in the US since 1939 and during that time had developed his 'orgone energy accumulator', a wooden cupboard lined with metal and insulated with steel wool. Although Albert Einstein, who Reich invited to try out the accumulator, was sceptical about its inventor's claim that it could improve the users' 'orgiastic potency' and, thereby, their mental health, many leading male, post-war American writers – including Norman Mailer, J. D. Salinger, Saul

Bellow, Allen Ginsberg and Jack Kerouac – hailed the benefits of going into Reich's closet. Later William Burroughs wrote in a magazine article called 'All the Accumulators I have Ever Owned': 'Your intrepid reporter, at age 37, achieved spontaneous orgasm, no hands, in an orgone accumulator built in an orange grove in Pharr, Texas.' If women gained orgiastic potency from the machine, satirised by Woody Allen in the 1973 movie *Sleeper* as an orgasmatron, we didn't get to hear about it.

By the mid 1950s, however, Reich, suffering from paranoid delusions that the world was under attack by UFOs, was being investigated by the Food and Drugs Administration for making fraudulent claims about the orgone energy accumulator. 'If his claims for the orgone accumulator were no more than ridiculous quackery', asks Christopher Turner, author of *Adventures in the Orgasmatron: Wilhelm Reich and the Invention of Sex*, 'as the FDA doctors suggested, and if he was just a paranoid schizophrenic, as one court psychiatrist concluded, why did the US government consider him such a danger?'[3] One possible answer is that the sexual liberation proselytised for by a Marxist psychoanalyst might have seemed a clear and present red danger to an increasingly paranoid America at the height of the Cold War. Another is that Reich's idea of sexual liberation was a threat to such cherished American values as the work ethic and monogamy. A third possibility is that a charlatan making money from a quack cure-all is intolerable in pretty much any polity.

Reich died of a heart attack in November 1957 in Lewisburg Federal Penitentiary in Pennsylvania, while serving a two-year jail sentence for breaking an injunction stopping him from hiring out or selling his machine. We don't know if Herbert Marcuse stepped inside Reich's accumulator, still less if he felt its benefits, but neither sounds likely. Marcuse, though he knew and had been influenced by Reich's writings, was less genitally fixated than his fellow exile. In *Eros and Civilisation*, he wasn't arguing for a greater quantity and quality of orgasms. Reich's mistake, he argued, was to take 'sexual liberation per se as a panacea for individual and social ills': 'The problem of sublimation is minimised; no essential distinction is made between repressive and non-repressive sublimation, and progress in freedom appears as a mere release of sexuality.'[4]

In his 1930 book *Civilisation and its Discontents*, Freud claimed that civilisation involves the subordination of happiness and sexual pleasure to work, monogamy and social restraint. He argued that social constraints are necessary for the flourishing of human society. Resources are scarce, so hard labour is required. The untrammelled indulgence of human biological and psychological needs, in accordance with what Freud called the pleasure principle, infringed on the freedom of others and so had to be curtailed by rules and discipline, or, as he called it, the reality principle. The Freudian narrative of how individuals repress and sublimate their needs goes like this. Initially, our instincts (what Freud called the id) drive us to seek pleasure and avoid pain. But during its development, as Marcuse notes, 'the individual comes to the traumatic realisation that full and painless gratification of needs is impossible'. And so the reality principle (represented by the ego in the individual's psyche) intervenes to instruct the individual on what is socially acceptable. In the process, the individual becomes not just pleasure-fixated but 'a conscious, thinking subject, geared to a rationality imposed on him from the outside'.[5]

Freud thought these instincts were unchangeable. Marcuse, though, argued that if instincts can be repressed, they are not immutable; more importantly, that the kind of society in which an individual develops as a conscious thinking subject plays a role in shaping the instincts. Effectively, Marcuse was historicising Freud from a Marxist perspective, suggesting that the instincts that Freud hypostatised could change with the social system. This became clear when Marcuse made his key distinction between basic and surplus repression (precisely the distinction he thought Reich failed to make in his eulogies to the orgasm as the supreme good). The former is the sort of repression of the instincts necessary, wrote Marcuse, 'for the perpetuation of the human race in civilisation'. But the latter, surplus repression, has the purpose of shaping the instincts in accordance with the 'performance principle' which, for Marcuse, was the prevailing form of the reality principle.

Marcuse's idea was that the reality principle mutates into a new form under capitalism. He wrote in *Eros and Civilisation*:

> The performance principle, which is that of an acquisitive and antago-
> nistic society in the process of constant expansion, presupposes a long
> development during which domination has been increasingly rational-
> ised: control over social labour now reproduces society on a large scale
> and under improving conditions . . . For the vast majority of the popu-
> lation, the scope and mode of satisfaction are determined by their own
> labour; but their labour is work for an apparatus which they do not
> control, which operates as an independent power to which individuals
> must submit if they want to live. And it becomes the more alien the
> more specialised the division of labour becomes. Men do not live their
> own lives but perform pre-established functions. While they work, they
> do not fulfil their own needs and faculties but work in *alienation*.[6]

Marcuse thus linked Freudian repression with Marxist alienation –
the worker is manipulated in such a way that the restrictions on the
libido seem to be rational laws which are then internalised. The
unnatural – that our pre-established function is to produce commodities and profit for the capitalist – becomes natural to us, a second
nature. Hence, the individual defines him or herself in conformity
with the apparatus. Or, as Marcuse put it: 'he desires what he is
supposed to desire . . . Neither his desires nor his alteration of reality
are henceforth his own: they are now "organised" by his society. And
this "organisation" represses and transubstantiates his original
instinctual needs.'[7]

Marcuse was writing in 1950s America in which, he thought,
advertising, consumerism, mass culture and ideology integrated
Americans into a peaceful subordination to the social system of the
bourgeois world and made them desire things that they didn't need.
Although he was teaching at American universities, Marcuse maintained close links with his former colleagues Adorno and Horkheimer
in Frankfurt, and in key respects, their critique of America is similar.
For all three, the rugged individualism of US society that was pitted
rhetorically against the collectivism of the Soviet bloc during the Cold
War was a myth: Americans were infantilised, repressed pseudo-indi-
viduals. During 1952 and 1953, for instance, Adorno spent ten months
in California analysing newspaper astrology columns, radio soap

operas and the new medium of television, and what he had to say about them bore closely on what Marcuse wrote in *Eros and Civilisation*. Adorno found in all these forms of mass culture a symmetry with fascist propaganda: both mass culture and fascist propaganda, he argued, meet and manipulate the dependency needs of the pseudo-individual character, 'promoting conventional, conformist and contented attitudes'.[8]

If you were an American, of course, this might have seemed incredibly patronising. Adorno, at least, praised astrology columnists for their ingenuity. Their readers weren't utterly witless: they realised from their own lives that 'everything does not run so smooth as the column seems to imply it does and that not everything takes care of itself'; rather, they experience life as making contradictory demands on them. In a manner similar to Nazi propagandists, 'the column has to take up these contradictions themselves if it really wants to tie the readers to its own authority'. One way the astrology columnists did this was to recommend different activities for different times of day: AM is for work, reality and the ego principle, Adorno noted; PM is apparently for 'the instinctual urges of the pleasure principle'. He also noted that the pleasures of the PM are rewards or compensations for the work of the AM. But the pleasures of the PM are only justified if they ultimately served the 'ulterior purpose of success and self-promotion'.[9] As a result, pleasure itself becomes a duty, a form of work: what looked like afternoon delight following a morning's labours was really anything but. Eros bowed to Logos. Instead of a freed-up pleasure principle, this division served to extend the dictates of the reality principle over every aspect of life. What psychoanalysis calls bi-phasic behaviour is a symptom of compulsive neurosis, Adorno argued. Astrology columns seemed to offer their readers tools to deal with the contradictions of everyday life, but were really, he thought, making them compulsive neurotics who internalised those contradictions rather than confronting them.

Adorno took this compulsive neurotic division into AM and PM to be emblematic of American mass culture. Instead of confronting the contradictions of society, its citizens neurotically internalised them; by dividing days into work and pleasure, they became, not self-fulfilled, but self-alienated. What Adorno found in the American astrology columns, Marcuse took to be more generally true of American and indeed any advanced industrial society. His hope in *Eros and Civilisation* was for a radical transformation of those societies, for the pleasure principle to be liberated from the dictatorship of the performance principle, for humans to become re-eroticised – whole, fulfilled and free.

Freud had argued that this kind of transformation was impossible, that civilisations must trade freedom for security. The United States of the 1950s seemed to be a civilisation that had oscillated towards security and away from freedom, while rhetorically posturing otherwise. Richard Yates suggested that his novel *Revolutionary Road*, published in 1961 but set in 1955, was about an era that embodied 'a kind of blind, desperate clinging to safety and security at any price'.[10] America was terrified of communism and nuclear war; Nixon and McCarthy's work on the House Un-American Activities Committee made men and women afraid to speak freely or act independently. The American society, or any other civilised society for that matter, that postured in the 1950s as free and affluent was, so Marcuse argued, straitjacketed by conformity.

The key point of Freud's *Civilisation and Its Discontents* was that the ostensible progress of civilisation involved a repression from which there was no escape. Marcuse argued against such pessimism. In advanced industrial societies such as the United States, he claimed, the scarcity of resources that Freud had cited as one reason why the pleasure principle needed to be curtailed by the reality principle was no longer a concern. 'The very progress of civilisation under the performance principle has attained a level of productivity at which the social demands upon instinctual energy to be spent in alienated labour could be considerably reduced', he wrote.[11] Freud's point about scarcity may have had some validity in earlier times, he argued, but now ostensible scarcity functions ideologically to keep us working when some of that work is surplus to requirements, a surplus that supports the domination of worker by capitalist.

The ideological function of hard labour is arguably still with us. In a 2013 article called 'On the Phenomenon of Bullshit Jobs', the anarchist, anthropologist and Occupy movement activist David Graeber noted that, in 1930, the economist John Maynard Keynes predicted that by the end of the century technology would have advanced sufficiently that in countries such as the UK and the US we'd be on fifteen-hour weeks. Graeber, like Marcuse, argued that in technological terms we are quite capable of reducing our working ours thus. And yet it didn't happen. 'Instead', Graeber argued, 'technology has been marshalled, if anything, to figure out ways to make us all work more. Huge swathes of people, in Europe and North America in particular, spend their entire working lives performing tasks they believe to be unnecessary. The moral and spiritual damage that comes from this situation is profound. It is a scar across our collective soul. Yet virtually no one talks about it.'[12] What Marcuse called 'the dreariness and injustice of work conditions' and workers' 'peaceful subordination to the social system of the bourgeois world' is no less true today than it was sixty years ago.

But in *Eros and Civilisation* Marcuse wasn't indicting bullshit jobs per se; rather he was arguing that increased productivity by means of alienated labour had eliminated the scarcity that required us to work hard. Our problem in advanced industrial societies then as now is not scarcity, but the absence of a fair and just distribution of resources. Marcuse's optimistic vision is one in which the working day is shortened and everybody's needs are met by improved distribution of goods and services and a better division of labour, such that, as a result, erotic energies are released. Releasing erotic energies in this way, Marcuse argued, would liberate us from the kind of genital fixation to which Wilhelm Reich had been prone. Freed from being a mere instrument of labour, the body could be resexualised. Marcuse suggested that for too long philosophy has treated 'being' as pure, abstract consciousness. Eros had been subdued by Logos. Capitalism, too, limited Eros, by constraining it under genital supremacy and by putting it to work in the service of monogamy and reproduction.

It's not very clear, though, how sexual practices would change if Eros was liberated. Marcuse didn't condemn, for example, coprophilia or homosexuality but argued that in the non-repressive civilisation he advocated they may take 'other forms compatible with normality in high civilisation'.[13]

But invoking 'normality' is problematic: if there are sexual norms in Marcuse's non-repressive world wouldn't they stem the erotic energies that have just been unleashed? He was clearly not suggesting the establishment of a vice squad to police his non-repressive utopia, but presumably rather suggesting that in it sexual practices will evolve from what they are now. What forms they will take is difficult – for us, as repressed, alienated subjects under the yoke of monopoly capitalism – to imagine.

One casualty of the end of repressive civilisation and the release of libidinal energy, Marcuse tantalisingly suggested, would be that iconic institution of 1950s America, the nuclear family. 'The body in its entirety would become an object of cathexis, a thing to be enjoyed – an instrument of pleasure', Marcuse wrote. 'This change in the value and scope of libidinal relations would lead to a disintegration of the institutions in which the private interpersonal relations have been organised, particularly the monogamic and patriarchal family.' Sex would no longer be 'in the service of production' but would have the 'function of obtaining pleasure from zones of the body'.[14] And that wouldn't be the end of the matter: not just the whole body would be eroticised, but everything one did would be too – social relations, work and creating culture.

Even more intriguing was what Marcuse's non-repressive civilisation meant for the notions of production and fulfilling labour discussed earlier. For Hegel, man realises his identity through production 'translating itself from the night of possibility into the day of actuality', and Marx too urged that fulfilling oneself as a human involves producing something. Erich Fromm also put forward the ideal of a 'productive man', a normative character who is alive to the extent he is 'in the act of expressing his own specific human powers'. For Marcuse, however, this emphasis on production reinforced the capitalist work ethic and the performance principle. His argument showed how far critical theory had departed from Marxist orthodoxy: Marx was effectively cast as a philosopher who bought into capitalist ideology by eulogising self-fulfilment through labour, albeit non-alienated labour. But Fromm rather than Marx was the explicit target:

Marcuse suggested that Fromm had smuggled capitalist values into his critique of the capitalist system – a point that he would later elaborate in a bitter dispute between the two men.

But Marcuse was not merely a hedonist arguing that we should play and not work. Rather, he was arguing that the division between work and play should be overcome. Following Schiller, he advocated play and art as emancipatory activities that could transform human beings and, in particular, change their relationship to labour. Instead of working, alienated, at jobs that diminish us spiritually and ruin us physically, he suggested that in a non-repressive society erotic energies would flow into sexual gratification, play and creative work. Marcuse took some of this utopian vision from the nineteenth-century French utopian socialist and pre-Marxist Charles Fourier, who sought a similar society to the one Marcuse dreamt of in *Eros and Civilisation*. Fourier sought, Marcuse wrote, 'the creation of "luxury, or the pleasure of the five senses"; the formation of libidinal groups (of friendship and love); and the establishment of a harmonious order, organising these groups for work in accordance with the development of the individual'. The main drawback of Fourier's utopia was that it was to be administered by a giant organisation that, Marcuse thought, would reproduce the repressive system it was designed to escape.[15]

None of this should be taken as suggesting, though, that Marcuse's non-repressive libidinal revolution was something that could be achieved without work. Freud, after all, had defined Eros as striving to 'form substance into ever greater unities, so that life may be prolonged and brought to higher development'.[16] That sounds like work, and Marcuse recognised as much – freeing up the pleasure principle as he suggested alters what work is and, yet, it is nonetheless work.

> The erotic aim of sustaining the entire body as a subject-object of pleasure calls for the continual revolution of the organism, the intensification of its receptivity, the growth of its sensuousness. The aim generates its own projects of realisation: the abolition of toil, the amelioration of the environment, the conquest of disease and decay, the creation of luxury. All these activities flow directly from the pleasure principle, and, at the same time they constitute work.[17]

What Marcuse described as continual revolution sounds like Sisyphean labour. But that labour, crucially, was not the alienated, repressive work that upheld the performance principle but more like the work of two other classical mythological figures Marcuse cited, Orpheus and Narcissus. Orpheus refuses repressive sexuality and seeks union with the object of his desire, while Narcissus has erotic impulses suffusing his entire personality. Strikingly too, for Marcuse, Narcissus is not separated from nature but part of it and he takes pleasure in seeing himself reflected in it. This part of Marcuse's analysis clearly connected with Adorno and Horkheimer's critique of the despoilation of nature in *Dialectic of Enlightenment*. For all three, any desirable transformation involved reuniting humans with nature rather than treating it, as it had been since Francis Bacon, as fit for nothing but domination. Orpheus and Narcissus were, for Marcuse, 'images of the Great Refusal: refusal to accept separation from the libidinous object (or subject). The refusal aimed at liberation – at the reunion of what has become separated.'[18] Eros has been sundered from Logos and subjugated by it; humanity has been divided from nature and dominated it. Arguably, the kinds of reunion Marcuse imagined involve labour, indeed the kind of self-actualising labour that Fromm described in his 1961 *Marx's Concept of Man*.

Eros and Civilisation saw Marcuse reconceptualising Marxism. For him in 1955, the history of all hitherto existing societies was not simply, as it had been a century earlier for Marx and Engels in *The Communist Manifesto*, the history of class struggles; it was also a fight over the repression of our instincts. Advanced industrial society is preventing us from reaching a non-repressive society 'based on a fundamentally different experience of being, a fundamentally different relation between man and nature, and fundamentally different existential relations'.[19] But, unlike Horkheimer and Adorno's philosophy, Marcuse's was optimistic, arguing that a non-repressive society was possible and that 'a new basic experience of being would change the human existence in its entirety'.

In *Eros and Civilisation*, Marcuse took Freud's pessimistic vision of what civilisation entailed and used it to imagine precisely the possibility Freud discounted, a non-repressive civilisation. That sounds very much like neo-Freudian revisionism. And yet his book ended with an epilogue entitled 'Critique of Neo-Freudian Revisionism' in which he accused several prominent psychoanalysts of revising Freud's work in such a way as to purge it of its critical implications. Among those in Marcuse's crosshairs once more was Erich Fromm. Marcuse believed that Fromm and the other neo-Freudians had rejected some of Freud's key insights such as his libidinal theory, the death instinct, the Oedipus complex, and the primal horde theory whereby in human pre-history a single domi-nant male was killed because of his sexual rights over women, generating a guilt that was passed down through human history.

Fromm – performing a Marxist critique of Freud not dissimilar to Marcuse's own in *Eros and Civilisation* – doubted that Oedipal strug-gle was the eternal truth of father–son relations, but saw it as a struggle to which the conditions of capitalist society made them more prone. But Marcuse went further in accusing Fromm of revisionism. He argued that his former colleague had moved away from the instinctual basis of human personality, instead embracing a 'positive thinking which leaves the negative where it is – predominant over human exist-ence'. Marcuse claimed that Fromm's distinctions between good and bad and productive and unproductive were taken from the very capi-talist ideology he was ostensibly critiquing. Worse, he accused Fromm of bowing before the conformist slogan 'accentuate the positive'.[20]

Is this fair on Fromm? Like Marcuse, Fromm had chosen to remain in his country of exile after the war. Indeed, of all the Frankfurt schol-ars, Fromm was the most comfortable in America – quicker to learn English (and latterly to write in that language with a greater ease and facility than not only his German colleagues but many native English speakers) and more ready to integrate into US society. Not that he was uncritical of that society: indeed, his exile writings were so critical that, initially, one would take him to be a natural ally of Marcuse. For instance, Fromm's 1941 *Fear of Freedom*, while explicitly indicting totalitarian societies and how they appeal to a deep-seated craving to escape from the freedom of the modern world and return to the womb, also recognised that capitalist democracies offered another form of escape from freedom. In his 1955 book *The Sane Society* he suggested that, while early capitalism had produced the 'hoarding character' who hoards both possessions and feelings, a new character type had emerged under post-war capitalism: the 'marketing character' who 'adapts to the market economy by becoming detached from authentic emotions, truth and conviction' and for whom 'everything is transformed into a commodity, not only things, but the person himself, his physical energy, his skills, his knowledge, his opinions, his feelings, even his smiles'.[21] Such people are not able to care, 'not because they are selfish, but because their relationship to each other and to themselves is so thin'.[22] Against the marketing character, Fromm juxtaposed his ideal character type, the 'productive character', who loves and creates, and for whom being is more important than having. Productive characters like this are discouraged in the market economy. In fact they are a threat to its values.

So much of this seems to be consistent with Marcuse's *Eros and Civilisation* that it is hard to understand why Fromm was targeted in its epilogue. Given Fromm's commitment to Marxism, it is not likely that he would have reduced psychoanalysis to a conformist psychology, and yet that is Marcuse's accusation. The epilogue was slightly modified and submitted to the journal *Dissent*, where it was published in 1955 and triggered an acrimonious dispute that was acted out in the magazine's pages over several issues. The roots of the conflict, however, go back to the 1930s when Fromm's growing distaste for Freudian orthodoxy led to a clash between him and Adorno and Horkheimer that led to his dismissal from the Institute in 1939. At that time, Adorno and Horkheimer had agreed with Freud's suggestion that there could be no harmony between the self and society. Instincts sought release, and society had to curtail that release in order to survive. Fromm, even in the 1930s, was suspicious of this Freudian orthodoxy: his concept of a social character involved external social structures shaping the inner self. But for Adorno and Horkheimer, and later Marcuse, this revision of Freud was socially conservative. Fromm had downgraded the importance Freud placed on early childhood sexual experiences and the unconscious, and Marcuse charged him with holding to an 'idealist ethics'. He argued that Fromm's call for human productivity, love and sanity suggested precisely what

Freud had denied, that there could be harmony between self and society. Fromm's revisionism defanged Freud, losing the critical edge of the latter's radical social critique. Fromm's 'road to sanity', Marcuse argued, represented palliatives for 'a smoother functioning of the established society'. Fromm retorted that Marcuse, in denying the possibility of creative productivity, happiness and genuine love under capitalism was thinking undialectically, taking his pessimism to the point of nihilism. Fromm argued that there are limited potentialities for self-transformation under capitalism that could eventually realise what he called a socialist humanism.

Marcuse's contention was that there is no such road to sanity. He reckoned Fromm's suggestion was premised on the idea of an autonomous individual capable of eluding the dominating structures of society. But Freud's point, echoed by critical theory, was that such a figure is a myth, invented in the nineteenth century under early capitalism and now an utter anachronism, a throwback to a pre-Freudian era. Invoking it now could only serve the interests of the dominating society Fromm was ostensibly out to excoriate. In *Dialectic of Enlightenment*, Adorno and Horkheimer compared the individual to a local shop made obsolete by a supermarket. The individual is 'the psychological corner shop' which emerged from feudal restraints as 'a dynamic cell of economic activity'. Freudian psychoanalysis 'represented the internal "small business" which grew up . . . as a complex dynamic system of the conscious and unconscious, the id, ego and super-ego'. Freudian psychoanalysis, for these critical theorists if not for Fromm, was the theory of the human psyche proper to capitalism as it evolved in the late nineteenth and twentieth centuries. In particular, psychoanalysis claimed that the autonomous individual is a chimera. We are not free either of our biological instincts, nor can we escape determination and domination by the social order. 'Decisions for men as active workers are taken by the hierarchy ranging from the trade associations to the national administration', wrote Adorno and Horkheimer, 'and in the private sphere by the system of mass culture which takes over the last inward impulses of individuals who are forced to consume what is offered to them'.[23] The autonomous individual, the figure that Fromm needed to construct his road to sanity, was programatically denied by critical theory. Adorno wrote: 'While they [the revisionists] unceasingly talk of the influence of society on the individual, they forget that not only the individual, but the category of individuality is a product of society.'[24]

The *Dissent* debate that marked Fromm's anathematisation by critical theory was so bitter that it ended Marcuse and Fromm's friendship. Years later Fromm saw Marcuse on a train and studiously ignored him. Wounding too for Fromm was the fact that the dispute was played out in the pages of a journal on whose editorial board he had served. Its editors, the New York Intellectuals Irving Howe and Lewis Coser, had become so disenchanted with their colleague and his views that they had no compunction about offending him by publishing Marcuse's attack. They even allowed Marcuse to write a rebuttal to Fromm's rebuttal. That may seem a minor issue, but it showed the extent to which the deck was stacked against him. The *Dissent* row was thus experienced by Fromm as a double stab in the back. His biographer suggests that the exchange damaged his quest for academic respectability, casting him in a marginalised role – an experience comparable to what he felt as a child in his parents' home or what he had experienced when he was dismissed by the Institute in 1939.[25] But if Fromm was damaged in academic circles by the dispute and became, as one critic put it, 'the forgotten intellectual',[26] that chiefly shows how unimportant academic reputation was to his growing role as what we have learned to call a public intellectual. After the *Dissent* debacle, Fromm carried on regardless, writing books that argued for the kind of socialist humanism his former colleagues denied was possible. He nonetheless achieved remarkable successes with many of them.

Although he would spend most of his life after exile in 1933 to his death in 1980 living in the United States, in 1950 he took up a post at the National Autonomous University in Mexico City. He moved there for the benefit of his second wife Henny Gurland, whom he had married in 1944. She had been advised by her doctor to take trips to the radioactive springs near Mexico City to aid her recovery from high blood pressure, cardiac problems and depression. In September 1940, Gurland, a photographer, had been among the group of refugees including Walter Benjamin who fled on foot across the Pyrenees, and may have been the last person to see him alive before he, reportedly, took his own life. During several trips to Mexico, the climate and warm mineral waters soothed Henny's pain and apparently eased her depression. For Fromm, Mexico seemed to be his last hope to restore his own happiness and hers. Yet in 1952 Henny died, possibly from heart failure, though more likely, as his biographer suggests, she committed suicide.

It's difficult not to read Fromm's most successful book, *The Art of Loving*, in the light of his Mexican years, the death of Henny and the misery it caused him. He wrote the book in part to counter the increasingly common notion that establishing a relationship does not require work. Love had been poisoned like everything else in commodity capitalism, reified and neutered of its otherwise deranging power. He wrote of the prevailing form of coupledom as an *égoisme à deux*, in which two self-centred people come together in marriage or partnership to escape loneliness, as though love were a full comprehensive insurance policy that could protect both parties from the vicissitudes of the real world of loss and disappointment. Neither egoist works, though, to arrive at what Fromm called a 'central relationship'. He argued that the very language of love connived with this lie: 'This attitude – that there is nothing easier than to love – has continued to be the prevalent idea about love in spite of the overwhelming evidence to the contrary.'[27] In Marxist terms, society treated love as a commodity rather than realising it was an art that took time, skill and dedication to master. The beloved too became reified, an object serving instrumental purposes rather than a person.

All the five types of love Fromm identified in *The Art of Loving* were becoming similarly debased – brotherly love by the commodification of humans; motherly love by narcissism; self-love by selfishness; love of God by idolatry; and erotic love by the absence of tenderness. The death of the tenderness in erotic love, he charged, came from the refusal of personal responsibility, the insistence on entitlement and the tendency to look outward in demand rather than inward in obligation.

It scarcely needs saying that we have not, as a society, learned the art of loving. Indeed, one suggestion is that we have abolished love in favour of sex, since for us capitalists of anti-romance, love involves too much work, commitment and risk. As a result, Fromm's book, six decades after its publication, reads like a challenge and a refreshing rebuke: in an age of disposable lovers, where calculated sexual pleasure has supplanted the unpredictability of love, where looking for love is like shopping and we demand from it what we have come to expect from our other purchases – novelty, variety, disposability. In his book *Liquid Love*, the sociologist Zygmunt Bauman argues that our society has failed to learn the lessons of Fromm's book: 'Attempts to tame the wayward and domesticate the riotous, to make the unknowable predictable and enchain the free-roaming – all such things sound the death knell to love. Eros won't outlast duality. As far as love is concerned, possession, power, fusion and disenchantment are the Four Horsemen of the Apocalypse.'[28]

IN MAY 1958, the twenty-eight-year-old Jürgen Habermas addressed a political protest in Frankfurt. The Federal Republic's Bundestag had voted that March to allow German armed forces to be equipped with NATO's atomic weapons. The Federal Republic's army had only existed since 1955 and from its inception the question of whether it should have nuclear weapons was a vexed issue. A protest group called The Göttingen Eighteen, consisting of Germany's leading atomic scientists, claimed that each one of the weapons being considered had the destructive power of a Hiroshima bomb, and declared that they had no place in Germany.

The question of whether the Frankfurt School should become involved in such matters was vexed. Adorno, for his part, seemed to suggest that silence was better than being misunderstood. He wrote: 'It is difficult to even sign appeals with which one sympathises, because in their inevitable desire to have a political impact, they always contain an element of untruth . . . The absence of commitment is not necessarily a moral defect; it can also be moral because it means insisting on the autonomy of one's own point of view.'[29] The high value Adorno put on such autonomy and aloofness from political commitment sounds akin to the free-floating quality Mannheim ascribed to intellectuals in the early 1930s, but such qualities also became exasperating to those who sought to change society – not least Adorno's own students during the university protests of the next decade, as we will see.

Adorno and his co-director Horkheimer weren't devoid of political commitment when they felt like it. In 1956, for instance, they wrote to the German news magazine *Der Spiegel* to defend France and Britain's military assault on Egypt which had been condemned by the United Nations. 'No one even ventures to point out that these Arab robber states have been on the lookout for years for an opportunity to fall upon Israel and to slaughter the Jews who have found refuge there.'[30] But for the most part, the two men remained aloof.

Neither shared the mounting distaste among some German intellectuals over the risks of a new German army, particularly one that had nuclear weapons. Indeed, they upset some younger members of the Institute by having no scruples about carrying out a study for the German Defence Ministry designed to find out how to select volunteers for the army on the basis of their democratic attitudes. Habermas feared that Horkheimer, the Frankfurt School's director for a quarter of a century, in particular, had become too allied with the Federal Republic. 'His public demeanour and his policy for the institute seemed to us to be almost the expression of an opportunist conformity which was at odds with the critical tradition which, after all, he embodied.' Adorno and Horkheimer wrote to Marcuse explaining why they were more comfortable in West Germany than in East Germany where, as critics of society, 'they would long since have been killed'. They went so far to argue that the freedom of thought they enjoyed in the west was paradisal.[31]

But what to do with that freedom? After he addressed the Frankfurt protest, Habermas wrote an article for a student magazine headlined 'Unrest is the Citizen's First Duty', in which he invoked the words of his teacher Adorno that the task of contemporary philosophy 'has its lifeblood in resistance'. Habermas's article was a counterblast to a simultaneously published article by Franz Böhm, who was not only a Christian Democrat Bundestag member, but, counterintuitively, chairman of the board of the Institute's Research Foundation.[32] Böhm accused the protesters of rabble rousing against his party (the CDU) and of collaborating with dictators opposing the west, brutalising political discussion and preparing the way for a new form of Nazism. In short, Böhm was accusing protesters such as Habermas of left fascism, a decade before Habermas himself would accuse student protesters like Rudi Dutschke of the same. Habermas argued that the protests were against 'the statesmen ruling in our name' and called for a plebiscite on the army being equipped with nuclear weapons (a plebiscite that West Germany's Constitutional Court ruled out later that year).[33]

But Habermas's political activity rankled inside Café Max. It wasn't just his speechifying and polemicising that worried Horkheimer, but also the political commitments expressed in his research papers for the Institute. In 1957, Habermas had written a paper entitled 'On the Philosophical Debate over Marx and Marxism'. In it, he appeared to call for 'the development of formal democracy into material democracy, of liberal democracy into social democracy'.[34] But these were not Habermas's orginal words, Horkheimer suspected. Indeed, Horkheimer was convinced that Habermas's original call for revolution in the paper had been edited out by Adorno and replaced with the words quoted above to spare the Institute's blushes. If so, that edited version was in line with the Institute's long-term commitment to Aesopian language. But Horkheimer wasn't placated: any reader could spot the call for revolution that remained. 'How is a people which is being held in the shackles of bourgeois society by a liberal constitution to change the so-called political society for which, according to H. [Habermas], it is "more than ripe", other than by violence?' Horkheimer wrote in a letter to Adorno. 'It is simply not possible to have admissions of this sort in the research report of an Institute that exists on the public funds of this shackling society.'[35] Quite so: calls for violent revolution weren't going to help the Institute get research contracts from the German Defence Ministry.

Horkheimer, in short, wanted Habermas out. And he managed to achieve his aim, even in the face of Adorno's misgivings, with a clever pretext. Habermas was planning to write his postdoctoral thesis on changes in the bourgeois public sphere (which would become, when published in 1962, his influential book *The Structural Transformation of the Public Sphere: An Inquiry into a Category of Bourgeois Society*), but Horkheimer insisted that he first do another study that would have taken three years. Exasperated, Habermas resigned and went to finish his thesis at Marburg University under the Marxist jurist Wolfgang Abendroth.

What had irritated Horkheimer about Habermas's writings was that his junior was criticising the political structure of the society on which the Institute depended for its financial survival. His work was too Marxist. Habermas had also written an introduction for an empirical sociological study called 'Students and Politics' aimed at investigating students' political participation and attitudes to democracy. There he argued that German society was at a crossroads between an authoritarian welfare state and substantive democracy. For Habermas, the Federal Republic had accorded many fundamental rights to the West German people under its so-called Basic Law and had given them access to politics at the federal level by means of elections to the Bundestag. But, as Rolf Wiggershaus notes, the Bundestag had lost power to the executive, the bureaucracy and lobbying groups.[36] Elections, then, seemed to confer democratic political power, but in fact made a mockery of it. 'With the decline of open class antagonisms, the contradiction has taken a new form: it now appears in the depoliticisation of the masses with an increase in the politicisation of society', wrote Habermas.[37] This critique of liberal democracy as a sham, along with the coded call for revolution, was too much for Horkheimer. He decided that the Institute would not publish 'Students and Politics'. When it was later published elsewhere, the Frankfurt School scarcely received a mention.

Café Marx was dead. Long live Café Max. What the role of the Frankfurt School and critical theory would be in the 1960s was less clear.

PART VI:

THE 1960s

15

Up Against the Wall, Motherfuckers

In the summer of 1964 on the Adriatic island of Korcula, Herbert Marcuse posed an interesting question: 'Why should the overthrow of the existing order be of vital necessity for people who own, or can hope to own, good clothes, a well-stocked larder, a TV set, a car, a house and so on, all within the existing order?'[1] More than forty years earlier, in the Thuringian town of Ilmenau, a Marxist summer school had confronted a crisis for revolutionary socialism in the wake of the failure of the German Revolution, and the success of the Bolshevik one. That so-called Erste Marxistische Arbeitwoche led a year later to the foundation of the Institute for Social Research and the reconfiguring of Marxism.

Now, in Korcula, another group of Marxists was struggling to comprehend another crisis for revolutionary socialism in a Cold War world divided between the capitalist west and the Soviet bloc. In the former, the masses had become too comfortable; in the latter, if Marcuse's 1958 *Soviet Marxism* or Fromm's 1961 *Marx's Concept of Man* were anything to go by, citizens were being spiritually crushed by a totalitarian bureaucracy enacting a perversion of Marx's philosophy.

For all the ideological heat expended in the Cold War between the two sides, Marcuse detected something like Freud's notion of the narcissism of small differences. He adhered to the Frankfurt School orthodoxy that monopoly capitalism was as much a form of totalitarianism as National Socialism or Soviet Marxism. Indeed, Marcuse self-consciously regarded his 1964 book *One-Dimensional Man* as the western counterpart to his *Soviet Marxism*. He held that the capitalist west had consolidated itself in opposition to its foe, Soviet society. But he also held that the 'totally administered' advanced industrial society, with its consumerism, militarism and sexual repression masquerading as erotic free-for-all, was a response, and a parallel, to the proverbial grimness of life under Stalin and his henchmen.

The venue was significant. Korcula is a Croatian island, and was, at the time of Marcuse's talk, part of the Socialist Federal Republic of Yugoslavia. Since 1948, when its leader Josip Tito had broken with Stalin and the Eastern bloc, Yugoslavia had been a non-aligned country. The summer school took place in a buffer state between the two sides in the Cold War. It was organised by a Yugoslav group of philosophers called Praxis, who described themselves as humanist Marxists. That term signified a return to the works of the young Marx, notably his *Economic and Philosophic Manuscripts* of 1844 in which he stressed worker alienation, in contrast to the later works which emphasised structural features of capitalism. Many of the attendees were humanist Marxists, but not all: one of the guests was a Father Gustav Wetter from the Vatican. Also present was the Marxist philosopher Ernst Bloch, who had left East Germany for the west after the Berlin Wall was built in 1961, and the French Marxist philosopher Lucien Goldmann, as well as Frankfurt School thinkers past and present, including Marcuse, Fromm and Habermas, who had been lured back to Frankfurt by Adorno in 1964 to take over Horkheimer's job as professor of philosophy and sociology at the Institute after the latter's retirement.

To the orthodox Soviet Marxists of post-Khrushchev Moscow, Marxist humanism was a dangerous heresy. To the French Marxist Louis Althusser, whose renowned structuralist, scientific account of Marxism, *For Marx*, would be published the following year, humanist Marxism focused on texts by Marx that should be set aside in favour of his supposedly more mature work. And yet it was precisely these early works that had catalysed the thoughts of the neo-Marxists of the Frankfurt School and underpinned the development of critical theory in the 1930s. True, since then, it might have been hard to make a case for the Frankfurt School as being Marxist at all; after all, as we have seen, it had airbrushed terms such as capitalism and Marxism from its texts while in American exile, and since its return to Frankfurt Horkheimer himself had frowned on texts that even implicitly endorsed revolution since they would risk scuppering funds and contracts from the Federal Republic. By the early 1960s, however, two members of the Frankfurt School, Habermas and Marcuse, were seeking to do something counterintuitive: to reconfigure Marxism without the proletariat and without, as a result, the class struggle.

In his essay 'Between Philosophy and Science, Marxism as Critique', published in 1963, Habermas acknowledged that Marxism may seem redundant due to the fact of widespread prosperity in advanced industrial societies. That prosperity meant that 'the interest in the emancipation of society can no longer be directly articulated in economic terms'. It also meant that 'the designated executor of the socialist revolution, the proletariat *as* proletariat has been dissolved'. But if the proletariat has been dissolved, doesn't that mean that Marxism should be wound up too? Maybe not: 'Liberation from hunger and misery does not necessarily converge with liberation from servitude and degradation.'[2]

For Habermas, Fromm and Marcuse, consumerism in the west had become the new opiate of the masses. Advanced industrial society had mass produced not just consumer goods, but mass acceptance of its order. As Marcuse wrote in his *One-Dimensional Man: Studies in the Ideology of Advanced Industrial Society*:

> If the worker and his boss enjoy the same television programme and visit the same resort places, if the typist is as attractively made up as the daughter of her employer, if the Negro owns a Cadillac, if they all read the same newspaper, then this assimilation indicates not the disappearance of classes, but the extent to which the needs and satisfactions that serve the preservation of the Establishment are shared by the underlying population.[3]

The triumph of consumer capitalism and the dearth of serious economic crises that might have threatened its future during the 1950s and 1960s meant that Marxists had once more to rethink their philosophy.

In particular, as Marcuse recognised, the proletariat was no longer to be viewed as Marx or Lukács had done. Marx had predicted a working-class revolution because it represented the absolute negation of the bourgeois order. One problem: that hadn't happened. Certainly, between the 1920s and the 1960s, the working classes in the advanced western industrial societies had not become the gravediggers of capitalism. As early as his 1941 book *Reason and Revolution*, Marcuse had argued that in these societies, since about the turn of the century, the advance of capitalistic productivity had stopped the development of revolutionary consciousness. 'Technological progress multiplied the needs and satisfactions, while its utilisation made the needs as well as their satisfactions repressive: they themselves sustain submission and domination', he wrote. This wasn't what classical Marxism had envisaged. Central to Marx's idea of socialism, Marcuse argued in *Reason and Revolution*, was 'the maturity of the internal contradictions of capitalism and the will to their abolition.'[4] But without the former, the latter had little urgency. Rising standards of living, at least in developed countries, had made the working classes too comfortable to revolt. But, as Marcuse said in Korcula, if the proletariat is no longer the negation of capitalism, then it is no longer different from other classes and so no longer capable of creating a better society.[5]

But rising living standards among the working classes in the advanced industrial west did not necessarily mean that Marxism was obsolete. Long before Habermas had argued that it was a misrepresentation of Marxism to articulate the emancipation of society only in economic terms, Marcuse had written in *Reason and Revolution*: 'Marx's notion of impoverishment implies consciousness of the arrested potentialities and of the possibility of their realisation – consciousness of alienation and dehumanisation.'[6] Such impoverishment was compatible with rising living standards: thus conceived, poverty and greater material prosperity were in a positive, rather than as you'd expect an inverse, relationship.

Marcuse's suggestion was, effectively, that those living in the rich west, among the cars, washing machines and stay-press trousers of advanced industrial society, were the most poor. And not just poor, but very nearly demented. Oliver Sacks' *The Man Who Mistook his*

Wife for a Hat describes a case history in which one of the clinical neurologist's patients' dealt with an ontological error betokening mental illness; Marcuse was describing something similar: in one-dimensional society we mistake ourselves for our consumer durables. 'The people recognise themselves in their commodities; they find their souls in their automobiles, hi-fi sets, split-level homes, kitchen equipment', he wrote.[7]

In the Hegelian philosophy of the subject, on which Marcuse relied, it was otherwise. The Hegelian subject is both being-in-itself and being-for-itself. It is the latter to the extent that it is a self-conscious subject capable of developing its powers and potentialities through action rather than contemplation or consumption. The subject manifests its nature by exercising its capacities on the objective world. In *Marx's Concept of Man*, Fromm argued that Hegel, Marx, Goethe and Zen Buddhism all have this vision of man overcoming self-alienation by relating to the objective world. He wrote: 'What is common to them is the idea that man overcomes the subject-object split; the object is an object, yet it ceases to be an object, and in this new approach man becomes one with the object, although he and it remain two.'[8]

In one-dimensional society, there is no such freedom to create oneself as an authentic individual because, Marcuse argued, its members do not know their true needs. Marcuse distinguished true needs from false ones. The former involve 'nourishment, clothing, lodging at the attainable level of satisfaction'. The latter are 'those which are superimposed upon the individual by particular social interests in his repression'. Marcuse's dismal notion was that we lack the freedom to know what is good for us, and his critics were quick to roll their eyes at the implication that he, at least, knew better. He wrote: 'In the last analysis, the answer to the question of what are true and false needs must be answered by the individuals themselves, but only in the last analysis; that is, if and when they are free to give their answer.'[9] The implication was that while individuals may seem to be free, they are in fact everywhere in chains – shackled to their washing machines and TVs. Everyone except, presumably, Marcuse.

For Marcuse, then, freedom from material want has been transformed into a means of producing servitude. Consumerism, advertising and mass culture help stabilise capitalism and, more than that, change the personality structures of those living under that system to turn them into pacified, obliging dupes.

> The products indoctrinate and manipulate; they promote a false consciousness which is immune against its falsehood. And as these beneficial products become available to more individuals in more social classes, the indoctrination they carry ceases to be publicity; it becomes a way of life. It is a good way of life – much better than before – and as a good way of life, it militates against qualitative change.[10]

Not all products are like this, of course. A significant counter-example is *One-Dimensional Man*. 'The central oddity of *One-Dimensional Man*', the Scottish moral and political philosopher Alasdair MacIntyre drolly remarked, 'is perhaps that it should have been written at all. For if its thesis were true then we would have to ask how the book came to have been written and we would certainly have to enquire whether it would find any readers. Or rather, to the extent that the book does find readers, to that extent Marcuse's thesis does not hold.'[11] The book involves a performative contradiction: if it had not been read its thesis would have been true; if not published, more true; if not written, even more true yet. But maybe MacIntyre misses the point of the book's success: perhaps this grimly pessimistic book was Marcuse's bestselling work not for its bleak diagnosis, but because it could be aberrantly decoded as a how-to guide for living in a one-dimensional society.

Some critics of *One-Dimensional Man* thought the book intolerably patronising. 'The masses have no egos, no ids, their souls devoid of inner tension or dynamism: their ideas, their needs even their dreams are "not their own": their inner lives are "totally administered", programmed to produce exactly those desires that the social system can satisfy and no more.' So wrote the New York Marxist professor Marshall Berman, best known as author of *All That is Solid Melts into Air: The Experience of Modernity*.[12] Berman attacked what he called the 'one-dimensional paradigm' for its elitism, for its lazy presumption that the masses are lumpen blobs incapable of subverting the controlling, consumerist messages of the advertising and public relations industries. For all that *One-Dimensional Man* became an essential text for the 1960s New Left, read by students from Berkeley to Frankfurt, Berman argued that its author, their putatively radical hero, had the same scorn for the masses as the 'would-be aristocrats of the twentieth-century right'. T. S. Eliot had his 'hollow men', Marcuse had his 'one-dimensional man': both were symbols, Berman argued, of a contempt for modern men and women.[13]

From *One-Dimensional Man* onwards, Marcuse returned to the notion of an intellectual dictatorship again and again.[14] In the year before his death, for example, he was very much attracted by the ideas of the East German dissident writer Rudolf Bahro who, in his 1978 book *The Alternative in Eastern Europe*, developed the notion of surplus and subordinate consciousnesses. The idea was that the masses are too mired in consumerism, popular culture and the struggle to get paid to be interested in creative work, cultural ideals or social transformation. The primary bearers of surplus consciousness are a broad group of intellectuals – in which he included scientists, technicians, cultural workers and, presumably, critical theorists – who could become a ruling elite.

In 1964 Marcuse was still looking for a new proletariat surrogate and hoping to find it in 'the substratum of outcasts and outsiders, the exploited and persecuted of other races and other colours, the unemployed and the unemployable. They exist outside the democratic process; their life is the most immediate and the most real need for ending intolerable conditions and institutions.'[15] Only they could qualify as a revolutionary vanguard because they were 'supposedly untouched by modernity's kiss of death'.[16] But such is Marcuse's pessimism in *One-Dimensional Man* that he thought even they could not be relied upon to be that vanguard, because 'the economic and technical capabilities of the established societies are sufficiently vast to allow for adjustments and concessions to the underdog, and their armed forces sufficiently trained and equipped to take care of emergency situations.'[17]

What's extraordinary, in retrospect, is that the writer of these dismal words could have become, for a moment, as much the subject of quasi-religious adulation as Jagger, Lennon or Dylan. Berman, for all his suspicions about the one-dimensional paradigm and Marcuse's elitism, recalled waiting one Friday evening in the 1960s for a concert to begin at Brandeis University near Boston, Massachusetts:

> word suddenly came up the line: 'Marcuse's here!' At once there was a hush, and people divided themselves up to clear a path. A tall, erect, vividly forceful man passed down the aisle, smiling here and there to friends, radiant yet curiously aloof, rather like an aristocrat who was a popular hero as well, perhaps Egmont in the streets of Brussels. The students held their breaths and gazed at him in awe. After he had got to his seat, they relaxed again, flux and chaos returned.[18]

Reading these words, it's hard not to think of the scene in *Annie Hall* in which Woody Allen's Alvy Singer ill-advisedly goes on a date to a Bob Dylan gig with a *Rolling Stone* reporter. 'Reporter: He's God! I mean, this man is God! He's got millions of followers who would crawl all the way across the world just to touch the hem of his garment. Alvy: Really? It must be a tremendous hem.'

Those who sought to touch Marcuse's hem were deluded. Berman, by 1981 uncontaminated by Marcusean awe, argued that the young radicals who fought to change society so that people could control their own lives had failed to read Marcuse closely enough. If they had they would have realised that his '"one-dimensional paradigm" proclaimed that no change was possible and that, indeed, these people weren't really alive.'[19] In *One-Dimensional Man*, Marcuse came not to praise but to bury the swinging sixties. The permissiveness of 1960s society was not what it seemed – a liberation from straight society – but an instrument of domination. 'This society', wrote Marcuse, 'turns everything it touches into a potential source of progress and of exploitation, of drudgery and satisfaction, of freedom and of oppression. Sexuality is no exception.'[20]

Whereas in the past, frustrated sexuality was a threat to social order since it created a reservoir of discontent, in the society Marcuse described the threat to social order had been overcome by liberalising sexuality. But that liberalising sexuality, he thought, was not subversive, but rather helped keep the existing oppressive order in place.

Hegel wrote of the 'unhappy consciousness', by which he meant a consciousness torn between what could be and what is. Sexual frustration was one form of unhappy consciousness. In repressively desublimated society, though, the unhappy consciousness had been overcome. The members of one-dimensional society become happy consciousnesses who get, sexually and otherwise, what they want, ignorant of the fact that, according to Marcuse, what they want is what they have been predisposed to accept.

Freud had the idea that the pleasure principle and the reality principle were at war. The untrammelled indulgence of human biological and psychological needs, in accordance with the pleasure principle, infringes the freedom of others and so has to be curtailed by rules and discipline, that is, by the reality principle. According to Marcuse, in advanced industrial society, something as counterintuitive as squaring the circle or as unlikely as finding the philosopher's stone had happened: the pleasure principle had absorbed the reality principle. The diabolical genius that Marcuse detected in one-dimensional society was such that pleasure had become a tool of oppression. In that society, sex and sexual display were everywhere. As a result, one-dimensional man (and perhaps one-dimensional woman, though Marcuse said little about her societal role) comes to think of himself as a sexual revolutionary who has overturned centuries of repression, triumphed over the inhibitions and evasions, the whalebone and the bustles, of yesteryear. One thing that has made this sexual display possible, for Marcuse, is the reduction of heavy physical labour: 'Without ceasing to be an instrument of labour the body is allowed to exhibit its sexual features in the everyday work world and in work relations. This is one of the unique features of industrial society – rendered possible by the reduction of dirty and heavy physical labour; by the availability of cheap, attractive clothing, beauty culture and physical hygiene.'[21]

It's as though deindustrialisation and desublimated sexuality are engaged in some hard-faced, glumly raunchy, lubricious lambada across the workplace carpet tiles. The worker has exchanged miner's helmet and steel toe-caps for mini skirt and kinky boots, and, while Marcuse certainly didn't overtly clinch the point that this newly sexualised workplace is one in which more of the workers than ever before are women, nor that it is women's bodies that are the must-have commodities in that dismal milieu, all that is implicit in what he wrote: 'The sexy office and sales girls, the handsome, virile junior executive and floor walker are highly marketable commodities, and the possession of suitable mistresses – once the prerogative of kings, princes and lords – facilitates the career of even the less exalted ranks in the business community.'[22]

Quite so: it's not only Don Draper who gets his leg over in the one-dimensional sexual marketplace that is the 1960's office of Marcuse's philosophy, but even his juniors. Marcuse didn't consider the possibility of sexual display as radical action against such commodification of women's bodies, nor is it likely he would have seen raunch culture as a protest by women against one-dimensional man and his reified sexuality.

It's worth at this point considering Herbert Marcuse's sex life. After all, if we learned one thing from the 1960s, it was that the personal is the political. Following the death of his first wife Sophie in 1951, Marcuse, who could neither drive nor cook, moved in with his friend Franz Neumann and Neumann's wife Inge. This was one feature of the Grand Hotel Abyss that Lukács didn't pick up on – if the service was excellent at the Grand Hotel while its residents comfortably contemplated the abyss, that service was provided by women. After Franz Neumann died in a car crash in 1954, Herbert went on to marry Inge. Later, he had an affair with a graduate student and when Inge found out she banned the student from the house, though that didn't end the affair. 'In so far as [he had] a carnal, genital, sexual drive it was concealed', reported his stepson Osha Neumann. 'It was certainly there in terms of his affairs, but it was concealed.'[23] Osha Neumann was sceptical about the philosopher as prophet of libidinal liberation, not least because his stepfather loved stuffed toys. 'He felt a particular kinship with hippos, not as they actually shit and fight in the forest, but as some teddy bear version', recalled Neumann (unwittingly raising the diverting question as to whether hippos do actually fight in forests). 'He would sit with this one stuffed hippo on his lap and project this image of a non-aggressive, non-genital sexuality.'[24] Marcuse shared that fondness with Adorno who, as noted earlier, in letters to his mother would address her as 'My dear, faithful Wondrous Hippo Cow' and, occasionally, sign himself off as 'Hippo King Archibald'. Why did the Frankfurt School fetishise hippos so much? We may never know.

Osha Neumann rejected one-dimensional society and joined a counter-culture many of whose members hero-worshipped his stepfather.[25] He dropped out of Yale, where he was studying history, to become an artist, and eventually joined an anarchist protest group known as Up Against the Wall Motherfuckers, based in New York's Lower East Side. The anarchist, activist and Youth International Party co-founder Abbie Hoffman described the group as 'the middle-class nightmare . . . an anti-media media phenomenon simply because their name could not be printed'. The Motherfuckers described themselves as a 'street gang with analysis'. Among their protests, they forced their way into the Pentagon in 1967, occupied Columbia University in 1968, dumped uncollected refuse from the Lower East Side into a fountain outside Lincoln Center in the Upper West Side during a garbage strike the same year, and cut the fences to the Woodstock Festival in 1969 to allow many to enter for free. 'We saw ourselves at war with the system, with all the conventions that kept people tied to commodities', Osha Neumann said. 'We lived the revolution 24 hours a day and we were willing to give up our lives for our beliefs and through our actions we wanted to show the possibility of overcoming fear and directly challenging the institutions.'[26] In a sense the Motherfuckers were counter-culturally resisting what Marcuse had called one-dimensional society.

But let's not get carried away with the Motherfuckers' protests. Someone, and it wasn't Osha or the rest of his 'street gang', wound up cleaning the trash from Lincoln Center's fountains. Marcuse's stepson later went on to become a prominent civil rights lawyer, specialising in representing homeless people in the Bay Area. His youthful protest against straight society seems, in part, Oedipal and similar to the rebellion of many of the Frankfurt School thinkers against their fathers. Indeed, Osha's rebellion involved the rejection of the repressive, bourgeois lifestyle that he detected in his stepfather – a lifestyle that Herbert Marcuse insisted upon even as he wrote books indicting bourgeois repression. Osha recalled that his childhood household was 'very repressive. Herbert, in terms of his personal life, insisted on a level of distance and a level of bourgeois order in his life that was very protective of him. I remember him telling me very approvingly of Thomas Mann, who, at least according to Herbert, would get up every morning and put on a jacket and tie and then sit down at his desk and write books about people led by passion.'[27]

And those books had a message for the loved-up members of the putatively permissive society in the 1960s, namely that, sex wise, they were doing it all wrong. Consider, Marcuse suggested in *One-Dimensional Man*, the difference between making love in a meadow and in an automobile, or between making love on a lovers' walk outside the town walls and on a Manhattan street:

> In the former cases, the environment partakes of and invites libidinal cathexis and tends to be eroticised, libido transcends behind the immediate erotogenic zones – a process of nonrepressive sublimation. In contrast, a mechanised environment seems to block such self-transcendence of libido. Impelled in the striving to extend the field of erotic gratification, libido becomes less 'polymorphous', less capable of eroticism beyond localised sexuality, and the *latter* is intensified.[28]

Here Marcuse was following a line of thought from *Eros and Civilisation* in which he suggested that Eros had become dominated by the 'monogamic genital supremacy' and that if we were truly liberated from sex as reproduction and/or genital satisfaction, all of our body and all of our lives could be eroticised. By the time he wrote *One-Dimensional Man*, Marcuse seemed to be suggesting that men and women in advanced industrial society were having the wrong kind of orgasm, albeit one more intensely pleasurable than the libidinal cathexis Marcuse was recommending as an alternative. Again, I can't resist quoting Woody Allen. In his film *Manhattan*, a woman at a party says: 'I finally had an orgasm, and my doctor told me it was the wrong kind.' 'Really?' retorts Isaac Davis (Allen). 'I've never had the wrong kind, ever. My worst one was right on the money.'

Marcuse's point – and it's one that risks falling prey to a rustic nostalgia for pre-industrial society – was that the intensified sexual energy experienced by, say, Isaac Davis in his mechanised environment (in his case, Manhattan) limits his scope for sublimation. Wilhelm Reich might have thought that the orgasm is the supreme good, but Marcuse did not. To sublimate, that is, to divert sexual energy into a more social, moral or aesthetic use, far from being a bad thing, has a utopian resonance for Marcuse. He wrote in *One-Dimensional Man*: 'In contrast to the pleasures of adjusted desublimation, sublimation preserves the consciousness of the renunciations which the repressive society inflicts upon the individual, and thereby preserves the need for liberation.'[29] He had in mind here the artist who, according to Freud, sublimates his sexual impulses in the creation of works of art. Sublimating sexual energy is different from repressing it and yet both are, Freud thought, evident in and even necessary for civilisation. Some repression, involving pushing a desire into the subconscious, is necessary: unchecked satisfaction of libidinal drives, which is what Freud called the programme of the pleasure principle, 'is at loggerheads with the whole world'. Happiness-wise, we are the bungled products of an inept creator. Freud wrote in *Civilisation and Its Discontents*:

> One feels inclined to say that the intention that man should be 'happy' is not included in the plan of 'Creation.' What we call happiness in the strictest sense comes from the (preferably sudden) satisfaction of needs which have been dammed up to a high degree, and it is from its nature only possible as an episodic phenomenon . . . We are so made that we can derive intense enjoyment only from a contrast and very little from a state of things. Thus our possibilities of happiness are already restricted by our constitution. Unhappiness is much less difficult to experience.[30]

Marcuse finessed these Freudian thoughts in Marxist terms, suggesting that there was basic and surplus repression – the former necessary for civilisation, the latter a tool of domination in advanced industrial society. Sublimation, by contrast, involves not so much hiding desires in the unconscious as diverting them into other activities that are, ostensibly, valuable for civilisation. In *Civilisation and Its Discontents*, the book that fired Marcuse's thoughts in *Eros and Civilisation* and *One-Dimensional Man*, Freud wrote that sublimation is 'what makes it possible for higher psychical activities – scientific, artistic or ideo-logical – to play such an important part in civilised life.'[31] Marcuse's radical take on Freud's thought is that such sublimation in art, the area of human activity he's most concerned with in *One-Dimensional Man*, is not just a socially acceptable way of expressing libidinal drives, not a kind of psychic safety valve that enables the existing order to function better, but oppositional and alien to that order. Ultimately though, such art does not threaten that order. For Marcuse, the artist – or at least the great artist – is an unhappy consciousness, bearing witness to defeated possibilities, hopes unfulfilled and promises betrayed. What he unapologetically called 'higher culture' existed as a kind of unofficial opposition to the existing order – a rebuke to reality and a refutation of it. 'The two antagonistic spheres of society have always coexisted; the higher culture has always been accommodating while the reality was rarely disturbed by its ideals and its truth.'[32]

It is as though Marcuse was imagining that the higher, two-dimen-sional culture could operate as a sort of semi-autonomous republic because it didn't represent a serious threat to prevailing reality. In that sense, Auden was right: poetry changes nothing; rather, it creates an imaginative space where reality can be seen for what it is, where it can be fictively indicted and fictively punished. Marcuse wrote that higher culture subverts everyday experience and shows it to be 'mutilated and false.'[33] But he argued that this two-dimensional culture, that functions as a kind of unofficial and unthreatening opposition to the lies and distortions of reality, is liquidated in technological society. The second dimension is incorporated into the prevailing state of affairs. 'The works of alienation are themselves incorporated into this society and circulate as part and parcel of the equipment which adorns and psychoanalyses the prevailing state of affairs. Thus, they become commercials – they sell, comfort, or excite.'[34]

This is the culture industry described by Horkheimer and Adorno, whose role, like that of repressively desublimated sexuality, is to make capitalism run more smoothly. This is also the fate, in one-dimensional society, of even putatively avant-garde political art: think of the fate of Brecht and Weill's *Mahoganny*, an opera written by men who didn't quite realise that what they were producing wouldn't – as they hoped – catalyse revolution, but would become part of the culinary principle they so derided.

But what has this liquidation of higher culture to do with sex and sublimation? The liberation of sexuality in the permissive 1960s was, Marcuse argued, a controlling mechanism that made us happier, even more sexually fulfilled. But a precondition of that greater happiness and sexual fulfilment is greater conformity. The first casualty of this growing conformity is the unhappy consciousness, in particular the artist who through his or her unhappiness and discontent could, in their works, 'elucidate the repressive power of the established universe of satisfaction'.[35] For Marcuse, repression still existed in advanced industrial societies, but sublimation increasingly did not: the former required humans to bend the knee to the prevailing order; the latter, by contrast, required a degree of autonomy and comprehension. For Marcuse, sublimation became in accomplished art that valuable if paradoxical phenomenon – a power that was capable of defeating 'suppression while bowing to it'.[36]

But there is no artistic sublimation any more. To demonstrate the point, Marcuse compared how artists in the post-war era and their predecessors depicted and dramatised sex. In Baudelaire's *Les Fleurs du Mal* or Tolstoy's *Anna Karenina* sexual pleasure is sublimated rather than fulfilled. Perhaps the best example of this sublimated sexuality is a work he does not mention, Wagner's *Tristan und Isolde*, in which sex and death, Eros and Thanatos, are locked in an eternal embrace. In such sublimated artworks, as Marcuse wrote, 'Fulfillment . . . is beyond good and evil, beyond social morality and thus it remains beyond the reaches of the established Reality Principle'.[37] Compare the way sexuality is portrayed in such works with its depiction in advanced industrial society, Marcuse suggested. He cited 'O'Neill's alcoholics and Faulkner's savages', *A Streetcar Named Desire*, *Cat on a Hot Tin Roof*, *Lolita* and 'all the stories of Hollywood and New York orgies, and the adventures of suburban housewives' as examples. The sexuality depicted in the latter cases is, for Marcuse, 'infinitely more realistic, daring, uninhibited' than its portrayal in classical or romantic literature. It is desublimated, unmediated, unremittingly present in its banal explicitness, uninterestingly and unashamedly what it is.

What has got lost between the two eras of literature? Negation. The former has images that negate the societies they represent; the latter does not. Or so Marcuse argued. In classical literature there were characters like prostitutes, devils, fools, rebel-poets – characters who disrupted the existing order. But in the literature of advanced industrial society such antinomian characters, while they still exist (Marcuse cites the 'vamp, the national hero, the beatnik, the neurotic housewife, the gangster, the star, the charismatic tycoon') perform a contrary function to their predecessors: 'They are no longer images of another way of life but rather freaks or types of the same life, serving as affirmation rather than negation of the existing order.'[38]

Stanley Kowalski's primal howl, then, is very different from Tristan and Isolde's *liebestod*. The former can be answered with electrodes, jail time or the University of Minnesota spankalogical protocol; the latter resists such methods of correction – it is societal negation until the fat lady stops singing. Sex in the art of advanced industrial society is therefore 'surely wild and obscene, virile and tasty, quite immoral – and, precisely because of that, perfectly harmless'.[39] 'Perfectly harmless' is an odd description of, say, Humbert Humbert's paedophilia, but Marcuse's point is that *Lolita* is not a negation of that society.

What's striking here is that Marcuse's examples pit old Europe against new America, as if to say the former culture was the unhappy sublimated one, the latter happy and desublimated. An old European sigh of what has been lost blows through the pessimistic pages of *One-Dimensional Man*. The high European culture that indicted pre-industrial society cannot be recaptured.[40] Indeed, pessimism is the book's keynote. In the face of a one-dimensional society without a plausible revolutionary subject, all that remained was what Marcuse, borrowing the term from the surrealist André Breton, called The Great Refusal and which he concedes is, like great oppositional art, politically impotent. He does not set out what that refusal means, but he has been taken by his interpreters to be suggesting a rejection of forms of oppression and domination. The term, for all its vagueness, impotence and impracticality is suggestive: it captures the mood of revolt sweeping through advanced industrial societies during the 1960s, embracing opposition to the Vietnam War, the Campaign for Nuclear Disarmament, the New Left, the hippies, and student protestors. Such opposition is 'an elementary force which violates the rules of the game and, in doing so, reveals it as a rigged game'.[41]

Civil rights protestors, though hardly politically impotent, are roped into Marcuse's Great Refusal: 'When they get together and go out into the streets, without arms, without protection, in order to ask for the most primitive civil rights, they know that they face dogs, stones, and bombs, jail, concentration camps, even death.' Marcuse hoped that 'the fact that they start refusing to play the game may be the fact which marks the beginning of the end of a period'.[42] But the civil rights protests were not just a refusal to play the game: they were an insistence that African-Americans should have the same rights as everybody else – in that sense the civil rights struggles were affirmative, not negative.

AMONG MARCUSE's American students in the 1960s was Angela Davis, who later became an African-American activist, feminist and revolutionary, for a while one of the FBI's ten most wanted, a woman Richard Nixon called a terrorist and one whom Ronald Reagan tried to fire from her academic post. Davis was born in 1944 and brought up in racially segregated, pre-civil-rights Birmingham, Alabama, a city notorious during the civil rights struggles for setting dogs and turning hoses on African-Americans seeking the vote – and worse: 'I grew up at a time when, as a response to an interracial discussion group I was involved in, the church where we were having the discussions was burned. I grew up at a time where black people would move in to the white neighbourhood right across the street from where we lived, and bombs would be set in those houses.'[43]

Later, she was awarded a scholarship to Brandeis University and came across Marcuse at a rally during the 1962 Cuban Missile Crisis, during which American and Soviet confrontation over Soviet deployment of ballistic missiles in Cuba brought the two nations close to nuclear war. She then became his student. What resonated for her in Marcuse's writings was, in part, what she called 'the emancipatory promise of the German philosophical tradition', but also his ability to reveal the barbarous underside to the American dream. As she put it in her preface to a collection of Marcuse's letters: 'precisely because he was so concretely and immediately involved in opposing German fascism, he was also able and willing to identify fascist tendencies in the US.'[44] Among those fascist tendencies in her homeland, she argued, was the prominent structural role of racism.

One could interpret some of Davis's later writings and campaigning as a continuation of her one-time teacher's analysis of fascist tendencies. Davis would go on to argue that what she called the 'prison-industrial complex' militated against the civil rights for which African-Americans fought during the civil rights struggles. But the over-incarceration of people of colour, she argued, was a result of a shift of capital from human services, from housing, jobs, education, to profitable arenas. 'It has meant there are huge numbers of people everywhere in the world who are not able to sustain themselves. They are made surplus, and as a result they are often forced to engage in practices that are deemed criminal. And so prisons pop up all over the world, often with the assistance of private corporations who profit from these surplus populations.'[45] Marcuse didn't live to see the prison-industrial complex flourish, but doubtless he would have approved of his student's astute diagnosis and condemnation.

Like many other students in the 1960s, Davis was an enthusiastic reader of Marcuse's 1965 essay 'Pure Tolerance', which argued that in a putatively liberal society, tolerance is a form of mystification, making society accept a subtle form of domination. What was needed, he argued, was a new kind of tolerance including tolerance for revolutionary violence. Like *The Thoughts of Chairman Mao*, his essay was bound like a prayer book or missal and became devotional reading at student sit-ins.[46] But its message was scandalous to some critics such as Alsadair MacIntyre:

> The truth is carried by the revolutionary minorities and their intellec-
> tual spokesmen, such as Marcuse, and the majority have to be liberated

by being educated into the truth by this minority who are entitled to suppress rival and harmful opinions. This is perhaps the most dangerous of all Marcuse's doctrines, for not only is what he asserts false, but his is a doctrine which if it were widely held would be an effective barrier to any rational progress and liberation.[47]

Angela Davis took a different message from Marcuse. 'Herbert Marcuse taught me that it was possible to be an academic, an activist, a scholar, and a revolutionary.'[48] She studied with Marcuse in Brandeis and with Adorno in Frankfurt, and then, in 1966 when the Black Panther Party was founded, she felt drawn back to the United States, in part, to work in radical movements. Adorno had been sceptical: 'He suggested that my desire to work directly in the radical movements of that period was akin to a media studies scholar deciding to become a radio technician.'[49]

Undaunted, she joined the Black Panthers and the Che-Lumumba Club, an all-black group within the US Communist Party. She also became professor of philosophy at the University of California in Los Angeles, but was fired because of her membership of the Communist Party. She was later reinstated and then, in June 1970, fired again for using inflammatory language in speeches describing the police as pigs and murderers for their role in suppressing a student protest at the People's Park on the Berkeley campus the previous year. By August 1970, she was a fugitive from justice. Davis was then put on the FBI's ten most wanted list, sought for her alleged role in supplying guns to the Black Panthers who had sprung three men, the so-called Soledad Brothers, from a courthouse where they were being tried for the murder of a prison guard. She was finally arrested and faced charges of conspiracy to kidnap and murder, for which she could have been executed. At her trial in 1972 she was acquitted, while other co-defendants, former Black Panthers, were jailed – some for more than half a century.

For Davis, her former professor was an intellectually liberating figure:

Marcuse played an important role during the late sixties and early seventies in encouraging intellectuals to speak out against racism,

against the Vietnam War, for student rights. He emphasised the important role of intellectuals within oppositional movements, which, I
believe, led more intellectuals to frame their work in relation to these
movements than would otherwise have done so. And Marcuse's
thought revealed how deeply he himself was influenced by the movements of his time and how his engagement with those movements
revitalised his thought.[50]

But perhaps the most surprising aspect of his influence on Davis was
how it shaped her vision of the utopian possibilities contained in art,
literature and music. But wasn't he too steeped in high European
culture for that? Surely, I asked when I interviewed Davis in 2014, he
had no sense of popular music as being resistant to the status quo, but
rather regarded it as Adorno regarded jazz, as part of the culture
industry that kept the status quo in place? Davis explained that 'He
started to change. He had this very classical, European formation, so
culture for him was high culture, but I think he later began to recognise that we shouldn't be concerned with high versus low culture. We
should be concerned with the work that culture does.'[51] In her 1998
book *Blues Legacies and Black Feminism*, Davis wrote about how singers such as Gertrude 'Ma' Rainey, Bessie Smith and Billie Holiday
'provided a cultural space for community-building among working-class black women . . . in which the coercions of bourgeois notions
of sexual purity and "true womanhood" were absent'.[52] Marcusean
notions of art as a semi-autonomous zone or another dimension
where utopias could be imagined in opposition to the dominant
cultures it indicted infuse this book.

Marcuse, following Adorno, who was in turn following Stendhal,
wrote of art as offering *promesse du bonheur*. He explained what that
meant in *One-Dimensional Man*, writing that the prevailing order
was 'overshadowed, broken, refuted by another dimension which was
irreconcilably antagonistic to the order of business, indicting it and
denying it'.[53] Marcuse found that *promesse du bonheur* in seventeenth-century Dutch painting, Goethe's *Wilhelm Meister*, the English
novel of the nineteenth century, and Thomas Mann; Angela Davis
heard it in Bessie Smith and Billie Holiday. But, as the 1960s unfolded,

Marcuse dared to imagine that the *promesse du bonheur* could be realised only in the aesthetic dimension (the title of Marcuse's last book was *The Aesthetic Dimension: Toward a Critique of Marxist Aesthetics*), but that utopia was at hand. In 1969's *An Essay on Liberation*, he committed the greatest Frankfurt School heresy: he indulged in positive thinking. 'What is denounced as "utopian" is no longer that which has "no place" and cannot have any place in the historical universe, but rather that which is blocked from coming about by the power of the established societies', he wrote. 'Utopian possibilities are inherent in the technical and technological forces of advanced capitalism and socialism: the rational utilisation of these forces on a global scale would terminate poverty and scarcity within a very foreseeable future.'[54]

Frankfurt School critical theory was not supposed to be like this. Critical theory had something built into it akin to the Jewish taboo on calling God by his name: to do so would be premature since we are not yet in the messianic age. Similarly for critical theory, setting out a utopian vision would be premature; its self-imposed task was to negate the truth of the existing order rather than producing blueprints for a better one. And yet in *An Essay on Liberation*, Marcuse dared to imagine a new type of man who rejected the values of established societies. This new man was not aggressive, was incapable of fighting wars or creating suffering, and worked happily both collectively and individually for a better world rather than to further his own interests.[55]

And what about women? In his 1974 essay 'Marxism and Feminism', Marcuse argued that 'feminine' qualities such as non-violence, tenderness, receptivity and sensitivity represent a negation of masculine values. 'Socialism, as a qualitatively different society, must embody the antithesis, the definite negation of aggressive and repressive needs of capitalism as a form of male-dominated culture.'[56]

Perhaps it was his very celebrity as the so-called Father of the New Left (an honorific he disavowed) that tempted Marcuse to imagine utopias. Some found his vision ridiculous: in his *Main Currents of Marxism: Its Origins, Growth and Dissolution*, the historian of ideas Leszek Kołakowski described Marcuse's utopia as anti-Marxist, and one that inverted Freud so that social rules could be discarded in favour of a 'New World of Happiness'. At the same time, it was a new world that was 'to be ruled despotically by an enlightened group [who] have realised in themselves the unity of Logos and Eros, and thrown off the vexatious authority of logic, mathematics, and the empirical sciences'.[57]

For all Marcuse's radical chic and counter-cultural celebrity, his rival for the title of hero of the New Left and the student movement was not seduced. When Jean-Paul Sartre and Marcuse arranged to meet at the Coupole in Paris in the late 1960s, Sartre worried how he could get through lunch without revealing the truth. 'I have never read a word Marcuse has written', he told his future biographer John Gerassi. 'I know he has tried to link Marx and Freud. And I know he supports activist students. But I can't possibly read his books by next week. Besides I don't want to stop my research on Flaubert. So you join us. And if Marcuse gets too philosophical, if he uses the word *reification* just once, interrupt and say something provocative and political.'

In the event, over cassoulet, Sartre came up with an ingenious strategy for concealing his ignorance. He asked questions that suggested a greater familiarity with Marcuse's works than he actually had. 'Each time he answered, I picked out an apparent flaw in his answer to ask another question. But since the flaw was only apparent, he could answer my question to his great satisfaction. Thus his vanity soared happily.' Indeed it did: as Gerassi put Marcuse into a taxi, the latter 'shook both of my hands with genuine gratitude and said: "I had no idea he knew my work so well." '[58]

16

Philosophising with Molotov Cocktails

While Marcuse dreamed of utopia in America, Adorno despaired in Europe. 'No universal history leads from savagery to humanitarianism, but there is one that leads from the slingshot to the megaton bomb',[1] he wrote in *Negative Dialectics*, the book he published in 1966 under the long shadow of Auschwitz and the threat of nuclear Armageddon. The Holocaust imposed what he called a 'new categorical imperative' that human beings arrange their thought and action so that 'Auschwitz would not repeat itself, [that] nothing similar would happen'. In Adorno's corner of Frankfurt, there was no future in Marcuse's Californian dreaming. *Negative Dialectics* is an untimely meditation – anti-systemic, anti-utopian and devoid of hope. 'There can be few works of philosophy that give such an overpowering sense of sterility as *Negative Dialectics*', wrote Kołakowski in *Main Currents of Marxism*.[2] Marcuse may have thought that utopia could be realised in this world and soon, but Adorno's implicit counter suggestion in *Negative Dialectics* was that it could only be realised in art, and there by definition only imaginatively.

'Negative dialectics flouts tradition', he wrote in the book's preface. 'As early as Plato, dialectics meant to achieve something positive by means of negation . . . This book seeks to free dialectics from such affirmative traits without reducing its determinacy.'[3] Before Plato, Heraclitus had proposed that the world is constantly in flux. The dialectical imagination takes this thought and tries to impose order on the change: for dialecticians, and Adorno was a lifelong member of that dialectical club, the question is, if the world essentially involves change not stasis, then where is that change heading?

The suggestion from Plato onwards was that change, and in particular historical change, has a goal or telos. Hegel's idea was that history unfolds through dialectical process. The paradoxical German term 'aufheben', which means three different and contradictory things – to preserve, to elevate and to cancel – and which, in its philosophical usage, is usually translated as 'sublate', is important here. The translator and philosopher Walter Kaufmann wrote: 'Hegel may be said to visualise how something is picked up in order that it may no longer be *there* just the way it was, although, it is not cancelled altogether but lifted up to be kept on a different level.'[4] Crucially for Hegel, nothing is discarded in this process – everything is taken up from one historical age to the next. For him, history is the unfolding of human freedom towards the Absolute and, what is the same thing, the expression of the *Weltgeist*, or world spirit. For Hegel 'everything that is real is rational', by which he means that everything has its place in the unfolding dialectical process. The result is that there is an 'identity of identity and non-identity'. History, thus conceived, is like a cosmically large recycling project in which nothing is allowed to become mere landfill. For Hegel, consequently, the whole is the true. For Adorno, in a typically perverse aphorism, the opposite is the case: 'The whole is the false.'[5]

Throughout his writings Adorno is suspicious of those philosophies that offer harmonious reconciliations. He was doubtful, as Martin Jay put it, of the young Lukács's vision of epic wholeness in ancient Greece, of Heidegger's notion of a fulfilled being now tragically forgotten, and of Walter Benjamin's faith in a prelapsarian oneness of name and thing.[6] But in *Negative Dialectics*, he was chiefly concerned, not with deconstructing such regressive fantasies, but with opposing the idea that dialectical historical processes had to have a goal. In particular, he rejected the idea that the narrative of history was destined to conclude with a happy ending. Thus, in opposition to Hegel's 'identity of identity and non-identity', Adorno proposed the even more baffling notion of 'the non-identity of identity and non-identity'. In making this suggestion, Adorno was asserting that the object does not go into its concept without remainder. And yet an object has to be subsumed without remainder if identity thinking is to make sense. If the object does not go into its concept without remainder then, because all thinking is conceptual, all concepts misrepresent their objects and all thinking involves an act of brutality to its object. Such, at least, was Adorno's inference.

Effectively, Adorno was deploying Marx's account of the exchange principle retrospectively to put holes in Hegelian identity philosophy: in achieving identity, Adorno suggested, Hegelian philosophy asserts the equivalence of what is not equivalent.[7] Instead of such brutal identity thinking, Adorno tentatively proposed a different approach to knowledge, what has become known as a constellational theory, borrowing the term 'constellation' from Walter Benjamin's *The Origin of German Tragic Drama*. Constellational thinking rejects the identity thinking that understands an object by subsuming it under a concept. To understand an object, for Adorno, was not to subsume it under concept but to set it in dialectical historical relationship with a constellation of other objects. In this sense, there is a strong parallel between constellational thinking and Benjamin's notion of the dialectical image. This use of the term constellation bears affinities with the devices of modernist art and literature that appealed to Benjamin – such as cinematic montage, cubist collage, Baudelaire's *correspondances* or Joyce's epiphanies.

In particular, Benjamin's constellations were akin to Proust's notion of involuntary memory. When he tastes a madeleine, the narrator of Proust's *À la recherche du temps perdu* involuntarily brings his whole childhood to life. These sudden flashes of insight were what Adorno hoped for in his constellational theory of knowledge. Through such changing constellations and such evanescent flashes, the truth about an object would emerge to the sympathetic observer. Adorno unveiled this approach to cognition in his inaugural lecture at the Institute for Social Research in Frankfurt in 1931 to be greeted with incomprehension by his listeners. In *Negative Dialectics*, he tried to expound a new version, using an analogy that made him sound like a combination of a safe-cracker labouring in a bank's vault after working hours, a Buddhist virtuoso of mindfulness, and a quantum physicist aware that his investigation is going to change the nature of what he's investigating. He wrote:

> The history locked in the object can only be delivered by a knowledge mindful of the historic positional value of the object in its relation to other objects – by the actualisation and concentration of something which is already known and is transformed by that knowledge. Cognition of the object in its constellation is cognition of the process stored in the object. As a constellation, theoretical thought circles the concept it would like to unseal, hoping that it may fly open like the lock of a well-guarded safe-deposit box: in response, not to a single key or a single number, but to a combination of numbers.[8]

Insight, if it was to be attained at all, was to be reached by adepts who had transcended identity thinking. But even then insight was only to come in flashes – constellations. These, like mobile armies of metaphors, were always changing, flickering in and out of the beholders' grasp. But the corollary of *Negative Dialectics* was that such flashes of insight were the only means by which we could step outside what was otherwise a total system of delusion.

This is all quite tough stuff and, even for adepts of critical theory, hard to swallow. Indeed, it was the very evanescent quality of the non-identity thinking proposed in *Negative Dialectics* that made Adorno's young colleague Jürgen Habermas draw back. In a 1979 interview he said he no longer agreed with 'the premise that instrumental reason has gained such dominance that there is really no way out of a total system of delusion in which insight is achieved only in flashes by isolated individuals'.[9]

If the foregoing sounds maddeningly abstruse, it is worth pointing out that Adorno was drawn to theorise non-identity thinking in order to 'lend a voice' to suffering that was otherwise silenced. 'The need to let suffering speak is a condition of all truth. For suffering is objectivity that weighs upon the subject.'[10] The suffering Adorno had in mind was that unseen in our one-dimensional world – that caused by the inhuman oppression of others. But, if all thought involves brutality since it is inherently conceptual, it's difficult to understand how

Adorno could even frame his critique of identity thinking, since to do so involves using the concepts that he disdained. Habermas wrote that Adorno was quite aware of the performative contradiction in his philosophical writing.[11] That, in a sense, was the crazy nature of the Frankfurt School's notion of immanent critique, whereby the ideology that was deconstructed was demolished with its own tools. In *Dialectic of Enlightenment*, he and Horkheimer raged that reason had become instrumental during the Enlightenment and thus yielded to power. In so doing it had lost its critical force. But, as Habermas noted in *The Philosophical Discourse of Modernity* in 1985, Adorno and Horkheimer's critique was odd since 'it denounces the Enlightenment with its own tools'.

In *Negative Dialectics*, Adorno remained faithful to this paradoxical philosophical strategy – to take the corpse of reason and make it speak of the circumstances of its own death. According to the *Stanford Encyclopaedia of Philosophy*:

> Adorno does not reject the necessity of conceptual identification . . . nor does his philosophy claim to have direct access to the nonidentical. Under current societal conditions, thought can only have access to the nonidentical via conceptual criticisms of false identifications. Such criticisms must be 'determinate negations', pointing up specific contradictions between what thought claims and what it actually delivers.[12]

The utopian dreaming that Marcuse was tempted to do in the 1960s was not for Adorno.

It was not only Hegel's philosophy that Adorno attacked in *Negative Dialectics*; Marx, too, was a target. Marx substituted class struggle for the Hegelian World Spirit while retaining the dialectical conception of history. The telos of history's dialectical process was, for Marx, the liberation of humanity in communist society. That utopia is realised in the proletarian revolution that abolishes the ruling class. In *Negative Dialectics*, Adorno turned his back to the future, rejecting Hegel and Marx's conception of history as moving dialectically towards a happy ending. But that did not mean, as one critic wrote, that Adorno was involved in the 'diabolisation of history' nor that *Negative Dialectics* replaced the history of salvation with the history of damnation: 'What was condemned in Hegel is once more turned on its head: radical evil – Evil as such is promoted to the status of the World Spirit.'[13]

But there is no World Spirit in *Negative Dialectics*. There is no necessity for things to turn out a certain way, although German philosophers had often supposed they would. Marx, for instance, had hoped that theory and practice could be reunited by means of revolution. For Adorno it had failed in that task. Hence the opening statement of his introduction: 'Philosophy, which once seemed obsolete, lives on because the moment to realise it was missed . . . the summary judgment that it had merely interpreted the world, that resignation in the face of reality had crippled it in itself, becomes a defeatism of reason after the attempt to change the world miscarried.'[14]

When Gershom Scholem read *Negative Dialectics*, he wondered if critical theory now amounted to Marx's analysis of capitalism without the class struggle. If so, that could equally be said of Marcuse's *One-Dimensional Man*. But while Marcuse spent the 1960s looking for a revolutionary subject to replace the proletariat, Adorno's philosophy was a reversal of Marxism: it could never help change the world, but only interpret it more profoundly. If it had a role, it was to reduce the systems of other philosophers to rubble and thus help cure the faithful of their delusions.

In his 1964 book *Jargon of Authenticity*, for instance, Adorno attacked the post-war tendency in German philosophy to find delusive succour in subjective inwardness. That kind of existential turn in philosophy – which he had critiqued in his pre-war works on Husserl and Kierkegaard – he found especially intolerable in the writings of Heidegger, Martin Buber and Karl Jaspers. He took their works to be self-mystificatory. Each in their own way devised elitist philosophies with abstruse terms in order to avoid confronting social realities, basking in the purported glow of such words as angst and leap, and thereby distracting themselves from the darkness of the times. What Wittgenstein said of his mission was also true of Adorno's in *Jargon of Authenticity*: 'This sort of thing has got to be stopped. Bad philosophers are like slum landlords. It's my job to put them out of business.'[15]

IN 1961, ADORNO met Karl Popper in Tübingen at the German Sociological Association. Both were principal speakers at a symposium to debate the methodology appropriate to social science research. It should have been a bruising encounter, a prize fight between two representatives of hostile philosophical positions or a Cold War era confrontation between the representatives of the rival ideologies of liberal democracy and Marxism.[16]

In the blue corner was the Viennese-born Popper, professor of logic and scientific method at the University of London, of whom his British disciple Bryan Magee once said: 'He puts me in mind of a blowtorch.'[17] Popper was the defender of the Open Society against various forms of totalitarianism, champion of scientific method, acerbic excoriator of what he called pseudo-sciences such as psychoanalysis, and insistent that the dialectical thinking in which the Frankfurt School specialised was not only false but dangerous.

In the red corner was Adorno, a man whom even his dedicated and sympathetic follower Martin Jay found painfully capable of the 'withering rant'.[18] Adorno doubted that the liberal, putatively open society that Popper extolled against totalitarianism was so very different from the latter. He, like other Frankfurt School critical theorists, had been impressed by Freudian psychoanalysis. Most significant, as the two men squared up, was that Adorno was sceptical about the pretensions of scientific method to be an objective means of establishing truth. 'The idea of scientific truth cannot be split off from that of a true society', Adorno wrote.[19] The corollary being that, given that we do not live in the latter, the former is beyond us. This conception of scientific truth was to have ramifications, not just for the natural sciences, but for the topic of the symposium – namely how sociology should work.

For the Frankfurt School, the sciences, be they natural or social, had become tools used by capitalism's oppressors to keep the true society from coming into being. Philosophy too, by abandoning a critical perspective on social reality, became a tool of oppression rather than liberation. This perspective was most punchily expressed in a chapter in *One-Dimensional Man* in which Marcuse excoriated what he called 'one-dimensional philosophy'.[20] Formal logic, the linguistic turn of the Vienna Circle of logical positivists, and the analysis of ordinary language by philosophers such as Wittgenstein and J. L. Austin, were all designed, Marcuse argued, 'to coordinate mental operations with those in the social reality' and so had an 'intrinsically ideological character'. Formal logic therefore wasn't so much a way of ordering our thoughts to ensure we don't collapse into philosophical error or illusion as a tool of domination. 'The idea of formal logic itself is a historical event in the development of the mental and physical instruments for universal control and calculability', wrote Marcuse. In this, his views on formal logic were akin to Adorno's critique of identity thinking developed in *Negative Dialectics*. At best, for the Frankfurt School, positivism was quietistic: as practised in Vienna, Oxford, Cambridge and certain American colleges, philosophy had become an absorbing game that distracted philosophers from rational criticism of an irrational society. Science was hardly exempt from this critique: rather, scientific method was the foremost means of both dominating nature and human beings.

This was hardly a new thought; it was a fundamental commitment of the Frankfurt School of critical thinking, developed by Max Horkheimer first in his 1937 paper 'Traditional and Critical Theory', and then in lectures at Columbia University in 1944 which became the basis for his 1947 book *Eclipse of Reason*. The German title of Horkheimer's book *Zur Kritik der instrumentellen Vernunft* (On the Critique of Instrumental Reason), gives a better flavour of what, by 1961, was the unshakeable commitment of the Frankfurt School. Horkheimer's book was a critical description of how reason collapses into irrationality through its emphasis on instrumental concerns. Instrumental reason was devoted to determining the means to a goal, without reasoning about ends in themselves. Horkheimer distinguished between subjective and objective reason (or in German between *Vernunft* and *Verstand*): the former is only concerned with means, the latter with ends.

But why is the former called subjective? Because, Horkheimer, thought, it was concerned with the subject's self-preservation, while objective reason seeks to root truth and meaning in terms of a comprehensive totality. Horkheimer once wrote: 'Social philosophy is confronted with the yearning for a new interpretation of a life trapped in its individual striving for happiness.'[21] The task facing the Frankfurt School was to free oppressed, suffering humanity from that trap, from a mindset that ensnared individuals in the pursuit of happiness rather than questioning why they sought such an end. Because there was no critical reflection on the irrationality or otherwise of such ends, Horkheimer thought, the project of Enlightenment became self-defeating. Enlightenment was supposed to involve the use of reason to help humans free themselves from myth and superstition; instead, it replaced one form of myth with another.

In the same year as he published *Eclipse of Reason*, he and Adorno wrote at the beginning of *Dialectic of Enlightenment*: 'Enlightenment, understood in the widest sense as the advance of thought, has always aimed at liberating human beings from fear and installing them as masters. Yet the wholly enlightened earth is radiant with triumphant calamity.'[22] But what do these thoughts about the nature of Enlightenment have to do with scientific method and formal logic? For Horkheimer, all parts of nature that cannot be calculated and formalised fall out of the Enlightenment's scientific picture of the world. In effect, the Enlightenment creates a world the better to fit its scientific picture of it. But that created world is a distortion. The inexorable drive of instrumental reason – including scientific method, mathematics and formal logic – causes this distorted picture to be seen as the only true picture of the world. We have a false sense of connectedness with the world that gives us a limited sense of how the world can be. In other words, we know some things only at the expense of others.[23] What seems to be a project dedicated to freeing humans from delusion can better be understood as exchanging one set of mental shackles for another. In Marcuse's gloss on this thought, we had become one-dimensional men and women, more or less drones in advanced industrial societies and happy with our lots.

While Adorno, Horkheimer and Marcuse comprehended scientific method as part of a triumphant calamity and the leading means by which capitalists achieve their domination of nature and oppress humanity, Karl Popper was working on his defence of scientific method. He argued that there can, should be, and was progress in science. It was as though he had never read *Dialectic of Enlightenment* or, if he had, thought it beneath contempt. In his first speech at the Tübingen conference, he ended with a quotation from Xenophanes that made his vision of scientific progress plain:

> The gods did not reveal from the beginning,
> All things to us; but in the course of time,
> Through seeking we may learn, and know things better . . .[24]

But, crucially for Popper, that project of knowing things better, which he thought was the basis of science,

> does not start from perceptions or observations or the collection of data or facts, but it starts, rather, from problems. One might say: No knowledge without problems; but also, no problems without knowledge. But this means that knowledge starts from the tension between knowledge and ignorance. Thus we might say not only, no problems without knowledge; but also, no problems without ignorance.[25]

That said, Popper's views about science were as challenging to scientific orthodoxy as to the Frankfurt School. His 1934 book *The Logic of Scientific Discovery* followed the Scottish Enlightenment philosopher David Hume who had pointed out that there is a contradiction in the notion that all knowledge is derived from experience and that general statements, including scientific laws, are verifiable by reference to experience. This notion was the foundational commitment of empiricism and indeed of positivism. And yet, Hume argued, no scientific hypothesis could be finally confirmed and so no scientific law could be definitively true.[26] For example, if all the swans we have seen are white, that doesn't mean the proposition 'All swans are white' is true. This was the problem of induction, and yet, Hume suggested, we cannot help but use inductive reasoning even if we cannot justify its results as knowledge.

Hume's scepticism about the rational basis of induction was inspiring to Popper because it challenged the prevailing view that only what can be proved by reason and experience can be accepted. This perspective on how science worked, called justificationism, and forming the rhetorical basis for much of science's endeavour to understand the world (the better, as the Frankfurt School would argue, to dominate it), was opposed by Popper. Like the Frankfurt School, if for utterly different reasons, he sought to clip the wings of science, to undermine its pretensions. For him, the progress of science did not so much expand the frontiers of human knowledge as reveal the vast empire of our ignorance. As he said at Tübingen, 'Indeed, it is precisely the staggering progress of the natural sciences . . . which constantly opens our eyes anew to our ignorance, even in the field of the natural sciences themselves.'[27]

For Popper, every test of a scientific hypothesis involves an attempt to refute or to falsify it, and one genuine counter-example will falsify the whole theory. He argued that the same scientific method of testing hypotheses did not apply in the case of psychoanalysis or Marxism. Rather, because there was no evidence that could count as false in either theory, he thought, nothing could refute them. Both psychoanalysis and Marxism were for Popper akin to astrology: by refusing to countenance any counter-examples they made themselves unfalsifiable and therefore superficial.

To be sure, Popper's account of the logic of scientific discovery is hardly uncontroversial and it was questioned by later philosophers of science, in particular the American Thomas Kuhn, who pointed out that scientists are more loath to give up cherished hypotheses than Popper suggested. Instead of taking one counter-example to spell doom for a hypothesis, scientists tend to shore it up with auxiliary hypotheses. This so-called 'conventionalist stratagem' makes a lot of sense, not least if you have spent a lot of time, intellectual effort and money testing a beloved hypothesis. Scientists, and this is something readily forgotten in the philosophy of science, are human too.

Indeed, Kuhn argued in his 1962 book *The Structure of Scientific Revolutions* that science involves competing paradigms, each of which consists of a core theory and auxiliary hypotheses.[28] The latter change but the former remains constant until that upsetting moment when it proves impossible to support the core theory through modified hypotheses. Then something unusual happens, which Kuhn called a 'paradigm shift', wherein the core theory is abandoned or radically changed. That often happens, he thought, when the old guard who defended the core theory retire or die. Kuhn's account, apart from anything else, is a refreshing antidote to the Frankfurt School's perspective on science as an efficient tool for the despoilation of nature and the domination of human beings. It also makes science seem less overtly rational than Popper's vision of it.

Popper's perspective on how science worked is important because his 1961 meeting with Adorno was heralded as the start of the *Positivmusstreit* or Positivism Dispute that rumbled on until the end of the decade at a series of conferences in German universities. The name of the dispute might suggest a clash between the Frankfurt School and the defenders of the hubristic scientific project that arose during the Enlightenment, premised on submitting the world to human understanding and control, but the truth is more complicated. In fact, the Positivism Dispute is really a misnomer. Popper, for all that he had written for the Vienna Circle in the 1930s, was no positivist, or at least refused the description. Indeed, Otto Neurath had called Popper the official opposition to the Vienna School. Popper's *The Logic of Scientific Discovery*, republished in an updated English language version only two years before the Tübingen symposium, included an eviscerating attack on the very basis of logical positivism, namely the verification principle, which asserts that a proposition is only cognitively meaningful if it can be definitively and conclusively determined to be either true or false, that is, either verifiable or falsifiable. It was a principle that applied a blowtorch to vast tracts of human discourse: if the verification principle held, then the judgements of ethics and aesthetics were meaningless, perhaps most charitably construed as more or less grunts of approval or disapprobation. And any talk of religion was similarly devoid of sense.

Popper would have none of this. He applied his own blowtorch to the principle, arguing that instead of verificationism what was needed was falsificationism. The latter meant, as we have seen, that hypotheses can be accepted as probable but never utterly confirmed. Human knowledge, he argued, is never conclusive but only conjectural, hypothetical, aspiring to certainty perhaps but achieving only probability. Human knowledge in Popper's perspective was like the British Empire or the Third Reich – it may have seemed to its most blinkered supporters that its borders were conclusively established, that once territory was captured it need never be surrendered, but the truth was that it was provisional and liable to change.

But if Popper was no positivist, that didn't stop Adorno and his acolytes during the dispute from describing him and his supporters, including the German philosopher Hans Albert, as such. 'It must be restated in advance here', wrote Adorno in a footnote to his introduction to a book about the dispute published in German in 1969 after hostilities had ceased, 'that Popper and Albert distance themselves from the specific position of logical positivism. The reason why they are nevertheless regarded as positivists should be evident from what follows.'[29] What was evident was that Adorno called Popper and Albert positivists because they disdained to do what the dialecticians of the Frankfurt School did, namely to question the authority of science.[30]

Popper, for his part, described himself as a critical rationalist, which makes drawing up the battle lines in Tübingen a marvellously challenging business. Adorno, after all, described himself as a critical theorist. But what is the difference between a critical rationalist and a critical theorist? Horkheimer in his essay 'Traditional and Critical Theory' distinguished between the Savant who doesn't realise that the economic (and thus currently capitalist) structure of society shapes scientific work, and the critical theorist who does. For the Frankfurt School, a self-styled critical rationalist like Popper was just as much a Savant in that sense as other self-declared positivists were. But how did Popper understand the term critical rationalist? He made his own distinction between critical rationalism and 'uncritical or comprehensive rationalism'. The latter was really another term for positivism, at least as the latter pertained to philosophy and science. It maintained that information derived from sensory experience, interpreted through reason and logic, forms the exclusive source of all authoritative knowledge.

In his opening address at Tübingen, Popper had set out twenty-seven theses and invited Adorno to support or dissent from them. He argued that the social sciences, just as much as the natural ones, could be and often were devoted to the pursuit of truth through objective procedures. But his eleventh thesis declared that it was a mistake to assume that the objectivity of a science depends upon the objectivity of the scientist. Popper doubted, then, Mannheim's notion of the free-floating intellectual who could rise above class or other interests, just as much as, if for different reasons, the Frankfurt School did. 'We cannot rob the scientist of his partisanship without also robbing him of his humanity', argued Popper, 'and we cannot suppress or destroy his value judgments without destroying him as a human being and as a scientist. Our motives and even our purely scientific ideals, including the ideal of a disinterested search for truth, are deeply anchored in extra-scientific and, in part, in religious evaluations. Thus the "objective" or the "value-free" scientist is hardly the ideal scientist.'[31] But Popper thought that science rose above such value judgements and class interests: 'What may be described as scientific objectivity is based solely upon a critical tradition which, despite resistance, often makes it possible to criticise a dominant dogma.' That critical tradition consisted in 'the social result of [scientists'] mutual criticism, of the friendly-hostile division of labour among scientists, of their co-operation and also of their competition.'[32] The objectivity of science, be it natural or social, and the disinterested pursuit of truth was guaranteed by the existence of such a flourishing critical tradition.

But this was precisely what Adorno, in his reply, denied existed, at least in sociology. He argued that the founder of sociology, the nineteenth-century Frenchman August Comte, was also the man who had devised the discipline of positivism. Both disciplines, Adorno argued, originated to help serve class interests as capitalism took hold. Each seemed, though, that they had a more innocent purpose: namely to aid human enlightenment by pushing back the frontiers of knowledge. In his reply to Popper, Adorno said:

> If in Comte, the outline of a new discipline was born out of the desire to protect the productive tendencies of his age, the unleashing of

productive forces, that is, from the destructive potential which was emerging in them at that time, then subsequently nothing has altered in this original situation unless it has become more extreme, in which case sociology should take this into account.[33]

In Adorno's view, sociology must turn critical if it was not merely to help uphold the status quo or, worse, provide the groundwork for totalitarianism. 'In view of the nakedly emergent coercive force of relations', he added, 'Comte's hope that sociology might guide social force reveals itself as naïve except when it provides plans for totalitarian rulers.'[34]

The conflict between the two men boiled down to a difference of perspective on the nature of the advanced industrial western nations in which they had lived and worked throughout their lives. Popper conceded that the critical tradition necessary for scientific objectivity may not exist in some societies. 'The existence of that tradition depends', he argued in his opening address, 'on a number of social and political circumstances which make this criticism possible.'[35] In his books *The Open Society and Its Enemies* (1945) and *The Poverty of Historicism* (1957), Popper defended open societies (by which he included liberal democracies such as the US, the UK and West Germany) against closed societies such as the one Plato called for in the *Republic* and which, he argued, characterised twentieth-century totalitarian regimes such as Nazi Germany and the Soviet Union. It was only open societies, Popper thought, that preserve reason, that is, criticism. As a consequence, it is only open societies that can be civilised, only they can engage in the rational pursuit of scientific truth, or rather the falsification of scientific error, because only in such societies is that quest objectively guaranteed by competition between scientists, mutual criticism and free discussion.

This, he thought, was equally true of the social as much as the natural sciences. 'The method of the social sciences, like that of the natural sciences, consists in trying out tentative solutions to certain problems: the problems from which our investigations start, and those which turn up during the investigation.'[36] This, Adorno countered, was a naive universalisation of the scientific method. He cited what Marx wrote in *A Contribution to the Critique of Political Economy*: 'It is not the consciousness of men that determines their being, but their social existence that determines their consciousness.' Adorno took this to be important for science and the social sciences: what look like neutral investigations are nothing of the kind. What this meant for sociology was that the social existence of the scientist, social scientists in particular, determined their mindset, what they chose to investigate and how they investigated it. Adorno was profoundly sceptical about Popper's idea that this social existence could be overcome in the name of scientific objectivity through mutual criticism and open discussion. Peer review was no panacea for Adorno, particularly if a discipline was in the service of existing, oppressive society.

And that was just what Adorno thought sociology was. Whether the kind of reason Popper extolled here is that of *Vernunft* or *Verstand* is unclear, but Adorno certainly took sociology to have collapsed into the latter – never questioning the ends to which reason, instrumentally, was put. He feared that sociology had abandoned 'a critical theory of society' and so was 'resignatory'. This was the unaddressed, central difference between Popper and Adorno: the latter thought that advanced industrial western societies involved 'conditions of unfreedom'; Popper thought that it was in such open societies that the freedom existed for the scientifically objective pursuit of truth to take place.

At the end of round one in the *Positivmusstreit*, many had the impression of two boxers failing to connect. 'One must doubt', said Ralf Dahrendorf, then professor of sociology at Tübingen and the symposium's rapporteur, 'whether Popper and Adorno could even agree upon a procedure with the aid of which their differences could be decided.'[37] The dispute, though, was a tag match in which Adorno and Popper were replaced by their more waspish juniors. In 1963, during a *Festschrift für Adorno*, Jürgen Habermas accused Popper of political and intellectual naivety in his framing of the nature of scientific and social scientific research, especially during a period of increasing social unrest. Habermas asserted the superiority of the Frankfurt School's 'dialectical' critique over what they took to be Popper's critical rationalism. This prompted Popper's followers to demonise Adorno's followers as irrationalists and totalitarians.[38] Hans Albert, for instance, damned the Frankfurt School's assumption of intellectual superiority over Popperian critical rationalism: 'The dialectical cult of total reason is too fastidious to content itself with "specific" solutions. Since there are no solutions which meet its demands, it is forced to rest content with insinuation, allusion and metaphor.'[39]

Adorno, very sensibly, waited until he came to edit the book containing these vituperative speeches to deliver his judgement on Albert's outburst. He argued that dialectical theory 'does not indulge in a cult of total reason; it criticises such reason. But whilst arrogance towards specific solutions is alien to it, it does not allow itself to be silenced by them.'[40] But after the dispute was over, none of the tag teams seemed to have learned much from each other. Certainly the Frankfurt School was never tempted into sharing Popper's vision of science as a kind of marketplace where, thanks to intellectual competition and mutual criticism, the worst hypotheses are falsified. Instead, as Adorno put it, the School considered itself to be on the right path. 'Dialectics remains intransigent in the dispute since it believes that it continues to reflect beyond the point at which its opponents break off, namely before the unquestioned authority of the institution of science.'[41]

ON 5 APRIL 1969, Marcuse wrote from his office at the University of California at San Diego to Adorno in Frankfurt. 'Dear Teddy, I find it really difficult to write this letter, but it has to be done and, in any case, it is better than covering up differences of opinion between the two of us.'[42] The differences were over the student protests at the time sweeping Europe and America. In particular, Marcuse was scandalised that Adorno had called in the police to evict a group of protesting students from the Institute for Social Research's building in January of that year. Marcuse had written to his old friend, expressing disappointment that he had chosen the wrong side in the struggle: 'I still believe that our cause (which is not only ours) is better taken up by the rebellious students than by the police, and, here in California, that is demonstrated to me almost daily (and not only in California).'

It was the latest in an exchange of letters between the two men that would end only in August that year with Adorno's death. This remarkable correspondence shows each man responding very differently to what both recognised as an attempted patricide by student protesters. 'We cannot abolish from the world the fact that these students are influenced by us (and certainly not least by you) – I am proud of that and am willing to come to terms with patricide, even though it hurts sometimes', Marcuse had written to Adorno. The leading lights of the Frankfurt School had rebelled against their fathers and now their students were similarly challenging the authority of their symbolic fathers.

The student movement opposed America's imperialist war in Vietnam, Cold War militarisation and the threat of nuclear Armageddon, while supporting Third World liberation movements and using sit-ins to demand the democratic restructuring of education. The question of how critical theory should respond to the protests was a vexed one. Habermas suggested that it might involve 'a strategy of hibernation' – keeping their heads down while everyone else was, apparently, losing theirs. Marcuse, by contrast, thought critical theory's cause was really the same as those of the protesters. If he was right, then the Frankfurt scholars ought to have checked out of the Grand Hotel Abyss and joined the students at the barricades. Adorno, with typical waspishness, poured scorn on that suggestion, writing in his essay 'Marginalia to Theory and Practice' that 'the barricades are a game, and the lords of the manor let the gamesters go on playing for the time being'.[43]

And yet, in the early days of the protests, Adorno had expressed solidarity with the student protesters. In one of his sociology seminars in 1967, he went so far as to say that 'the students have taken on something of the role of the Jews'. He had also prefaced a lecture in June that year by inviting his students to stand in memory 'of our dead colleague Benno Ohnesorg'. Ohnesorg had been shot in the back by a police officer during a student-led demonstration in Berlin against the security measures put in place for the state visit to West Germany by the Shah of Iran, the dictator who tortured opponents and crushed freedom of expression.[44]

Nor was Adorno unsympathetic to the students' demand for an overhaul of obsolete authoritarian university structures. Certainly, students were exasperated at the undemocratic power wielded over them by their professors. In one protest, for example, a ceremony honouring a rector at the University of Hamburg was interrupted by two students carrying a banner bearing the slogan: 'Beneath their robes: two thousand years of mustiness.' Adorno was less sympathetic to disruptions of lectures and the forcing of university staff to undergo self-criticism. He told students in an aesthetics lecture that there had to be some rules and that formalised statutes could not be viewed entirely negatively by anyone who knows 'what it means when the doorbell rings at 6am and you do not know whether it is the Gestapo or the baker'. For all that critical theory had long suggested that there were parallels between fascism and the totally administered advanced industrial society, Adorno chose this moment to stand up for the Federal Republic against those who called it a fascist state. He warned his students not to make the mistake of 'attacking what was a democracy, however much in need of improvement, rather than tackling its enemy'.[45]

But protesting students weren't the only ones to invoke the spectre of fascism. Habermas, whom Adorno had lured back to Frankfurt in 1964, to take over the retired Max Horkheimer's job as professor of philosophy and sociology, did just that in June 1967 when he shared a platform in Hanover with the student leaders Rudi Dutschke and Hans-Jürgen Krahl to discuss the topic 'University and Democracy: Conditions and Organisation of Resistance'. Habermas spoke in support of the student radicals' programme, but not their means. He rounded on Dutschke for pursuing revolution by 'any means necessary', arguing: 'In my opinion, he has presented a voluntarist ideology which was called utopian socialism in 1848, but which in today's context . . . has to be called left fascism.'[46]

Adorno didn't dissociate himself from Habermas's words and, partly as a result – for all his meetings with students to discuss educational reform and the sympathetic noises he made in interviews – he became one of the leading targets of the Sozialistische Deutsche Studentenbund (SDS). When he gave a talk at the Free University of

Berlin on Goethe's *Iphigenie in Tauris* later that year, two students unfurled a banner: 'Berlin's left-wing fascists greet Teddie the Classicist.' They urged him to speak out in support of student and self-styled *spaßguerrilla* (fun guerrilla) Fritz Teufel, who had been on hunger strike in jail facing a charge of treason over his role in the demonstration that had led to the death of Benno Ohnesorg.[47] Teufel had become a celebrity in Germany for his involvement in the so-called 'pudding assassination' of US vice-president Hubert Humphrey in which he and other protestors had planned to throw bags of pudding and yogurt during a state visit. But Adorno refused and carried on with his lecture, at the end of which a woman tried to present him with a red teddy bear. Adorno claimed to be unshaken by what he called this 'abusive behaviour'. He was nevertheless becoming exasperated by the students, writing to Marcuse that many of them tried 'to synthesise their practice with a non-existent theory, and thus expressed a decisionism that evokes horrific memories'.[48] Not for the first time, he was seeing fascism behind the flower power student movement.

The following year, 1968, the student rebellion escalated across the west, with the May revolt in Paris. In Frankfurt, strikes were organised by students in the hope that they would inspire workers to do the same. It was in this context that at the Frankfurt Book Fair in September that year, Adorno, along with Habermas and the future Nobel Laureate Günter Grass, shared a platform with one of his student protégés, Hans-Jürgen Krahl, to discuss the topic 'Authority and Revolution'. The discussion went Oedipal as Krahl turned on his mentor. 'Six months ago, when we were besieging the council of Frankfurt University, the only professor who came to the students' sit-in was Professor Adorno', recalled Krahl. 'He made straight for the microphone, and just as he reached it, he ducked past and shot into the philosophy seminar. In short, once again, on the threshold of practice, he retreated into theory.' Adorno replied: 'I do not know if elderly gentlemen with a paunch are the right people to take part in a demonstration.'[49] He later wrote to Günter Grass, noting that 'I have nothing in common with the students' narrow-minded direct action strategies which are already degenerating into abominable irrationalism. In truth, it is they who have changed their position rather than I mine.'[50]

Greater humiliation was to come. His sociology seminar was taken over by striking students calling for the reform of their course. 'Critical theory has been organised in such an authoritarian manner that its approach to sociology allows no space for the students to organise their own studies', said a leaflet distributed by the occupying students. 'We are fed up with letting ourselves be trained in Frankfurt to become dubious members of the political left who, once their studies are finished, can serve as the integrated allies of the authoritarian state.'[51] This was a shattering rebuke for a critical theorist like Adorno. After all, before the First World War, as a student leader Walter Benjamin had rebelled against a university education that churned out obliging state functionaries. 'We have to wake up from the existence of our parents', Benjamin wrote later in *The Arcades Project*. This, in a sense was what Krahl and his fellow SDS protesters were doing, awakening from the parental authority of Adorno and asserting that education had to be more than the Institute for Social Research was offering. In these charged circumstances, Adorno wrote to Marcuse inviting him to Frankfurt in the hope that the presence of the darling of the student movement, the Father of the New Left, might have a mollifying effect on the putative children of the revolution.

But Marcuse started to get compunctions about helping Adorno after he heard about what happened at the Institute in January 1969. It was then that a group of SDS students led by Krahl occupied a room and refused requests from Adorno and Habermas to leave. 'We had to call the police, who then arrested all those who they found in the room', Adorno wrote to Marcuse. The students were outraged at his betrayal. 'Adorno as institution is dead', declared a flyer distributed by a radical group of sociology students in April of that year. And Marcuse, too, thought his friend had made a mistake. He wrote to Adorno: 'Occupation of rooms (apart from my own apartment) without such a threat of violence would not be a reason for me to call the police. I would have left them sitting there and left it to somebody else to call the police.' More profoundly, Marcuse disagreed with his former Frankfurt School colleagues on their analysis of the students' tactics, and with Adorno on the relationship between theory and practice. He wrote:

> You know me well enough to know that I reject the unmediated trans-
> lation of theory into praxis just as emphatically as you do. But I do
> believe that there are situations, moments, in which theory is pushed
> on further by praxis – situations and moments in which theory that is
> kept separate from praxis becomes untrue to itself . . . But this same
> situation is so terrible, so suffocating and demeaning, that rebellion
> against it forces a biological, physiological reaction: one can bear it no
> longer, one is suffocating and one has to let some air in . . . And I would
> despair about myself (us) if I (we) would appear to be on the side of a
> world that supports mass murder in Vietnam, or says nothing about it,
> and which makes a hell of any realms that are outside the reach of its
> own repressive power.[52]

In such circumstances, Marcuse decided not to go to Frankfurt to help Adorno out of a fix and ease the conflict between him and his students.

Adorno replied angrily, saying that he had no regrets about call-ing the police. He accused the SDS of both Stalinism (for interrupting his lectures to demand that he engage in self-criticism) and fascism (because of their violence and silencing tactics). Adorno rounded on Marcuse for siding with the students, given their outrageous tactics and their jejune politics that his old, misguided friend seemed to share. He wrote: 'We withstood in our time, you no less than me, a much more dreadful situation – that of the murder of the Jews, without proceeding to praxis; simply because it was blocked for us. I think that clarity about the streak of coldness in one's self is a matter for self-contemplation.' Marcuse had complained about Habermas's use of the term 'left fascism' to describe the students. 'But you are a dialectician, aren't you?' Adorno snarled back in his reply. 'As if such contradictions did not exist – might not a move-ment, by the force of its immanent antinomies, transform itself into its opposite? I do not doubt for a moment that the student move-ment in its current form is heading towards that technocratization of the university that it claims it wants to prevent, indeed quite directly.'

But if Adorno thought himself a better dialectician than Marcuse, able to see how *spaßguerrilla* tactics, flower power and erotic liberation could mutate into their own kind of oppression, then he wasn't to enjoy being proved right. On April 22, he endured his bitterest humiliation. He started his lecture series 'An Introduction to Dialectical Thinking' by inviting students to ask him questions at any point. Two students demanded he perform an act of self-criticism for having called the police to clear the Institute and for starting legal proceedings against Krahl. It was then that a student wrote on the blackboard: 'If Adorno is left in peace, capitalism will never cease.' Others shouted: 'Down with the informer!' Adorno said he would give everyone five minutes to decide if they wanted him to carry on with the lecture. Then three women protesters surrounded him on the platform, bared their breasts and scattered rose and tulip petals over him. He grabbed his hat and coat, ran off from the hall and later cancelled the lecture series.[53] Dialectics had been brought to a standstill, though not in quite the edifying way Benjamin had hoped for in *The Arcades Project*.

A report in the *Frankfurter Rundschau*, under the heading 'Adorno as an Institution is Dead: How the Consciousness Changer was Driven out of the Lecture Hall', compared what became known as the 'Busenaktion' (breast action) to fascism: 'The rowdy treatment of Adorno, far from signalling the emergence of a new post-bourgeois style . . . points to a pre-bourgeois, indeed pre-civilised, relapse into barbarism.' Adorno, for his part, couldn't quite believe he had been targeted: 'To have picked on me of all people. I who have spoken out against every kind of erotic repression and sexual taboo . . . The laughter that was aimed at me was basically the reaction of the philistine who giggles when he seeks girls with naked breasts.'[54] The incident drove Adorno into 'extreme depression' as he put it to Marcuse, who had travelled across the Atlantic for a lecture tour and was hoping to meet up with Adorno and Habermas during the summer.

While Adorno was humiliated, Marcuse, on his return to Europe was feted. The magazine *Konkret* described him as 'the only representative of the "Frankfurt School" who supports those who wish to realise the claims of Critical Theory: the students, young workers, persecuted minorities in the metropolises, and the oppressed in the Third World'. But a couple of weeks later the Marcusean love-in was rudely interrupted by Daniel Cohn-Bendit, leader of the May '68 Paris student uprisings. 'Marcuse, why have you come to the theatre of the bourgeoisie?' yelled Cohn-Bendit as Marcuse tried to give a lecture at the Teatro Eliseo in Rome. 'Herbert, tell us why the CIA pays you?'[55] Danny the Red was reacting to reports in a left-wing Berlin newspaper claiming that Marcuse had worked for the CIA long after he had ostensibly quit working for the US Secret Service in 1951. Could it really be that the radically chic excoriator of American imperialism was really its lackey? Was the man who theorised the one-dimensional society in fact one of those responsible for keeping it in place? That seems unlikely. Marcuse, though, clearly found the Roman experience uncomfortable, if not as humiliating as the 'Busenaktion' against Adorno: according to newspaper reports he walked out of the lecture, though in correspondence with Adorno he was keen to deny that it had been ended by student protest.

Marcuse, though upset by Adorno's rough treatment in Frankfurt and chastened by Danny-le-Rouge's ribbing in Rome, didn't revise his opinion of the student protestors. They were, if not the revolutionary subject he had been seeking to replace the disappointing working classes, then at least capable of 'a protest against capitalism'. He wrote to Adorno from the Provençal town of Cabris in late July:

Of course, I never voiced the nonsensical opinion that the student movement is itself revolutionary. But it is the strongest, perhaps the only, catalyst for the internal collapse of the system of domination today. The student movement in the United States has indeed intervened effectively as just such a catalyst: in the development of political consciousness, in the agitation in the ghettos, in the radical alienation from the system of layers who were formerly integrated, and, most importantly, in the mobilisation of further circles of the populace against American imperialism.[56]

Marcuse thought that the Frankfurt School should be helping the students, rather than demanding their arrest. 'I have fought publicly enough against the slogan "destroy the university", which I regard as a suicidal act. I believe that it is precisely in a situation such as this that it is our task to help the movement, theoretically, as well as in defending it against repression and denunciation.'[57]

If the Institute opposed the student movement, it would betray its radical heritage, argued Marcuse. He was worried already that its radical credentials had been tarnished by its apparent support for US foreign policy. Marcuse was furious, in particular, about the defence of America's role in Vietnam made by Horkheimer, who had retired as the Institute's director in 1964. According to Friedrich Pollock, Horkheimer regarded the Vietnam war as a 'justified attempt to halt the Chinese in Asia' and thought that US withdrawal would lead to a blood bath that 'would also expedite China's passage to the Rhine'.[58] For Marcuse, the student movement was fighting US imperialism and deserved the Frankfurt School's support. He wrote to Adorno:

> According to its own dynamic, the great, indeed historic, work of the Institute demands the adoption of a clear position against American imperialism and for the liberation struggle in Vietnam, and it is simply not on to speak of the 'Chinese on the Rhine', as long as capitalism is the dominant exploiter. As early as 1965, I heard of the identification of the Institute with American policy in Germany.[59]

Adorno replied to this in a hand-written letter that reached Marcuse on August 6, the day of Adorno's death. He and his wife Gretel had gone on holiday to the Swiss Alps, hoping that 'badly battered Teddie', as he described himself to Marcuse, could recover from his ordeals in Frankfurt with some extended Alpine walks. At a recent exam, he related, he 'got another dose of tear gas; that is most burdensome, given my severe conjunctivitis'. He wanted, in his final letter to Marcuse, to clear up a misunderstanding: he wasn't unsympathetic to the student movement, for all that it had made the past few years a merry hell for him. He had, though, an important caveat: 'But it is mixed with a dram of madness, in which the totalitarian resides teleologically, and not at all simply as a repercussion (though it is this too).'

Despite warnings from his doctor to avoid strenuous activity, Adorno travelled by cable car up a 3,000-metre Swiss mountain. At the summit he started to suffer pains and so later that day went to hospital in Visp, Switzerland, where the following morning he suffered a heart attack and died. He would have turned sixty-six the following month. The year before his death, Adorno had written to his friend Peter Szondi that he was becoming sick of student affairs and feared that they were manipulating him and his colleagues. 'It's a case of patricide deferred', he wrote.[60] It would be glib, though, to argue that the deferral was only brief and that Adorno was killed by his students.

In any case, not only would Adorno's and his colleagues' writings survive their authors' deaths, but, thanks to his former assistant, the Frankfurt School was about to take a new turn.

PART VII:

BACK FROM THE ABYSS – HABERMAS AND CRITICAL THEORY AFTER THE 1960s

17

The Frankfurt Spider

In January 2010, Jürgen Habermas fell prey to an internet hoax.[1] An anonymous prankster set up a fake Twitter feed purporting to be by Habermas, at the time professor emeritus of philosophy at the Johann Wolfgang Goethe University of Frankfurt. 'It irritated me because the sender's identity was a fake', Habermas told me when I interviewed him. Like Apple co-founder Steve Jobs, Zimbabwean president Robert Mugabe and former US secretary of state Condoleezza Rice before him, Habermas had been twitterjacked.

Twitter closed down the fake Habermas feed, but not before the philosophy blogosphere had become very excited. Could it be that the then eighty-year-old German thinker was joining the Twitterati? Was he really trying to explain his ethico-political theories in 140 characters or fewer? Some were taken in, others doubtful. One blogger wrote sceptically: 'Firstly, the sentence "Sprechen Sie Deutsch, bitte?" does not seem to be a sentence uttered by a native German speaker – he would have simply asked "Sprechen Sie Deutsch?" or said "Sprechen Sie bitte Deutsch?"'

Some of the tweets were authentic Habermas. For instance, at 5.38 p.m. on January 29, the account tweeted the following: 'It's true that the internet has reactivated the grass-roots of an egalitarian public sphere of writers and readers.' At 5.40 p.m.: 'It also counterbalances the deficits from the impersonal and asymmetrical character of broadcasting insofar as . . .' At 5.41 p.m.: '. . . it reintroduces deliberative elements in communication. Besides that, it can undermine the censorship of authoritarian regimes . . .' At 5.44 p.m.: 'But the rise of millions of fragmented discussions across the world tend instead to lead to fragmentation of audiences into isolated publics.'

Intrigued, I cut and pasted these tweets into Google and soon found that they were all taken from footnote three to the English translation of Habermas's 2006 paper 'Political Communication in Media Society: Does Democracy Still Enjoy an Epistemic Dimension?' Why would Habermas cut and paste from his own paper? Of course, it turned out that he hadn't.

To find out who had, I posted appeals for information on philosophy blogs from Chicago to Leiden. Would the real creator of the fake Habermas please stand up? After a few weeks, I received an email from someone called Raphael, a Brazilian studying for a PhD in politics in the US, confessing that he had created the feed. At first he used it to 'inform people about [Habermas's] most recent publications', as a form of flattery to the man he had admired since he was an undergraduate. But one day, an Austrian professor sent him a message asking if he was the real Habermas. 'I thought that it would be funny to pretend a little bit. Then I quoted the passage about the internet and the fragmentation of the public sphere. It was interesting to see people's reaction.'

Raphael didn't want to disclose his surname or where he was studying, out of embarrassment. But in tweeting Habermas's thoughts on the internet, he succeeded in getting the attention of many philosophers and sociologists. They were intrigued by how one of Habermas's key concepts, the 'public sphere', which he developed in his 1962 book *The Structural Transformation of the Public Sphere: An Inquiry into a Category of Bourgeois Society*, might apply to the internet age. This isn't a trivial matter: at a time when contempt for traditional democratic party politics runs deep and when the so-called democratic deficit makes European political integration look like a scheme concocted by self-serving elites, perhaps the internet offers hope for change.

Habermas uses the term public sphere in a particular sense. 'By the "public sphere" we mean first of all the realm of our social life in which something approaching public opinion can be formed', he wrote. 'Citizens behave as a public body when they confer in an unrestricted fashion – that is, with the guarantee of freedom of assembly and association and the freedom to express and publish their opinions – about matters of general interest.'[2] For Habermas, the public sphere briefly flourished at a specific historical moment. Just before the industrial revolution at the beginning of the eighteenth century, literary men and women met in London's coffee houses, Paris's salons and Germany's *Tischgesellschaften* ('table talks') for what Habermas calls 'rational-critical discussion'. It was also the era of literary journals and a nascent free press and these too were part of the public sphere that acted as a check on absolutist rulers.

'In its clash with the arcane and bureaucratic practices of the absolutist state', wrote Habermas in a sentence too long to be tweeted, 'the emergent bourgeoisie gradually replaced a public sphere in which the ruler's power was merely represented before the people with a sphere in which state authority was publicly monitored through informed and critical discourse by the people.'[3] This new sphere was made possible by new rights granting freedom of association and, to a limited extent, press freedom. The new social associations to which they gave rise were voluntary and, crucially for Habermas, united under a common aim, namely to make use of their reason in discussion. He argued that, for the first time, public opinion came out of these coffee-house associations and literary journals and led to the development of a notion of the common good. And that notion was used to critique the powers of what, in Europe at the time, were unrepresentative and closed forms of government.

But the eighteenth-century 'public sphere' was killed off during the twentieth century. Habermas found lots of different fingerprints on the murder weapon: the welfare state, mass media, the rise of public relations, the undermining of parliamentary politics by the rise of political parties. The fact that most of us know more about Kim Kardashian than post-endogenous growth theory probably doesn't help. The freedom of the press that allowed critical voices to be raised against absolutist rule also resulted in mass circulation newspapers that became profit-generating machines for capitalist organisations, and thus, for Habermas, the public sphere lost its autonomy and critical power.

But there's a problem with Habermas's story here. The early eighteenth-century public sphere he eulogised is scarcely a role model for us in the twenty-first century wondering how democratic politics can become something other than an oxymoron. Those coffee-house associations and literary journals were spaces for educated men who owned property or otherwise had ample means. Moreover, their notion of the common good was probably very different from those not included in the public sphere, notably women, peasants and the nascent proletariat. Habermas's thinking therefore had a nostalgic tenor: if only we were more like all those well-read, well-informed, critically minded coffee-house denizens, then democracy might have a chance in the twenty-first century. He argued that the principles of these associations were sound: in principle, they were voluntary and would admit anybody; in principle, status, class, gender and wealth were irrelevant to admission to this public sphere and to participation in informed and critical discourse. Principle and practice of course were very different, but the important thing was that people came together to reason in an unconstrained way. Habermas argued that this was where the ideal of democratic politics was born.

One can be sceptical about where he decided to locate the birthplace of that democratic ideal without doubting Habermas's utopian hopes and his commitment to revivifying democratic institutions. But utopian hopes and commitment to democratic revivification were not the currency in which the first generation of the Frankfurt School traded. Adorno and Horkheimer conceived of emancipation in a negative way: they could change little and instead only say no to the existing state of affairs. Marcuse was of a similar temper, writing about the power of negative thinking and dabbling unconvincingly in imagining utopias only when caught up in the giddy euphoria of the New Left in the late 1960s.

That first generation, though, was fast disappearing (Adorno died in 1969, Horkheimer in 1973, Marcuse in 1979 and Fromm in 1980) and being replaced by a second generation, led by Habermas. That said, Habermas left Frankfurt in 1971 to become co-director of the superbly named Max Planck Institute for Research into Conditions of Living in a Scientific and Technological World, in Starnberg, a small lakeside town near Munich. Habermas's conditions of living were certainly comfortable in this scientific and technological world. In Starnberg, which regularly tops lists of German towns with the highest disposable income per capita, he and his wife, Ute, whom he married in 1955, built a spectacular, pure-white house inspired by the Bauhaus architect Adolf Loos, filled with light and books. The house's austere optimism, not quite built to Neue Sachlichkeit principles but certainly of a modernist temper, suited him, juxtaposing coolly against a world of gimcrack postmodernism. There the Habermases raised three children, and kept the home even after he returned to teach at Frankfurt in 1983.

If Habermas had not rebelled against his teachers, he would have become yet another philosophical Cassandra; instead, he became more like the Frankfurt School's Pollyanna. This is surprising given that he came of age in post-war Germany. As his *Stanford Encyclopedia of Philosophy* entry notes: 'The Nuremberg Trials were a key formative moment that brought home to him the depth of Germany's moral and political failure under National Socialism.'[4] Shouldn't he, then, have despaired as his teacher Adorno did? It was Adorno who mused with the guilt of a Holocaust survivor on whether 'one who escaped [Auschwitz] by accident, one who by rights should have been killed, may go on living'.[5] Habermas's hopeful direction for German philosophy looked like a rebellious response to Adorno's philosophical despair. Adorno's negative dialectics was a style of thinking that scorned method and held out against creating just the kind of systematically theorised, rationally achieved consensus that has guided Habermas's work. But Oedipal rebellion is hardly all there is to this.

Significant too is the fact that Habermas is not Jewish. Nor is he a Holocaust survivor like those of the first Frankfurt School generation and, if there is anything to suggest that he felt guilt or shame for his adolescent role in fighting for Hitler (and there's no sense in his writings that he felt either), his feelings are very different from those Adorno experienced. The guilt of the survivor that Adorno described in a letter to his mother in 1946 after the death of his father, is not something that Habermas could share.

'It is well-known that the Jews were forbidden to look into the future', Walter Benjamin wrote in his 'Theses on the Philosophy of History'. 'The Torah and the prayers instructed them, by contrast, in remembrance. This disenchanted those who fell prey to the future, who sought advice from the soothsayers. For that reason the future did not, however, turn into a homogeneous and empty time for the Jews. For in it every second was the narrow gate, through which the Messiah could enter.'[6] Habermas was under no such prohibition. Jews focus, if Benjamin was right, on the remembrance of past sufferings rather than imagining futures in which suffering and injustice are not part of the programme. Not so for Habermas. Unlike Heidegger, he took responsibility; unlike Adorno, he declined to despair. Unlike his teacher, too, he has sought to develop system and method, and to work out how, as he described it to me, 'the citizens of a political community could still exercise collective influence over their social destiny through the democratic process'. Unlike Benjamin, Habermas dared to look into the future and imagine a utopia, even if it was one for which few shared his enthusiasm.

Never since Kant and Hegel has a German philosopher and social theorist developed such an elaborate intellectual system. And yet this multidisciplinary system is based on one simple idea, namely that through rational communication we can overcome our biases, our egocentric and ethnocentric perspectives, come to a consensus or community of reason, and develop thereby what the American pragmatist philosopher George Herbert Mead, who much influenced Habermas, called the 'larger self'. Nietzsche called Kant the 'catastrophic spider', entangling philosophy in a crazy web of intellectual constructs – phenomena, noumena, transcendental unities, imperatives, categories and judgements. Habermas, though, is of a similar sensibility to the great Enlightenment systems builder: the hundreds of thousands of words he has written in the past half century in philosophy, social theory, political theory, ethics, moral theory and legal theory constitute a vast web – not a dismal intellectual trap but a heroic construction designed by one opposed to fascism, postmodernism and his masters' despair. The great difference between Kant and Habermas is that the former's system was monological, imagining that the individual could generate a whole, universalisable moral system from their own reasoned reflection, while the latter is dialogical: for Habermas, it is only through reasoned discussion in what he calls an 'unlimited communication community' that we can arrive at rational consensus, that professorial vision of utopia. Habermas might well then be thought of as a post-Kantian philosophical spider if not a catastrophic one.

One of his foremost American critics, Stanley Fish, professor of English and law at Duke University, has been particularly critical of Habermas's notion that we might talk our way past our biases in rational discussion. In order to enter into a conversation in which you might lose your prejudices, Fish argued, you would have to begin by putting aside your prejudices – as Habermas assumed those coffee-house denizens of the early eighteenth-century public sphere did. Fish doubted the possibility of doing this:

> The trouble with Habermas' way of thinking is that you couldn't possibly take this first step. This first step is in fact the last step. I have always been mystified by the attention that Habermas receives. His way of thinking about these matters seems to me to be obviously faulty. The only way I can explain it to myself is that Habermas represents something that a lot of people would like to buy into: He seems to offer a way out of corrosive relativism.[7]

But even if Fish is right and Habermas's way out is just yet another cul de sac, the impulse to avoid relativism – whereby there is no truth but many truths, no correct moral judgement but only a competing clamour of different value claims – has been an important part of what has kept Habermas spinning his web of words more than half a century. Habermas's fight against the relativism of postmodern thought is central to understanding his work.

More important, though, in understanding Habermas, is the thought articulated, as we have seen, by Adorno: 'Hitler imposes a new categorical imperative on human beings in their condition of unfreedom: to arrange their thought and action that Auschwitz would not repeat itself, [that] nothing similar would happen.'[8] It is this thought, and this moral duty, that has impelled Habermas to work to ensure that human beings never stoop to such barbarism again. It's striking that Adorno spoke of a categorical imperative, the notion that Kant made central to his moral theory, because Adorno temperamentally disdained what Habermas embraced, not only the system building of German philosophy and social theory, but also the hopeful Enlightenment commitment to the use of reason as a way of safeguarding human beings from domination, be that domination by superstition or political oppression. Kant's idea was that a moral system could be generated by means of reason, and so, because it was free of personal biases, interests and passions, become universalisable: reason was a court in which every human being was guaranteed to be treated fairly and that produced results that were incontestable.

David Hume had argued that reason is the slave of the passions and thus, effectively, rubbished the possibility of the Kantian moral system before the spider of Königsberg had even started work on it. For the latter, if an action was founded on the passions, it was by definition not moral; only those actions that were in accord with the categorical imperative and thus arrived at by means of reasoned reflection were universalisable and thus capable of being truly moral. But what if Hume is right and all our reasoned judgements are premised on mere passions? Then, you might think, the Kantian system collapses. Hume's moral psychology was intolerable to Kant. For him, such slavery to the passions is improper if man is to become mature, self-mastering and autonomous. Passions are to be mastered and, if we are not mature enough to master ourselves, then others must help us. The categorical imperative was at the heart of his moral theory, one that expressed his Enlightenment commitment to the use of reason to achieve individual autonomy. He took the use of reason to demonstrate *Mündigkeit*, or the ability to think for oneself.

But while Adorno took *Mündigkeit* in an entirely negative way, as meaning a refusal to adjust to the existing order, Habermas insisted it was the foundation for the creation of truly democratic institutions. He conceded that rationality may have been the cause of our problems, but insists too that it must be the solution to them. Only through the kind of communicative reason Habermas imputes to eighteenth-century public spheres and yearns for in a contemporary society beset by democratic deficit, can humanity become what Adorno feared it never would be – mature, autonomous, free.

But then Adorno and Habermas had very different attitudes to what the Enlightenment was. Indeed, much of Habermas's writing can be taken as an overturning of Adorno and Horkheimer's *Dialectic of Enlightenment*, that foundational text written in the 1940s when what they took to be the barbarisms of Nazism, Stalinism and the totally administered society were making a mockery of the Enlightenment heritage. The eighteenth-century Enlightenment of Rousseau, Voltaire, Diderot and Kant was supposed to liberate man from myth, to allow him to think for himself (women weren't part of the Enlightenment's purportedly emancipatory narrative). But, with the rise of industrialisation and capitalism in the later eighteenth and early nineteenth century came more bureaucracy, administration and thus control. Using a form of immanent critique (i.e. critiquing a phenomenon using its own values), Adorno and Horkheimer argued that the Enlightenment hoisted itself on its own petard, because in supposedly achieving that very freedom from domination by myth and sacrifice, man was forced to repress his instincts and natural drives.[9]

Hence their focus on the episode in *The Odyssey* in which Odysseus orders his shipmates to chain him to the mast so that he can't surrender to the Sirens' seductive song. Although Homer's epic was written about ten centuries before the European Enlightenment, it is in *The Odyssey* that Adorno and Horkheimer find the birth of humanity's impulse, characteristic of the Enlightenment, to liberate itself from myth and to dominate nature. As Habermas put it: 'The permanent sign of enlightenment is domination over an objectified nature and a repressed internal nature.'[10] In *The Odyssey*, man separates himself from nature the better to dominate it. For Adorno and Horkheimer, we are all little Odysseuses, chained to our masts, sundered from nature and from our own instincts and drives. With the exceptions, of course, of Adorno and Horkheimer.

Habermas demurred. He had read *Dialectic of Enlightenment* as a young man and was excited by it, only later coming to regard its immanent critique as having gone too far. But it was only after the deaths of its authors that he dared publish his misgivings. Even then, in a lecture published in his 1985 book *The Philosophical Discourse of Modernity*, he admitted how difficult it is not to be overwhelmed by his masters' rhetoric, to step back and see how simplistic it was. Habermas, then, is a new Odysseus, hearing the Siren call of that rhetoric and overcoming his natural impulse to be seduced. His masters had argued that reason itself destroys the humanity it first made possible and that this happened because 'of a drive to self-preservation that mutilates reason, because it lays claim to it only in the form of a purposive-rational mastery of nature and instinct – precisely as instrumental reason'. But, for Habermas, there were other forms of reason he wanted to salvage from the Enlightenment heritage – notably communicative reason, of the kind that thrived in and supposedly produced consensus in the public sphere of the early eighteenth century and which he regards as the basis for hope in the revival of democratic ideals in our age.

The term instrumental reason is key here. Habermas defined it in his 1968 book *Technik und Wissenschaft als Ideologie* as the interest in understanding the necessities of nature and the potential for technically harnessing natural laws, and manipulating living and dead nature, constitutive of the natural sciences.[11] That sounds anodyne, but Horkheimer, in his 1947 book *The Eclipse of Reason*, gave it a rhetorical, perhaps even histrionic spin, suggesting that instrumental reason has two opposing elements, namely 'the abstract ego emptied of all substance except its attempt to transform everything in heaven and on earth into means for its preservation, and on the other hand an empty nature degraded to mere material, mere stuff to be dominated, without any other purpose than that of this very domination'.[12]

The Enlightenment was supposed to have freed us from myth and disenchanted the world, slain the gods and made humans masters of their domains. But, so the writers of *Dialectic of Enlightenment* argued, it had failed. In 1797, Goya produced one of the Enlightenment's most terrifying and emblematic images, that of a dozing man beneath a roomful of terrifying winged creatures, and called it *The Sleep of Reason Produces Monsters*. Adorno and Horkheimer's suggestion was that the awakening of reason had produced other monsters. Max

Weber, Habermas noted, imagined the ancient, disenchanted gods rising from their graves in the guise of depersonalised forces to resume their irreconcilable struggles with the demons. Those depersonalised forces – rationalisation, administration, the very workings of capitalism – properly understood, show we have not killed the old gods, just allowed them to put on new masks. Such is the Enlightenment's perversion of its own values.

Habermas went along with this, but only up to a point: 'It is true that with the capitalist economy and the modern state the tendency to incorporate all questions of validity into the limited horizon of purposive rationality proper to subjects interested in self-preservation and to self-maintaining systems is strengthened.'[13] But the rhetorical leap Adorno and Horkheimer made from this is unwarranted: 'This does not yet prove that reason remains subordinated to the dictates of purposive rationality right into its most recent products – modern science, universalistic ideas of justice and morality, autonomous art.'[14] There is more to science than the deployment of instrumental reason, more to art than the culture industry, and the universalistic foundations of the law and morality as well as constitutional government are worthy of much more than censure. The Enlightenment, that is to say, has for Habermas 'a sound core'. But it is one that Adorno and Horkheimer's 'oversimplified presentation' skated over. '*Dialectic of Enlightenment* holds out scarcely any prospect of an escape from the myth of purposive rationality that has turned into objective violence.'[15]

That, though, is what Habermas tries to do in his writings – namely, to theorise his way from beneath the shadow of that intimidating German compound noun *Verblendungszusammenhang*, or total system of delusion. In a 1979 interview he said: 'I do not share the basic premise of Critical Theory, the premise that instrumental reason has gained such dominance that there is really no way out of a total system of delusion, in which insight is achieved only in flashes by isolated individuals.'[16] That kind of insight sounded by turns both elitist and hopeless. Habermas was sceptical about how the first generation of Frankfurt scholars were able to step outside the influence of this total system of delusion in order to provide a critique of it: if it was so total, then surely they were deluded too? He used a similar argument against postmodernists: if, as they claimed, all truth was relative then even the claim that truth is relative becomes relative in its turn. For the Frankfurt School's first generation, this total system of delusion could only be overcome with the collapse of advanced industrial society and the arrival of socialism. Habermas rejected this perspective, arguing instead for reform of the existing system: for him, the eighteenth-century idea of the public sphere could be revivified to resist the ideological apparatuses of the system. *Mündigkeit* or maturity, the self-mastery and autonomy that Kant had extolled, could be realised in our time to overcome the total system of delusion that was late capitalism.

But in holding to the 'sound core' of the Enlightenment in this way Habermas was a man out of time – opposed not just by student radicals in the late 1960s but by postmodernist thinkers in the following decades. Postmodernism was never Habermas's bag, for two reasons. Firstly, he saw it as a means of silencing oppositional voices. His critique of postmodernism in this sense was akin to that of the American Marxist thinker Fredric Jameson, who argued that postmodernism was less a theory than a systemic modification of capitalism, one that countered the critical force of what Habermas took to be the project of modernity.[17] For Jameson, without such a project, without a critical stance, we are defenceless against global capitalism. But while Jameson still maintained a Marxist vision of a new international proletariat rising up against globalised capital and postmodern decadence, Habermas had moved on from his earlier Marxism. Secondly, Habermas poured scorn on postmodernism because like Rudi Dutschke's politics (which Habermas had called left fascism), it seemed to him to flirt with irrationalism and nihilism and so reminded him of the Nazi era.

The postmodernists, for their part, were equally scornful of Habermas's project. The French philosopher Jean-François Lyotard, author of *The Postmodern Condition*, wrote: 'After the enormous massacres we have experienced, no one can any longer believe in progress, in consensus, in transcendent values. Habermas presupposes such a belief.'[18] In this, it was as though Lyotard was the inheritor of Adorno's philosophy rather than Habermas. But perhaps not:

arguably it is Habermas, more than any other European intellectual, who has tried to adhere to Adorno's new categorical imperative.

IN 1980, HABERMAS gave an ardent speech in Frankfurt after he received the Adorno Award, a prize set up to recognise outstanding achievement in philosophy, theatre, music and film. It was called 'Modernity: An Unfinished Project'.[19] In it he defended what he took to be the values of modernity against various postmodernists – among them Lyotard, Michel Foucault and Jacques Derrida – as well as against certain neoconservative thinkers who blamed those values for corrupting western society. In *The Philosophical Discourse of Modernity*, he wrote: 'Modernity can and will no longer become the criteria by which it takes its orientation from the models supplied by another epoch: it has to create its normativity out of itself'.[20] That didn't mean modernity was anti-historical; rather that it was directed only against, as he put it in his Frankfurt speech, 'the false normativity of a historical understanding essentially oriented towards the imitation of past models'.

Walter Benjamin dreamed of exploding the continuum of history; modernity similarly has a transformed notion of time, one that frees itself from the authority of tradition. With the rise of modern science from the seventeenth century onwards, involving the growth of new techniques of measurement, hypothesis-testing and mathematical theorising, and the increase of technically useful knowledge, the authority of the Church waned, as did the previous Aristotelian approach to scientific inquiry. The authority of both was replaced by that of reason. More specifically relevant to Habermas's thesis was that modernity freed humans from traditional roles and enabled them to choose their own ends and become autonomous. In this, Kant's moral philosophy was key: he insisted that we treat others 'never merely as a means, but always at the same time as an end' and so for him, from the moral point of view, the most distinctive feature of human nature was our ability freely to choose our own ends. This is precisely the story of the Enlightenment that Horkheimer countered in *Eclipse of Reason* with his description of how reason collapsed into irrationality through its emphasis on instrumental concerns. Instrumental reason, as

Horkheimer understood it, was devoted to determining the means to an end, without reasoning about ends in themselves.

Habermas's thesis about modernity, then, overturned the Frankfurt School's most distinctive shibboleth. He countered his teachers by arguing that reason had freed rather than enslaved us. For Habermas, modernity freed us in particular from the monotheistic Judaeo-Christian tradition and saw the emergence of a secular morality. That secular morality also decoupled humanity from a substantial conception of the good life. The good was different from the right or the just – indeed from the Enlightenment onwards there was a competing plurality of conceptions of the good. It's striking that aspects of Kant's moral theory, forged in the Enlightenment, were seized on by two leading philosophers – one American, the other German – nearly simultaneously two centuries later. It is almost as if both philosophers were reviving it as they tried to imagine how to hold together, in a just and fair way, western societies that otherwise seemed destined to fragment. Certainly the plurality of conceptions of the good was not something anyone could miss if they were raised, like Habermas and the American philosopher John Rawls, in the increasingly multicultural, multi-faith west after the Second World War. Modern societies were not held together by overarching traditions; rather they consisted of individuals who took themselves to be autonomous subjects.

What, then, could hold such societies together? A leading feature of Rawls's account, set out in his his hugely influential 1971 book *A Theory of Justice*, was that there is a priority of the right over the good. By that Rawls meant that claims based on the rights of individuals were more important than and thus prior to claims based on the good that would result to them, or to others, from violating those rights. The first duty of the liberal state was to safeguard the individual's basic civil liberties. This entailed, as Rawls put it, that 'the loss of freedom for some' could never be 'made right by a greater good shared by others'. The impartiality of the concept of the right ensured, for Rawls, social stability or harmony.

Habermas agreed with much of this: clearly modern societies could not be held together by one overarching concept of good as earlier ones had been. What's more, inviolable liberties and rights are essential to ensure human flourishing and autonomy, to the *Mündigkeit* Kant extolled. For Habermas, all that was necessary but not sufficient. His philosophy, social theory and political theory was devoted to protecting us from the bad consequences of the Enlightenment. That is what he meant by insisting that modernity is an unfinished project: we have benefited from becoming modern in terms of technical progress, economic growth, rational administration, greater autonomy, but we have been scarred by that transformation too.

In his Adorno Prize talk, Habermas said: 'The project of modernity as it was formulated by the philosophers of the Enlightenment in the eighteenth century consists in the relentless development of the objectivating sciences, of the universalistic foundations of morality and law, and of autonomous art, all in accord with their own immanent logic.' He cited Max Weber who argued that, with the collapse of religious and metaphysical worldviews as a result of the Enlightenment, three value spheres or discourses open up to replace them – the natural sciences, morality and law, and the arts. Each of these has become institutionalised and so the preserve of experts, scarcely on speaking terms with each other let alone laypersons. 'The distance between these expert cultures and the general public has increased', he pointed out.[21]

The result? What Habermas called the 'lifeworld' has become impoverished. This is of great importance for his social theory. The lifeworld is one of two distinct spheres of social life, the other being the system. For him lifeworld means the pre-theoretical everyday world of family and household, of shared meanings and understandings, of the unconstrained conversations that take place in the public sphere. The system by contrast means structures and patterns of instrumental rationality and action, notably money and power, whose chief function is the production and circulation of goods and services. The system then includes the economy, state administration and state-sanctioned political parties. The relationship between lifeworld and system is important for Habermas: the former, which is the home of communicative reason and action, risks being colonised by the latter, which is the home of instrumental reason. But that is disastrous for the project of modernity.

The optimistic dream of Enlightenment thinkers such as Condorcet, Habermas argued, was that the arts and sciences would 'not merely promote the control of the forces of nature, but also further the understanding of self and world, the progress of morality, justice in social institutions and even human happiness'.[22] That, he argued, hasn't happened. Instead, systems of power and money have imposed constraints on human action. Systems are dominated by instrumental rationality. Instead of reflecting on our ends and changing them, the system takes on an internal logic that escapes human control.

This distinction between lifeworld and system owes much to Heidegger and also to Marx, but mostly it owes a great deal to Habermas's Frankfurt School predecessors. It was they who took those living in advanced industrial societies to have been utterly colonised by the system to the extent that the lifeworld no longer existed: we have become one-dimensional men and women, mere functionaries of a capitalist system rather than autonomous beings capable of the proper autonomy and self-mastery Kant envisaged.

Habermas differs from his predecessors on two counts. Firstly, he thinks that humanity has gained from the Enlightenment and the rise of science. Secondly, he refused to give up hope as they did. In his Adorno Prize talk, he characterised his former colleague as a man for whom 'the emphatic claim to reason has withdrawn into the accusatory gesture of the esoteric work of art, morality no longer appears susceptible to justification, and philosophy is left solely with the task of revealing, in an indirect fashion, the critical content sealed up within art'.[23] That shrinking from politics into esoterica was not for Habermas: he held rather to the grand promise of the Enlightenment that Adorno thought he and Horkheimer had obliterated. Halfway through 'Modernity: An Unfinished Project', Habermas asked two rhetorical questions:

> should we continue to hold fast to the intentions of the Enlightenment, however fractured they may be, or should we rather relinquish the entire project of modernity? If the cognitive potentials in question do not merely result in technical progress, economic growth and rational

administration, should we wish to see them checked in order to protect a life praxis still dependent on blind traditions from any unsettling disturbance?[24]

But even if we should continue the project of modernity as Habermas counselled, what is less clear is how the impoverishment of lifeworld by system is to be halted. For it is in the lifeworld that Habermas finds the potential bulwarks against the evisceration of social life by capitalism, state and what his colleague Marcuse called one-dimensional society. It is there that he finds the public sphere that once offered a utopian hope for a rational, autonomous, voluntary association where we might, through communicative reason and communication action, become more than one-dimensional men and women.

Shortly after he had been twitterjacked, I asked Habermas if the internet and social media might function as a public sphere. He was sceptical. 'The internet generates a centrifugal force', he replied.

It releases an anarchic wave of highly fragmented circuits of communication that infrequently overlap. Of course, the spontaneous and egalitarian nature of unlimited communication can have subversive effects under authoritarian regimes. But the web itself does not produce any public spheres. Its structure is not suited to focusing the attention of a dispersed public of citizens who form opinions simultaneously on the same topics and contributions which have been scrutinised and filtered by experts.

Perhaps social networking websites might help create that solidarity? 'As regards its impact on the public sphere, accelerated communication opens up entirely new possibilities for organising activities and for large-scale political mobilisations of widely dispersed addressees . . . However, they remain contingent on their relation to the real decision-making processes that take place outside the virtual space of electronically networked monads.'[25]

Maybe Habermas was wrong to be so dismissive of the potential of the internet and social media to function as public spheres, to serve as virtual spaces for discussion untainted by status and spin. Certainly nowadays, the kind of interventions in political matters that Habermas has made in performing his role as a public intellectual throughout his career increasingly take place in cyberspace. When I interviewed him, he was concerned rather about the risk of newspapers being rendered obsolete as a result of the rise of the internet. 'In our own countries, too, the national press, which until now has been the backbone of democratic discourse, is in severe danger. No one has yet come up with a business model that would ensure the survival of the important national newspapers on the internet.' That worry was understandable given how much hope he had placed in the idea that newspapers might (just sometimes) facilitate 'ideal speech situations' in which citizens are able to raise moral and political concerns and defend them by rationality alone. His hope was that newspapers would act as a counterbalance to the erosion of lifeworld by system, or to put it another way, that they would ward off the disenfranchisement of the modern party political system. Certainly Habermas, perhaps more than any other public intellectual of his generation, took his role seriously as a participant in that public sphere. In the revivification of that sphere, the role of intellectuals was key. They must guide debate towards a rational consensus, rather than allowing spin doctors and other media manipulators to stifle freedom of expression and undermine democracy. Habermas argued that rationally achieved consensus, which Adorno's *Negative Dialectics* implacably refused, was necessary and possible for human flourishing post-Auschwitz. The barriers preventing the exercise of reason and mutual understanding could be identified, comprehended and reduced.

Typical of Habermas's public engagement in the German press was his intervention in the *Historikerstreit*, or Historians' Dispute, about how the Holocaust should be interpreted, that raged for four years from 1986. The German historian Ernst Nolte argued that 'Auschwitz . . . was above all a reaction born out of the annihilating occurrences of the Russian Revolution . . . the so-called annihilation of the Jews during the Third Reich was a reaction or a distorted copy and not a first act or an original'. Nolte argued that the Gulag Archipelago preceded Auschwitz and inferred from this that Germany had 'reasonably' turned to Nazism in face of the Bolshevik threat.[26]

Four decades after the fall of Hitler, Habermas sensed that Nolte and other right-wing historians were trying to exonerate their nation for responsibility for the Third Reich's atrocities. Worse yet, some of the historians against whom Habermas wrote were intellectuals who had contacts in West German chancellor Helmut Kohl's Christian Democrat government. For Habermas, their revisionist account of the Final Solution represented the misuse of academic history for political ends. And those ends, quite possibly, involved bolstering Kohl's popularity at home and serving to justify a cessation of West Germany's reparation payments to Israel for the Holocaust.

Habermas described his opponents as trying to normalise German history and attempting to erase what Nolte had called the 'past that refused to go away'. Habermas argued that these historians were trying to get a nation off the hook by suggesting that Nazism was a breach with German history by a small criminal clique. In a series of articles attacking this attempt 'to make Auschwitz unexceptional', he wrote of 'the obligation incumbent upon us in Germany – even if no one else were to feel it any longer – to keep alive, without distortion and not only in an intellectual form, the memory of the sufferings of those who were murdered by German hands'.[27] The spectre of Adorno's new categorical imperative was never far from his mind as Habermas wrote these articles.

What angered him in particular during the *Historikerstreit* was the revival of something he found intolerable – German nationalism. Nationalism in general nauseated Habermas, but German nationalism was worse. One concern for him was that a nation-state, particularly one founded on an ethnic unity, is exclusionary. Another is that the bonds of solidarity between members of a nation are emotional, sentimental and affective and therefore not open to the communicative reason he takes to be necessary for a flourishing public sphere or civil society that can act as a check on the state. Nationalism, then, serves an important function in smoothing the workings of what Habermas calls the system, notably the state administration, since it gives citizens a sense of belonging to a unitary political community, rather than equipping them with the social spaces and intellectual tools to be a critical check on state power. In

Habermas's technical terms, this pre-discursive nationalism is a phenomenon that arises in the lifeworld but can be colonised by the system. Put more simply, nationalist feelings can always be readily manipulated by political elites: Hitler had done just that and Habermas was understandably queasy about history repeating itself.

The rise of nationalism in Germany in particular subverted the idea of communicative rationality that Habermas set out in his 1981 masterpiece *The Theory of Communicative Action*, whereby participants in argument learn from others and from themselves and question suppositions typically taken for granted. In the aftermath of one of the most brutal centuries in recorded history and with the threat of worse to come, this sounded welcome – like an ongoing version of South Africa's Truth and Reconciliation Commission. But that seemed to be precisely what was not happening as, at the end of the 1980s, Germany hurried towards reunification. Here, Habermas repeatedly sounded a cautionary note, fearing that reunification was a polite word for an economically successful republic in the west annexing a former Soviet satellite state.[28] His fear was that reunification was happening so quickly that East German citizens would be incorporated into the Federal Republic by West German bureaucrats without having any say in the kind of society they might want to live in. There was, or so he hoped, more to reunification than economic advantage for the citizens of the former GDR. For him the manner of reunification may have served West German political elites, but it thwarted communicative rationality, the dialogical consensus he took to be the mark of a mature polity. In other words, system was once more impoverishing lifeworld.

In his writings from the 1980s and 1990s, he worried that a pre-discursive nationalism was undermining what he liked about how his homeland had developed since the Second World War. He took some measure of pride in the fact that the Federal Republic had rejected nationalism in favour of what he called 'constitutional patriotism'. 'For us in the Federal Republic', he wrote in *Die Nachholende Revolution* (The Catch-up Revolution) in 1990, 'constitutional patriotism means, among other things, pride in the fact that we have succeeded in permanently overcoming fascism, establishing a just political order, and anchoring it in a fairly liberal political culture.'[29] His hope was that constitutional patriotism could take the place of nationalism.

Only an academic, you might well think, could find constitutional patriotism inspiring. And yet one can understand Habermas's impulse in trying to find a substitute for rising nationalism. The unspeakable crimes committed by the German nation between 1933 and 1945 had, at least, given its citizens an opportunity to confront the delusions of nationalism in a way other Europeans have not. Certainly the British, in part thanks to the triumphalist national narrative that was among the toxic spoils of winning the Second World War, have rarely reflected on the pitfalls of the exclusive, racist nationalism to which we are so frequently prone. There is something, then, if not inspiring, then admirable, about Habermas's constitutional patriotism, not least at a time when western Europe becomes more multicultural. If multicultural societies are to work, then nationalism has to be overcome with something like a democratic constitution in which all different ethnicities, religions and cultures can feel at home.

Habermas also insisted that that constitution must conform with the ethical understanding of all groups in the political community. No longer could western European countries be held together by the (traditionally Christian-based) conception of the good of a majority. His notion of constitutional patriotism was intended as a bulwark against the bad nationalism he loathed since in it he saw the impulses that had been harnessed by Hitler. Moreover, constitutional patriotism was neither exclusionary, nor premised on one single conception of the good: it was something that everybody in a polity could share since it was an expression of pride in the free and fair workings of the state, which was always held to account by a flourishing public sphere or civil society. That, at least, was Habermas's purportedly inspirational notion. Clearly, though, it wasn't inspirational to the racists who attacked foreign guest-workers in the former East German cities of Rostock and Hoyeswerda after reunification, when the new Germany struggled with rising unemployment.

Habermas's scepticism about nationalism also underpinned his dream of European unification – something that, as the millennium reached its teens, looked utopian, as the Greek debt crisis threatened to destroy the eurozone and thus the foundation of political integration. In his 2010 book *Europe: The Faltering Project*, he argued that the 'monstrous mass crimes of the twentieth century' meant that nations can no longer be presumed to be innocents and thus immune to international law.[30] Constitutional patriotism, then, is a way station to the greater goal of replacing petty nationalisms with a better, more rational organisation based on worldwide consensus.

Habermas's hope was that a more unified Europe could work closely with the US to build a more stable and equitable international order. He told me in 2010 that Europe should be bolstering US President Barack Obama in his international goals, such as disarmament and securing peace in the Middle East, as well as encouraging Washington to lead efforts to regulate financial markets and stem climate change. 'But as so often is the case, the Europeans lack the political will and the necessary strength. Measured against the expectations which it encounters at the global level, Europe is a major failure on the international stage.'[31]

Significantly, the German title of the book was *Ach, Europa*. The transnational community he yearned for as a means of overcoming the European nationalist nightmare that had led to two world wars and the Holocaust wasn't likely to exist on the continent any time soon. Ever the Pollyanna, though, Habermas snatched optimism from the jaws of seeming hopelessness, when I suggested to him that the European Union was too remote from its citizens to be inspiring and that, in any case, the Greek crisis and his own government's attitude to it menaced the EU's future existence. 'Greece's debt crisis has had a welcome political side-effect', he said. 'At one of its weakest moments, the European Union has been plunged into a discussion concerning the central problem of its future development.' But he did concede that one of the EU's biggest problems, and a stumbling block to the transcending of national borders he favours, is his homeland's renewed narcissism. The spectre of German nationalism that had made him queasy in the late 1980s was having the same effect again. He told me he thought Angela Merkel's Germany was as nationalistic as Thatcher's Britain. 'The German elites apparently seem to be enjoying the comforts of self-satisfied national normalcy: "We can be like the others once again!" . . . The willingness of a totally defeated people to learn more quickly has disappeared. The narcissistic mentality of a complacent colossus in the middle of Europe is no longer even a guarantee that the unstable status quo in the EU will be preserved.'[32] His fear, here and during the *Historikerstreit*, was that Germany's singular shame – its responsibility for the Holocaust – which imposed on it a singular, chastened identity, was being forgotten.

But in any case, how could European unification serve his dream of extending and enriching democracy when it remains an elite project? Habermas believes that, like the internet, Europe has created no public sphere in which citizens can express their views freely and without regard to status. How can this be changed? He argued that 'a co-ordination of the economic policies in the eurozone would also lead to an integration of policies in other sectors. Here what has until now tended to be an administratively driven project could also put down roots in the minds and hearts of the national populations.' Again the Pollyanna hope: the system can serve the lifeworld, which can enrich the system, in a virtuous spiral or feedback loop. But that seems a remote possibility, especially as Europe's leaders revel in cross-border sniping and remain mired in nationalism.

Why did Habermas pin so much hope on an integrated Europe? Why not plump for a neoliberal network of European states, each just one selfish player in a capitalistic world? 'Aside from the insensitivity to the external costs of the social upheavals that [neoliberal policy] casually takes for granted', he replied,

> what annoys me is the lack of a historical understanding of the shifts in the relationship between the market and political power. Since the beginning of the modern period, expanding markets and communications networks had an explosive force, with simultaneously individualising and liberating consequences for individual citizens; but each such opening was followed by a reorganisation of the old relations of solidarity within an expanded institutional framework.

This is typical Habermas: instead of wallowing in the hopelessness of a Marxist-inspired philosopher confronted with a capitalism endlessly rampant and utterly destructive of the kind of egalitarian politics he wants to see, he told me a story about the past that seems to suggest things weren't as hopeless as we might have feared. 'Time and again, a sufficient equilibrium between the market and politics was achieved to ensure that the network of social relations between citizens of a political community was not damaged beyond repair. According to this rhythm, the current phase of financial market-driven globalisation should also be followed by a strengthening of the international community.'[33] It's a dialectical story of recent history, but hardly one that Adorno could have written.

Unlike his teachers, Habermas has always found reasons to be positive and ambitious about political reform. His career might be seen as a heroically hopeful response to his teachers' pessimistic works and to the prevailing intellectual zeitgeist in Europe. While Adorno, like Marx, said little about what a good or rational society should look like, and poststructuralists like Foucault were highly suspicious of institutions in general, Habermas has spent a lot of his career writing books that identify the conditions that best foster individual autonomy and thereby give individuals the capacities to enable them to resist the homogenising nature of capitalism and the corrosive effects of state administration. While Horkheimer and Adorno linked emancipation to refusing to adapt to current social reality, Habermas's extraordinary hope is that social reality can be changed by means of creating truly democratic institutions that are capable of withstanding the corrosive effects of capitalism.

But perhaps Adorno was right to despair. True, we may have left the Third Reich behind, but we live in an era in which commitment to democracy appears to be at a low ebb. The notion of a well-functioning public sphere seems the barmy dream of a cock-eyed optimist. 'There are good reasons to be alarmed', retorted Habermas when I put this to him:

> Some people already think that authoritarian mass democracies will provide the functionally superior model under conditions of a globalised world economy . . . Today many people are intimidated by a growing social complexity which is ensnaring individuals in

increasingly dense contexts of action and communication. In this mood, the notion that the citizens of a political community could still exercise collective influence over their social destiny through the democratic process is also being denounced by intellectuals as a misguided Enlightenment inheritance. Liberal confidence in the idea of an autonomous life is now confined to the individual freedom of choice of consumers who are living off the drip-feed of contingent opportunity structures.[34]

But that freedom of choice, as Habermas understood from the first generation of Frankfurt scholars, and from Marcuse in particular, was no freedom at all. Like Marcuse, Habermas was struggling to theorise his way out of one-dimensional society.

Eminent critics such as the philosophers Richard Rorty and Slavoj Žižek have argued that the vast intellectual web of theory Habermas has spun is inadequate. They contended that the public sphere as a place of purely rational independent debate never existed, and that his cherished and meticulously theorised notion of communicative action was a professorial utopian dream that will never be realised. The possibility of untrammelled debate as the foundation of political legit-imacy is a beautiful, but deluded, hope. Against such criticisms, Habermas – a man out of time, a utopian modernist living in a post-modern dystopia, but also the most engaged of European public intellectuals – retorted in an interview: 'If there is any small remnant of utopia that I've preserved, then it is surely the idea that democ-racy – and its public struggle for its best form – is capable of hacking through the Gordian knot of otherwise insoluble problems. I'm not saying we're going to succeed in this; we don't even know whether success is possible. But because we don't know, we still have to try.'[35]

HABERMAS'S COMMITMENT to keep hacking through that Gordian knot has had one unexpected consequence. A few years after 9/11, he published *An Awareness of What is Missing: Faith and Reason in a Post-Secular Age*, which marked an extraordinary break with his former philosophy. He had once argued that 'the authority of the holy is gradually replaced by the authority of an achieved consensus'.[36]

That, so he had thought, was one of the good legacies of the Enlightenment: the rise of secular morality and the decline of religious authority allowed us to think for ourselves and develop our own conception of the good.

In the first decade of the new millennium, however, he was rethinking the role of religion in public life. 'Postmetaphysical thinking', he wrote, 'cannot cope on its own with the defeatism concerning reason which we encounter today both in the postmodern radicalisation of the "dialectic of the Enlightenment" and in the naturalism founded on a naïve faith in science'.[37] Worse, he argued, the liberal state, resting on a base of procedural rationality, cannot inspire its citizens to virtuous (as opposed to self-interested) acts because it has lost 'its grip on the images, preserved by religion, of the moral whole' and is unable to formulate 'collectively binding ideals'.[38] His notion of constitutional patriotism had involved such an ideal, one that might inspire different groups in a multicultural society even as each one pursued its own conception of the good, but clearly that constitutional patriotism was less inspiring to citizens than to the professor. Enter religion, to do what reason, and the Enlightenment, apparently could not.

Habermas didn't stop there in his engagement with religion. In 2004, two elderly Germans, both former members of the Hitler Youth, met at the Catholic Academy of Bavaria to debate the topic 'Pre-political moral foundations of the liberal state'. One was Habermas, the leftist professor; the other was Cardinal Ratzinger, who would soon become Pope Benedict XVI. Habermas argued that the liberal state should 'treat with care all cultural sources on which the normative consciousness and solidarity of citizens draws', not least because they were important allies in its own struggle against the alienating forces of the modern world. Ratzinger, equally emolliently, argued that the 'divine light of reason' had a role to play in controlling the 'pathologies of religion'.[39]

Reading the transcript of their conversation makes one think, uncharitably, of the end of Orwell's *Animal Farm*, when the creatures outside the farmhouse looked 'from man to pig, and from pig to man again; but already it was impossible to say which was which'. Sometimes, as Ratzinger and Habermas debated, it was hard to tell which was the cardinal and which the one-time defender of the Enlightenment's secular legacy.

Habermas went so far as to suggest that religious notions had their parallels in secular reason and that, as a result, the Enlightenment was infused with Judaeo-Christian values. For instance, the Biblical vision of man as made in the 'image and likeness' of God finds its profane expression in the principle of the equal worth of all human beings. But in the translation, something went missing: 'When sin was converted to culpability, and the breaking of divine commands to an offence against human laws, something was lost.' It was as though Habermas was arguing that the Enlightenment had a God-shaped hole and that the secular needed what it had programmatically disowned, i.e. the religious, if it was to flourish. 'Among the modern societies', he wrote, 'only those that are able to introduce into the secular domain the essential contents of their religious traditions which point beyond the merely human realm will also be able to rescue the substance of the human.'[40]

But what could that mean? In 2007 Habermas took part in a dialogue with four Jesuit academics in Munich that was later published as *An Awareness of What Is*. In it he recalled the funeral of a friend who in life 'rejected any profession of faith', and yet indicated before his death that he wanted his memorial service to be held at Saint Peter's Church in Zurich. Habermas suggested that his friend 'had sensed the awkwardness of non-religious burial practices and, by his choice of place, publicly declared that the enlightened modern age has failed to find a suitable replacement for a religious way of coping with the final rite de passage'. The story isn't very convincing: many atheists and agnostics have mourned loved ones at funerals that did not take place on hallowed ground without sensing the kind of awkwardness or failure Habermas imputed to his friend. But still, he took it 'as a paradoxical event which tells us something about secular reason'.[41]

What Habermas wanted to tell us about secular reason, which he had spent most of his career extolling, and indeed about the modern secular state, was that both lack what religious authority offers the faithful – not just salvation but, he argued, virtuous lives. Secular reason suffered from a 'motivational weakness' in that it could not inspire its citizens to virtuous acts. Not that he was junking secular reason. He wanted to hold on to the 'cognitive achievements of modernity' – tolerance, equality, individual freedom, freedom of thought, cosmopolitanism and scientific advancement. He wanted to counter, too, the fundamentalisms that willfully 'cut themselves off' from everything that is good about the Enlightenment project. But he was proposing something more. It was characterised by Stanley Fish as

> something less than a merger and more like an agreement between trading partners: ... the religious side must accept the authority of 'natural' reason as the fallible results of the institutionalised sciences and the basic principles of universalistic egalitarianism in law and morality. Conversely, secular reason may not set itself up as the judge concerning truths of faith, even though in the end it can accept as reasonable only what it can translate into its own, in principle universally accessible, discourses.[42]

In this, Habermas was suggesting a tolerant attitude towards faith akin to what the American journalist H. L. Mencken once wrote: 'We must accept the other fellow's religion, but only in the sense and to the extent that we respect his theory that his wife is beautiful and his children smart.'[43] Such tolerance was, after all, an Enlightenment achievement worth holding on to.

That said, Habermas was arguing that the great product of the Enlightenment, secular reason, is 'unenlightened about itself', it doesn't know what it is for. That's to say, he had found at the centre of his intellectual web what critical theorists virtuosically discovered in other thinkers' theories, namely an aporia (a word taken from the Greek for 'no passage', and often signifying perplexity). Two of his interpreters tried to pinpoint the aporetic nature of Habermas's account of secular reason. If the modern west is to be perceived as more than merely 'godless', Edward Skidelsky wrote, 'if it is to inspire not just fear, but also respect, it must recover its ethical substance'. This, he thought, demanded a reconciliation with its religious inheritance.[44] Stanley Fish argued: 'The problem is that a political structure that welcomes all worldviews into the marketplace of ideas, but holds itself aloof from any and all of them, will have no basis for judging the outcomes its procedures yield.'[45]

But surely Habermas's elaborate intellectual systems – his discourse theory of ethics and his programme of political theory – were expressly devised to ensure that what Fish called the worldviews welcomed into the marketplace of ideas flourished in so far as they didn't overturn the moral order of liberal society. Habermas distinguished ethics from morality: the former concerns questions of individual happiness and the good of communities; the latter has to do with deciding which actions are right or wrong according to valid norms. Moral order depends on most agents being disposed to adhere to those norms and they will only do so if those norms clearly demonstrate a universalisable interest.

Morality, thus conceived, is Kantian; ethics an Aristotelian notion of the good life and the good community. Fish's characterisation of Habermas's secular reason, then, wasn't quite right: the political structure that allows all worldviews into its marketplace of ideas *does* have a procedure for judging the outcomes its procedures yield: an action is right or wrong according to whether it is permitted or prohibited by a demonstrably valid norm to which agents adhere, and they adhere to those norms that embody a universal interest – such as don't be cruel to your children or be kind to friends. Precisely because they embody such a universal interest they can help hold society together, even one comprised of different faiths, ethnicities and conceptions of the good life. Such norms, then, are likely to be very general in character. Just as Rawls prioritised the right over the good in part to ensure the fairness and stability of modern liberal society, so Habermas prioritised the moral over the ethical, and his suggestion was that valid norms are prior to substantial conceptions of the good that, properly understood, are distinctively ethical.

But this is where Habermas's discourse ethics gets tricky. He wants to separate norms from values – norms are universalisable and thus moral, whereas values are non-universalisable and thus ethical. But the distinction between norms and values, as critics including Thomas McCarthy and Hilary Putnam have argued, is not as sharp as Habermas wanted to make it because moral norms develop from values such as friendship and kindness.[46] Habermas's project was a kind of immunisation project aimed at protecting the moral order from infection by ethical values. His hope was that such immunisation would stop the spread of conflicts in modern multicultural societies. But the suggestion of critics like McCarthy and Putnam was that the moral order of the secular state upholds norms already infused with ethical values, some of them religious.

Habermas's point in *An Awareness of What is Missing* was that, as we move from the secular to a post-secular age (and he thought we should), those religious values should be respected since they can help hold societies together. The liberal state should 'treat with care all cultural sources on which the normative consciousness and solidarity of citizens draws'. Not for him the militant atheism of Richard Dawkins or the late Christopher Hitchens who took religion to be a phenomenon that needed to be anathematised in the secular society: 'the liberal state must expect its secular citizens, in exercising their role as citizens, not to treat religious expressions as simply irrational'.[47] Rather, religion could be useful; his hope was that it could be used to help overcome social disruptions and the alienation from the modern liberal state. In effect, religion was being instrumentalised by Habermas. In a 2001 lecture, he described 9/11 as a reaction to 'an accelerated and radically uprooting modernisation'.[48] The terror attacks and the rise of religious fundamentalism were responses to an alienation from that modernisation, and his hope was that non-fundamentalist religion could help overcome that alienation. Whether the Catholic Church was prepared to be co-opted thus is less clear.

Habermas's encounter with religion highlighted many poignant things – not least, the failures of his own intellectual system and the difficulty of making modern liberal societies work. For our purposes, too, it highlighted the long journey the Frankfurt School of critical theory has taken since its inception as a Marxist research institute in the early 1920s. Instead of regarding religion as an opium of the masses that would be abolished in a communist society, the Frankfurt School was now treating it as an invaluable ally.

18

Consuming Passions: Critical Theory in the New Millennium

In Jonathan Franzen's 2001 novel *The Corrections*, Chip Lambert liquidates his library. He sells off his collection of Frankfurt School books, as well as 'his feminists, his formalists, his structuralists, his poststructuralists, his Freudians, and his queers', in order to raise money to impress a new girlfriend. Lambert is just the kind of guy who would have yards of Marxist cultural critical tomes on his shelves. Former assistant professor in Textual Artifacts, teacher of Consuming Narratives, lecturer on phallic anxiety in Tudor drama, he has just given up academia in favour of screenwriting. Parting with his Frankfurt School books, in particular, though, is a painful business. 'He turned away from their reproachful spines, remembering how each one of them had called out in a bookstore with a promise of a radical critique of late-capitalist society . . . But Jürgen Habermas didn't have Julia's long, cool, pear-tree limbs, Theodor Adorno didn't have Julia's grapy smell of lecherous pliability, Fred Jameson didn't have Julia's artful tongue.'[1]

I know what you're wondering: if Adorno did have Julia's grapy smell of lecherous pliability, would Chip Lambert have kept his copy of *Dialectic of Enlightenment*? Not, I suspect, even then.

Lambert takes his books to the Strand Bookstore in Lower Manhattan. His library cost nearly four thousand dollars to acquire; the books' resale value is sixty-five. He puts the proceeds towards 'wild Norwegian salmon, line caught' for $78.40 at an upmarket grocery called the Nightmare of Consumption. This is the 1990s, a time,

Franzen seems to suggest, of a consumerism so brazen that it's advantageous, brand-wise, for high-end grocers to appropriate ironically the rhetoric of capitalist critique for their stores' names.

It is also a decade in which the Frankfurt School's nightmare came true. There was, as Margaret Thatcher put it, no alternative. No alternative to capitalism, to one-dimensional society, to liberal democracy. As if to clinch that point, in the 1990s the American political scientist Francis Fukuyama decided to erase a question mark. In 1989, he had written a paper called 'The End of History?', arguing that there can be no new stage beyond liberal democracy precisely because it is that system which guarantees the greatest possible level of recognition of the individual. Three years later, when Fukuyama published his book *The End of History and the Last Man*, the question mark had gone. He may have smuggled his neoconservative agenda into his post-ideological thesis, but Fukuyama's suggestion that the great ideological battles between east and west were over, and that western liberal democracy had triumphed, seemed incontestable.

All that remained was an eternity of what sounded very much like boredom: 'The end of history will be a very sad time', he wrote. 'The struggle for recognition, the willingness to risk one's life for a purely abstract goal, the worldwide ideological struggle that called forth daring, courage, imagination, and idealism, will be replaced by economic calculation, the endless solving of technical problems, environmental concerns, and the satisfaction of sophisticated consumer demands.'[2] Perhaps the prospect of that boredom, Fukuyama mused, might restart history.

That question of the struggle for recognition was a key concern for Fukuyama. It was also central for the latest director of the Institute for Social Research, Axel Honneth, whose book *The Struggle for Recognition: The Moral Grammar of Social Conflicts* appeared (in German) in the same year as *The End of History*.[3] The question of recognition goes back to Plato, for whom the psyche could be divided into three parts – reason, eros and what he called thymos, or recognition. Any political system that created inequality satisfied the human need for recognition of some members while denying it to others. Megalothymia means the need to be recognised as superior to others, while isothymia is the need to be recognised as merely equal to others. Nietzsche in *Thus Spake Zarathustra* juxtaposed the megalothymia of his imagined superior being, the übermensch, with the isothymia of the last man, and excoriated the latter. The last man, Nietzsche thought, thrived in the isothymia of democracy wherein, he thought, there is no longer a distinction between ruler and ruled, strong and weak, or the supreme and the mediocre.

In that sense, the end of history Fukuyama triumphantly imagined is the hell Nietzsche excoriated in Zarathustra: 'The earth has become small, and on it hops the Last Man, who makes everything small. His species is as ineradicable as the flea; the Last Man lives longest. "We have discovered happiness" – say the Last Men, and they blink.'[4] For Fukuyama, liberal democracy allied to capitalism was the best means of achieving a balance between material equality and thymos, guaranteeing the maximum possible recognition of the individual. For Nietzsche, that system killed off any recognition that was worthwhile: instead of struggling for recognition through daring, courage, imagination and idealism, he thought the Last Men had diminished humans by making them aspire to equal rights, comfort and security.

Axel Honneth came to the notion of recognition with a different perspective from that of Fukuyama, one that drew on child psychology. He also dusted off the notion of reification, which had catalysed the thoughts of his Frankfurt School predecessors when, half a century earlier, they had read about it in Lukács's *History and Class Consciousness*. Honneth supposed that we come to recognise others as persons as babies and suggested this was a normative attitude. Only later, he argues in *Reification: A New Look at an Old Idea*, may the subject become blind to this 'antecedent recognition'[5]. There can be a 'forgetfulness of recognition', Honneth suggests, caused either by reifying social practices which prompt individuals to perceive subjects merely as objects or by ideological belief systems that depict some human beings as non- or sub-human. For Honneth, there was a parallel between maternal love and the need for recognition from society: 'Just as, in the case of love, children acquire, via the continuous experience of "maternal" care, the basic self-confidence to assert their needs in an unforced manner, adult subjects acquire, via the experience of legal recognition, the possibility of seeing their actions as the universally respected expression of their own autonomy.'[6] True, this wasn't the recognition commanded by Nietzschean übermenschen, but rather of those whom Nietzsche would deride as the Last Men. Any recognition they received from the state was given as a precondition of that system's fairness, rather than imperiously snatched as an expression of one's personal glory.

For Honneth, then, the task was not revolution but improving capitalism and democracy to the point where we can get full recognition as human subjects. At least one of his Frankfurt School predecessors, Adorno, would have demurred: for him there could be nothing true within a false system and this system was totally reified. But Adorno died in 1969, and the Frankfurt School, under Habermas and then Honneth, has ever since committed itself not to revolution but to ameliorating the conditions of capitalism and liberal democracy.

In this, Chip Lambert, by purging his library, mutated from a follower of Adorno to a man more in tune with Honneth's late Frankfurt School ethos. Lambert 'no longer wanted to live in a different world; he just wanted to be a man with dignity in this one'.[7] That 'dignity' is a give away – dignity is thymos, the need for recognition. But the dignity Lambert seeks is of a grubby kind. Indeed, if dignity involves having a flush bank account and being hooked salmon-like by the gimcrack delusions of late capitalism, is it worth having? Dignity here seems conceived as an intentionally self-deluded, pathically healthful approach, or, as Adorno put it in *Minima Moralia*, as a 'successful adaptation to the inevitable, an equable, practical frame of mind . . . The only objective way of diagnosing the sickness of the healthy is by the incongruity between their rational existence and the possible course their lives might be given by reason.'[8]

Dignity, though, doesn't have to be thought of in this way. The dignity Honneth thought worth pursuing, by contrast, involves the possibility of seeing one's actions as the universally respected expression of one's own autonomy. That kind of recognition keeps the system in place rather than challenging it, but it involves more than shopping for salmon in a store called the Nightmare of Consumption.

And yet one can understand Lambert's impulse. Easier to get the the girl, the salmon and this commodified approximation of bliss than get entangled in, say, Adorno's hopeless paradoxes of happiness. The mark of the healthy, undamaged individual, Adorno suggested in *Minima Moralia*, is to be afflicted by the general unhappiness: 'What would happiness be that was not measured by the immeasurable grief at what is?'[9] But Lambert's point about dignity is that we cannot, or not for long, live in immeasurable grief at what is. As Virginia Woolf wrote in *The Waves*: 'One cannot live outside the machine for more perhaps than half an hour.'[10]

Better, then, to adjust oneself to living inside the machine. Or as Adorno put it, 'the sickness proper to the time' might well consist 'precisely in normality'.[11] One can imagine Chip Lambert exchanging his dismal Frankfurt School library for an upbeat new one. Out with *One-Dimensional Man*, *The Lure of Technocracy*, *Dialectic of Enlightenment*! In with upbeat new volumes enjoining us to get happy in the new millennium, such as Daniel Gilbert's *Stumbling on Happiness*, Richard Schoch's *The Secrets of Happiness*, Darrin McMahon's *The Pursuit of Happiness*, Jonathan Haidt's *The Happiness Hypothesis* and Richard Layard's *Happiness: Lessons from a New Science*. In this last, the London School of Economics professor measured happiness, not by immeasurable grief at what is, but in terms of the costs to GDP of depression. The Freudian psychoanalyst Adam Phillips once suggested to me that any culture obsessed with happiness must be in despair. 'Otherwise why would anybody be bothered about it at all? . . . Anybody in this culture who watches the news and can be happy – there's something wrong with them.'[12]

Lambert's dignity has another resonance. In purging his library of critical theory, he is setting aside childish – or at least sophomoric – things. To speak of 'late capitalist society' was in that era 'a mark of immaturity, an outworn college creed. The thing itself may grow old with us, but the term can't be used by middle-aged grown-ups participating in the real world (that is to say, the surface of the earth, minus college campuses)', wrote the critic Benjamin Kunkel. 'The same may go for "postmodernism", a word which by now provokes the weariness it once served in part to describe.'[13]

Grown-ups buy line-caught salmon, they don't read *Dialectic of Enlightenment*. History has stopped and we live, don't we, in the best of all possible worlds? In that best of all possible worlds, at the end of history, wrote Fredric Jameson in *Late Marxism* (1990), 'the question about poetry after Auschwitz has been replaced with that of whether you could bear to read Adorno and Horkheimer next to the pool'.[14] And, if Adorno was right about happiness, it consisted of setting aside his and Horkheimer's books as one relaxed. Adorno envisaged happiness thus: 'Rien faire comme une bête, lying on water and looking peacefully at the sky . . . None of the abstract concepts comes closer to fulfilled utopia than that of perpetual peace.'[15] If Virginia Woolf was right and one couldn't live outside the machine for more than half an hour, then such happiness would be equally unendurable.

In the new millennium, though, something changed. Instead of perpetual poolside peace, history restarted and revolution was on the agenda. 'What is going on?' asked the Maoist French philosopher Alain Badiou in *The Rebirth of History* in 2011. 'The continuation, at all costs, of a weary world? A salutary crisis of that world, racked by its victorious expansion? The end of that world? The advent of a different world?'[16] Boredom hadn't restarted history; a crisis in capitalism had. If only Henryk Grossman had been alive to witness it. Badiou was writing about the unexpected consequences of the global financial crisis, in particular movements such as Occupy, Syriza and Podemos. He might too have added the failure of the US and its allies to 'democratise' Iraq and Afghanistan, as well as the Bolivarian socialist renaissance in Latin America. Through such movements people demanded what they had been denied under neoliberal capitalism – recognition. To put it in Fukuyama's terms, what looked like a system premised on isothymia was in fact based on megalothymia. The legal recognition prized by Axel Honneth seemed, like liberal democracy, to guarantee a parody of recognition not the thing itself.

Hence the slogan devised by Occupy activist and anthropologist David Graeber: 'We are the 99%'. Hence too Occupy New York's 'experiment in a post-bureaucratic society' – an attempt at realising anarchism in a system that effectively denied the possibility of people seeing their actions as the universally respected expression of their own autonomy. 'We wanted to demonstrate we could do all the services that social service providers do without endless bureaucracy', Graeber told me.[17] Denied recognition by the system, the anarchists of Zucotti Park found it in self-organisation and thereby achieved a sense of solidarity. In *Valences of the Dialectic*, Jameson argued that when the fitful apprehension of history does enter the lives of individuals it is often through the feeling of belonging to a particular generation: 'The experience of generationality is . . . a specific collective experience of the present: it marks the enlargement of my existential present into a collective and historical one.'[18]

Benjamin dreamed of exploding the continuum of history; the experiences Jameson described involve that dream's realisation. The homogeneous, empty time Benjamin associated with the onward march of capitalism and positivism is halted, albeit briefly, and replaced by a more experientially rich and redemptive notion of non-linear time. That, at least, is what Jameson took from Zucotti Park.

In that rebirth of history about which Badiou wrote, Marxism made a comeback. As did critical theory. Perhaps if Chip Lambert had held on to his library until, say, 2010, he would have got a better price for it. Let's not go crazy: he might have got two salmons. But the hunger for books providing a critique of capitalism continues. In the nightmare of consumption that is Tate Modern's gift shop, for instance, there is now a huge section called critical theory. In it, the Frankfurt School no longer has a monopoly on the term – critical theory involves all the disciplines that were once represented in Chip Lambert's library.

A mini-boom in popularising critical theory books – including graphic guides, dictionaries, perhaps even this book – is one perverse consequence of the global capitalist crisis, as is a renewal of critical sociology premised on the Frankfurt School heritage. 'Wherever you look these days', write the German sociologists Klaus Dörre, Stephan Lessenich and Hartmut Rosa, 'the critique of capitalism has become quite fashionable.' Their book *Sociology, Capitalism, Critique* is not just quite fashionable, it also resuscitates critical theory for new times and takes the sides of the losers in the global financial crisis. 'Our analyses here may be best understood as a critique of the self-debasement, self-disempowerment and self-destruction wrought upon society under capitalism.'[19]

In our age, anyone resuscitating critical theory needs to have a sense of irony. Among capitalism's losers are millions of overworked, underpaid workers ostensibly liberated by the largest socialist revolution in history (China's) who have been driven to the brink of suicide to keep those in the west playing with their iPads. The proletariat, far from burying capitalism, are keeping it on life support. Again, were he still alive, Grossman would have noted that capitalism has deferred its demise through such outsourcing of the exploitation of labour. Perhaps in Lower Manhattan grocery stores thymos remains in ample supply. In other parts of the world it is sorely lacking. 'The domination of capitalism globally depends today on the existence of a Chinese Communist Party that gives de-localised capitalist enterprises cheap labour to lower prices and deprive workers of the rights of self-organisation', Jacques Rancière, the French Marxist and Professor of Philosophy at the University of Paris VIII, told me. 'Happily, it is possible to hope for a world less absurd and more just than today's.'[20]

And our world is absurd. 'When every single person in a train carriage is staring at a small illuminated device, it is an almost tacky vision of dystopia', wrote Eliane Glaser, author of *Get Real: How to See Through the Hype, Spin and Lies of Modern Life*. 'Technology – along with turbo-capitalism – seems to me to be hastening the cultural and environmental apocalypse. The way I see it, digital consumerism makes us too passive to revolt, or to save the world.'[21] Certainly, if Adorno were alive today he might well have argued that the cultural apocalypse has already happened, but that we are too blind to notice it. His fondest fears have been realised. 'The pop hegemony is all but complete, its superstars dominating the media and wielding the economic might of tycoons', wrote Alex Ross.

> They live full time in the unreal realm of the mega-rich, yet they hide behind a folksy façade, wolfing down pizza at the Oscars and cheering sports teams from V.I.P. boxes . . . Opera, dance, poetry, and the literary novel are still called 'élitist', despite the fact that the world's real

power has little use for them. The old hierarchy of high and low has become a sham: pop is the ruling party.[22]

Adorno and Horkheimer never lived to be twitterjacked or develop social media profiles, but they would have seen much of what the internet offers as confirmation of their view that the culture industry allows the 'freedom to choose what is always the same'. 'Culture appears more monolithic than ever, with a few gigantic corporations – Google, Apple, Facebook, Amazon – presiding over unprecedented monopolies', Ross adds. 'Internet discourse has become tighter, more coercive.'

In the late 1990s, as an arts editor at the *Guardian*, I commissioned an article to explore the perils of customised culture. The idea was to question the tailoring of cultural products to your tastes, the whole 'If you liked that, you'll love this' idea. Wasn't the point of art, I thought then, to blast through the continuum of one's tastes rather than pander to them? John Reith, the BBC's first director general, once said that good broadcasting gives people what they do not yet know they need. When the piece came in, many of my co-workers wondered – what is so very bad about customised culture? Isn't getting more of what we know we like a good thing? But, I wailed, good broadcasting and great art offers a kind of serendipity that expands your horizons rather than keeping you in an eternal feedback loop. Since that article appeared, the culture industry has triumphed in ways even Adorno and Horkheimer might not have envisaged. In the new millennium, the online culture industry seems expressly devised to help us hermetically seal ourselves from such serendipitous experiences. The internet is a means for achieving precisely that – a high-tech prophylactic against contamination by ideas that might challenge your worldview.

What has been steamrollered, too, is Adorno's esoteric vision of art. 'Stendhal's dictum about the *promesse du bonheur* says that art thanks existence by accentuating what in existence prefigures utopia', he wrote in his last book, the posthumously published *Aesthetic Theory*. 'This is a diminishing resource, since existence increasingly mirrors only itself. Consequently, art is ever less able to mirror existence. Because any happiness that one might take from or find in what exists is false, a mere substitute, art has to break its promise in order to keep it.'[23]

Art, that is to say, has become impossible thanks to the impoverishment of the existence that it sought to honour. Instead we are left with the readily consumable products of the culture industry. What Ernst Bloch called the spirit of utopia is expendable in the online culture industry for which, among others, Steve Jobs, Mark Zuckerberg and Jeff Bezos are responsible, and which gives us more of the same, develops algorithms the better to chain us to our tastes, and makes us desire our own domination. In such a customised culture, one that abolishes serendipity, makes a mockery of dignity and turns human liberation into a terrifying prospect, the best writings of the Frankfurt School still have much to teach us – not least about the impossibility and the necessity of thinking differently.

Further Reading

Books by Frankfurt School thinkers

Adorno, Theodor W., *The Authoritarian Personality*, Wiley, 1964.

——, *Prisms*, MIT Press, 1983.

——, *Quasi Una Fantasia: Essays on Modern Music*, Verso, 1998.

——, *Aesthetic Theory*, Athlone Press, 1999.

——, *Essays on Music*, University of California Press, 2002.

——, *The Stars Down to Earth and Other Essays on the Irrational in Culture*, Routledge, 2002.

——, *Negative Dialectics*, Routledge, 2003.

——, *Minima Moralia: Reflections from Damaged Life*, Verso 2005.

——, *Letters to his Parents*, Polity, 2006.

——, *The Culture Industry*, Routledge, 2006.

——, *Dream Notes*, Polity, 2007.

——, *Philosophy of Modern Music*, Bloomsbury, 2007.

Adorno, Theodor W. and Karl Popper et al. *The Positivist Dispute in German Sociology*, Harper & Row, 1976.

Adorno, Theodor W. and Max Horkheimer, *Dialectic of Enlightenment*, Verso, 1997.

Adorno, Theodor W. and Alban Berg, *Correspondence 1925–1935*, Polity, 2005.

Adorno, Theodor W. and Thomas Mann, *Correspondence 1943–1955*, Polity, 2006.

Benjamin, Walter, *Reflections: Essays, Aphorisms, Autobiographical Writings*, ed. Peter Demetz, Harcourt, 1986.

——, *Illuminations*, ed. Hannah Arendt, Fontana, 1992.

——, *The Correspondence of Walter Benjamin, 1910–1940*, ed. Gershom Scholem and Theodor W. Adorno, Chicago University Press, 1994.

——, *The Arcades Project*, Harvard University Press, 1999.

——, *Berlin Childhood around 1900*, Belknap, 2006.

——, *Radio Benjamin*, Verso, 2014.

Fromm, Erich, *The Art of Loving*, Unwin, 1981.

——, *Escape from Freedom*, Open Road Media, 2013.

——, *Marx's Concept of Man: Including 'Economic and Philosophical Manuscripts'*, Bloomsbury, 2013.

——, *The Sane Society*, Routledge, 2013.

——, *To Have or To Be*, A&C Black, 2013.

Grossman, Henryk, *Law of Accumulation and Breakdown of the Capitalist System*, Pluto Press, 1992.

——, *Fifty Years of Struggle over Marxism 1883–1932*, ed. Rick Kuhn and Einde O'Callaghan, Socialist Alternative, 2014.

——, *Marx, Classical Political Economy and the Problem of Dynamics*, ed. Rick Kuhn, Socialist Alternative, 2015.

Habermas, Jürgen, *Theory and Practice*, Beacon Press, 1973.

——, *The Philosophical Discourse of Modernity*, Polity, 1990.

——, *Autonomy and Solidarity: Interviews with Jürgen Habermas*, ed. Peter Dews, Verso, 1992.

——, *The Past as Future: Jürgen Habermas, interviewed by Michael Haller*, Polity, 1994.

——, *Technik und wissenschaft als 'ideologie'*, Suhrkamp, 1998.

——, *The Theory of Communicative Action*, Vols 1 and 2, Polity, 2004.

——, *Between Naturalism and Religion*, Polity, 2010.

——, *Philosophical-Political Profiles*, Polity, 2012.

——, *An Awareness of What is Missing: Faith and Reason in a Post-secular Age*, Polity, 2014.

——, *Europe: The Faltering Project*, Wiley, 2014.

——, *The Lure of Technocracy*, Polity, 2015.

Honneth, Axel, *The Struggle for Recognition: The Moral Grammar of Social Conflicts*, MIT Press, 1996.

——, *Reification: A New Look at an Old Idea*, Oxford University Press, 2008.

Horkheimer, Max, *Critical Theory: Selected Essays*, A&C Black, 1972.
———, *Dämmerung: Notizen in Deutschland*, Edition Max, 1972.
———, *Eclipse of Reason*, A&C Black, 2013.

Marcuse, Herbert, *Eros and Civilisation: A Philosophical Inquiry Into Freud*, Beacon Press, 1974.
———, *One-Dimensional Man: Studies in the Ideology of Advanced Industrial Society*, Routledge, 2002.
———, *Technology, War and Fascism: Collected Papers of Herbert Marcuse*, Vol. 1, Routledge, 2004.
———, *The New Left and the 1960s: Collected Papers of Herbert Marcuse*, Vol. 3, Routledge, 2004.
———, *Reason and Revolution: Hegel and the Rise of Social Theory*, Routledge, 2013.
———, *Marxism, Revolution and Utopia: Collected Papers of Herbert Marcuse*, Vol. 6, Routledge, 2014.

Neumann, Franz, *Behemoth: The Structure and Practice of National Socialism*, Oxford University Press, 1942.

Neumann, Franz, Herbert Marcuse and Otto Kircheimer, *Secret Reports on Nazi Germany: The Frankfurt School Contribution to the War Effort*, Princeton University Press, 2013.

Biographies/memoirs

Eiland, Howard and Michael Jennings, *Walter Benjamin: A Critical Life*, Harvard University Press, 2014.
Friedman, Lawrence J., *The Lives of Erich Fromm: Love's Prophet*, Columbia University Press, 2013.
Kuhn, Rick, *Henryk Grossman and the Recovery of Marxism*, University of Illinois Press, 2007.
Löwenthal, Leo, *An Unmastered Past*, California University Press, 1987.
Müller-Doohm, Stefan, *Adorno: A Biography*, Polity, 2014.
Neumann, Osha, *Up Against the Wall Motherf**er: A Memoir of the '60s, with Notes for Next Time*, Seven Stories Press, 2011.

Parker, Stephen, *Bertolt Brecht: A Literary Life*, Bloomsbury, 2014.

Scholem, Gershom, *Walter Benjamin: The Story of a Friendship*, New York Review of Books, 1981.

Histories of the Frankfurt School

Abromeit, John, *Max Horkheimer and the Foundations of the Frankfurt School*, Cambridge University Press, 2011.

Buck-Morss, Susan, *Origin of Negative Dialectics*, Simon and Schuster, 1979.

Connerton, Paul, *The Tragedy of Enlightenment: An Essay on the Frankfurt School*, Cambridge University Press, 1960.

Jay, Martin, *The Dialectical Imagination: A History of the Frankfurt School and the Institute of Social Research*, California University Press, 1973.

Tarr, Zoltán, *The Frankfurt School: The Critical Theories of Max Horkheimer and Theodor W. Adorno*, Transaction Publishers, 2011.

Wheatland, Thomas, *The Frankfurt School in Exile*, University of Minnesota Press, 2009.

Wiggershaus, Rolf, *The Frankfurt School: Its History, Theories, and Political Significance*, MIT Press 1995.

Studies of individual thinkers

Adams, Nicholas, *Habermas and Theology*, Cambridge University Press, 2006.

Benhabib, Seyla, Wolfgang Bonss and John McCole (eds), *Max Horkheimer: New Perspectives*, MIT Press, 1995.

Braune, Joan, *Erich Fromm's Revolutionary Hope: Prophetic Messianism as a Critical Theory of the Future*, Springer, 2014.

Ferris, David S. (ed.), *The Cambridge Companion to Walter Benjamin*, Cambridge University Press, 2004.

Finlayson, James Gordon, *Habermas: A Very Short Introduction*, Oxford University Press, 2005.

Jäger, Lorenz, *Adorno: A Political Biography*, Yale University Press, 2004.

Jay, Martin, *Adorno*, Fontana Modern Masters, 1984.

Kellner, Douglas, *Herbert Marcuse and the Crisis of Marxism*, University of California Press, 1984.

Leslie, Esther, *Walter Benjamin*, London, Reaktion Books 2007.

MacIntyre, Alsadair, *Marcuse*, Fontana Modern Masters, 1970.

Mittelmeier, Martin, *Adorno in Neapel: Wie sich eine Sehnsuchtslandschaft in Philosophie verwandelt*, Siedler Verlag, 2013.

O'Neill, Maggie (ed.), *Adorno, Culture and Feminism*, SAGE, 1999.

Outhwaite, William, *Habermas: A Critical Introduction*, Polity, 2009.

Passerin d'Entrèves, Maurizio and Seyla Benhabib (eds), *Habermas and the Unfinished Project of Modernity: Critical Essays on* The Philosophical Discourse of Modernity, MIT Press, 1997.

Rose, Gillian, *The Melancholy Science: An Introduction to the Thought of Theodor W. Adorno*, Verso, 1978.

Stirk, Peter M. R., *Max Horkheimer: A New Interpretation*, Rowman & Littlefield, 1992.

Hegelian neo-Marxism

Feenberg, Andrew, *The Philosophy of Praxis: Marx, Lukács and the Frankfurt School*, Verso, 2014.

Lukács, György, *History and Class Consciousness: Studies in Marxist Dialectics*, MIT Press, 1971.

Žižek, Slavoj, *Less Than Nothing: Hegel and the Shadow of Dialectical Materialism*, Verso, 2012.

Books by writers associated with the Frankfurt School

Bloch, Ernst, *The Spirit of Utopia*, Stanford University Press, 2000.

Davis, Angela Y., *Blues Legacies and Black Feminism: Gertrude Ma Rainey, Bessie Smith, and Billie Holiday*, Knopf Doubleday, 2011.

Dörre, Klaus, Stephan Lessenich and Hartmut Rosa, *Sociology, Capitalism, Critique*, Verso, 2015.

Kracauer, Siegfried, *The Mass Ornament: Weimar Essays*, Harvard University Press, 1995.

Mann, Thomas, *Doctor Faustus*, Vintage, 1999.

Mannheim, Karl, *Ideology and Utopia*, Routledge, 2013.

Introduction to Critical Theory

Macey, David, *Dictionary of Critical Theory*, Penguin, 2001.

Notes

Introduction: Against the Current

1. See Esther Leslie, 'Introduction to Adorno/Marcuse Correspondence on the German Student Movement', at platypus1917.org.
2. See Karl Marx, *The German Ideology: Including Theses on Feuerbach and Introduction to the Critique of Political Economy*, Prometheus Books, 1976, p. 571.
3. See György Lukács, 'Preface to *The Theory of the Novel*', at marxists.org.
4. Quoted in Stefan Müller-Doohm, *Adorno: A Biography*, Polity, 2014, p. 475.
5. See Theodor W. Adorno, 'Marginalia to Theory and Praxis' in *Critical Models: Interventions and Catchwords*, Columbia University Press, 2012, p. 263.
6. Ibid., p. 271.
7. Ibid., p. 263.
8. Ibid.
9. Quoted in Müller-Doohm, *Adorno: A Biography*, p. 463.
10. Walter Benjamin, 'Theses on the Philosophy of History' in *Illuminations*, ed. Hannah Arendt, Fontana, 1992, p. 253.
11. Adorno, 'Marginalia to Theory and Praxis', p. 263.
12. See Daniel Trilling, 'Who Are Breivik's Fellow Travellers', *New Statesman*, 18 April 2012, at newstatesman.com.
13. See Michael Minnicino, 'The Frankfurt School and "Political Correctness"', *Fidelio* 1 (1992), at schillerinstitute.org. See also the section 'Cultural Marxism conspiracy theory' in the Wikipedia entry for the Frankfurt School.

14. See Peter Thompson, 'The Frankfurt School, Part 1: Why did Anders Breivik fear them?', *Guardian*, 25 March 2013, at theguardian.com.

15. See Theodor W. Adorno, 'Introduction', in T. W. Adorno, Else Frenkel-Brunswik, Daniel J. Levinson and R. Nevitt Sanford, *The Authoritarian Personality*, Harper & Brothers, 1950, p. 7.

16. See Ed West, 'Criticising Cultural Marxism Doesn't Make You Anders Breivik', *Telegraph*, 8 August 2012, at blogs.telegraph.co.uk.

17. Theodor W. Adorno and Max Horkheimer, *Dialectic of Enlightenment*, Verso, 1997, pp. 166–7.

18. Ibid., p. 167.

19. See Müller-Doohm, *Adorno: A Biography*, p. 262.

1   Condition: Critical

1. Walter Benjamin, *Berlin Childhood around 1900*, Belknap, 2006, p. 62.

2. Ibid., p. 63.

3. Martin Jay, *The Dialectical Imagination: A History of the Frankfurt School and the Institute of Social Research*, California University Press, 1973, p. 22.

4. Rick Kuhn, *Henryk Grossman and the Recovery of Marxism*, University of Illinois Press, 2007, p. 2.

5. Walter Benjamin, *The Arcades Project*, Belknap, 2002, p. 389.

6. Benjamin, *Berlin Childhood*, p. 42.

7. Benjamin, *The Arcades Project*, p. 391.

8. Walter Benjamin, 'A Berlin Chronicle' in *Reflections: Essays, Aphorisms, Autobiographical Writings*, ed. Peter Demetz, Harcourt, 1986, pp. 10–11.

9. Benjamin, *Berlin Childhood*, p. 159.

10. See Walter Benjamin, *Selected Writings 1931–1934*, Vol. 2, ed. Michael W. Jennings, Howard Eiland and Gary Smith, Belknap, 2005, p. 621.

11. Benjamin, *Illuminations*, p. 248.

12. Howard Eiland and Michael Jennings, *Walter Benjamin: A Critical Life*, Harvard University Press, 2014, p. 13.

13. Benjamin, *Berlin Childhood*, p. 158.

14. See Eiland and Jennings, *Walter Benjamin*, pp. 314 ff., and Esther Leslie, *Walter Benjamin*, Reaktion Books, 2007, pp. 101 ff.

15. Benjamin, *Berlin Childhood*, p. 37.

16. See Terry Eagleton, 'Waking the Dead', *New Statesman*, 12 November 2009, at newstatesman.com.
17. Benjamin, *Berlin Childhood*, p. xii.
18. Leslie, *Walter Benjamin*, p. 130.
19. Benjamin, *The Arcades Project*, p. 463.
20. Benjamin, *Berlin Childhood*, p. 85.
21. See Benjamin, 'The Image of Proust', in *Illuminations*, p. 198.
22. Ibid., p. 198.
23. Ibid., p. 199.
24. See Szondi's essay in Benjamin, *Berlin Childhood*, p. 18.
25. Benjamin, *Illuminations*, p. 245.
26. Benjamin, *Berlin Childhood*, p. 37
27. Quoted in Paul Muljadi, *Epicureanism: The Complete Guide*, Pediapress, 2011.
28. See Adorno's 1950 Afterword to *Berlin Childhood around 1900* quoted at hup.harvard.edu/catalog and on the back cover of the English language edition.
29. Eiland and Jennings, *Walter Benjamin*, p. 327.
30. Benjamin, *Berlin Childhood*, pp. 39–40.
31. Axel Honneth, *Reification: A New Look at an Old Idea*, Oxford University Press, 2008, p. 62.
32. Benjamin, *Selected Writings*, Vol. 2, p. 576.
33. See T. J. Clark, 'Reservations of the Marvellous', *London Review of Books*, 22 June 2000, at lrb.co.uk.
34. Benjamin, *The Arcades Project*, p. 908.

2   Fathers and Sons, and Other Conflicts

1. Benjamin, *Illuminations*, p. 31.
2. See Jay, *The Dialectical Imagination*, p. 292.
3. See Benjamin, *Reflections*, p. xiii.
4. Leo Löwenthal, *An Unmastered Past*, California University Press, 1987, pp. 17–18.
5. Ibid., p. 19.
6. Ibid., p. 19.

7. Vincent Geoghegan, *Ernst Bloch*, Routledge, 2008, p. 79.
8. David Biale, *Gershom Scholem: Kabbalah and Counter-history*, Harvard University Press, 1982, p. 9. Rolf Wiggershaus, *The Frankfurt School: Its History, Theories, and Political Significance*, MIT Press, 1995, p. 41.
10. John Abromeit, *Max Horkheimer and the Foundations of the Frankfurt School*, Cambridge University Press, 2011, p. 25.
11. Ibid., p. 22.
12. Ibid., p. 26.
13. Ibid., pp. 31-2.
14. Wiggershaus, *The Frankfurt School*, p. 43.
15. E. M. Forster, *Howards End*, Penguin, 1984, p. 147.
16. Wiggershaus, *The Frankfurt School*, p. 43.
17. Alfred Schmidt, 'Max Horkheimer's Intellectual Physiognomy', in *On Max Horkheimer: New Perspectives*, ed. Seyla Benhabib, Wolfgang Bonss and John McCole, MIT Press, 1995, p. 26.
18. Ibid.
19. Ibid.
20. Arthur Schopenhauer, *The World as Will and Representation*, Vol. 2, Dover, 1969, p. 357.
21. Arthur Schopenhauer, *On the Basis of Morality*, Hackett Publishing, 1995, p. 166.
22. Cited in Abromeit, *Max Horkheimer*, p. 35.
23. Max Horkheimer, 'Materialism and Metaphysics' in *Critical Theory: Selected Essays*, A&C Black, 1972, p. 10.
24. Abromeit, *Max Horkheimer*, p. 32.
25. See Arendt's essay in Benjamin, *Illuminations*, p. 31
26. Eiland and Jennings, *Walter Benjamin*, p. 18.
27. Franz Kafka, *Letter to his Father*, in an edition of Kafka's writings (including *The Trial, In the Penal Settlement, Metamorphosis, The Castle, The Great Wall of China, Investigations of a Dog*, and the *Diaries 1910-23*), Secker and Warburg, 1976, p. 566.
28. Ibid., pp. 584-5.
29. Ibid., p. 558.
30. Franz Kafka, *The Judgment*, at records.viu.ca.
31. Benjamin, *Illuminations*, p. 110.
32. See 'Biographical Notes on Herbert Marcuse' at history.ucsb.edu.

33. Wiggershaus, *The Frankfurt School*, p. 96.

34. See Brian Magee, 'Philosophy: Men of Ideas', available on YouTube.

35. Müller-Doohm, *Adorno: A Biography*, p. 19.

36. Adorno and Horkheimer, *Dialectic of Enlightenment*, p. 169.

37. Müller-Doohm, *Adorno: A Biography*, p. 18.

38. Arendt, in Benjamin, *Illuminations*, p. 13.

39. Müller-Doohm, *Adorno: A Biography*, p. 39.

40. Ibid., p. 20.

41. Lawrence J. Friedman, *The Lives of Erich Fromm: Love's Prophet*, Columbia University Press, 2013, pp. 4 ff.

42. Erich Fromm, *The Art of Loving*, Unwin, 1981, p. 41.

43. Friedman, *The Lives of Erich Fromm*, p. 6.

44. Kuhn, *Henryk Grossman*, pp. 1 ff.

45. Ibid., p. 56

46. Ibid., p. 89.

47. Müller-Doohm, *Adorno: A Biography*, p. 35.

48. Zoltán Tarr, *The Frankfurt School: The Critical Theories of Max Horkheimer and Theodor W. Adorno*, Transaction Publishers, 2011, pp. 19-20.

49. See the entry for Karl Liebknecht at spartacus-educational.com.

50. Gershom Scholem, *Walter Benjamin: The Story of a Friendship*, New York Review of Books, 1981, p. 24.

51. See Leslie, *Walter Benjamin*, p. 33.

52. Eiland and Jennings, *Walter Benjamin*, p. 79.

53. See Ray Monk, *Ludwig Wittgenstein: The Duty of Genius*, Random House, 2012, p. 138.

54. See Douglas Kellner, *Herbert Marcuse and the Crisis of Marxism*, Macmillan, 1984, pp. 14 ff.

55. Wiggershaus, *The Frankfurt School*, p. 44.

56. Mary-Alice Waters (ed.), *Rosa Luxemburg Speaks*, Pathfinder, 1991, p. 7.

57. Cited in Stephen Parker, *Bertolt Brecht: A Literary Life*, Bloomsbury 2014, p. 121.

58. Kellner, *Herbert Marcuse*, pp. 17–18.

59. See Abromeit, *Max Horkheimer*, p. 419.

60. Ibid.

61. Theodor Adorno, *Minima Moralia: Reflections from Damaged Life*, Verso, 2005, p. 22.

62. See Kellner, *Herbert Marcuse*, p. 169.

63. Adorno, *Minima Moralia*, p. 22.

64. Ibid.

65. Ibid., p. 23.

66. Müller-Doohm, *Adorno: A Biography*, p. 31.

3   The World Turned Upside Down

1. See the history of Frankfurt at frankfurt.de.

2. See Dieter Rebellisch, *Ludwig Landmann. Frankfurter Oberbürgermeister der Weimarer Republik*, Wiesbaden, 1975.

3. Corina Silvia Socaciu, 'Der vergessene Oberbürgermeister', 4 March 2015, at fr-online.de.

4. See *Frankfurter Allgemeine Zeitung*, 10 December 2009, Nr. 287, p. 43, or Hans Riebsamen, 'Lehrbeispiel für menschliche Gemeinheit', 29 December 2009, at faz.net.

5. Ibid.

6. *Grundriss der Statistik*, Leipzig, 1862, p. 61.

7. Simon Winder, *Germania: A Personal History of Germans Ancient and Modern*, Picador, 2010, p. 86.

8. Bryan Magee, *The Philosophy of Schopenhauer*, Oxford University Press, 2009, p. 21.

9. See 'Brick by Brick: the building blocks of civilisation – in pictures', *Guardian*, 9 April 2015, at theguardian.com.

10. See Ben Mauk, 'The Name of the Critic: On Walter Benjamin: A Critical Life'', at theamericanreader.com.

11. Benjamin, 'Surrealism', in *Reflections*, p. 191.

12. Festung des Wissenschaft, *Neue Zürcher Zeitung*, 3 November 2012, Literatur und Kunst, p. 65, at nzz.ch.

13. Ibid.

14. Dennis Crockett, *The Art of the Great Disorder 1918–1924*, Pennsylvania State University Press, 1999, p. xix.

15. See Jay, *The Dialectical Imagination*, p. 11.

16. Adorno and Horkheimer, *Dialectic of Enlightenment*, p. 25.

17. See Frank-Bertolt Raith, *Der heroische Stil: Studien zur Architektur*

am Ende der Weimarer Republik, Verlag für Bauwesen, Berlin 1997, p. 238.

18. See Parker, *Bertolt Brecht: A Literary Life*, p. 439 and Kuhn, *Henryk Grossman*, p. 113.

19. See Wiggershaus, *The Frankfurt School*, p. 12.

20. See Jay, *The Dialectical Imagination*, p. 5

21. Ibid., p. 11.

22. Gillian Rose, *The Melancholy Science: An Introduction to the Thought of Theodor W. Adorno*, Verso, 1978, p. 2.

23. See Jay, *The Dialectical Imagination*, p. 5.

24. See V. I. Lenin, *The Second Congress of the Communist International, Verbatim Report*, at marxists.org.

25. György Lukács, *History and Class Consciousness: Studies in Marxist Dialectics*, MIT Press, 1971.

26. See '1913: Ford's Assembly Line Starts Rolling' at history.com.

27. Ibid.

28. See Benjamin, *Illuminations*, p. 241.

29. Ibid., pp. 83–4.

30. Ibid., p. 84.

31. See Parker, *Bertolt Brecht: A Literary Life*, p. 238.

32. Ibid., p. 229.

33. See David Macey, *Dictionary of Critical Theory*, Penguin, 2001, p. 67.

34. Ibid., p. 68.

35. Rose, *The Melancholy Science*, p. 39.

36. Lukács, *History and Class Consciousness*, p. 100.

37. Macey, *Dictionary of Critical Theory*, p. 326.

38. Slavoj Žižek, *Less Than Nothing: Hegel and the Shadow of Dialectical Materialism*, Verso, 2012, p. 245.

39. Karl Marx and Friedrich Engels, *The Communist Manifesto: A Modern Edition*, Verso, 1998, p. 26.

40. Kuhn, *Henryk Grossman*, p. 126.

41. See Parker, *Bertolt Brecht: A Literary Life*, p. 273.

42. Jay, *The Dialectical Imagination*, p. 18.

43. See Kuhn, *Henryk Grossman*, p. 122.

44. Georg Wilhelm Friedrich Hegel, *Phenomenology of Spirit*, Oxford University Press, 1977, p. 126.

45. Lukács, *History and Class Consciousness*, p. 88.
46. See Stuart D. Goldman, 'The Spy Who Saved the Soviets', 30 July 2010, at historynet.com.
47. See Jay, *The Dialectical Imagination*, p. 14.
48. Wiggershaus, *The Frankfurt School*, p. 123.

4   A Bit of the Other

1. Walter Benjamin and Asja Lacis, 'Naples' in *Reflections*, p. 171. The following quotations are from this essay unless specified otherwise.
2. Charles Pettman, *Africanderisms*, Longmans, Green & Co., 1913, at archive.org.
3. Benjamin, *The Arcades Project*, p. 9.
4. Martin Mittelmeier, *Neapel: Wie sich eine Sehnsuchtslandschaft in Philosophie verwandelt*, Siedler Verlag, 2013. See also Ben Hutchinson's review of the book in the *Times Literary Supplement*, 7 February 2014.
5. Ibid.
6. See Peter Thompson, 'The Frankfurt School, Part 2: Negative Dialectics', *Guardian*, 1 April 2013, at theguardian.com.
7. Müller-Doohm, *Adorno: A Biography*, p. 513.
8. See Benjamin, 'Moscow', in *Reflections*, pp. 97–130. The following quotations are from this essay unless specified otherwise.
9. See Tim Ashley, 'Too Scary for Stalin', *Guardian*, 26 March 2004, at theguardian.com.
10. Eiland and Jennings, *Walter Benjamin*, p. 138.
11. Ibid., p. 281.
12. See the selection from *One-Way Street* in Benjamin, *Reflections*, pp. 61–96.
13. See Benjamin, *The Arcades Project*, p. ix.
14. Eiland and Jennings, *Walter Benjamin*, p. 53.
15. Douglas Murphy, *Last Futures: Nature, Technology and the End of Architecture*, Verso, 2015, p. 207.
16. Benjamin, *The Arcades Project*, p. 406.
17. Ibid., p. 26.
18. Peter Sloterdijk, *In the World Interior of Capital*, Polity, 2013, p. 174.

19. Ibid., p. 171.

20. Giorgio Agamben, *Stanzas*, University of Minnesota Press, 1993, pp. xvii.

21. Karl Marx, *Capital: A Critique of Political Economy – The Process of Capitalist Production*, Cosimo Books, 2007, p. 83.

22. Max Pensky, 'Method and Time: Benjamin's Dialectical Images' in *The Cambridge Companion to Walter Benjamin*, ed. David S. Ferris, Cambridge University Press, 2004.

23. Ibid., p. 187.

24. Benjamin, *The Arcades Project*, p. 462.

25. See Pensky, 'Method and Time'.

26. See Marx's Letter to Ruge in Karl Marx and Friedrich Engels, *Collected Works*, Vol. 3, International Publishers, 1975, p. 144.

27. Benjamin, *The Arcades Project*, p. 389.

28. See Anthony Auerbach, 'Imagine no Metaphors', *Image and Narrative*, September 2007, at imageandnarrative.be.

29. See Benjamin, 'Marseilles' in *Reflections*, pp. 131–6. The following quotations are from this essay unless specified otherwise.

30. Basil Woon, *From Deauville to Monte Carlo*, Liveright, 1929.

31. See Guide to Marseille at eurostar.com.

32. See Benjamin, 'Hashish in Marseilles' in *Reflections*, pp. 137–45.

33. D. H. Lawrence, *The Complete Poems*, Wordsworth Editions, 1994, p. 367.

34. See Beatrice Hansse (ed.), *Walter Benjamin and the Arcades Project*, Bloomsbury Publishing, 2006, p. 282.

35. Max Horkheimer (under the pseudonym Heinrich Regius), *Dämmerung*, Zurich, 1934, p. 181.

36. Erich Fromm, *Marx's Concept of Man: Including 'Economic and Philosophical Manuscripts'*, Bloomsbury, 2013, p. 26.

37. Cited in ibid., p. 26.

38. See Benjamin, *Illuminations*, p. 261.

39. See Jay, *The Dialectical Imagination*, p. 57.

40. Herbert Marcuse, *Eros and Civilisation: A Philosophical Inquiry into Freud*, Beacon Press, 1974, p. 161. Cited in Marshall Berman, *All That is Solid Melts into Air*, Verso, 2010, pp. 126–7.

41. Ibid.

42. Berman, *All That is Solid Melts into Air*, p. 127.

43. Simone Weil, *Oppression and Liberty*, Routledge, 2001, and James Gordon

Finlayson, *Habermas: A Very Short Introduction*, Oxford University Press, 2005, p. 16.

44. Jürgen Habermas, *Theory and Practice*, Beacon Press, 1973, p. 169.

45. William Outhwaite, *Habermas: A Critical Introduction*, Polity, 2009, p. 17.

46. Milton, *The Complete Poems*, Penguin, 1998, p. 309.

5   Show Us the Way to the Next Whiskey Bar

1. See Theodor Adorno, 'Mahoganny' in *The Weimar Republic Sourcebook*, ed. Anton Kaes, Martin Jay and Edward Dimendberg, University of California Press, 1994, pp. 588 ff. The following quotations are from this essay unless specified otherwise.

2. Parker, *Bertolt Brecht: A Literary Life*, pp. 273 ff.

3. See Jay, *The Dialectical Imagination*, pp. 124 ff.

4. See Dirk Van Hulle (ed.), *The New Cambridge Companion to Samuel Beckett*, Cambridge University Press, 2015, p. 75.

5. Parker, *Bertolt Brecht: A Literary Life*, p. 277.

6. T. S. Eliot, 'Portrait of a Lady' at bartleby.com.

7. See Andrew Feenberg and William Leiss (eds), *The Essential Marcuse*, Beacon Press, 2007.

8. Kellner, *Herbert Marcuse*, p. 106.

9. Jay, *The Dialectical Imagination*, pp. 182 ff.

10. Theodor W. Adorno, *Quasi Una Fantasia: Essays on Modern Music*, Verso, 1998, p. 20.

11. Will Self, 'Opera Remains the Preserve of the Rich', *Guardian*, 13 March 2015, at theguardian.com.

12. See Lukács, 'Preface to *The Theory of the Novel*', at marxists.org.

13. See Mark Clark, 'Hero or Villain? Bertolt Brecht and the Crisis Surrounding June 1953', *Journal of Contemporary History* 41:3 (2006), pp. 451–75.

6   The Power of Negative Thinking

1. See Benjamin, *Illuminations*, pp. 211 ff.
2. Thomas Wheatland, *The Frankfurt School in Exile*, University of Minnesota Press, 2009, p. 138.
3. Adorno, *Minima Moralia*, pp. 27–8.
4. Max Horkheimer, 'The Present Situation of Social Philosophy and the Tasks of an Institute for Social Research', at marxists.org.
5. See Karl Korsch, 'Marxism and Philosophy', at marxists.org.
6. Müller-Doohm, *Adorno: A Biography*, p. 137.
7. Ibid., p. 139.
8. See Jay, *The Dialectical Imagination*, p. 54.
9. See Feenberg and Leiss, *The Essential Marcuse*, p. 66.
10. Max Horkheimer, 'The Present Situation of Social Philosophy and the Tasks of an Institute for Social Research', at marxists.org.
11. Horkheimer, *Critical Theory: Selected Essays*, p. 143.
12. See Abromeit, *Max Horkheimer*, p. 97.
13. Horkheimer, *Critical Theory: Selected Essays*, pp. 188 ff.
14. See Jay, *The Dialectical Imagination*, p. 61.
15. Herbert Marcuse, *Reason and Revolution*, Routledge, 2013, p. 47.
16. Kellner, *Herbert Marcuse*, pp. 92 ff.
17. See Kellner's introduction to Herbert Marcuse, *One-Dimensional Man*, Routledge, 2002, p. xvii.
18. Kellner, *Herbert Marcuse*, p. 124.
19. Horkheimer, *Critical Theory: Selected Essays*, p. 221.
20. Abromeit, *Max Horkheimer*, p. 4.
21. Karl Mannheim, *Ideology and Utopia*, Routledge, 2013, p. 143.
22. Benjamin, *Illuminations*, p. 249.
23. Marcuse, *One-Dimensional Man*, p. 261.
24. See Friedman, *The Lives of Erich Fromm*, p. 33.
25. See Stuart Jeffries, 'Angela Davis: "There is an unbroken line of police violence in the US that takes us all the way back to the days of slavery"', *Guardian*, 14 December 2014, at theguardian.com.
26. See Friedman, *The Lives of Erich Fromm*, p. 36.
27. Ibid., pp. 36–7.
28. See Jay, *The Dialectical Imagination*, pp. 116 ff.

29. Friedman, *The Lives of Erich Fromm*, pp. 43 ff.

30. See Mark and Engels, *The Communist Manifesto*, Chapter 2, at marxists.org

31. Adorno, *Minima Moralia*, p. 2.

32. Erich Fromm, 'The Authoritarian Personality', at marxists.org.

7   In the Crocodile's Jaws

1. See Eiland and Jennings, *Walter Benjamin*, pp. 314 ff., and Leslie, *Walter Benjamin*, pp. 101 ff.

2. See Benjamin, *Selected Writings*, Vol. 2, p. 846.

3. See Walter Benjamin, *Radio Benjamin*, Verso, 2014.

4. 'The Benjamin Broadcasts', at bbc.co.uk.

5. See Bertolt Brecht, *Poems 1913–1956*, Routledge, 2007, and Parker, *Bertolt Brecht: A Literary Life*.

6. Friedman, *The Lives of Erich Fromm*, p. 1.

7. Adorno, *Minima Moralia*, p. 104.

8. Ibid.

9. See Ehrhard Bahr, *Weimar on the Pacific: German Exile Culture in Los Angeles and the Crisis of Modernism*, University of California Press, 2008, p. 13.

10. Jay Parini, *Benjamin's Crossing*, Anchor Books, 1998, p. 28.

11. See Parker, *Bertolt Brecht: A Literary Life*, p. 437.

12. Arendt, in Benjamin, *Illuminations*, pp. 32 ff.

13. Ibid., p. 32–3.

14. Ibid., p. 32.

15. Ibid., p. 29.

16. Eiland and Jennings, *Walter Benjamin*, p. 121.

17. Arendt, in Benjamin, *Illuminations*, p. 32.

18. Ibid., p. 33.

19. Ibid., p. 22.

20. Eiland and Jennings, *Walter Benjamin*, p. 374.

21. Scholem, *Walter Benjamin: The Story of a Friendship*, p. 238.

22. Eiland and Jennings, *Walter Benjamin*, p. 315.

23. Gary Smith (ed.), *The Correspondence of Walter Benjamin and Gershom Scholem, 1932–1940*, Harvard University Press, 1992, p. 13.

24. See Benjamin, 'The Destructive Character' in *Reflections*, pp. 301–3.

25. Scholem, *Walter Benjamin: The Story of a Friendship*, p. 291.

26. Arthur Schopenhauer, 'On Suicide' in *On the Suffering of the World*, Penguin, 2004, p. 52.

27. See Chandak Sengoopta, *Otto Weininger: Sex, Science, and Self in Imperial Vienna*, Chicago University Press, 2000, p. 19.

28. Eiland and Jennings, *Walter Benjamin*, p. 70.

29. See 'One-Way Street' in *Reflections*, pp. 69–70.

30. Ibid., p. 70.

31. Schopenhauer, *On the Suffering of the World*, p. 53.

32. Adorno, *Minima Moralia*, p. 247.

33. Benjamin, *Illuminations*, p. 249.

34. See Avner Shapira, 'Walter Benjamin's Berlin 120 Years On', *Haaretz*, 12 July 2012, at haaretz.com.

35. See Benjamin, 'Karl Kraus' in *Reflections*, pp. 239 ff.

36. Benjamin, *Selected Writings*, Vol. 2, pp. 712 ff.

37. Gershom Scholem, 'Walter Benjamin and His Angel' in *Jews and Judaism in Crisis*, Schocken, 1978, pp. 198 ff.

38. See Eagleton, 'Waking the Dead'.

39. Gershom Scholem and Theodor W. Adorno (eds), *The Correspondence of Walter Benjamin, 1910–1940*, University of Chicago Press, 1994, p. 569.

40. Adorno, *Minima Moralia*, p. 87.

8   Modernism and All That Jazz

1. See Benjamin, 'The Work of Art in the Age of Mechanical Reproduction' in *Illuminations*, pp. 211–44. The following quotations are from this essay unless specified otherwise.

2. Theodor W. Adorno, 'On Jazz', in *Essays on Music*, University of California Press, 2002, pp. 470–95.

3. Lawrence, *The Complete Poems*, p. 366.

4. Benjamin, *The Arcades Project*, p. 364.

5. See the biography for Friedrich Kittler at egs.edu.

6. Richard Wollheim, *Painting as an Art*, Thames and Hudson, 1987, p. 8.

7. Mihaly Csíkszentmihályi, *Flow: The Psychology of Optimal Experience*, Harper, 1990.

8. Eiland and Jennings, *Walter Benjamin*, p. 517.

9. Roberto Calasso, *The Ruin of Kasch*, Harvard University Press, 1994, p. 139.

10. Adorno, 'On Jazz', in *Essays on Music*, p. 473. The following quotations are from this essay unless specified otherwise.

11. See Jay, *The Dialectical Imagination*, p. 186.

12. Adorno and Horkheimer, *Dialectic of Enlightenment*, p. 111.

13. Theodor W. Adorno, *Prisms*, MIT Press, 1983, p. 123.

9   A New World

1. See Festung des Wissenschaft, *Neue Zürcher Zeitung*, 3 November 2012, Literatur und Kunst, p. 65, at nzz.ch.

2. Friedman, *The Lives of Erich Fromm*, p. 39.

3. See Jeremy Noakes and Geoffrey Pridham (eds), *Nazism 1919–1945, Vol. 1, The Rise to Power 1919–1934*, University of Exeter Press, 1998, pp. 94–5.

4. Kellner, *Herbert Marcuse*, p. 98.

5. Jay, *The Dialectical Imagination*, p. 156.

6. Müller-Doohm, *Adorno: A Biography*, p. 178.

7. Theodor W. Adorno and Alban Berg, *Correspondence 1925–1935*, Polity, 2005, p. 193.

8. Müller-Doohm, *Adorno: A Biography*, p. 190.

9. Lorenz Jäger, *Adorno: A Political Biography*, Yale, 2004, p. 88.

10. A. J. Ayer, *Part of My Life*, Collins, 1977, p. 153.

11. Monk, *Ludwig Wittgenstein*, p. 271.

12. See David Edmonds and John Eidinow, *Wittgenstein's Poker*, Faber, 2014.

13. See Wheatland, *The Frankfurt School in Exile*, pp. 35 ff.

14. Lewis Feuer, 'The Frankfurt School Marxists and the Columbia Liberals', *Survey* 25:3 (1980), pp. 156–76.

15. See Stephen Koch, *Double Lives: Stalin, Willi Münzenberg and the Seduction of the Intellectuals*, Enigma Books, 2004.

16. Jay, *The Dialectical Imagination*, p. 8.

17. Ibid., p. 205.

18. Ibid., footnote to p. 162.

19. Walter Benjamin and Gretel Adorno, *Correspondence 1930–1940*, Polity, 2008, p. 211.

20. Ibid., p. 211.

21. See Wheatland, *The Frankfurt School in Exile*, pp. 35 ff.

22. Ted Honderich (ed.), *Oxford Companion to Philosophy*, Oxford University Press, 2005, p. 747.

23. See 'Herbert Marcuse on John Dewey & Positivism', at autodidactproject.org.

24. See Wheatland, *The Frankfurt School in Exile*, p. 109.

25. Wiggershaus, *The Frankfurt School*, p. 344

26. See Susan Cavin, 'Adorno, Lazarsfeld and the Princeton Radio Project' at citation.allacademic.com.

27. Hadley Cantril, *The Invasion from Mars: A Study in the Psychology of Panic*, Transaction Publishers, 2005.

28. Müller-Doohm, *Adorno: A Biography*, p. 247.

29. Ibid., p. 247.

30. Quoted in Müller-Doohm, *Adorno: A Biography*, p. 249.

31. Ibid., p. 250.

32. See Cavin, 'Adorno, Lazarsfeld and the Princeton Radio'.

33. Müller-Doohm, *Adorno: A Biography*, p. 254.

10 The Road to Port Bou

1. Theodor W. Adorno, *Letters to his Parents*, Polity, 2007, p. 33.

2. Ibid., p. 3.

3. Quoted in Yasemin Yildiz, *Beyond the Mother Tongue: The Postmonolingual Condition*, Fordham University Press, 2012, p. 85.

4. Adorno and Horkheimer, *Dialectic of Enlightenment*, p. xi.

5. See Benjamin, *Illuminations*, pp. 248–9.

6. See Eiland and Jennings, *Walter Benjamin*, p. 647.

7. See Benjamin, *Illuminations*, p. 23.

8. See Benjamin, 'Marseilles', in *Reflections*, p. 131.

9. Ibid., pp. 137 ff.

10. Quoted in Lisa Fittko's essay 'The Story of Old Benjamin', in Benjamin, *The Arcades Project*, p. 948.

11. See Eiland and Jennings, *Walter Benjamin*, p. 674.
12. Ibid., p. 675.
13. Müller-Doohm, *Adorno: A Biography*, p. 263.
14. See Stuart Jeffries, 'Did Stalin's Killers Liquidate Walter Benjamin?', *Guardian*, 8 July 2001, at theguardian.com.
15. Müller-Doohm, *Adorno: A Biography*, p. 269.
16. See Benjamin, *Illuminations*, p. 248. The Wikipedia entry for Walter Benjamin includes a photograph of the tombstone.

11 In League with the Devil

1. Brecht, *Poems, 1938–1956*, p. 367.
2. See Bahr, *Weimar on the Pacific*, p. 83.
3. Ibid., p. 35.
4. Brecht, *Poems, 1938–1956*, p. 382.
5. Otto Friedrich, *City of Nets: A Portrait of Hollywood in the 1940s*, Headline Books, 1987, p. xi.
6. Quoted in Robert Leckie, *Delivered from Evil: The Saga of World War II*, Harper & Row, 1987, p. 250. See also Antony Beevor, *Stalingrad*, Penguin, 1999, p. 80.
7. See Thomas Toughill, *A World to Gain: The Battle for Global Domination and Why America Entered WWII*, Clairview, 2004, p. 14.
8. Friedrich, *City of Nets*, p. xi.
9. Ibid.
10. See Müller-Doohm, *Adorno: A Biography*, p. 262. 'In view of what is now threatening to engulf Europe,' wrote Horkheimer, 'our work is essentially designed to pass things down through the night that is approaching: a kind of message in a bottle.'
11. Theodor W. Adorno, *Dream Notes*, Polity, 2007, p. 48.
12. Adorno and Horkheimer, *Dialectic of Enlightenment*, p. 149.
13. Ibid.
14. Ibid., p. 148.
15. Ibid., p. 138.
16. Ibid., p. 140.
17. Quoted in Müller-Doohm, *Adorno: A Biography*, p. 312.

18. See Peter Thompson, 'The Frankfurt School, Part 3: Dialectic of Enlightenment', *Guardian*, 8 April 2013, at theguardian.com.

19. See Richard Hoggart, *The Uses of Literacy*, Penguin, 2009, Chapter 7.

20. Adorno and Horkheimer, *Dialectic of Enlightenment*, p. 105.

21. Theodor W. Adorno, *Philosophy of Modern Music*, Bloomsbury Publishing, 2007, p. 147.

22. See J. M. Bernstein's introduction to Theodor W. Adorno, *The Culture Industry*, Routledge, 2006, especially p. 1.

23. Adorno and Horkheimer, *Dialectic of Enlightenment*, p. 18.

24. Ibid., pp. 7–8.

25. See Ray Monk, *Bertrand Russell: The Ghosts of Madness 1921–1970*, Vintage, 2000, pp. 219 ff.

26. Adorno and Horkheimer, *Dialectic of Enlightenment*, pp. 43 ff.

27. Ibid., pp. 81 ff.

28. Jay, *The Dialectical Imagination*, p. 265.

29. Adorno, *Minima Moralia*, p. 95.

30. Susan Buck-Morss, *The Origin of Negative Dialectics*, Simon and Schuster, 1979, p. 58.

31. Renée J. Heberle (ed.), *Feminist Interpretations of Theodor Adorno*, Penn State University Press, 2010, p. 5.

32. Adorno, *Minima Moralia*, p. 96.

33. Müller-Doohm, *Adorno: A Biography*, p. 316.

34. See Friedrich, *City of Nets*, p. 274.

35. See Andrea Weiss, *In the Shadow of the Magic Mountain: The Erika and Klaus Mann Story*, University of Chicago Press, 2010, p. 116.

36. See Craig R. Whitney, 'Thomas Mann's Daughter an Informer', *New York Times*, 18 July 1993, at nytimes.com.

37. See Steiner's blurb to Theodor W. Adorno and Thomas Mann, *Correspondence 1943–1955*, Polity, 2006, at polity.co.uk.

38. Quoted in Weiss, *In the Shadow of the Magic Mountain*, p. 103.

39. See 'From the Stacks: "Homage to Thomas Mann"' (April 1, 1936), *New Republic*, 12 August 2013, at newrepublic.com.

40. See *Letters of Thomas Mann, 1889–1955*, ed. Richard Winston and Clara Winston, University of California Press, 1975, pp. 205 ff.

41. See the *Encyclopaedia Britannica* entry for Thomas Mann at britannica.com.

42. See Bahr, *Weimar on the Pacific*, p. 244.

43. Thomas Mann, *Doctor Faustus*, Vintage, 1999, p. 481.

44. See Bahr, *Weimar on the Pacific*, p. 251.

45. See Mann, *Doctor Faustus*, pp. 406–7.

46. See Friedrich, *City of Nets*, p. 271.

47. See Adorno and Mann, *Correspondence*, p. vi.

48. Mann, *Doctor Faustus*, p. 52.

49. Ibid., p. 53.

50. See Bahr, *Weimar on the Pacific*, pp. 253–4.

51. Ibid., p. 258.

52. Quoted in Friedrich, *City of Nets*, p. 276.

53. Ibid., p. 256.

54. See Adorno and Mann, *Correspondence*, p. vii.

55. Mann, *Doctor Faustus*, p. 486.

56. See Bahr, *Weimar on the Pacific*, p. 260.

57. Ibid.

58. See Müller-Doohm, *Adorno: A Biography*, p. 319.

59. Quoted in Bahr, *Weimar on the Pacific*, p. 247.

60. Quoted in Ibid., p. 262.

61. Mann, *Doctor Faustus*, p. 510.

62. Müller-Doohm, *Adorno: A Biography*, p. 318

63. Jean-François Lyotard, 'Adorno as the Devil', *Telos*, Spring 1974, at www.telospress.com; quoted in Carsten Strathausen, 'Adorno, or The End of Aesthetics' in Max Pensky (ed.), *Globalising Critical Theory*, Rowman & Littlefield, 2005, p. 226.

64. Theodor Adorno, 'Reconciliation under Duress', in Adorno et al., *Aesthetics and Politics*, Verso, 1980, pp. 151 ff.

65. See James Hellings, *Adorno and Art: Aesthetic Theory Contra Critical Theory*, Palgrave Macmillan, 2014, p. 33.

66. See Theodor Adorno, *Aesthetic Theory*, Athlone Press, 1999, p. 229.

67. See Anthony Elliott (ed.), *The Routledge Companion to Social Theory*, Routledge, 2009, p. 242.

12 The Fight Against Fascism

1. Quoted by Maurice Brinton, 'The Irrational in Politics', at marxists.org.

2. See Friedman, *The Lives of Erich Fromm*, pp. 51 ff.

3. Ibid., p. 38.

4. Erich Fromm, *Escape from Freedom*, Avon, 1965, p. 173.

5. Ibid., pp. 19–20.

6. Kellner, *Herbert Marcuse*, p. 98.

7. Ernst Bloch, *Heritage of Our Times*, Wiley, 2009.

8. Benjamin, *Illuminations*, p. 235.

9. See Jay, *The Dialectical Imagination*, pp. 161 ff.

10. Franz Neumann, *Behemoth: The Structure and Practice of National Socialism*, Rowman & Littlefield, 2009, p. 227.

11. Ibid., p. 85.

12. Adorno, *Minima Moralia*, p. 106.

13. Müller-Doohm, *Adorno: A Biography*, p. 310.

14. Adorno and Horkheimer, *Dialectic of Enlightenment*, pp. 173–4.

15. Ibid., p. 199.

16. See Jay, *The Dialectical Imagination*, p. 232.

17. Kellner, *Herbert Marcuse*, p. 149.

18. Raymond Geuss, Foreword to Franz Neumann, Herbert Marcuse and Otto Kirchheimer, *Secret Reports on Nazi Germany: The Frankfurt School Contribution to the War Effort*, Princeton University Press, 2013, p. ix.

19. Ibid., p. 131.

20. See the entry on Franz Neumann at spartacus-educational.com.

21. Ibid.

22. Kellner, *Herbert Marcuse*, p. 152.

23. Quoted in *Trial of the Major War Criminals Before the International Military Tribunal, Nuremberg, 14 November 1945–1 October 1946: Proceedings*, AMS Press, 1947, p. 35.

24. Adorno, *Letters to his Parents*, pp. 258–9.

25. Müller-Doohm, *Adorno: A Biography*, p. 309.

26. Adorno, *Minima Moralia*, p. 234.

13 The Ghost Sonata

1. Müller-Doohm, *Adorno: A Biography*, p. 321.
2. Kuhn, *Henryk Grossman*, p. 209.
3. Ibid., p. 215.
4. Ibid., p. 221.
5. Müller-Doohm, *Adorno: A Biography*, p. 334.
6. Andreea Deciu Ritivoi, *Intimate Strangers: Arendt, Marcuse, Solzhenitsyn, and Said in American Political Discourse*, Columbia University Press, 2014, p. 163.
7. Saul Bellow, 'The French as Dostoevsky Saw Them', in *It All Adds Up*, Secker and Warburg, 1994, p. 41.
8. Saul Bellow, *The Adventures of Augie March*, Penguin, 1981, p. 3.
9. Müller-Doohm, *Adorno: A Biography*, p. 326.
10. See Maggie O'Neill (ed.), *Adorno, Culture and Feminism*, Sage, 1999, p. 95.
11. Peter Dews (ed.), *Autonomy and Solidarity: Interviews with Jürgen Habermas*, Verso, 1992, p. 46.
12. Müller-Doohm, *Adorno: A Biography*, p. 330.
13. Ibid., p. 565.
14. Quoted in 'Correspondence with Martin Heidegger', marcuse.org/herbert/pubs/40spubs/47MarcuseHeidegger.htm and in Berel Lang, *Heidegger's Silence*, Cornel University Press, 1996, p. 58.
15. Herbert Marcuse, *Technology, War and Fascism: Collected Papers, Volume 1*, ed. Douglas Kellner, Routledge, 2004, p. 263.
16. Jürgen Habermas, *Between Naturalism and Religion*, Polity, 2010, p. 20.
17. Dews, *Autonomy and Solidarity*, p. 78.
18. Müller-Doohm, *Adorno: A Biography*, p. 335.
19. Adorno, *Minima Moralia*, p. 233.
20. Müller-Doohm, *Adorno: A Biography*, p. 383.
21. Ibid., p. 383.
22. Ibid., p. 384.
23. Ibid.
24. Adorno, *Prisms*, p. 34.
25. Adorno, *Minima Moralia*, p. 44.
26. Primo Levi, *If This Is a Man*, Abacus, 2004, p. 57.
27. Müller-Doohm, *Adorno: A Biography*, p. 405.

28. Quoted in Brían Hanrahan, 'Review of Darkness Spoken: Collected Poems of Ingeborg Bachmann', *Harvard Review* 32 (2007), p. 162.

29. Theodor W. Adorno, *Negative Dialectics*, Routledge, 2003, p. 362.

30. Ibid., p. 365.

31. Adorno and Mann, *Correspondence*, pp. 45–6.

32. Müller-Doohm, *Adorno: A Biography*, p. 293.

33. Adorno, *The Culture Industry*, p. 141.

34. Adorno and Horkheimer, *Dialectic of Enlightenment*, p. 192.

35. See György Lukács, 'Class Consciousness', at marxists.org.

36. Erich Fromm, *The Sane Society*, Routledge, 2013, p. 166.

37. Adorno and Mann, *Correspondence*, p. 46.

38. Adorno et al., *The Authoritarian Personality*, p. 753.

39. Ibid., pp. 224 ff.

40. Ibid., p. 753.

41. You can do the F-test at anesi.com/fscale.htm.

42. Adorno et al., *The Authoritarian Personality*, p. 7.

14 The Liberation of Eros

1. Kellner, *Herbert Marcuse*, p. 155.

2. See Christopher Turner, 'Wilhelm Reich: The Man Who Invented Free Love', *Guardian*, 8 July 2011, at theguardian.com.

3. Christopher Turner, *Adventures in the Orgasmatron: Wilhelm Reich and the Invention of Sex*, Fourth Estate, 2011, p. 10.

4. See Herbert Marcuse, 'Epilogue: Critique of neo-Freudian Revisionism' at marxists.org.

5. Kellner, *Herbert Marcuse*, p. 158.

6. Herbert Marcuse, *Eros and Civilisation: A Philosophical Inquiry Into Freud*, Beacon Press, 1974, p. 45.

7. Ibid., p. 14.

8. Theodor W. Adorno, *The Stars Down to Earth and Other Essays on the Irrational in Culture*, Routledge, 2002, p. 12.

9. Ibid., p. 12.

10. Quoted in Mary VanderGoot, *After Freedom: How Boomers Pursued Freedom, Questioned Virtue, and Still Search for Meaning*, Wipf and Stock, 2012, p. 8.

11. Marcuse, *Eros and Civilisation*, p. 129.

12. See David Graeber, 'On the Phenomenon of Bullshit Jobs', 17 August 2013, at strikemag.org.

13. Marcuse, *Eros and Civilisation*, p. 203.

14. Ibid., p. 201.

15. Kellner, *Herbert Marcuse*, p. 185.

16. Ibid.

17. Ibid.

18. Marcuse, *Eros and Civilisation*, p. 170.

19. Ibid., p. 5.

20. Ibid., p. 250.

21. See Fromm, *The Sane Society*, pp. 99 ff.

22. Erich Fromm, *To Have or To Be*, A&C Black, 2013, p. 128.

23. Adorno and Horkheimer, *Dialectic of Enlightenment*, p. 203.

24. Theodor W. Adorno, 'Die Revidierte Psychoanalyse' in *Institut für Sozialforschung, Soziologische Exkurse*, Frankfurt, 1956, p. 30. Cited in Russell Jacoby, *Social Amnesia: A Critique of Contemporary Psychology*, Transaction Publishers, 1975, p. 33.

25. Friedman, *The Lives of Erich Fromm*, pp. 192 ff.

26. See Joan Braune, *Erich Fromm's Revolutionary Hope: Prophetic Messianism as a Critical Theory of the Future*, Springer, 2014, p. 3.

27. Fromm, *The Art of Loving*, p. 11.

28. See Zygmunt Bauman, *Liquid Love: On the Frailty of Human Bonds*, Polity, 2013, pp. 7–8.

29. Müller-Doohm, *Adorno: A Biography*, p. 414.

30. Ibid., p. 413.

31. Ibid., p. 415.

32. Wiggershaus, *The Frankfurt School*, p. 551.

33. Ibid.

34. Ibid., p. 554.

35. Ibid.

36. Ibid.

37. Ibid.

15 Up Against the Wall, Motherfuckers

1. Herbert Marcuse, *Marxism, Revolution and Utopia: Collected Papers, Volume 6*, Routledge, 2014, p. 179.
2. Cited in Outhwaite, *Habermas: A Critical Introduction*, p. 14.
3. Marcuse, *One-Dimensional Man*, p. 10.
4. See Kellner, *Herbert Marcuse*, p. 232.
5. Marcuse, *Marxism, Revolution and Utopia*, pp. 178–9.
6. See Herbert Marcuse, *Reason and Revolution*, at marxists.org.
7. Marcuse, *One-Dimensional Man*, p. 11.
8. Fromm, *Marx's Concept of Man*, p. 38.
9. Marcuse, *One-Dimensional Man*, p. 7.
10. Ibid., p. 14.
11. Alasdair MacIntyre, *Marcuse*, Fontana, 1970, p. 62.
12. Berman, *All That is Solid Melts into Air*, pp. 28–9.
13. Ibid., p. 28.
14. Kellner, *Herbert Marcuse*, p. 465.
15. Marcuse, *One-Dimensional Man*, p. 260.
16. Berman, *All That is Solid Melts into Air*, p. 29.
17. Marcuse, *One-Dimensional Man*, p. 261.
18. Kellner, *Herbert Marcuse*, p. 3.
19. Berman, *All That is Solid Melts into Air*, p. 29.
20. Marcuse, *One-Dimensional Man*, p. 81.
21. Ibid., p. 77.
22. Ibid., p. 78.
23. David Allyn, *Make Love, Not War: The Sexual Revolution, an Unfettered History*, Taylor & Francis, 2001, p. 204.
24. Ibid., p. 202.
25. See Osha Neumann, *Up Against the Wall Motherf**er: A Memoir of the '60s, with Notes for Next Time*, Seven Stories Press, 2011.
26. See Pooja Mhatre, 'Faces of Berkeley: Osha Neumann, activist lawyer', *The Daily Californian*, 28 June 2012, at dailycal.org.
27. Allyn, *Make Love, Not War*, p. 203.
28. Marcuse, *One-Dimensional Man*, p. 77.
29. Ibid., p. 79.
30. Sigmund Freud, *Civilisation and Its Discontents*, Penguin, 2004, pp. 16–17.

31. Ibid., p. 44.

32. Marcuse, *One-Dimensional Man*, p. 60.

33. Ibid., p. 65.

34. Ibid., p. 67.

35. Ibid., p. 77.

36. Ibid., p. 79.

37. Ibid., p. 80.

38. Ibid., p. 62.

39. Ibid., p. 81.

40. Ibid., p. 61.

41. Ibid., pp. 260–1.

42. Ibid., p. 261.

43. See Jeffries, 'Angela Davis: "There is an unbroken line of police violence . . .",' at theguardian.com.

44. Angela Davis, 'Marcuse's Legacies', Preface to Herbert Marcuse, *The New Left and the 1960s: Collected Papers, Volume 3*, Routledge, 2004, p. ix, at pages.gseis.ucla.edu.

45. See Jeffries, 'Angela Davis: "There is an unbroken line of police violence . . ."'.

46. Maurice William Cranston, *The New Left: Six Critical Essays*, Bodley Head, 1970, p. 87.

47. MacIntyre, *Marcuse*, p. 90.

48. See John Abromeit and W. Mark Cobb (eds), *Herbert Marcuse: A Critical Reader*, Routledge, 2014, p. 2.

49. Davis, 'Marcuse's Legacies', p ix.

50. Ibid.

51. See Jeffries, 'Angela Davis: "There is an unbroken line of police violence . . ."'.

52. Angela Y. Davis, *Blues Legacies and Black Feminism: Gertrude Ma Rainey, Bessie Smith, and Billie Holiday*, Knopf Doubleday, 2011, p. 44.

53. Marcuse, *One-Dimensional Man*, p. 62.

54. Marcuse, *An Essay on Liberation*, Beacon Press, 1971, p. 4.

55. Ibid., pp. 20 ff.

56. Kellner, *Herbert Marcuse*, p. 340.

57. Leszek Kołakowski, *Main Currents of Marxism: Volume III, The Breakdown*, Oxford University Press, 1981, p. 416.

58. John Gerassi, *Jean-Paul Sartre: Hated Conscience of His Century, Volume 1: Protestant or Protestor?*, University of Chicago Press, 1989, p. 9.

16 Philosophising with Molotov Cocktails

1. Adorno, *Negative Dialectics*, p. 320.
2. Kołakowski, *Main Currents of Marxism: Volume III*, p. 366.
3. Adorno, *Negative Dialectics*, p. xix.
4. Walter Kaufmann, *Hegel: A Reinterpretation*, Anchor, 1966, p. 144.
5. Adorno, *Minima Moralia*, p. 50.
6. See Martin Jay, *Adorno*, Fontana, 1984, p. 63.
7. See Renée Heberle's introduction to *Feminist Reinterpretations of Theodor Adorno*, p. 7.
8. Adorno, *Negative Dialectics*, p. 163.
9. Dews, *Autonomy and Solidarity*, p. 82.
10. Adorno, *Negative Dialectics*, p. 17.
11. Jürgen Habermas, *The Philosophical Discourse of Modernity*, Polity, 1990, p. 119.
12. See the entry for Adorno at plato.stanford.edu.
13. Paul Connerton, *The Tragedy of Enlightenment: An Essay on the Frankfurt School*, Cambridge University Press, 1960, p. 114.
14. Adorno, *Negative Dialectics*, p. 3.
15. Cited in Garth L. Hallett, *Essentialism: A Wittgensteinian Critique*, SUNY Press, 1991, p. 125.
16. See Steve Fuller, 'Karl Popper and the Reconstitution of the Rationalist Left', in Ian Charles Jarvie, Karl Milford and David W. Miller (eds), *Karl Popper, A Centenary Assessment, Volume 3: Science*, Ashgate, 2006, p. 190.
17. Bryan Magee, *Confessions of a Philosopher*, Random House, 1997, p. 183.
18. To clinch the point about Adorno's waspishness, see Martin Jay's essay 'The Ungrateful Dead' in his *Refractions of Violence*, Routledge, 2012, pp. 39–46. Decades after Adorno's death, Jay discovered a letter written by Adorno to Marcuse in 1969. In it, Adorno complained that Jay, whom he described as 'a horrible guy', had shown 'an unerring instinct to direct himself to the dirt' during their interview. Understandably, Jay, who spent much of his professional life extolling and interpreting the works of Adorno and the Frankfurt School, was more than a little wounded.
19. See Adorno's introduction to Theodor Adorno, Karl Popper et al., *The Positivist Dispute in German Sociology*, Harper & Row, 1976, p. 27.
20. See Marcuse, *One-Dimensional Man*, Chapter 7 (The Triumph of Positive Thinking: One-Dimensional Philosophy), pp. 174–203.

21. See the entry for Horkheimer at plato.stanford.edu.

22. Adorno and Horkheimer, *Dialectic of Enlightenment*, p. 1.

23. See Fuller, 'Karl Popper and the Reconstitution of the Rationalist Left', p. 191.

24. See Popper's first contribution to the Tübingen symposium in *The Positivist Dispute in German Sociology*, p. 104.

25. Ibid., p. 88.

26. David Hume, *An Enquiry Concerning Human Understanding*, Courier Corporation, 2004, p. 14.

27. See Popper's first paper in *The Positivist Dispute in German Sociology*, p. 87.

28. Thomas S. Kuhn, *The Structure of Scientific Revolutions*, University of Chicago Press, 1996.

29. Adorno, *The Positivist Dispute in German Sociology*, p. xi, footnote 4.

30. Ibid., p. 67.

31. Popper, *The Positivist Dispute in German Sociology*, p. 97.

32. Ibid., p. 95.

33. Adorno, *The Positivist Dispute in German Sociology*, p. 121.

34. Ibid.

35. Popper, *The Positivist Dispute in German Sociology*, p. 95.

36. Ibid., p. 89.

37. Ibid., p. 3.

38. See Fuller, 'Karl Popper and the Reconstitution of the Rationalist Left', p. 191.

39. Quoted in *The Positivist Dispute in German Sociology*, p. 65.

40. Ibid., p. 65.

41. Ibid., p. 67.

42. See Theodor Adorno and Herbert Marcuse, 'Correspondence on the German Student Movement' (1969), at platypus1917.org.

43. Müller-Doohm, *Adorno: A Biography*, p. 463.

44. Ibid., p. 452.

45. Ibid., p. 456.

46. Ibid., p. 453.

47. Ibid., p. 454.

48. Ibid., p. 456.

49. Ibid., pp. 460 ff.

50. Ibid., p. 461.

51. Ibid., p. 464

52. Adorno and Marcuse, 'Correspondence on the German Student Movement'.

53. Müller-Doohm, *Adorno: A Biography*, p. 475.

54. Ibid., p. 476.

55. See Leslie, 'Introduction to Adorno/Marcuse Correspondence on the German Student Movement', at platypus1917.org.

56. See Adorno and Marcuse, 'Correspondence on the German Student Movement'.

57. Ibid.

58. Peter M. R. Stirk, *Max Horkheimer: A New Interpretation*, Rowman & Littlefield, 1992, p. 179.

59. See Adorno and Marcuse, 'Correspondence on the German Student Movement'.

60. Müller-Doohm, *Adorno: A Biography*, p. 457.

17 The Frankfurt Spider

1. See Stuart Jeffries, 'A Rare Interview with Jürgen Habermas', *Financial Times*, 30 April 2010, ft.com.

2. See Stephen Eric Bronner, *Critical Theory and Society: A Reader*, Psychology Press, 1989, p. 136.

3. See the introduction to Jürgen Habermas, *The Structural Transformation of the Public Sphere: An Inquiry into a Category of Bourgeois Society*, Wiley, 2015.

4. See the entry for Habermas at plato.stanford.edu.

5. Adorno, *Negative Dialectics*, p. 363.

6. See Benjamin, *Illuminations*, p. 255.

7. See Mitchell Stephens, 'The Theologian of Talk', *Los Angeles Times*, 23 October 1994, at articles.latimes.com.

8. Adorno, *Negative Dialectics*, p. 365.

9. Adorno and Horkheimer, *Dialectic of Enlightenment*, pp. 44–5.

10. Habermas, *The Philosophical Discourse of Modernity*, p. 109.

11. Jürgen Habermas, *Technik und wissenschaft als 'ideologie'*, Suhrkamp, 1998.

12. Max Horkheimer, *Eclipse of Reason*, A&C Black, 2013, p. 68.

13. Habermas, *The Philosophical Discourse of Modernity*, p. 113.

14. Ibid., p. 111.

15. Ibid., p. 114.

16. Dews, *Autonomy and Solidarity*, p. 82.

17. See Fredric Jameson, *Postmodernism, or, The Cultural Logic of Late Capitalism*, Verso, 1991.

18. See Stephens, 'The Theologian of Talk'.

19. Maurizio Passerin d'Entrèves and Seyla Benhabib (eds), *Habermas and the Unfinished Project of Modernity: Critical Essays on The Philosophical Discourse of Modernity*, MIT Press, 1997, pp. 38 ff.

20. Habermas, *The Philosophical Discourse of Modernity*, p. 7.

21. Passerin d'Entrèves and Seyla Benhabib, *Habermas and the Unfinished Project of Modernity*, p. 45.

22. Ibid.

23. Ibid., p. 46.

24. Ibid., pp. 45–6.

25. See Jeffries, 'A Rare Interview with Jürgen Habermas'.

26. Cited in Igor Primoratz and Aleksandar Pavkovic (eds), *Patriotism: Philosophical and Political Perspectives*, Ashgate, 2013, p. 140.

27. Quoted in Lewis Edwin Hahn (ed.), *Perspectives on Habermas*, Open Court Publishing, 2000, p. 355.

28. See Finlayson, *Habermas: A Very Short Introduction*, pp. 126 ff.

29. Cited in ibid., p. 127.

30. Jürgen Habermas, *Europe: The Faltering Project*, Wiley, 2014

31. See Jeffries, 'A Rare Interview with Jürgen Habermas'.

32. Ibid.

33. Ibid.

34. Ibid.

35. Michael Haller, *The Past as Future: Jürgen Habermas*, Polity, 1994, p. 97.

36. Cited in Nicholas Adams, *Habermas and Theology*, Cambridge University Press, 2006, p. 79.

37. Jürgen Habermas, *An Awareness of What is Missing: Faith and Reason in a Post-Secular Age*, Wiley, 2014, p. 18.

38. Ibid., p. 19.

39. See Edward Skidelsky's article 'Habermas vs the Pope: The darling of the 68ers and Benedict XVI find a surprising amount to agree on', *Prospect*, 20 November 2005, at prospectmagazine.co.uk.

40. Cited in Habermas, *An Awareness of What is Missing*, p. 5.

41. Ibid., p. 15.

42. See Stanley Fish, 'Does Reason Know What it is Missing?', *New York Times*, 12 April 2010, blog at opinionator.blogs.nytimes.com.

43. Cited in Richard Dawkins, *The God Delusion*, Random House, 2009, p. 50.

44. Skidelsky, 'Habermas vs the Pope'.

45. Fish, 'Does Reason Know What it is Missing?'

46. See Finlayson, *Habermas: A Very Short Introduction*, pp. 104–5.

47. Habermas, *An Awareness of What is Missing*, p. 22.

48. Cited in Skidelsky, 'Habermas vs the Pope'.

18 Consuming Passions: Critical Theory in the New Millennium

1. Jonathan Franzen, *The Corrections*, HarperCollins UK, 2010, p. 93.

2. Francis Fukuyama, 'The End of History?', *National Interest* 16, 1989, pp. 3–18.

3. Axel Honneth, *The Struggle for Recognition: The Moral Grammar of Social Conflicts*, MIT Press, 1996.

4. Friedrich Wilhelm Nietzsche, *Thus Spake Zarathustra*, Penguin, 1969, p. 46.

5. Honneth, *Reification: A New Look at an Old Idea*, p. 75.

6. Ibid., p. 118.

7. Franzen, *The Corrections*, p. 94.

8. Adorno, *Minima Moralia*, p. 59.

9. Ibid., p. 200.

10. Cited in Alex Ross, 'The Naysayers: Walter Benjamin, Theodor Adorno, and the Critique of Pop Culture', *The New Yorker*, 15 September 2014, at newyorker.com.

11. Adorno, *Minima Moralia*, p. 58.

12. See Stuart Jeffries, 'Happiness is Always a Delusion', *Guardian*, 19 July 2006, at theguardian.com.

13. Benjamin Kunkel, 'Into the Big Tent', *London Review of Books*, 22 April 2010, at lrb.co.uk.

14. Fredric Jameson, *Late Marxism: Adorno, Or, the Persistence of the Dialectic*, Verso, 1996, p. 248.

15. Adorno, *Minima Moralia*, pp. 58, 157.

16. Alain Badiou, *The Rebirth of History: Times of Riots and Uprisings*, Verso, 2012, p. 1.

17. See Stuart Jeffries, 'David Graeber Interview', *Guardian*, 21 March 2015, at theguardian.com.

18. Fredric Jameson, *Valences of the Dialectic*, Verso, 2009, p. 525.

19. Klaus Dörre, Stephan Lessenich and Hartmut Rosa, *Sociology, Capitalism, Critique*, Verso, 2015, p. 1.

20. See Stuart Jeffries, 'Why Marxism is on the Rise Again', *Guardian*, 4 July 2012, at theguardian.com.

21. See Elaine Glaser, 'Bring Back Ideology: Fukuyama's "end of history" 25 years on', *Guardian*, 21 March 2014, at theguardian.com.

22. See Ross, 'The Naysayers: Walter Benjamin, Theodor Adorno . . '.

23. Adorno, *Aesthetic Theory*, p. 311.

Index

Abendroth, Wolfgang 299
Adair, Gilbert 105
Adenauer, Konrad 265
Adorno, Gretel (née Karplus) 168, 195, 199, 216, 220, 349
Adorno, Theodor 1, 6, 10, 17, 47–9, 55, 111, 131–2, 272, 359–60, 376; *Aesthetic Theory* 230, 243, 391–2; American exile 7, 9, 61, 157, 197, 198, 198–9, 203–7, 211–12, 218–19, 220, 223–38; on art 175, 186–9, 246; *The Authoritarian Personality* 4, 7–8, 275, 276–9, 280; and Benjamin 30, 216; California F-scale 274–5, 276–8; conception of history 163, 329–30; conception of labour 117; conflict with Popper 331; critique of America 284–6; 'Culture, Critique and Society' 271; *The Culture Industry* 230; Davis and 321; death 349–50, 356; death of father 257; dialectical method 141; *Dialectic of Enlightenment* 10, 47–8, 74, 151, 186, 188, 212, 218–19, 223–36, 252–3, 275, 280, 290, 293, 329, 333, 361–3; as director of the Institute for Social Research 268–9; and disintegration 101–2; the *Dissent*

debate 292–4; and the family 8, 62–3, 157; on Germany 263–4, 273–4; the Group Experiment 270–1, 280; and happiness 387, 388; 'In Search of Wagner' 194; at the Institute for Social Research 139, 140–1; *Jargon of Authenticity* 330–1; *Kierkegaard: Construction of the Aesthetic* 129–30; *Lamentation of Doctor Faustus* 242–3; and Lukács 246; and *Mahoganny* 125, 128, 129, 130–1, 132–3; and Mann 236–45; 'Marginalia to Theory and Praxis' 3, 342; and mass-produced culture 83; *Minima Moralia* 60–3, 138–9, 157, 162–3, 172, 226–7, 235, 251, 257–8, 269, 271, 386–7; 'Motifs' 133; 'Music in Radio' 205; musicological writings 129–30, 130–2, 186–9, 194, 205–6, 230, 240; Neapolitan holiday 100–2; *Negative Dialectics* 101, 273, 325–30, 370; 'Note on Anti-Semitism' 253; Oedipal struggle 47–9; 'On Jazz' 175–6, 186–9; 'On the Question "What is German?"' 263–4; 'On Twelve-tone Technique' 102; Oxford exile 194–5;